The Teaching for Social Justice Series

Construction Sites:
Excavating Race, Class, and Gender Among Urban Youths
LOIS WEIS AND MICHELLE FINE, EDITORS

The Public Assault on America's Children:
Poverty, Violence, and Juvenile Injustice
VALERIE POLAKOW, EDITOR

Walking the Color Line:
The Art and Practice of Anti-racist Teaching
MARK PERRY

A Simple Justice:
The Challenge of Small Schools
WILLIAM AYERS, MICHAEL KLONSKY, AND GABRIELLE H. LYON, EDITORS

Holler If You Hear Me:
The Education of a Teacher and His Students
GREGORY MICHIE

CONSTRUCTION SITES

Excavating Race, Class, and Gender Among Urban Youth

Lois Weis and Michelle Fine

EDITORS

TEACHERS
COLLEGE
PRESS

Teachers College, Columbia University
New York and London

Published by Teachers College Press, 1234 Amsterdam Avenue, New York, NY 10027

Chapter 1 has appeared previously as "Writing on the Bias" by Linda Brodkey in *College English*, volume 56, number 5, pp. 527–547. Copyright 1994 by the National Council of Teachers of English. Reprinted with permission.

Chapter 3 has appeared previously as "Raising Resisters" by Janice Victoria Ward in *Urban Girls*: *Resisting Stereotypes, Creating Identities*, N. Way and B. Leadbeater, Eds. Reprinted by permission of New York University Press.

Chapter 14 has been reprinted from THE HOUSE OF JOSHUA: MEDITATIONS ON FAMILY AND THE PLACE by Mindy Thompson Fullilove by permission of the University of Nebraska Press. © 1999 by the University of Nebraska Press.

Chapter 16 is adapted from *The Color of Privilege: Three Blasphemies on Race and Feminism*, by Aída Hurtado. Reprinted with permission of the University of Michigan Press.

Lines from NIGGERS ARE SCARED OF REVOLUTION copyright © 1970, DOUGLAS MUSIC CORP. All rights reserved. Used by permission.

Lines from SUCKA NIGGA, by Kamaal Fareed, Ali Shaheed Muhammed, Malik Taylor, F. Hubbard. © 1993 Zomba Enterprises Inc., Jazz Merchant Music, Hub-Tones Music. All Rights on behalf of Jazz Merchant Music administered by Zomba Enterprises, Inc. All Rights Reserved. Used by Permission. WARNER BROS. PUBLICATIONS, U.S. INC., Miami, FL 33014.

Lines from TRUE TO THE GAME, by Ice Cube. © 1991 WB Music Corp. (ASCAP), Gangsta Boogie Music (ASCAP). All Rights administered by WB Music Corp. All Rights Reserved. Used by Permission. WARNER BROS. PUBLICATIONS U.S. INC., Miami, FL 33014.

Lines from "Song No. 3" by Sonia Sanchez, from *Under a Soprano Sky*, published by Africa World Press, Trenton, NJ, are reprinted with permission.

The poem "Women Word," by Elba Rosario Sánchez, is reprinted with permission of the author.

Lines from "Letting Go" and "To live in the Borderlands means you" are from *Borderlands/La Frontera: The New Mestiza*, © 1987 by Gloria Anzaldúa.

Lines from "Loose Woman" from *Loose Woman*. Copyright © 1994 by Sandra Cisneros. Published by Vintage Books, a division of Random House, Inc., and originally in hardcover by Alfred A. Knopf, Inc. Reprinted by permission of Susan Bergholz Literary Services, New York. All rights reserved.

Library of Congress Cataloging-in-Publication Data

Construction sites : excavating race, class, and gender among urban youth / Lois Weis
    and Michelle Fine, editors.
        p. cm. — (The teaching for social justice series)
    Includes bibliographical references and index.
    ISBN 0-8077-3979-0 (cloth : alk. paper)—ISBN 0-8077-3978-2 (pbk. : alk. paper)
    1. Urban youth—Education—Political aspects—United States.   2. Urban youth—United
States—Social conditions.   3. Educational anthropology—United States.   4. Identity
(Psychology) in youth—United States.   I. Weis, Lois.   II. Fine, Michelle.   III. Series.
LC5141 .C65 2000
    306.43—dc21   00-030238

ISBN 0-8077-3978-2 (paper)
ISBN 0-8077-3979-0 (cloth)

Contents

Series Foreword

Teaching for social justice might be thought of as a kind of popular education—of, by, and for the people—something that lies at the heart of education in a democracy, education toward a more vital, more muscular democratic society. It can propel us toward action, away from complacency, reminding us of the powerful commitment, persistence, bravery, and triumphs of our justice-seeking forebears—women and men who sought to build a world that worked for us all. Without them, liberty would today be slighter, poorer, weaker—the American flag wrapped around an empty shell—a democracy of form and symbol over substance.

Rousseau argues in regard to justice that equality "must not be understood to mean that degrees of power and wealth should be exactly the same," but only that with respect to *power*, equality renders it "incapable of all violence" and only exerted in the interest of a freely developed and participatory law, and that with respect to *wealth*, "no citizen should be so opulent that he can buy another, and none so poor that he is constrained to sell himself." The quest for equality and social justice over many centuries is worked out in the open spaces of that proclamation, in the concrete struggles of human beings constructing and contesting all kinds of potential meanings within that ideal. Nothing is settled, once and for all, but a different order of question presents itself: Who should be included? What do we owe one another? What is fair and unfair?

This series gathers together examples of popular education being practiced today, as well as clear and new thinking concerning issues of democracy, social justice, and educational activism. Many contributions will be grounded in practice and will, we hope, focus on the complexities built into popular education: difficulties, set-backs, successes, steps forward—work that reminds us of what Bernice Johnson Reagon calls "the sweetness of struggle." We seek as well, developing theoretical work that might push us all forward, to grasp anew the meaning of democracy in changing times, the demands of justice, and the imperatives of social change. We want to encourage new voices and new ideas, and in all cases to contribute to a serious, grounded, thoughtful exchange about the enduring questions in education: Education for what? Education for whom? Education toward what kind of social order?

If society cannot be changed under any circumstances, if there is nothing to be done, not even small and humble gestures toward something better, well, that about ends all conversation. Our sense of agency shrinks, our choices diminish. What more is there to say? But if a fairer, more sane, and just social order is both desirable and possible, that is, if some of us can join one another to imagine and build a participatory movement for justice, a public space for the enactment of democratic dreams, our field opens slightly. There would still be much to be done, for nothing would be entirely settled. We would still need to stir ourselves from passivity, cynicism, and despair; to reach beyond the superficial barriers that wall us off from one another; to resist the flattening effects of consumerism and the blinding, mystifying power of the familiar social evils (such as racism, sexism, and homophobia); to shake off the anesthetizing impact of most classrooms, most research, and of the authoritative, official voices that dominate the airwaves and the media; and to, as Maxine Greene says, "release our imaginations" and act on behalf of what the known demands, linking our conduit firmly to our consciousness. We would be moving, then, without guarantees, but with purpose and with hope.

Education is an arena of struggle as well as hope—struggle because it stirs in us the need to look at the world anew, to question what we have created, to wonder what is worthwhile for human beings to know and experience—and hope because we gesture toward the future. Education is where we ask how we might engage, enlarge, and change our lives, and it is, then, where we confront our dreams and fight out notions of the good life, where we try to comprehend, apprehend, or possibly even change the world. Education is contested space, a natural site of conflict—sometimes restrained, other times in full eruption—over questions of justice.

The work, of course, is never done. Democracy is dynamic, a community always in the making. Teaching for social justice continues the difficult task of constructing and reinvigorating a public. It broadens the table, so that more may sit together. Clearly, we have a long, long way to go. And we begin.

William Ayers, Series Editor

Therese Quinn, Associate Series Editor

Acknowledgments

Ideas are created in rich social relationships; manuscripts require the relentless commitments of a few. With broad thanks to many for sharing and creating ideas, we must acknowledge Amy Ferry, Steven Fine, Jenni Hoffman, and Susan Weseen for their remarkable dedication to turning this book around in short time and with great care. Thanks also to Carole Saltz for her everlasting support and Susan Liddicoat for her meticulous editing. And of course we owe this book to the many teachers, community-based activists, students, and youth who let us into their lives.

We dedicate *Construction Sites* to educators working inside and beyond schools, trying to craft with youth a life of pleasure and justice.

Construction Sites: An Introduction

LOIS WEIS AND MICHELLE FINE

Ask a 14-year-old to tell you a story about what she's most proud of, what she knows and what she's good at. Ask him what he yearns to understand, where he's likely to learn it, and from whom. Chances are, in either case, you won't get a story about school. As critical ethnographers of urban youth and community life, we begin with a recognition that much of what youths learn, teach, believe in, long to know—and, most fundamentally, how they form and re-form identities—takes shape within spaces both within and outside school. It is to the politics and practices of such spaces that we dedicate this book.

Having edited *Beyond Silenced Voices* (Weis & Fine, 1993), we recognize that much work goes on within schools. We have also been impressed that much of the pedagogical and political work of forming self and communities, by youth, takes place well outside the borders of schooling. As educators—whether preservice, new to the field, or possessing years of experience and wisdom—we need to deepen our understandings of the many contexts that are meaningful to youth if we are to engage with them intellectually and ethically. In this text we focus on sites both within and outside school as critical spaces of educational practice. And we insist that, as educators, we recognize that learning takes place in varying spaces.

There is much talk these days about school–community relations for adolescents, and yet relatively little is known about life at the borders of school and community, much less the stories of youth as they sojourn between. While there have been some forays into this intellectual area (Christian-Smith & Roman, 1988; Giroux & McLaren, 1994; McLaughlin & Brice-Heath, 1993; Seller & Weis, 1997), a sustained look at the ways in which youth develop political and social identities, investments, and relations, both within and outside school contexts, is noticeably absent from the literatures on education and on adolescence. How young people take up public spaces (Kelley, 1997) and how they carve out "private" ones have been relatively underexplored. It is the vibrancy in the "in-between," as

Maxine Greene would tell us, that youths' sense of possibility, imagina-tion, social critique, outrage, despair, aesthetics, and social action lie. It is in these spaces that youths engage with a kind of deliberate agency, some-times an urgency, in which reciprocity is assumed, mastery—of spirit, arts, the body, activism—is sought, voices can be heard, and differences can be articulated; deficit models are left at the door. It is into these spaces that our work carries us.

Construction Sites is an invitation to explore the many lives lived by youth—to wander along the sidewalks they travel, into the corners where they seek solace, onto the fields and rinks where they play and perform, into the schools in which they learn, the libraries where they devour books, the parks where they spend time, the clubs where they hang out in; to discover the spaces they long to find as well as the institutions they adore and those they resist. Recognizing the long arm of global capitalism and the rapid and devastating state retreat from public spaces for poor and working class youth, we feel and hear the tainted corporatization of both "public" and "private" spaces. As such, no space can be romanticized as innocent, uncontaminated, or "free." At the same time, however, we can't help but notice the power of these often subterranean spaces, some in school, many not, within which youth work out the politics of mind, body, soul, and pleasure. Within these spaces we witness deeply educa-tive pedagogies, politics, moves toward self and community, a reshaping of borders, fractures, and social realignments.

Construction Sites represents an intellectual and political project crafted to reveal and theorize spaces for and by youth, in and out of schools. We pry open both a theoretical framework and a set of the "really real," to use William James's language, spaces within which youth form and re-form identities, develop and reframe social relations, and, in some cases, spawn the seeds of youth organizing.

This book travels across sites with a strong sense of possibility for con-temporary youth. These young men and women, raised in the Reagan, Bush, and Clinton years, have been saturated with the disappointing lega-cies of feminism, civil rights, and the most hopeful (if backlash-filled) gay/lesbian rights movement. These are the young people who were fed conservative ideologies and survived the right-wing politics of the late-twentieth century, dedicated to tax relief for the wealthy, the expansion of global capitalism, the demise of public spaces, the undermining of public education, assaults on affirmative action, curtailment of immigration, un-raveling of the welfare state, police harassment, and the swelling of prison construction. This generation has witnessed a vicious national assault, dis-cursive and material, on poor and working-class people of all races and ethnicities (Fine & Weis, 1998). They are a generation for which the moral community of concern and connection has shrunk dramatically (Fine, Weis, & Powell, 1997).

And yet many of this generation refuse to be shut out. Cultivating social critique and action in their own small spaces, they toil sometimes under the caring eyes of organizers, teachers, parents, or peers. As often, they do so despite adults, often quite alone. Boys and girls of color, poverty, or both challenge perverse representations of themselves and their "deficits" and "pathologies," organizing in quiet spaces. Girls across race and class lines are taking back their bodies and public spaces. Gay, lesbian, and bisexual youth demand spaces for visibility and comfort in high schools and in college. So here we look at the movements of youth, as they shape and reshape identities, as they challenge our stereotypes of them, as they imagine and build possibilities for the future.

The book is divided into three major sections. In the first part, "Spaces for Identity Work," we focus on those spaces where youth seek a respite from social assault, a space to grow, critique, and just relax with others of similar background. In Part II, "Spaces for Border Crossing," we visit those spaces where youth come together across difference, interrogating their many identities through ethical, spiritual, athletic, intellectual, and/or political projects. Part III, "Spaces of Privilege and Resistance," offers cautionary tales revolving around sites of historic privilege where "others" have been recently invited, only to be further marginalized. By offering these three sections we examine the potential power of such spaces, across similarity and difference, and the types of difficulties that may arise within them.

We use this set of essays to appreciate and remind ourselves about the vivid range of spaces in which youth learn and teach. Shaping and being shaped by youth, these spaces include schools, cultural settings, the library, streets, the poetry workshop buried in the neighborhood high school, the skating rink, the barber shop, the gay club next to the Christian Coalition group, the basketball court, the dining room table at home, the girls' baseball diamond. While the volume recognizes and honors important projects within school, it refuses to see schools as the only site in which youth are educated. It also refuses to view youth as only the recipients of knowledge, by insisting that youth are also producers and educators themselves. The chapters in this text acknowledge that there are no neutral spaces, that all spaces are "political" insofar as they are infused with questions of power and privilege. All spaces suffer the burdens of social contradictions. None are insulated from racism, sexism, homophobia, and classism. As such, all spaces carry the capacity and power to enable, restrict, applaud, stigmatize, erase, or complicate threads of youth identity and their ethical commitments.

In times of shriveled state responsibility for youth and the evaporation of public spaces especially for poor and working class youth, we offer these essays to implore educators, community activists, youth, and youth workers to imagine sites for youth work and not to rely on schools, families, or religious institutions alone. Youth need spaces to work through the pains of oppressed identities, to explore the pleasures of not-yet identities, and to organize movements we can't even imagine. Young people deserve to engage in ethical projects larger than self, around difference, for freedom and social justice. In this spirit, we end with an inviting essay by Maxine Greene that allows us to imagine what public space must be for today's youth.

REFERENCES

Christian-Smith, L., & Roman, L. (1988). *Becoming feminine: The politics of popular culture*. Philadelphia: Falmer.

Fine, M., Weis, L., & Powell, L. (1997). Communities of difference: A critical look at desegregated spaces created for and by youth. *Harvard Educational Review, 67*(2), 247–284.

Fine, M., & Weis, L. (1998). *The unknown city: The voices of poor and working class young adults*. Boston: Beacon Press.

Giroux, H., & McLaren, P. (1994). *Between borders: Pedagogy and the politics of cultural studies*. New York: Routledge.

Kelley, R. (1997). *Yo' mama's disfunktional*. Boston: Beacon Press.

McLaughlin, M., & Brice-Heath, S. (1993). *Identity and inner-city youth: Beyond ethnicity and gender*. New York: Teachers College Press.

Seller, M., & Weis, L. (1997). *Beyond Black and White: New faces and voices in United States schools*. Albany: State University of New York Press.

Weis, L., & Fine, M. (1993). *Beyond silenced voices: Class, race, and gender in United States schools*. Albany: State University of New York Press.

PART I

SPACES FOR IDENTITY WORK

The chapters in this section escort us into spaces in which youth create, invent, reconstruct, critique, and reassemble identities. Trying on different ways of wearing adolescence, they play with sexualities, being smart, marginal, biracial, cool, Latina, pregnant or not, immigrant, gay, lesbian, or bisexual. They wander across spaces where they perform very different selves: from the family kitchen table to a neighbor's house, traveling from the gay youth group to church, dressing for the Chinese New Year celebration, talkin' trash on the basketball court, searching for safe talk in a group designed to promote sexual abstinence, or floating onto the ice to skate. Across spaces, these young women and men craft selves of complexity, subversive conformity, and safe resistance. They shed, appropriate, and create shawls and caps of identity that slide comfortably, delicately, and sometimes awkwardly from space to space.

We know from speaking with youth that, having been raised in a generation of identity politics, they refuse, as often as not, singular, binary, or essentialist notions of identity. Instead they yearn for spaces that stretch open at their messy intersections. And yet for many urban youth, racial, sexual, class, and cultural markers prevent them from experiencing affirmation or engaged recognition in any "public space"—schools, buses, parks—or in the eyes of police, teachers, strangers, ministers, and sometimes family. For youth of color, "public spaces"—streets, parks, subways—may be treacherous and ironically more treacherous with "police protection." So they carve their own sites and navigate their own journeys, away from danger—for a moment. By virtue of being Black and male, Puerto Rican and gay, Vietnamese and first generation, pregnant and young, White working class and smart, or just female, these young people know the gaze they endure just walking down the street, the suspicions they provoke just by being. Some hide. Some play with representations. Some talk back in public. All seek spaces of meaning, recognition, and comfort.

Given the micro-aggressions (Franklin, 1999) of daily life for these youth, it would be theoretically and politically irresponsible to dismiss these spaces as evidence of narrow identity politics. On the contrary, a profound moral and ethical praxis is underway within and across these spaces. These youth are simply sustained in sites in which their very existence is not in question and not assumed deficient, in which their language is not assumed unintelligible, their sexualities dangerous, their class status a mark of "lack"—spaces in which they are neither invisible nor hypervisible. There are no victims here, but there are lots of cultural critics. In this section, you will meet historically and currently marginalized young people who take up much-deserved spaces to grow roots, develop, flourish, engage, critique, and just relax with similarly situated others. These are places in which young people congregate with peers, families, and community to laugh, satirize, reclaim, unravel, and prepare themselves emotionally, politically, and intellectually for the next day's excursions.

Concerning the micro-politics of home, school, and community, the first three essays reveal the power and variety of youth spaces, in which young women sew together threads of identity and possibility, alone and with peers. Linda Brodkey takes us through a critical autoethnography, across neighborhoods, kitchens, libraries, schools, and dance classes, as she becomes a writer. Lois Weis and Doris Carbonell-Medina invite us into an "abstinence" support group, peeking into a girls-only conversation, learning much about the treacherous routes urban girls have to traverse in order to satisfy—and survive—family, school, boyfriends, and peers. Janie Ward reveals the rich, counterhegemonic labor over dinner taking place every night in the homes of some African American girls, in conversations with families, strategizing how to confront and resist day-to-day encounters with racism and sexism, how to generate a resistance for liberation.

Writing with and for youth who have been marginalized by culture, sexuality, teen pregnancy, gender, and racism, the next five essays explore the complexity of spaces in which youth are affirmed for their "differences" and out of which youth gain the strength to venture into less welcoming corners of the world. Craig Centrie offers us a close ethnographic look inside homes, schools, and community celebrations, as we marvel at the worlds, values, and languages traversed by Vietnamese immigrant youth. Richard Barry writes with and for a group of gay, lesbian, bisexual youth and "friends" who dare to work through issues of sexual politics on their campus, narrating how much such a space allows them to wander outside and then back to home, family, church, and school with a sense of grounding. Amira Proweller allows us to peer inside a school for pregnant and parenting teens, an unsuspected site of dignity and resistance. Sarah Carney speaks with young women skaters, alternating between discourses of anorexia/disease and athletics/strength, searching for a language on the ice in which to take back their bodies and performances that, at once, reproduce and resist the strictures of femininity. Finally, Antwi Akom takes us onto urban basketball courts, into barber shops, and inside the lyrics and meanings of rap, to perform a genealogy on the use of the word "nigger," trying to extract where, how, and with what intent youth deploy language that, at once, joins friends and comrades and rejects race-traitors. Ironically, like the discourse on pathology and anorexia that Sarah Carney finds with her White young women, the discourse of "nigger" or "nigga" that Antwi Akom examines reveals the muscles of resistance and the victories of social reproduction.

In these spaces of identity work, in which the power of "difference" is explored, we hear affirmation, contradiction, and the capacity to resist relentlessly. These essays testify to youths' need for and ability to construct spaces in which they engage in a kind of critical consciousness, challenging hegemonic beliefs about them, their perceived inadequacies, pathologies, and "lacks" and restoring a sense of possibility for themselves and their peers, with and beyond narrow spaces of identity sustenance.

REFERENCE

Franklin, A. J. (1999). Invisibility syndrome and racial identity development in psychotherapy and counseling of African American men. *The Counseling Psychologist, 27,* 761–793.

CHAPTER 1

Writing on the Bias

LINDA BRODKEY

If you believe family folklore, I began writing the year before I entered
kindergarten, when I conducted a census (presumably inspired by a visit
from the 1950 census taker). I consider it a story about writing rather than,
say, survey research, because while it has me asking the neighbors when
they were going to die, in my mind's eye I see myself as a child recording
their answers—one to a page—in a Big Chief tablet. As I remember it, my
mother sometimes told this story when she and her sister were of a mind
to reflect on their children's behavior. Since in my family the past provided the only possible understanding of the present, the story was probably my mother's way of talking about her middle daughter's indiscriminate extroversion and perfectionism. On the one hand, these inborn traits
would explain my performance in school, for teachers like gregarious
children who approach all tasks as worth their full attention. On the other
hand, my mother, who claims to have found me engaged in conversations
with strangers on more than one occasion, would have been worrried
about such wholesale friendliness. Innocence was not first among the virtues my mother admired in her children. That I view the census story as
my mother's does not erase faint outlines I also see of myself as a little
girl, who leaves her mother's house to travel the neighborhood under the
protective mantle of writing.

Writing was the girl's passport to neighbors' houses, where she whiled
away the long and lonely days chatting up the grown-ups when the older
children were at school, and otherwise entertained herself with this
newfound power over adults, who responded to her even if they did not
also answer her question. As naive as the question may seem, as startling
and by some standards even unmannerly, a child asking grown-ups when
they were going to die was probably considered a good deal less intrusive
in the White, working-class neighborhood in the small midwestern city
where I grew up than the federal government's sending a grown man to
ask questions about income, education, and religion. Forty some years later,

stories are all that remain of that childhood experience. I remember nothing: not if I ever met an official census taker, not if I believed grown-ups *knew* when they would die, not if I was a 4-year-old preoccupied by death, not even if I took a survey. And while it seems to me of a piece with other family narratives explaining human behavior as inborn, whether it is a "true" story interests me a good deal less than how it may have affected me and my writing.

I would like to think that the story of my preschool experience sustained me through what I now remember as many lean years of writing in school. Yet when I look back I see only a young girl intent on getting it right, eager to produce flawless prose, and not a trace of the woman who years later will write that school writing is to writing as catsup is to tomatoes: as junk food to food. What is nutritious has been eliminated (or nearly so) in processing. What remains is not just empty but poisonous fare because some people so crave junk that they prefer it to food, and their preference is then used by those who, since they profit by selling us catsup as a vegetable and rules as writing, lobby to keep both on the school menu. Surely a child possessed of a Big Chief tablet would be having a very different experience of writing than the one who keeps her lines straight and stays out of margins, memorizes spelling and vocabulary words, fills in blanks, makes book reports, explicates poems and interprets novels, and turns them all in on time. In the neighborhood I was fed food and conversation in exchange for writing. At school I learned to trade my words for grades and degrees, in what might be seen as the academic equivalent of dealing in futures—speculation based on remarkably little information about my prospects as an academic commodity.

Lately I seem to have come full cycle, for I am sometimes reminded of the little girl whose writing seemed to make food appear and people talk when something I write appears in print or when I give a paper. I never think of her when I write annual reports on my research and teaching or revise my curriculum vitae (that's school all over again), but when someone writes back or talks back, I'm in the old neighborhood again, back where writing is playing is eating is visiting is talking, back where the pleasures of writing are many and school just another game I played. While the census may have taught me *to* write, taught me that writing is worth doing, I learned things about *how* to write in school. That some children who already see themselves as writers can appropriate skills, which when presented *as* writing would arguably alienate most children from writing, should not be construed as a testimonial for teaching writing as skills. To this day, when a copyeditor invokes an in-house rule I feel shame, as if my not having mastered a rule that I could not have known even existed means I must not be much of a writer. As a child I trusted teachers and distrusted myself, as girls are known to do. And to make matters even worse, I was a child who lived by rules.

I suspect I loved rules because I loved the idea of controlling events. Step on a crack and break your mother's back. Hop over it and save her. You are safe from all harm as long as you cross only on green. Say a perfect act of contrition immediately before dying and you will go directly to heaven. Say it too fast or too slow, misspeak a word, forget one, or remember something you should have confessed and you will go directly to hell or, worse, languish in purgatory. Better yet, live such an exemplary life that confession will be moot. The new rules for spelling, grammar, and punctuation were simply added to injunctions against stepping on cracks in sidewalks and crossing against the light, not to mention the rules for saying a perfect act of contrition. Write perfectly spelled and punctuated grammatically correct sentences and you are a writer. I fetishized the rules of grammar, spelling, and punctuation as I did the others, believing that if they governed me they also governed reality/eternity/writing.

A tendency to fetishize rules at once fueled my childhood enthusiasms and threatened to extinguish the pleasure of the most powerful of my desires: to be a ballerina. My long affair with dance began where all my childhood enthusiasms with art began—in the children's room of the public library, where in the summer of the fourth grade I found the holdings, as I now say, on dance. As I remember, these included biographies of dancers (Anna Pavlova and Maria Tallchief) and probably choreographers, and at least one illustrated book, which I studied and as a result of which forced my body to assume the positions illustrated, until I could complete with relative ease my rendition of a *barre*. Above all else, what I seem to have learned from those hours of painstaking and excruciating self-instruction, in addition to a number of habits that later had to be just as painstakingly unlearned, is that dance is discipline, and discipline a faultless physical reenactment of an ideal. Perfect *barres*, perfect acts of contritions, perfect sentences. Without diminishing the importance of the *barre* to dance, prayer to religion, or grammar to writing, the danger of making a fetish of rules is in the illustrated book of ballet, the Baltimore Catechism, and English handbooks, in codifications that purport to instruct, but as often as not ground a ritual fascination with rules, the perfection of which is in turn used as a standard against which to measure someone's devotion to dance, religion, or writing rather than their performances as dancers, *religeuses*, or writers.

In the mid-1950s when I was checking ballet books out of the children's library, I had seen ballet performed only on "The Ed Sulllivan Show," that is, seen tiny dancers flit across a snowy screen. Other than that, there was the seemingly spontaneous, effortless, and flawless dancing in movies. But the dance I tried to re-create from the photographs in the book resembled neither these professional performances nor even the amateur recitals staged by local dance studios. Others who grew up in small midwestern cities (Quincy, Illinois: population 41,450 according to the 1950 census; 43,743 according to the census taken in 1960) may have also attended recitals where top billing was given to adolescent girls adept at toe-tap, origins unknown to me. I consider it still a quintessential spectacle of White lower-middle-class female sensuality. The girl danced solo, and the din created by the plates on the points of her toe shoes was as riveting as it was raucous. For all I know, the plates were there to warn the weary women who usually operated dance studios that a child was not *en pointe*. Or perhaps since toe-tap recitals are as noisy as they are vigorous, the taps, which would disguise the noise of moving feet and creaking bones, were there to distract audiences and dancers alike from the painful reality of being *en pointe*, which is not unlike that of running in 5-inch heels. I secretly admired the girls I publicly condemned, and in my mind's eye I can still see them flaunting their sexual independence before a captive audience of family and friends. As wildly different as toe-tap is from ballet, they are nonetheless alike in being performing arts, even if the flagrant sensuality of the one now seems to me a burlesque of the sexual sensibilities of the other. By contrast, the book I read illustrated ballet as a set of discrete skills to be learned and then routinely deployed in seemingly endless and sexless reenactments of tableaux—bodies transfixed in rather than moving through space.

When I finally studied dance—with the only teacher in town who disdained toe-tap—I learned the rules and followed them religiously. I loved the discipline of ballet with all the fervor of an S/M enthusiast, for I can recall making no distinctions between pleasure and pain. Inasmuch as ballet is discipline, I learned to be a reasonably good dancer. If I didn't fly as often as I wished, perhaps it was because I was a good Catholic girl who translated the discipline of ballet into ritual enactments, for my understanding of religion and dance alike was radically diminished by my experience of, and faith in, the absolute power of rules.

The child's confusion of discipline for dance is understandable, for it can be traced to her reading, which represented dance as a natural progression from the *barre* to the stage. It's not so much that the child misunderstood the illustrations, but that she misread the book, which was not a manual for dancers, but one from which children who attended performances were to learn to appreciate ballet. Fortunately for me, my autodidacticism was modified enough by performance that I gradually revised my understanding of dance. And fortunately for me, my mother's narrative of my preschool writing as a social performance worth remembering and telling probably enabled me to learn rules and eventually to resist mistaking them for writing. Over the years, the schools have probably quelled a desire to write in a good many children by subjecting them to ritual performances of penmanship, spelling, grammar, punctuation, oraganization, and most recently thinking. Every generation mixes its own nostrums, and passes them off as writing. The fetishes may change but not the substitution of some formal ritual performance for writing.

When I was in elementary school, before children were allowed to write, they were expected to learn to read, write cursive, spell, diagram sentences, punctuate them, and arrange them in paragraphs. The first writing assignment I remember was in the fifth grade—"Write about your favorite country"—and my essay on "Africa" was a compilation of sentences copied in my own hand from encyclopedia entries. Apparently neither the teacher nor I knew that Africa is not a country. And apparently neither of us noticed that the Africa in the encyclopedias was populated by precious goods and wild animals, not people. I would have produced that essay around the time that I gave up on the novel I was secretly writing, featuring the heroine Susan Saint, because while I wanted her to drive away in her roadster (she bore a striking resemblance to Nancy Drew), she could not because I did not know how to drive. By the time I learned to drive, however, I had already learned to write fluent essays and to keep Susan Saint and her problems to myself.

I am sometimes reminded that I nearly became a reader rather than a writer in a vivid memory of myself as young girl slowly picking her way down the stairs of the Quincy Public Library. I know I am leaving the children's library and am en route to the rooms reserved below for adults. The scene is lit from above and behind by a window, through which the sun shines down on the child whose first trip to the adult library saddens me. On mornings when I wake with this memory, I am overcome by sorrow even though I know the actual trip to have been a childish triumph of sorts. I literally read my way out of the children's library in the summer of the fifth grade—every book, or so I used to think, with the twin exceptions of *Tom Sawyer* and *Huckleberry Finn*. I was averse to neither adventure books nor stories about boys, and read plenty of books about boy athletes, castaways, orphans, princes, presidents, kings, and cowboys, not to mention boy detectives, boy horses and dogs, boy wonders and boy friends. The problem was Mark Twain, a man I held personally responsible for the Tom Sawyer–Huck Finn–Becky Thatcher–Injun Joe diners, motels, historic houses, along with a detestable cave, that plagued my childhood, the Mark Twain roadside attractions in the nearby town of Hannibal, Missouri, a few miles down the Mississippi River from Quincy, Illinois. When as an adult I finally forced myself to read *Huckleberry Finn*,

I came to believe that Twain would have appreciated the enterprising uses the town had made of its native son, perhaps because by then I believed that Huck's desire to "light out for the territories" was of a piece with other tropes of the West, which could justify anything from genocide to servitude to souvenirs in the name of civilization.

This memory of myself is carefully staged. I can only be looking at the loss of innocence. A young girl. A descent. Away from the light. That I set the scene in a library suggests a loss specific to literacy. Yet here is a child who reads so much that the librarians have declared her an honorary adult and sent her to the adult library where there are even more books than in the children's library, some of them not suitable, she hopes, for children. She should be dancing down that stairway, as I may actually have done, full of herself and in full possession of the token of her recent enfranchisement—a card good for all the books in the adult library. Indeed there were more books there, so many more than the child imagined that she found she could not read her way out, not that summer, not soon, not ever. I can see the girl is on the brink of learning that the books are not hers, that books, even children's books, are copyrighted, someone's property. And, since she already knows that some properties are more valuable than others, before long she will confound their imputed value and her desire, and want only the best books.

I must have suspected even in the children's library that *someone* wrote the books I read, since I had refused even to borrow those written by Mark Twain, and left my own Susan Saint sitting at the curb. Maybe I refused to read his books not simply because I loathed Twain tourist attractions, but also because his books were the only ones advertized as belonging to an author. The others were my stories: I lifted them off the shelves, checked them out, took them home, read them, and returned them a few days later in exchange for more. In the child's economics of literacy, the cycle of exchange depended entirely on *her* reading. It is a childish and even a dangerous view of literacy, for it entirely ignores the labor of producing books (with the possible exception of the material facts of books themselves), and yet it is one that libraries and schools promote when they base children's experience of literacy solely on reading.

Finding out that every book belonged to an author made the adult books different from the children's books I had regarded as public property and treated as I did the equipment on the school playground or neighborhood park. I didn't think I owned the swings, but I believed they were mine while I used them. I read the children's books seriatim—fiction and nonfiction, off the shelves, one after the other, section by section, top to bottom, left to right. There must have been a card catalogue, but I do not remember consulting it. Shelves rather than Dewey guided my reading, aided and limited by my height and what my mother called my "boarding house reach." What I could reach I read. And at some point, the librarians decided that I had read them all, or more likely that my grasp exceeded my reach, and sent me downstairs. Or more likely still, they probably ran out of prizes, having rewarded me for the most books read by a child in my school, my age, in a week, a month, over a summer, during a year.

Things were not the same in the adult library. Not just the books but the place. It smelled the same (of paste and glue and paper and must), but it neither looked nor felt the same. The books were tightly wedged on shelves, lined up like the aisles of supermarkets. There was just enough room between shelves to make a selection, but not enough to linger, and nothing like enough to stretch out on the floor and read. Truth to tell, I never felt I really belonged in the adult library, and I wonder now if that's because the loss of human space figured the loss of books as stories. I was not ready to give up stories. If I didn't actually read *all* the children's books, I read every one I checked out—from the first word to the last. Today the only books I still read that way are mysteries. I am a proper grown-up about all the other books and journals I use in my work. Like a good librarian, I order and maintain them, and even replace those that disappear. They are shelved according to topic in alphabetical order. I can almost always find what I'm looking for. But the mysteries are shelved to replicate the children's library, or at least my memory of it. I am not usually looking for any one in particular, and so I read what catches my eye. And when I want a particular book, I tear the shelves apart looking for it, happier than I care to admit wallowing in the stacks of books surrounding me.

It is only in the occasional glimpses of myself cautiously descending those library stairs that I realize that if I am uneasy about what I will learn in the adult library that may well be because I had yet to learn that I could write as well as read books. I am on the brink of believing instead that if I could not read them all, I could at least read the right ones. The right books are literature. Most of Shakespeare's plays and sonnets, some of Donne's lyrics, some of Wordsworth's, *The Canterbury Tales, Paradise Lost, Jane Eyre, David Copperfield,* and *The Scarlet Letter* are literature. I was working from a list. They were on it. It was only later that I learned that it's not that simple, that there is also *the literature,* as in the literature of a field or discipline, the right books *and* the right articles—about history, literature, physics, sociology, law, medicine. And it was much later still that I even thought to ask who made the lists, on which women rarely appear and people of color even more rarely, where America is a far flung replica of an English village, and most of the rest of the world not even that.

The economics of literature is entirely different than that of stories. Frankly, one animal story was as good as the next as far as I was concerned, one biography, one mystery, one romance, one adventure (except *Tom Sawyer* and *Huckleberry Finn*). But the value of stories as measured against literature is very low indeed. Stories are a dime a dozen. Almost anyone can tell or write stories (even a child can do it). Not just anyone can write literature (most adults cannot), and not just anyone can read it. Literature is an acquired taste, it seems, and like a taste for martinis and cavier, it is acquired leisurely through associating with the right people whose discernment guarantees a steady demand for a limited supply of literature. I used my adult card to check out *The House of the Seven Gables*, which I probably chose on the recommendation of my fifth-grade teacher but which I read—with some difficulty. I read it not because I liked it, but because I wanted to be someone who liked literature, an experience not unlike that of wondering, while taking the first sip of martini or bite of cavier, if other people actually like the taste of turpentine or cat food, and immediately denying the thought.

Looking back, however, I would not want to have missed a single one the stories dressed up as literature or, for that matter, all that many of those billed as the literature. But I do sometimes wish, on the mornings I wake to watch myself descending those stairs, that I understood why, when I realized I could not read all the books in the adult library, I took smug comfort in believing that only some of them were worth reading. What was my stake in the great books, the ones on the recommended lists distributed to honors students at my school? For years I read exclusively from those mimeographed lists, except for an occasional mistake like *Green Mansions* and some occasional lapses like *Gone with the Wind* and *Peyton Place*, and for many years I was comforted by the list, secure in my choices and certain that I was making progress. No sooner had I knocked off a great book than I had it recorded on a three-by-five card. One per book. Vital statistics on the front—author, title, main characters, and plot—a short memorable quote on the back.

My devotion to that file bears a suspicious resemblance to my dedication to the *barre*, and I realize now that ballet and literature must be early tokens of my longing to replace the working-class fictions of my childhood with a middle-class fiction in which art transcends class. I see in that file, for instance, the evidence of my desire and struggle to acquire the middle-class habit of privileging authorship. That I more readily remember novels I read in adolescence by title than author is probably evidence that I retained, despite my files, my earlier belief in stories, and possibly even the economic theory in which stories belong to the people who animate them in their reading. In the world of English professors whose ranks I sought to join, however, such mundane matters as the labor of literary production—the work of writing, placing, selecting, editing, printing, marketing, and distributing books—were thought to be distasteful, akin to asking the host how much the caviar cost. Only when I began studying and teaching writing did I finally remember that aesthetics can be as effective a hermetic seal against the economic and political conditions of authorship as are industrial parks and affluent suburbs against the economic privation and desperation of the urban and rural poor.

Sometime during the second year of college I quit recording and filing my reading, probably around the time I began reading books that were banned, or that I believed were: *Tropic of Cancer, Lady Chatterly's Lover, Fanny Hill, The Story of O, The Hundred Dollar Misunderstanding*. But until then no one needed to monitor my reading. I policed myself. Worse, I set out to police my family, whose knowledge of and interest in literature I found sadly lacking. So caught up was I in the promise of literature that I chided unconscionably the same mother who first took me to the library and walked me there until I was old enough to go alone, who had the good sense not to tell the first-grade teacher I could already read, so she could "teach" me, who read *War and Peace* with me in the eleventh grade, just to keep me company (I only read *Peace*, but she read both), and who never issued any of those dire warnings—about ruining my eyes, turning into a bookworm, or ending up a spinster—that must have kept generations of female and male children alike from reading much at all.

The list that identified some stories as literature also cast its readers as superior to those who, like my mother, preferred mysteries and romances. I suspect I desperately wanted her to read literature because I believed that if she didn't have her own passport to the middle class I would have to leave her behind when I went away—to college. There are times when I see each great book I filed as also recording an inoculation against the imputed ills of the working-class childhood that infected me and that in turn threatened the middle-class children with whom I studied. I do not think people in the 1950s believed poverty was contagious. They had not yet been taught to see poverty as something people bring on themselves and to spurn the poor as people who didn't get and stay with the program. But I probably did represent a threat to middle-class sensibility that can be ascribed to growing up in a working-class house.

We were a family of five, my parents and three girls, in a four-room house—a kitchen, a living room (known as the front room), two bedrooms, and a bathroom. In such small quarters, interior space is social by definition, since to be in a room is to be in either the company or proximity of others. That I knew how to read when I entered school can probably be attributed as much to this social arrangement of space as to any unusual interest or precocity on my part. I would have been there while my mother checked my older sister's homework. My sister may have even taught me to read. But I would not have simply learned to read. I would have learned to read in the social space of the kitchen.

In a middle-class household, a child who insisted on reading in the kitchen during, say, meal preparation would probably be perceived as hostile, and would no doubt either be asked to set the table or shunted off to another room, possibly even her own room. My mother was usually surrounded by her children. So, while I regularly read in the kitchen in the company of my mother and sisters, and was often more attentive to what I was reading than what they were saying or doing, I can recall no one suggesting that the act itself was hostile, or that I read someplace else. It's not just that there was no place to send me. It's that I wasn't held responsible for my reading. Some kids sing, some cook, some read. It was a gift, like perfect pitch, not a skill I was honing or my mother nurturing. What was considered wonderful was my ability to read in the midst of conversation, what my mother called my "remarkable power of concentration." It was not cause for wonder, however, when I focused on grievances, for then my "remarkable power of concentration" became my "one-track mind."

My reading was not cause for wonder or concern at home because my mother believed she could always call me back if she wanted or needed me. But it was cause for concern at school, in fact, according to my mother, a source of considerable consternation for a beloved first-grade teacher who, exhibiting none of my mother's admiration for my unbridled reading, went to extraordinary lengths to break me of the habit. She took particular exception to my practice of "reading ahead" to find out what happened to the children and household pets in the basal reader. It seems strange to me now that I could have confused a primer for a story, but I took it very hard when the teacher taped the unread portion of book closed to prevent me from "reading ahead" without her permission. I never untaped the book or directly challenged her right to regulate my reading. But in a rare act of childhood defiance, I remember promptly "reading ahead" when I happened on a copy of the reader in the children's library.

If my "reading ahead" concerned the teacher enough to justify taping the book closed, my habit of interrupting the other children while they were reading must have driven her to distraction, since I can still feel the heat of my humiliation and recall my terror as I stood alone and in tears in the cloakroom, where I had been sent for talking during reading. That happened only once that I can remember. The door that isolated me from the others may have terrified me more than it would have a child accustomed to closed doors. I was not in a dark or windowless room, but I could not hear what was being said in the classroom with the door closed. By some standards the punishment fit the crime. Yet it ignores the conflict that the middle-class practice of reading alone and in silence, only what is assigned when it is assigned, creates in a working-class child whose reading had, until then, been part and parcel of the social fabric of home and whose choice of reading matter had been regulated by the holdings of the children's library and her reach.

I was not taught to read in the first grade, but was instead taught to unlearn how I already read and to learn to read again by a well-meaning and dedicated teacher authorized by the state to regulate my reading. My father once complained that he never understood me after I went to school. I always thought he was referring to the speech lessons in the second grade that radically altered my dialect, from the southern midland dialect spoken at home to the northern midland spoken by most of my teachers. But now I wonder whether it was a class rather than regional dialect that stood between us, whether the door that temporarily isolated me from the other children also threatened to closet me permanently from my family. That the ostensible autonomy of middle-class professionals depends on children internalizing the rules that regulate reading (and writing) seems obvious to me. Less obvious, however, is what part reading and writing practices learned at home, and at variance with those learned at school, continue to play in my intellectual life.

There is no denying that I re-create the cloakroom everywhere I live. It is not uncommon, of course, for academics to furnish their homes with books. It is not even uncommon for academics to read several at a time. But the inordinate pleasure I take from littering all available surfaces with books makes it seem unlikely that in my case books are indexing only my academic enthusiasms. It seems more likely to me, now that I've remembered and reflected on the cloakroom, that the books are there to keep me company, that they are tokens of the absent family and friends whose voices have been muted by time and space. If so, it gives me a measure of satisfaction to believe that this lifelong habit simulates reading as I learned it at home, that even as I read the literature that took me so far from home, I have been protecting myself from total class annihilation.

As a young girl, I was not just reading about other people, other places, and other lives. I was reading about people, places, and lives utterly unlike mine. Virtually everything in the fiction I read was fantastic: their houses, their families, their neighborhoods, their neighbors, their clothes, their food, their amusements, their feelings, their romances, their friendships, their conversation, their desires, their problems, their prospects. These things were different not just because literature is not life, but because the drama in the books on the recommended list, at least in the nineteenth-century novels I preferred, either happened in middle-class houses—*Emma* and *Middlemarch*—or, so I now realize, in defense of the middle class and their houses—*Great Expectations* and *War and Peace*. I loved most those novels that held literary open house, the ones that toured prime literary real estate. I doted on the rooms reserved for specific uses—parlors, drawing rooms, sitting rooms, libraries—and only incidentally considered the heroines who retired there to hold conversations, closeted from parents, relatives, and siblings.

I skimmed descriptions of gardens or grounds, I skipped altogether descriptions of cottages inhabited by tenant farmers, and I seem to have either ignored or forgotten descriptions of servants' quarters and kitchens. The uncertain course of romance and courtship, the tedium of manners, the ceaseless rounds of social obligations also went largely unnoticed. But not interior space, nor threats of its loss. The unheard of privilege of privacy made palpable by the rooms middle-class heroines occupied made an immediate and lasting impression on me. I have no idea if many other children from working-class homes also acquired from their reading an appetite for privacy. But I am certain that the literature that fascinated me kindled and shaped a desire for privacy in me so acute that only hearing my mother's voice reminds me that not only I but an entire family paid the price of my replacing the sociality of my working-class home with the books that now keep me company at home.

I wonder what it must have been like to have witnessed rather than experienced my reading. Unlike the heroines in the novels I was reading, the women in my family, in my neighborhood for that matter, lived in rather than visited the kitchen. My sisters and I would sit at the kitchen table talking, reading, studying, drawing, writing, sewing, taunting one another, tattling, boasting, snapping beans, kneading bags of margarine, cutting cookies, cutting out paper dolls and their clothes while our mother talked to us as she fixed meals, baked, mended, cut patterns, sewed, talked on the phone. It now seems to me that all serious conversations were held in the kitchen. My father sometimes quizzed us at supper, gave us words to spell, word problems to solve, multiplication tables to recite. It was easy for me to accommodate him. Since he visited only at meal times, he never participated in our kitchen conversations, never knew we were picking at and picking up the threads of earlier conversations.

My mother usually let us sit at the table and listen while she and the neighbor women, or female relatives, told the stories that made the kitchen that I remember the hub of our familial and social life. There were stories about pregnancy and childbirth, childhood (theirs and their children's), stories recounting the antics of local doctors, politicians, cops, bosses, nuns, priests, and ministers and their children, and stories encoding the exigent dangers of sex—going too far, getting into trouble, having to get married. Teachers were the only authorities who were never challenged in my presence, though sometimes in my hearing. I wonder now if the absence of critique meant the mothers believed the classroom to be an even more important room, though they must at least have suspected they could lose their children, their daughters as well as their sons, to teachers and to the middle class.

My father's familial domain was the living room, where most evenings he would read the local paper and union materials or study car repair manuals and report cards, and where he alone napped, in his chair. The children sometimes also came there to read, perhaps because my mother read there in the daytime, but we were not allowed to talk or play in the living room when my father was there. The family began gathering in the living room only after the television arrived, which would make it 1955. In what now seems a blink of the eye, the television displaced my father in a spate of family programs. My mother, my sisters, and I must have learned a fair number of middle-class scripts from television, and then rehearsed them on my father.

Working-class houses are not miniatures of middle-class houses, neither of real ones nor of those created by literature or constructed for television. So in one of those remarkable generalizations to which children are prone, I seem to have concluded that since middle-class mores governed the dramatic action in fiction, nothing of real consequence could happen to anyone who does not reside in a middle-class house. Little wonder then that I also fervently believed that my parents had only to acquire such a house to assume consequence and persisted in making plans for moving the family into it, despite my parents' quite reasonable insistence that I well knew that they had not the money to do so. I wonder now if my terror of working-class inconsequence was not aggravated by two interdependent, historical events in the 1950s: the escalating cold war and the end of the postwar recession. The first event radically altered my education and the second, my neighborhood.

By the late 1950s, some of our neighbors had sold or left their rented homes without dining rooms and a bedroom for each child and taken out government-insured, low-interest mortgages on the ideal two-story middle-class house or, barring that, the ersatz middle-class tract houses that developers and realtors were selling the unwary. The ideal had a foyer, a free-standing staircase, and hardwood floors throughout, a fireplace in the living room, a formal dining room, a large kitchen with a walk-in pantry on the first floor, three or four bedrooms upstairs, a bathroom up and down, a screened veranda, a full basement and attic, and a detached garage. The house was made of either brick or stone. While the tract houses possessed none of the virtues of the two-story houses I had encountered in my reading and seen advertised on television, save the illusory privacy of bedrooms with doors, that they were known locally as doll houses would have appealed not to my sense of irony but to my fantasy (apparently shared by the many adults who purchased them) that a new house would reinvent us as a middle-class family. Such houses did not, of course, even exist in the neighborhood, so those who moved up also moved out.

My family stayed in the neighborhood until well after I left for college. But they must have known as early as the ninth grade that I would move out, when the public schools tracked me into college preparatory classes on the basis of my test scores (I forget which tests) and my performance in classes. It seems, though I remember no one saying so at the time, that I was being drafted for the cold war, which precipitated an educational reform, at least in Quincy, Illinois, that cut across class lines with a flourish that only seems imaginable during periods of extreme nationalism. Nationalism even extended to putting one male and one female Negro on the college track. A fair amount of money was lavished on the education of cold war recruits. Classrooms were well furnished and well maintained, the science and language laboratories (where I studied Russian) were well equipped, the teachers were well educated (most had MAs, a few had PhDs), and the student–teacher ratio must have been excellent, for I never wanted for attention.

My schoolday began at 8:00 A.M. and I was rarely back home before 5:00 P.M. There were few electives, and the ones I chose (like journalism) required more, not less, time than required courses. While I continued to study dance until my senior year (when I finally had to admit that diligence is no substitute for talent), I gradually became the school's daughter: National Honor Society, editor of the school newspaper, Student Council, Latin Club, Russian Club, Pep Club, and other societies and clubs that I am grateful to have forgotten. The homework for these cold war classes took from three to five hours most evenings, which I dutifully completed without fail at the kitchen table and checked and/or completed on the phone. Most of the daily assignments were graded, and the scheduled tests and pop quizzes were buttressed by periodic batteries of standardized achievement and IQ tests. So thoroughly prepared was I for college during my four years of high school that my first two years at the small state university from which I graduated were mostly review, except for writing.

I had not written much besides journalism in high school, and my professors, who did not much admire my mastery of the inverted pyramid, were looking for an essay whose paragraphs elaborated what I now think of as the *generic-corrective-display-thesis*: A good many scholars/critics have concluded X, but X ignores Y, which is essential/critical to fully understanding Z (the structure of a poem or the universe, the precipitating causes of the Civil War, the Enlightenment, progress, overpopulation). A student can use this thesis in any class because it both corrects errors in previous scholarship or criticism and displays the student's knowledge of the literature. It took me nearly a year to (re)invent the thesis and three more years to perfect it. It kept my grades high and it probably kept me from learning as much as I might have about writing, even though it gave me plenty of time to perfect my style. Not to put too fine a point on it, this quintessentially modern thesis assumes that reality, which exists entirely separate from and independent of language, is superficially complicated but ultimately governed by simple, underlying principles, rules, and/or verities. I no longer believe the thesis, but I believed it then, if only because I desperately wanted to believe in middle-class houses, wherein everything seemed to conspire to protect the inhabitants from any of the complications that beset the people in my house and neighborhood.

I probably visited my first middle-class houses the summer my younger sister and I lay in bed listening to the couple next door read *Gone with the Wind* to each other in their bedroom. They are recorded in my memory as reading voices, one male, one female, quietly enuciating just loud enough for us to hear. I never spoke of my affection for the couple next door or of anything that happened at home in the houses of my new classmates or at school. By then I was old enough to know better, old enough to realize that any story I told would incriminate my family and indict my neighborhood. For by then, we had been visited by the social worker, who I remember as a singularly humorless man in a suit, asking my mother questions and writing down her answers. He didn't smile when she described the decor as early Halloween, and she didn't contradict him when he pointed out there were no bookcases. She didn't tell him that she and her children borrowed books from the library or that the ones we owned were stored under our beds. I had a complete set of Nancy Drew mysteries under my bed, and among us my sisters and I had collected a fair number of the classic girls' books—*Heidi, Little Women, Anne Frank*—along with the adventures of Trixie Beldon, Ginny Gordon, and Sue Barton. Although I never asked my mother why she let the social worker think what he would, I must have taken her reticence as a given because I never attempted to explain home to anyone who didn't live there.

Since none of my classmates had gone to my neighborhood elementary school, my parents knew none of their parents or, more precisely, my mother knew none of their mothers. My mother had made it her business to meet and chat with the mothers of my new working-class girl friends in junior high. But I made no new friends among the other White working-class recruits in my college preparatory classes and was forbidden, for the usual racist reasons, to do anything more than mention that the Negro girl was also Catholic. All through high school I kept up with working-class girl friends from the neighborhood school. I even coached my best working-class girl friend from junior high on her dance routine for the "Miss Quincy Pageant" the summer I went to college. But I kept the old friends separate from the new ones, for the worlds were by then as distinct to me as the children's library and the adult library, as stories and literature. Like reading, tracking radically displaced me, conferring on me honorary middle-class privileges on the order of those afforded by my early admission to the adult library.

Alone, I entered houses made familiar by my reading. I particularly enjoyed living the fiction that food is served rather than prepared and floors, windows, dishes, and clothes endlessly clean rather than cleaned endlessly. These were phenomena already known to me from my reading. Also familiar were ambitious mothers who took their daughters shopping in St Louis or Chicago, where they were fitted for gowns that the local newspaper would describe in lavish detail. Familiar though I may have found these customs, my interest in fictional real estate had obscured the importance of manners, no less important in the twentieth-century middle-class houses where my new girl friends lived than in nineteenth-century novels. The talk was of honors, grade point averages, colleges, sororities, SATs, country clubs, clothes, dances, and dates. In the light of these topics, I could no longer avoid concluding that in this culture, and in the fictional one on which it seemed to rest, the present is a dress rehearsal for a future whose value will ultimately be determined by whether getting into the right sorority at the right school results in marrying the right man.

My own class-based experience of family shielded me from envying any but the material comforts of my middle-class girl friends. I learned to speak fluent bourgeoisie in those houses. And what I learned there contributed to my college grades and probably even my academic career. Fluency has not, however, made me a native speaker, for when left to my own devices I continue to measure the value of the present in terms of itself rather the future. The future only interests me when the present becomes intolerable. That I still consider material conditions the sine qua non of my intellectual life is doubtless a legacy of my viewing the middle classes with a literary map of their houses in hand rather than a copy of their conduct book committed to memory. That I never fully assimilated the bourgeois belief that rehearsal predicts the future is without a doubt a working-class legacy. This is not to say that I neither plan nor rehearse. But since neither raises any expectations about my literal ability to control events, I am more inclined to view plans and rehearsals as the moments when I am forcibly reminded of my devotion to contingencies—to the possibility that the essay will be better than the plan and the performance a considerable improvement over the rehearsal, acknowledging all the while essays and performances that fell flat.

It is probably a measure of their extraordinary faith in education that my parents, who regularly challenged the authority of medicine, the church, and the state, never resisted the tracking of their middle daughter into college preparatory classes, even though they could ill afford either the new courses or friends. The courses radically diminished my chances of fully developing or properly valuing the domestic competencies that other working-class girls acquired at home (cooking, baking, cleaning, ironing, sewing, mending) or those that the girls in my family learned during summers spent on our aunt and uncle's farm (truck gardening, canning, preserving, tending livestock). To make matters worse, the middle-class houses seeded unspeakable desires having to do with the pleasures of romance, solitude, and economic independence that would naturally follow from the "college education" vaunted at school and taken for granted by my new friends and their parents.

The educational opportunities that thrilled me contradicted most of what was expected of me at home. Yet my parents accepted the economic privations that accompanied my tracking. I paid for my ballet classes by teaching younger children, and the part-time job I held as an honors student neither required that I work the hours nor that I work as hard as my older sister had. My going to college meant not just that my parents would contribute to my support beyond the usual age of 18, but that I would not be contributing to theirs in return for room and board. There is a sense in which my parents reconciled my prolonged economic dependence by turning me into the youngest daughter. They guarded me so carefully that even serious problems and illnesses went unmentioned until I was home on break. Little wonder, then, that I was younger at 20 than I had been at 16, or that I began to prefer school to home, the more so since many of my college courses indulged my fantasy of America as a society where I could reinvent myself as a classless, genderless, raceless scholar. I wanted little more during that time than to be free of the town that had held me in thrall, where neighborhoods mapped class and race with a ruthless precision neither acknowledged nor validated by my reading and where the prospects for women at either my house or the houses of my friends had begun to look equally uninviting.

At my house gender was defined in terms of money and work. Among themselves, women talked about neither the accumulation of capital nor the consolidation of wealth and privilege through marriage. Women like my mother saw their work as steering adolescent girls through the present tense dangers of dating and pregnancy, rather than the future tense possibilities of marrying well. Marriage posed financial problems, and its topics were employment, housing, the care and feeding of children, and in my case the loss of financial independence. These working-class marriage-narratives did not hold the same promise of untroubled futures that the middle-class ones seemed to hold for my girl friends. Bearing and raising children are not nearly as attractive propositions for girls who watch and even help their mothers do the work. Nor, for that matter, is keeping house, if the old carpet is a threadbare heirloom and the provenance of the second-hand furniture unknown.

Since it was the body of neither a working-class mother nor a middle-class wife but that of the female dancer that had attracted me from childhood through adolescence, I cannot but wonder if on realizing that I would not be a dancer, I somehow imagined that as a professor I could turn myself inside out like a reversible garment and cloak my female body in what I believed (via courses and grades) to be my genderless and classless mind. While traces of this desire remain, it nonetheless comes as something of a surprise to realize that I am never more my mother's daughter than when I am writing the essays, papers, lectures, books that organize my academic life. For it is not when I talk but when I write that I perform uncanny re-enactments of my mother sewing, and then that I realize I must have learned to write from watching her sew. What I saw, or now believe I must have seen, was a woman whose pleasure while sewing matched mine while playing. I suppose what I remember is seeing her thoroughly at ease, for the woman who sewed was entirely different from the one who cooked, cleaned, shopped, talked, and cared for her children. That woman was preoccupied, often weary and worried, and awkward in the presence of strangers. The woman who sewed was none of these. This woman would discuss ideas that animated her long before she ever spread out the newspapers she saved for her patterns, and this woman had discarded all but one by the time she bought the fabric, laid out the pieces on the bias, cut the cloth, hand basted and machine stitched the darts and seams of a garment.

Sewing relieved the tyranny of money over my mother's life. She made all her children's clothes, by copying ready-to-wear clothing, except her seams were more generous and her hems deeper, so they could be let out as we grew. My mother never thought of herself as (or allowed anyone to call her) a seamstress. It may have been undue modesty on her part, or she may have preferred her high standing among local amateurs to joining the ranks of anonymous professionals. But I like to think it is because she knew seamstresses do not sew to please themselves. And my mother pleased herself when she sewed. I can remember no time during my childhood when my mother was *not* sewing: our clothes, our doll clothes, our costumes for Halloween and school plays and my dance recitals, not to mention First Communion dresses, confirmation dresses, "outfits" for Easter and Christmas, party dresses, and formals. Dresses, skirts, blouses, and trousers hung perfectly, we were given to understand, only when she found and cut the cloth on the bias. The clothes, the doll clothes, and the costumes were all given equal attention, each made as if it were to last forever and to be viewed by an eye as appreciative of detail as my mother's. When I think about this aesthetic as a tribute to her children's acuity, I regret even more the careless indifference each of us assumed during adolescence to these tokens of her esteem. She was literally outclassed by the inexpensive ready-to-wear clothing that devalued and finally supplanted "home-made" clothes, and simultaneously the one domestic practice at which my mother thrived.

None of my mother's children would fully appreciate her aesthetic again until we were adults, and my own appreciation has been tempered with varieties of remorse. I lack the skill, the capital, and even the patience to clothe myself with the rigorous attention to detail I learned from my mother. Yet I am never more confident than when I am wearing something I believe she would admire. It is less a particular style of clothing than the certitude that my mother could tell just from the hang of it that I had not forgotten how much depends on the bias. While few garments I own would please my mother, that my best essays are written on the bias would. Even more than what I finally produce, that I do not even attempt to write an essay until I have found a bias would please her, for my practice as a writer is as intricately tied to seeking and following oblique lines that cut across the grain as was my mother's.

A girl can, it seems, learn a great deal about work and its pleasures from watching her mother sew. While I never learned to sew, that I write as my mother sewed probably explains why I take a good deal more obvious pleasure in the intellectual work of being an academic than those of my peers who have difficulty believing writing to be real work. If I enjoy the labor of writing, that can at least in part be explained by my writing as my mother sewed. She made clothes. I make prose. There is a sense in which just as my mother was always sewing, I am always writing. I understood her to be sewing in even her most casual remarks.

Writing begins for me with something once heard or seen or read that recurs in my mind's eye as a troubling image—myself as a little girl cautiously descending a staircase, which in turn prompts me to seek a narrative explanation for its persistence. My search for a narrative is guided by the bias of the image, in this essay by the inexplicable sorrow the child evoked in me. As I trace lines of inquiry that depend on the bias, I can see there are others besides mine, for there are at least as many biases woven into the fabric of a life as into poplins, wools, and satins. I can see differences in how from one bias I construe the cloakroom as an effort to eradicate traces of working-class sociality from a classroom and from yet another I could justify the teacher who sent me there, for I am also a teacher. That I follow my bias does not mean that I cannot see others. It means instead that rather than extol the triumph of the child, I meet my sorrow by sorting the details of her longing to be middle class from those of her struggle against the indiscriminate eradication of the intellectuality of her family at school.

I wish everyone were taught to write on the bias, for finding and following a bias is as critical to writing as sewing. Yet if bias seems even more counterintuitive in writing than in sewing, that is because students are taught that third-person statements are unbiased (objective) and those in the first person are biased (subjective). Little wonder then that by the time they reach college, most students have concluded that to avoid bias they have only to recast their first person claims into the third person. Delete "I believe" from "racism is on the rise in this country" or "racism has virtually disappeared in this country" and the assertion assumes a reality independent of the writer, who is no longer the author but merely the messenger. Students learn what they have been taught, and they have been taught that grammatical person governs the objectivity and subjectivity of actual persons. Step on a crack. Break your mother's back. Hop over it. Save her life.

Most students have learned rules that readers rather than writers believe govern prose. They have not been taught what every writer knows, that one writes on the bias or not at all. A bias may be provided by a theory or an experience or an image or an ideology. Without a bias, however, language is only words as cloth is only threads. To write is to find words that explain what can be seen from an angle of vision, the limitations of which determine a wide or narrow bias, but not the lack of one. Far from guaranteeing objectivity, third-person assertions too often record an unexamined routine in which the writers who follow a bias provided by, say, the "objectivism" of journalism or science confound that worldview/theory/ideology with reality. The bias that is or should be treated as pejorative rather than honorific is that which feigns objectivity by dressing up its reasons in seemingly unassailable logic and palming off its interest as disinterest—in order to silence arguments from other quarters.

It seems to me that middle-class culture and schooling gratuitously and foolishly rob children of the pleasures of the physical and intellectual work of learning generally and writing in particular. Most successful students learn to disown their labor (to claim they have not read the assignment or studied for the test). They disdain their own scholastic achievement as luck or intelligence, and grudgingly accept in its stead the tokens to be exchanged for symbolic opportunities. Take tests for grades, exchange the grades for credentials, use the credentials to a launch a career, measure the career by the number of promotions and the size of the paychecks and the amount of stock. Writing is only incidental in this cycle. It is incidental because the cycle deflates the value of the intellectual work of practices like writing in order to artificially inflate the value of ritual performances (achievement tests, reading scores) that can be calculated and minted as cultural currency.

That the present is hostage to the future in any culture that devalues labor seems to me both obvious and tragic. That this country has historically substituted tokens of literacy for literacy practices and then cloaked its anti-intellectualism in alarming statistics about illiteracy and illiterates makes it all the more important that those of us who learned to write teach ourselves to remember how and where that happened, what it was we learned, and especially how the lessons learned material. Just as a piece of cloth can be fashioned into any number of garments, the essay I construct from language is not the only one I could have written. The pleasures in playing out possibilities are matched only by the labor taken to complete one garment or essay.

CHAPTER 2

Learning to Speak Out in an Abstinence-Based Sex Education Group: Gender and Race Work in an Urban Magnet School

LOIS WEIS
with DORIS CARBONELL-MEDINA

Lois: Oh, Donna [a young woman in the group] was saying . . . looking at a sheet that you had given them, you know, instead of having sex, you go for a bike ride, watch television, et cetera, et cetera. And Donna looked at the sheet and said, "Well, we can't do these things. We're poor. We don't have bikes . . . we don't have a car." And you [Doris, the group leader] turned to her and, without missing a beat, said, "Well, you're going to be even poorer if you have a baby or get AIDS."

Recent research on sexuality education in schools suggests that the current state of affairs is dismal. From Michelle Fine's (1988) research on what she terms the missing "discourse of desire" to work by Mariamne Whatley (1991) and, more recently, Bonnie Nelson Trudell (1993), we learn that in these curricula young men are painted as biologically programmed sexual aggressors, while young women are scripted as passive victims whose only possible position is that of not provoking easily sexually aroused males. While it is generally acknowledged that there is not nearly enough sexuality education in schools, what does exist leaves much to be desired (Emihovich, 1998). In addition, research shows that compulsory heterosexuality is inscribed throughout the school curriculum and most prominently in the sexuality education curriculum, where AIDS is often presented solely as a disease of homosexuals (Friend, 1993).

Taking into account these observations and working from this perspective, it is clear that the sexuality education curriculum is about to become even worse. Due to the passage of recent legislation, abstinence-only programs are slated to receive millions and millions of dollars under the Family Adolescent Life Act (AFLA, Title XX of the Public Health Act) and the Personal Responsibility and Work Opportunity Reconciliation Act of 1996 (otherwise known as "welfare reform"). Despite this massive funding, there has been little research concerning the effectiveness of one type of program versus another (Kirby, 1997; Wilcox, 1997) and even less research on the day-to-day delivery of those programs that do exist (for the exception, see Trudell, 1993).

The fact remains, though, that millions of dollars are being poured into abstinence-only sex education programs in schools without any idea of outcomes. Currently, most sex education programs in schools are *abstinence-based*, including the one examined here. While "abstinence-based" and "abstinence-only" may appear to be a minor language difference, there is, in fact, a major difference in content. *Abstinence-only* programs present abstinence as the only option for adolescents and offer no additional content, such as contraceptive information, for those adolescents who may not be abstinent. In addition, such programs often use fear tactics to make their points. *Abstinence-based* programs, on the other hand, make up most of the sexuality education programs in schools and offer information about safer-sex techniques and contraception in the event that adolescents do not "choose" abstinence.

In this chapter I investigate one such abstinence-based program, My Bottom Line, and suggest that the space carved out by this program for girls is being used to promote the deconstruction of taken-for-granted gender and race meanings.[1] In this space teenage women struggle to avoid the lives that they fear will be theirs, under the careful guidance of a Latina group leader whom I observed and worked closely with. In this urban magnet arts school, abstinence-based programming (mainstream sexuality education programming) is being used for some very progressive ends, ends that encourage young women across race and ethnicity to explore their own gendered subjectivities and, most of all, to resist the violence and control that they feel lies ahead of them. Writing with deep respect for the work of Michelle Fine (1988), Mariamne Whatley (1991), Bonnie Nelson Trudell (1993), and others who have pointed out the difficulties with mainstream sexuality education curricula, I want to suggest here that such curricula can potentially be used in more progressive ways and, in fact, offer a space for uses that abstinence-only programs do not. While there may be great problems with mainstream sexuality education curricula, it is important to focus on the space that such curricula *could* offer if opened up and used in a more progressive manner.

It must be clear from the beginning, though, that hegemonic definitions of heterosexuality were not questioned in the particular group studied. This group was aimed, unofficially, at helping young women to gain strength and control within the boundaries of heterosexual relationships. It did not, therefore, broach alternative sexual orientations.

Data were gathered during the spring semester of 1997 at "Arts Academy," a grades 5–12 magnet school geared toward the arts in Buffalo, New York. Students must be accepted into the school on the basis of an audition, either in dance, theater, music or visual arts, or radio and TV. The school draws broadly from the city of Buffalo, although many of the students reside in poor and/or working-class neighborhoods within a 10-minute ride of the school. The school is located just south of downtown Buffalo and, like all magnet schools in the city, as part of the desegregation plan, ostensibly acts as a magnet for White students to attend school in neighborhoods populated by people of color. The school is highly mixed racially and ethnically, having 45% White, 45% African American, 8% Latino/Latina, 1% Native American, and 1% Asian students. The ethnic and racial montage is everywhere visible as students from varying backgrounds participate in academic and arts endeavors spanning jazz combo to ballet.

Data were drawn from the within-school program My Bottom Line, whose officially stated goal is "to prevent or delay the onset of sexual activity, build self-esteem, and increase self-sufficiency in young women through an abstinence-based, gender-specific prevention education program." The program stresses abstinence as the preferred "choice" but does not steer totally clear of topics related to contraception and/or safer sex.

The school guidance counselor, Shirley, actively recruited Woman-focus, a nonprofit agency designed to deliver the program to local area schools, to establish My Bottom Line at Arts Academy. It has the strong backing of the guidance counseling staff, and group meetings were held in the large, centrally located conference room of the guidance office. Students voluntarily attend the program during study halls, participating one or two times a week, depending on their schedules.

As Shirley, the guidance counselor states:

> I really want these girls to take good risks with their lives and
> escape negative situations. I want them to be empowered to make

good choices, to be able to leave town for college, to take intern-
ships, to take advantage of opportunities, to be able to leave their
neighborhoods. Too many are trapped. I want them to delay sexual
activity without being a prude so that they will be able to live fuller
lives. Too many of these girls don't realistically see what a baby
does to one's life. They have babies to make up for their own lost
childhood and want to give to the baby what they themselves did
not have. But they do not have the resources or maturity to give
to their baby what they didn't have.

Shirley used all school resources possible to support My Bottom Line.
She talked with teachers on a regular basis, urged them to send students
during their study halls, and worked with teachers to facilitate this.

My Bottom Line is run by Doris Carbonell-Medina, a Latina Woman-
focus staff member. I participated in all meetings for a full semester and
acted, at times, as co-facilitator of the group. The program runs for 15 weeks.
Although the program targets young women in seventh, eighth, and ninth
grades, young women ranging from grades 7–12 participated, at the explicit request of Doris. Seventh- and eighth-graders meet together, and high
school students meet in a different session.

The officially stated goal of the program is to reduce sexual activity
among youth. As stated in the proposal for funding (My Bottom Line,
1995):

> The alarmingly high rate of teenage pregnancy, the risk of AIDS and other
> sexually transmitted diseases have served to open up and intensify the de-
> bate in this country and in the Buffalo community over what to do about
> the sexual activity of adolescents and the associated problems. What was once
> a moral issue is clearly a public health issue. Educators, parents, politicians,
> and health officials share concern and agree that clearly our current systems
> are failing to adequately equip our young people to handle the choices and
> the consequences they face in 1994.
>
> Current peer standards of sexual behavior, stronger media messages,
> shifting society values, and changing family configurations have all helped
> to confuse our teens as to how to handle their emerging sexuality. Abstinence,
> or refraining from sexual intercourse, has become a lost and understated
> option for many teens. At best, our teens are not getting balanced messages
> about their choices with regard to sexual activity. At worst, there is no evi-
> dent, consistently reachable "face saving" support for the teens who want to
> abstain or delay the onset of sexual activity.
>
> Education for sexual abstinence, life skills to empower young women
> to assert their honest choices with regard to sexual activity, and the poten-
> tial impact on adolescent sexual activity is the focus of the proposed My
> Bottom Line program. (p. 3)

The expressed intention of the program is, then, one of encouraging abstinence among girls who are not yet sexually active, generally those in the seventh, eighth, and ninth grades. However, Doris insists on working with the older girls as well, specifically tying her decision to the rhetoric of abstinence:

> Many people interpret abstinence-based program as, you know, very conservative, sort of right-wing, concepts. Like that abstinence means they have to be "clamped shut," and you're saying, "that's it." And that's why we target those seventh-, eighth-, and ninth-grade girls, because those are the years that they're going to be facing those crucial decisions in their life, as to whether or not they want to be having sex. And those are the years that girls choose this for their lives. But, on the other hand, those high school girls that have already made that choice [to have sex], or some that haven't, they also need some sort of intervention, and that knowledge that simply because you've been sexually active in one relationship doesn't mean that you have to be sexually active in another relationship. And, you know, young girls need to be given that information, or at least to be given the confidence to say, "Hey, you don't have to sleep around with every single guy." There are some standards that you should have. There are some criteria that you should have in establishing your relationships. And I think those lines get blurred once you become sexually involved, and once you get into that whole world of adolescence and sex.

Tying her insistence on working with girls beyond ninth grade to a strongly held notion that these young women need to be given choices about relationships and sex even *after* they have had a sexual relationship, Doris works hard to let young women know that they do not have to be sexually available to every man simply because they are not virgins. In doing so, she stretches, intentionally, the purpose of the program:

Doris: You know, it's not that I don't care if they are having sex. If they are having sex, I just want them to be prepared to answer, if they are engaging in adultlike activity, that they should have adultlike responsibility. And that's where my focus is. Adultlike responsibility if you are, you know, assuming this way of life. And I think that they need the confidence to know that they don't have to have sex with every guy that they go out with.

Lois: What do you mean by adultlike responsibility? You say it would be better if they didn't engage in sex, but if they engage in sex, then they have to, number one, you don't always have to have sex, but number two, you have to do so in an adultlike way. Can you say a little bit about what you mean by that?

Doris: Sure. Adultlike way, you have to be able to protect yourself from unwanted pregnancies, that you have to protect yourself from STDS [sexually transmitted diseases] and other related diseases. That you have to understand that you're placing yourself in a very emotional and vulnerable position when you begin to, you know, act, and you conduct yourself in your relationship with him, yeah. And that, a lot of times there can be some positioning that goes on [in the relationship; she is speaking of control], and even some abuse. And, I mean . . . you might think this [abuse] is normal, that it's OK for them [the young women] to be treated badly, or to be controlled. So that if, in fact, this is happening to you, then you have to recognize that this [abuse] is not right. And you have to take responsibility for yourself and get out. And tell somebody about this problem. So that's adultlike responsibility if you have a relationship with a member of the opposite sex, particularly if he's older than you. But now, [in the program] we're doing this thing that they're [the young women] signing a contract [laughs] . . . I devised this contract we outlined at the beginning of September. And we talked about it, that the girls agreed not to have sex until they can take care of themselves. And then I go on into it and define "take care of yourself."

This space, then—in addition to dealing with issues of sexual absti-nence—was intentionally established to empower young women, particu-larly in their relationships with young men. For Doris and Shirley, women's bodies must be under the control of women themselves and should not be a site for male control, abuse, or exploitation. Both state strongly that women need to make choices about their bodies and minds and that the lack of such choices means that these young girls/women will never ven-ture outside their neighborhoods or escape their economic marginality. Empowering them to stay away from situations of abuse lies at the center of the unofficial programming. This is not, then, simply a program about abstinence, although the abstinence strain is there. Here, mainstream sexu-ality education curricula are used as the basis for important discussions about gender, sexuality, and, indirectly, race.

In the midst of a society moving in increasingly polarized directions (Fine & Weis, 1998), such spaces are potentially important in this regard. The question is posed here: What is the nature of the "gender work" going on in this space? In this bold program designed to push at the very walls of specific gendered meanings, what are the implications for "race work" given that it is taking place in the particular context of the urban magnet school?

This project is part of a broader study of "urban spaces" (many aspects of which appear as chapters in this volume) and theoretically derives from the work of Sara Evans and Harry Boyte (1992), Nancy Fraser (1993), and others. Fraser (1993) argues that it is advantageous for "marginals" to create what she calls "counterpublics" where they may oppose stereotypes and assert novel interpretations of their own shifting identities, interests, and needs. She theorizes that these spaces are formed, ironically, out of the very exclusionary practices of the public sphere. We, too, have found that in the midst of disengagement by the public sector and relocation of private-sector jobs "down south" or overseas, it is into newly constructed "free spaces", as Evans and Boyte (1992) call them, that poor and working-class men and women have fled from sites of historical pain and struggle and reconstituted new identities (Fine & Weis, 1998).

In the broader study, we stretch across spaces that are sites of explicit political resistance, such as those Boyte and Evans describe, to those that are more nearly recuperative spaces, as more aptly described by Oldenburg (1989). These are places for breathing, relaxing, or sitting on a couch without the constant arrows of stereotypes and social hatred. Many of the spaces we have investigated, however, are spaces carved in conscious opposition by adults *for* adults (see, e.g., Christmas, 1999). In My Bottom Line we have a space set up as oppositional by adults *for* young women. In this space, which adults establish and facilitate, teens actively interact. Although the official intent of My Bottom Line is sexual abstinence, there is much other work going on in this site, by both adults and youth, that makes it a powerful space for re-visioning gender and race subjectivities as students gain a set of lenses and allies for doing social critique. As we have argued elsewhere, most youth have the potential for social critique, but this critique fizzles as they grow older (Fine, 1993; Fine & Weis, 1998; Weis & Fine, 1996). Here we focus on the preliminary consolidation of critique and enter the site, as I lived in it and worked with it, for 6 months. It is the gender and race work we examine here, work done under the explicit tutelage of Doris Carbonell-Medina.[2]

BARING SECRETS

A cornerstone of the group is confidentiality, a confidentiality that enables the girls to bare secrets without fear of recrimination or gossip. As Doris states:

I tell them at the very beginning that this issue I take very seriously. And when we say that in order to build trusting relationships, in order to build relationships [in the group] where we can open up and tell our stories, that we have to be mature. And mature means that you don't go around and you gossip and stuff. Then I say that I get so crazy about this stuff that if it comes back to me that you've opened your mouth and blabbed—and that's how it's seen—you know, we'd ask you to leave. And that would be the way that we separate you from us, because we don't want you to be in our group if you can't keep our secrets. They're very careful about it I tell you. And they don't reveal anything [in group] that they don't want people to know. And then, if they've really got to get it out—and many of them have done this to me—they have said, "Can I talk to you after the group?"

Embedded in the weaving of a new collective of young women across race lines is the baring of secrets. The group is a space within which young women tell a great deal about their personal lives—the illnesses within their homes, the violence in their relationships, their fears spoken aloud when their "stepfather's moving back in with mom." Girls share secrets as they share strength and hope, jumping in to help each other with problems, sometimes life-threatening ones, and other times, mundane. As they share secrets, they examine self and weave new identities, individual and collective. What is particularly striking in these data is the extent to which young White women reveal pieces of their lives normally not told. Although they are relatively quiet in group, as compared with African American girls, for example, those who do open up contest the suffocating silence that envelops them. White women, whether adolescents or adults, are the most silent/silenced group with which we have worked (Fine & Weis, 1998; Weis & Fine, 1998), speaking softly about the horrors in their lives only in one-to-one interviews, never in a group context. But not so here. White girls are cracking that silence so typical of the group, sharing secrets in protected environments, working beyond the one-to-one encounters. They are hearing each other out as they unburden their problems. White girls from a variety of backgrounds unravel their stories within the group context, as did Tiffany:

Tiffany: I love my mother dearly. But, OK, she's manic-depressive, but I love her dearly.
Lois: Is she really manic-depressive?
Tiffany: Yeah, like she's got medication and everything. She's a manic depressive and my dad is schizophrenic—which is great for me (*sarcasti-*

cally) . . . She doesn't make friends easily. I have to watch what I say, because I don't want to get her in a bad mood. She's on medication now. She's very caring, but she's smothering. Like, it's my birthday Monday, right. I'm like, since I was like 9, I have like, each birthday, I have a half an hour later that I can stay up. I mean, right now it's 9:30, and all my friends are sitting there going to bed at 11:00. And on Monday, I get to go to bed at 10:00 and that makes me so happy because I can go to bed at ten (*laughs*).

Tiffany goes on to tell us that she went through a bout of clinically diagnosed depression a couple of years ago:

Tiffany: Well, in the summer of the freshman year, 2 years ago, I like, it was like, well, the court thing, everybody's separate. They [my parents] go to court. And I have to choose who I want to stay with for this part of the summer and that part of the summer. And that's how I was just like, usually I'm all happy, you know, kind of like this [as she is now], kind of perky (*laughs*). . . . And so, like all of a sudden, I just . . . I remember sitting there on the bed and going, you know, "I can't do it anymore." Because I wasn't really happy. I was just getting tired. And I went into a slight, it wasn't a severe depression, but it was depression. I had medication and everything. And I just distanced myself from it and I went to a doctor—a psychiatrist—and everything, 'cause I like burst into tears at the slightest criticism.
Lois: Did they send you to a doctor?
Tiffany: Yeah, they sent me to a doctor. I went to a doctor because I was losin' weight, because I weighed 108. And I'm 5'8". And I dropped like 20 pounds that summer.

Tiffany speaks candidly about her clinically ill parents, weaving through the discussion her own feelings as she attempts to live in her mother's house. She is not the only one who speaks so openly about home-based problems, and the uniqueness of this, particularly among White girls, should not be underestimated. My Bottom Line offers a space in which such secrets can be shared. Tiffany, of course, does not receive professional help in a group of this sort. What she does receive is support and under-standing from her peers, monitored by an adult who is sensitive to these issues. In addition, and perhaps most important, someone like Tiffany feels less alone with her problems since she has shared them and learned, oftentimes, that she is not the only one with such problems. While teen-agers, to be sure, often complain about their parents, this should not be seen simply as a "gripe session." Tiffany's parents are ill, and the sharing of this information, like the sharing of incidents of domestic violence, of violence in a personal relationship, represents one step toward acknowledging the problem and obtaining long-term help. Doris meets regularly with the girls outside the group, urging them, in a more confidential context, to seek additional help.

Within this same context, at another session, Connie, a White girl, talks about her parents' chronic drinking and her own fears about possibly drinking too much. We urged her, within group, to pursue Al-Anon, a support group for families of alcoholics, within which she can begin to sort out the effects her parents' drinking have had on her and, at the same time, concentrate on her own health. Sharing in this sense can be turned into direct action.

DISTANCING

Able to bare secrets, young women use the space of My Bottom Line to fashion and refashion individual and collective identities. Under Doris's expert guidance, it is a space within which selves are tried on, experimented with, accepted and rejected. A key piece of this identity work among participants involves distancing self from those perceived as "not like us." In this space, in this time, they pull away from others. Unlike previous work, however, which suggests that this form of identity work in urban schools takes place largely along we–they racial lines (Bertram, Marusza, Fine, & Weis, 2000; Fine & Weis, 1998; Fine, Weis, & Powell, 1997; Weis, 1990), particularly among working-class Whites and most particularly among boys and men, the specific form this identity work takes here is that of distancing from other neighborhood youth and, more broadly, from other girls/ women thought to be heading down the wrong path. Virtually all the teen women, irrespective of race and ethnicity, who attend group use the space to distance themselves explicitly from those they perceive to be "other" than themselves—those who will not make it, those who will end up pregnant at an early age, those who will be beaten by men. This is not an idyllic presentation of cross-race interactions and friendships, but rather reflects the observation that when "difference" is constructed in group, it is not constructed along racial lines. Girls from all communities articulate carefully that they wish to be different from those in their neighborhoods, those they leave behind in their pursuit of schooling and success. While this may not translate into intimate friendships across racial and ethnic lines, it does mean that the racial "other" is not constructed as the "fall guy" for any of the groups under consideration, contrasting sharply with Julia Marusza's data on girls in a White lower-class community center

(1998). None of the groups under consideration erect racial borders specifically against which their own identity is then elaborated. Rather, identity is elaborated *across* racial and ethnic group as girls distance self from
the "other," whether male or female, who will not make it. Certainly there
is much racial identity work going on in other sites that reaffirms Whiteness, for example, in opposition to Blackness, much as previous work suggests (Bertram et al., 2000; Weis, Proweller, & Centrié, 1997). However,
in this site alternative positionalities are developed.

Witness Connie and Ayisha below. Connie is a White girl of modest
means who lives in one of the racial borderlands of Buffalo, a place formerly Italian but now largely Puerto Rican and African American. Although Connie draws an "other," this "other" is racially like herself:

> We live in a really small house. I don't have the things my friends
> have, like all of them at this school are having big graduation
> parties; I asked my mom to get some small invitations from Party
> City so that we could at least have the family over; she hasn't even
> done that. I guess I won't have any celebration. All my friends are
> having these really big parties. They all have much more money
> than we do. We live in a really small house; I have a really small
> bedroom. My one sister lives with us with [her] two kids; another
> sister lives in a house owned by my father on 14th street. All my
> sisters are on welfare. We have been on welfare when my father
> wasn't driving truck. When he lost his job, we didn't even have
> food in the house. I would go over to my boyfriend's house to eat.
> His parents are real nice to me. I have no friends in the neighbor-
> hood. All I know is that I don't want to be like my sisters and my
> mother. Their lives have gone nowhere. I don't want to be like
> them. I want to have lots of money—and food. I want to go to
> college.

Connie spends much time in the group discussing her own emotional
and physical distancing from her alcoholic father, her immediate family,
and her neighborhood. The group offers a "safe space" in which she can
air these problems and receive support for remaining emotionally separate from her family, for not being dragged down. At the moment, her
boyfriend also offers this "safe space." He is 23; they are engaged, having
met 3 years ago. The group, although concerned that Connie might fall
into a pattern of drinking like her father, supports this couple. Doris and
the other group members check to make certain that Arturo (her boyfriend) is not abusing her physically. Unlike other White girls and women
we have interviewed extensively, Connie and other group members talk

relatively freely about family histories of alcoholism and physical and/or sexual abuse, thus engaging in a language through which one's own and others' circumstances can be understood. In putting this language on the table, they bury such histories far less often than previous research suggests (Weis, Fine, Bertram, Proweller, & Marusza, 1998). Additionally, in breaking the silence about alcoholism, welfare, and/or violence in the White family, they shatter the myth that the White family has no problems, thereby encouraging young women across race and ethnicity to understand that such problems are indeed shared, as well as helping young women to face their own situations. Young women share their stories of pain and hope in group; the group becomes a space within which this dialogue takes place.

Ayisha, an African American young woman of 16 who has a 1-year-old daughter, also sees her task as one of distancing herself from the neighborhood in which she grew up. This distancing is nuanced, however, since she is entirely dependent on her family, boyfriend, and her boyfriend's family in order to raise her daughter. She walks a fine line—needing to distance herself from those who will hold her back but simultaneously to recognize and respect those who help her move forward. All live in the same neighborhood, which Ayisha describes:

> Actually there is a small percent who are going to do something with their lives. I hate to see 'em like that, but it's like they're all going to go off, smoke weed and drink, go to parties, and hang around the fellows. You know, my mother always told me, "It's not ladylike to sit there and drink on the corner." It's just . . . I mean, they just don't care about their body. It's terrible to see. And I'll be trying to say, you know, I have some friends and they go do that. And I'll be like "You all shouldn't do that." "Well, just because you don't do it . . ." "OK. Whatever. Whatever you decide to do, I'm behind you. If that's what you're doing, OK, that's what you're going to do." But they're always calling me a preacher or something, you know, every time I try to talk to them.

Ayisha has a somewhat contradictory relationship with her neighborhood. She is supportive of others and understands that they are supportive of her. At the same time, she knows many are going down the wrong path:

> At the rate they're going, they're either going to wind up in jail or dead, because they're always into something; they're always doing something wrong, always. There's never a time that our neighbor-

hood is peaceful, unless it's during the early morning. . . . All this, it's like they'd be on the corner selling drugs, or some of them turn to using drugs. And I keep telling them, "That's not the life you want to live. But I mean, you have kids, you really have to think about what you are doing."

Many of these young women, particularly the African Americans, are very much connected to their families and neighborhoods, passionately caring about what happens in their communities, while at the same time drawing discursive boundaries around themselves in relation to others their age, boundaries that enable them to go to school and stay on the right track. They engage the "other" constantly, telling them that they are going down the wrong path, while at the same time setting them up as radically different from themselves. Mindy, a White girl living in a largely Polish neighborhood, expresses sentiments similar to those of Ayisha:

Mindy: Oh, the girls. I'm the oldest girl in my neighborhood by 2 years, and the youngest ones have just turned 13, no, they're going to be 14 this summer. And all of them are pot heads and I try so hard, like, [to them] "You know, you're so young." And I feel like, I mean, I'm not that old either, but I've been through a lot of things that they're going through at that age. And I was like, I was like, you know, "I had sex at this age," and, you know, "I regret it," you know. And all this and that.

Lois: How old were you when you had sex?

Mindy: I was like 15 and a half. I had just turned 15. And I told them, "I regret it." And even when I first had sex, I just didn't go out with this guy and have sex. I waited a while and I still told them, I was like, "I regretted it." You know, "you're going to regret it. Sooner or later, you're going to regret all these things that you're doing, and I'm just trying to help you." But they don't care. They'll just do what they want to do anyways. Like my ex-boyfriend's sister, she is getting a reputation of being a whore, and all this and that. And I tried tellin' her, "You know, Carla, you got to calm down a little bit." She is 15. And she messes with guys that are really like 26, you know. And I said, "What does a 26-year-old want to do with a 15-year-old?" And she said, "I don't know, they really like me." I was like, "Get out of here!"

Mindy talks with the other girls in the neighborhood, trying to help them while at the same time using them as a foil against which to elaborate what she sees as her own currently appropriate behavior. While not denying that she did many of the same things at a younger age, she now weaves her femininity and sexuality differently, constructing herself explicitly in relation to others in her neighborhood. In Mindy's case, it is other *girls* who are centrally located in her discursive constructions. Others in the group focus on boys *and* girls in the neighborhood as they elaborate what they want themselves to look like in the present and the future. For some, though, like Mindy, it is specifically with the girl/woman subject that they are concerned.

This work of "othering" is done similarly across race and ethnic lines in the group, thus rewriting dominant race scripts of difference in poor areas at one and the same time as they sculpt alternative forms of femininity/womanhood (Fine & Weis, 1998). All are concerned with elaborating a positive present and future for themselves and see themselves in relation to community "others"—those who do drugs, drink to excess, wear tight clothes, sleep with a lot of guys, walk the streets, don't take school seriously, see older men. The group provides an arena within which these actual constructions get worked through, between, and among participants. Witness, for example, the following comments of an eighth-grade group, most of whom are African American at this particular session:

Lois: OK, talk to me about the women in your community.

Krista: About 10:20 they come out. (*laughter*)

Danielle: Just about every girl, like, on my street, had babies when they were about 14, 15

Krista: And I know this one girl, she doesn't live on my street anymore, but she had a baby when she was like 14 or 15, and she went back to the same guy and got pregnant again, so now she's got two kids. And I don't know a lot like that. But I know her, because I think she used to baby-sit me when I was little, but I don't know if he's there and will come back to her, you know, better and everything. But she got pregnant again.

Lois: What about some of the other women?

Shantelle: Well, some of 'em is fast. They talk to the boys on the corner. All boys on the corner is not bad. They wear a lot of showy clothes.

Tonika: I was watching Jenny Jones, this 12-year-old girl, she wore so much makeup, she acts like she's about 23. And the makeup and stuff. All these girls had these shirts like this [indicates very short], their chest sticking out. I mean, all these short shorts, look like underwear.

Tish: My underwear is not going to be that short.

Tonika: I mean, they're wondering why they'd be getting raped and stuff, even though it's [rape] wrong, but if you walk out of there with your chest sticking out in some short shorts, which is what they do, it's kind of like, what kind of attention you're going to get? You think you're going to get positive attention, you know?

Shantelle: OK. A lot of girls like have babies around my neighborhood. They don't have an education, so like they are kind of, they're low educated, ain't got no money, broken-down house and everything, and they're talking to the people in the weed house and everything.

Gloria: The girls around my neighborhood, they all 'hos.' And they wear nasty outfits, and they go out with older guys.

Delores: They [older guys] just be using, they use you, and they have like three other girlfriends, and they try to play it off. When they get caught, they'd be trying to like, well, you shouldn't have been doing all this, and all that stuff. And they [the girls] can't do nothing about it.

This eighth-grade group uses the space to talk about "other" girls and women in the neighborhood, carefully distancing themselves from them and asserting, through discussion, that they are different. By publicly solidifying the boundaries of good behavior, they hope to hang together and remain without problems.

This actual (and potential) discursive work takes place across racial and ethnic groups. The fall guy is not a constructed racial other, as is so common in urban (and suburban; Kress, 1997) schools, but rather those neighborhood youth who are perceived to be headed down the wrong path. In the case of young women, it is those other girls and women—those who are fast, wild, wear tight clothes—who enact femininity and sexuality differently from what they feel is appropriate and safe, who provide the primary "other" against which their own individual and emerging collective self is created. While this may seem to mirror the good girl–bad girl distinction that is so deeply etched in male culture—and indeed it does in some ways—the fact is that these young women are working cross-racially to live productive lives, lives that enable choices to be made and that are free from abuse. The young eighth-graders know that the "older guys just be using them [these other girls]"; they have "three other girlfriends, and they try to play it off." When the guys are caught, they blame the young women for doing something wrong—"You shouldn't have been doing this and that." These 13-year-old girls understand this full well and use the group to talk about it. It is exactly this situation that they are trying to avoid, and they know that things only get worse as women grow older. They want to stay in school in order to assert some control over their lives, enabling them to make choices regarding sexuality, men, marriage, and a future devoid of physical and sexual abuse and harassment. While the officially stated goal of My Bottom Line is to encourage abstinence, much more is happening in this context; young women are weaving a form of collective strength that goes beyond individual abstinence—they are gaining a set of lenses through which to do social critique and opening up the possibility of cross-race political work in the future.

It is most interesting in this regard that while race work is not in the official curriculum of this project, it is done all the time. The distancing discussed above, which is a by-product of baring secrets, encourages a form of gender collectivity that works across traditionally antagonistic race lines. Abstinence work, on the other hand, which is the official curriculum, is done some of the time, raising interesting questions as to what constitutes the lived curriculum as opposed to the intended curriculum of this or any other project. Curriculum theorists (Cornbleth, 1990; McNeil, 1986) have, of course, alerted us to the fact that what forms the curriculum in actual classrooms at times bears little resemblance to what is seen as the legitimate curriculum (that which is written). The same dynamic is at play here.

The girls, too, stretch the project in that they interact with what is presented and create something new—in this case, a girls' collectivity that works across race lines. By baring their secrets, they create a community, at least in this space at this time, that transcends individual racial and even social-class identities. It is the dialectic of lived curriculum creation that is so noteworthy in this particular context—the context of teaching about abstinence. We will see this even more clearly in the next section.

In a contradictory way, of course, these young women, while struggling for their own future health and safety are positioning themselves as different from "like others" in their communities of origin, thus cutting themselves off potentially from what Robinson and Ward (1991; and Ward in this volume) refer to as group based "resistance for liberation." At the moment, though, any potential future psychic pain involved in this move and possible inability to do future political work around categories of community of origin cannot be acknowledged. Indeed, it can be argued that these young women must engage in such a move, even if only temporary, in order to save themselves from what they fear is their fate. The moment of disruption chronicled here is not, though, without its own contradictions.

CONTESTING SOCIAL STEREOTYPES

Spaces such as the one explored here can offer places where trite social stereotypes are contested, where individuals and collectivities challenge definitions and constructions perpetuated through the media, popular culture, and so forth. This is highly evident in this group, in that the girls use the space, under the guidance of Doris, to challenge hegemonic constructions of femininity, race, and teenagers in general.

Doris's role here is important. She urges these young women not to accept prevailing constructions of femininity and masculinity, and to challenge race and gender scripts directly. Note her comments as recorded in my fieldnotes:

> Doris and I were waiting for the girls to come in for the high school group. Just then Tia [age 16] walked in for the fifth-period meeting. Tia talked about her former boyfriend who got a 13-year-old girl pregnant and "now it is too late to do anything about it since it is her fourth month." The girl lives two doors down from her. Her mother's best friend is the mother of the young man involved, and that is how she found out. They had broken up already because she [Tia] had no time to see him, with school and working at Wegmans, but she still cares for him. The boy, as it turns out, is 19. Tia can't even look at the girl. She considers her a "slut." She forgives the boy, because "she made him do it," but not the girl.

Doris: What do you mean, you forgive the boy but not the girl?
Tia: But she *made* him do it!
Doris: She made him put his penis into her vagina? He had *nothing* to do with it at all?

> Tia admitted that he had *something* to do with it, finally, but she still hates the girl since she is a "slut." Since the baby will live only two doors from her, she will see the baby a lot, and she is angry about it. "How is she going to take care of a baby at only 13? She is a slut."

Working from prevailing understandings that boys are not responsible for their sexual activity because they are hormonally programmed to want sex—unlike girls, whose job it is to make sure that boys do not get aroused—Tia's response mirrors notions of sexuality and gender circulating in the broader society and available, as Fine (1988) and Whatley (1991) note, in sexuality education curricula. These understandings have it that if girls get in trouble, it is their fault, since they have the responsibility of ensuring that boys are not enticed by sex. This positions women as sexual victims of hormonally programmed males. Under this formulation, the only role for females is to keep men from becoming aroused. In this particular instance, of course, it is arguably the case that Tia employs this stereotype to avoid admitting that she is jealous of her neighbor because her ex-boyfriend had sex with her. Doris intentionally interrupts the framing of the girl as the *only* problem here by posing the question: "She made him put his penis into her vagina? He had *nothing* to do with it at all?" Consider how, in the group, Doris, as leader, challenges the notion of victim in a variety of ways:

Doris: Is it good to be friends before having a boyfriend–girlfriend relationship?

Delores: I think you should be friends first, then if it don't work out, you can still be friends.

Ayisha: That don't work.

Patrice: I hate it when you make friends with a boy and then he doesn't want to take you out because he think you like a little sister.

Tonika: I hate it; most of the guys are taken, conceited, or gay (*all laugh*).

Doris: How old are you? [She already knows how old they are.]

Group response: Thirteen.

Doris: Don't you have a long way to go?

Tonika: No.

Ayisha: This one guy likes me. Everywhere I go, he right there. When I go to my friend Phalla's, he right there.

Doris: Why is that a problem?

Ayisha: Cuz I don't like him. I don't want him to be around me.

Doris: Is this a form of sexual harassment? We walk down the street and someone calls after us. Don't we want real romance? You meet and fall in love?

Tish: But then you find out he's married.

Patrice: He's married and he's got a girlfriend.

Delores: He's married, got a girlfriend, and got kids by both of them.

Doris: What do we do when someone is in an unhealthy relationship?

Tish: Try to help them out.

Patrice: Get a restraining order.

Tonika: Talk about violence! When my mom was pregnant, her boyfriend hit her.

Patrice: My mom got beat up, then she left.

Doris: Well, we all know that relationships are bad if there is physical abuse.

Doris introduces, in the above, the language of sexual harassment and makes certain that the girls understand that violence in relationships should not be tolerated. While these are obviously complicated issues with no easy solutions, it is key that these discussions are taking place in a public space, indeed a school, under the guidance of a trained adult, who is suggesting that women need to develop their own power in relationships rather than passively accept the idea that whatever happens to them is their fault. She is, through the group, encouraging the girls to reconstruct what it means to be a woman/girl, working against the grain, offering an alternative voice to the deafening victim mentality. She is helping the girls establish their *bottom line*—the bottom line that women ought not be victims.

The young women further the reconstruction of gender within this site, contesting what they see as male surveillance of women's bodies:

Susan: I'm uncomfortable around guys.

Lois: Why?

Susan: Oh, I don't know. Like, I had my dress, you know, not low cut, because that's not the way I feel comfortable, it's just like guys are always thinking about sex, and it drives me crazy. Because you know, with these guys on my street, I'm like, if they say "hi," or I went over, and going to talk to them, and I realized through the whole conversation this guy is just like staring at my breasts, you know. And they were staring, and I was like, "OK, bye," and I left. He was just staring at my breasts. Was he looking for them to see if they were there? They're so small, or what? I was "Hello." I just kept on with the conversation and I was like, looking down, looking up. What, guys? They're driving me crazy.

Kathy also resents what she sees as the male gaze:

It's hard. It's like, especially when what you believe if it's not like what everybody else is doing. It's like really hard to like keep your word to it. There's a lot of pressure out there. It's hard to really go out without like guys looking at you or something like that. I mean, I get freaked out. Like all the news about rape and everything. I get freaked out whenever I see like a guy just standing on the corner. I go out driving and I like lock all my doors when I see some guy just standing there by himself. But I get scared. I'm really scared.

Working through sensitive issues cross-racially encourages more open attitudes toward race issues in general, serving to contest and rewrite social scripts of race difference (Fine et al., 1997). Although very little specifically "race work" is done in the group, such work is very much in the minds of participants. Mindy, introduced earlier as a White young woman from a predominantly Polish area in Buffalo, has this to say:

Mindy: And my best friend is Black. And a lot of guys from my neighborhoods try to get with her . . . and they're all White. It's different . . . a guy will be prejudiced, but he'll be more prejudiced against a guy that's a different race, not the girl. You know, it's supposed to be, especially in my neighborhood, "These [White girls] are *our* girls," you know. And

if you [girls] go outside the neighborhood, they are mad. The thing
about the guys not wanting the girls to be with people from a different
race is because if we're with guys from a different race, then it kind of
leaves them [White guys] out. I don't know if that makes sense, but
that's the way I look at it. Like a lot of the guys in my neighborhood
expect the girls to be with them, like from my neighborhood. And they
[the guys] can have girls on the side.

Lois: And these girls—Puerto Rican girls, Black girls, they're the ones on the side?

Mindy: Uh-huh. And when we're messing with other guys, whatever, they
get so, I don't know, they don't get violent, but they start saying things
like . . . my one friend Jean . . . all she does is date Black people.
They'll call her "nigger lover."

Mindy connects racism among neighborhood boys directly with expressed notions of male superiority, with male desires to stake out and
control women as property while at the same time having sex on the side
with girls of their choice, often girls of color. She comments further:

Mindy: Like there's this thing now where girls are expected to share boyfriends, especially in my neighborhood. Like you have this boyfriend, but
he'll be going out with another girl. But it really doesn't matter, you
know, because she's from a different neighborhood, and he'll go to see
her on the weekends.

Lois: What about the opposite? Like what about you, if you have more than
one boyfriend?

Mindy: That's not how it works. It's kind of going back to the old days,
where they're superior.

For Mindy, young men are attempting to stake out the right to have
as many women as they want, while at the same time controlling the sexuality of neighborhood girls, calling them "sluts" if they see boys outside
the neighborhood, particularly boys of color. She understands this as a way
of reestablishing male superiority in relationships wherein men/boys control all the actions/desires/sexual behavior of girls/women.

Situated in the middle of a girls' group in a public school, young women
traverse a variety of subjects regarding race, gender, sexuality, and men.
Moving through these issues, under the watchful and caring eye of Doris
Carbonell-Medina, young women begin to form a new collective—a collective based on a stronger woman/girl, one who is different in many ways
from those left behind emotionally in the neighborhood. It is a collective
that surges cross-race, although not necessarily in terms of intimate friendships. But these young women nevertheless share the most intimate pieces

of themselves in the group setting, creating a form of friendship that may or may not transcend the bounds of the school, or even the group. And they think it is important—they think My Bottom Line gives them the space they need to think things out.

CONCLUDING THOUGHTS

I have focused here on a group within a public school, one that offers opportunities to construct alternative gender and race meanings from those "naturally" distributed in such settings. Doris—supported by Shirley, the guidance counselor—and the young women discussed here are working against the grain, challenging representations and inventing new ones, playing with and against hegemonic notions of gender and, at times, race, so as to live productive lives free from male abuse. It is the desire to live such lives that brings these young women to this space, a deeply held hope that life can be better than that which they see in much of their surroundings. They are in school, hope to stay there, and want to be different from those youth whom they see as lost. And it is this desire that keeps them coming to group and keeps them talking.

Questions can be raised, though: To what end does this type of group exist? Do the good parts of the group, the new expressions of collectivity, persist beyond school, or even beyond the group itself? To what extent can such a group *ever* challenge the existing distribution of power and resources, distributions that will ultimately determine the lives these young women will live? In other words, can such a group ever challenge fundamental structural inequalities? Or does a group like this only put a Band-Aid on a sore, one that cannot be healed by an intervention? To this I can only offer partial answers, of course. There are those who will argue strongly that such groups can never challenge the existing distribution of power and resources in society and therefore can never really do anything for the lives of these girls. In fact, some say, such groups only perpetuate a lie in that they do not really confront the kinds of inequalities facing youth like this, whether along race, social-class, or gender lines.

While I may have some sympathy for this argument, ultimately I come down differently on this set of points. These young women are struggling hard to escape what they see as a life filled with exploitation and abuse. They want choices—choices to go to school, to live productively, to live free from male violence and exploitation. And this, to some extent at least, they do control. By beginning the discussion around abuse, by beginning the discussion around victimization, welfare, men, alcoholism, and violence, they gain information that many women of our generation did not have. They gain a language—a language of what is abuse, of what is "normal" in relationships where sex is involved. They hear from trusted adults and their peers what the pitfalls in relationships can be and what to do when confronted with such pitfalls—what to do with male violence, whether from a boyfriend or a father; what to do when he has "only hit me once." They hear from Doris, publicly and quickly: "Believe me, ladies, if he hits you once, he will hit you again."

Speaking out and hearing from others also readies young women to continue to do so in the future. If they speak out once, they will be able to speak out again. If they listen to others about sensitive subjects once, they will be able to do so in the future. They will be able to share and build women's communities, communities that support their right to live with respect, free from exploitation and abuse. I and many others like me know that once we speak about horrors and tragedies in our lives, the monkey is off our back—it is easier to speak again. We know that we will not be rejected, be seen as "bad," because of what happened to us. And so these young women will learn, too. By speaking out now, it will be easier to speak out in the future. They have learned that no one will reject them because of what has happened. This represents a form of strength that should never be underestimated.

And we, as women, need to continue to speak out, individually and in groups, about our shared experiences. But this set of understandings takes many years to come to fruition. These young women have made a beginning in a group designed to encourage abstinence. But a new collective is forming—indeed, one that is based on cross-race interactions and one aimed at understanding and challenging gendered situations and meanings. And so this group is invaluable—it is the beginning of learning to speak out and trust, as we explore ourselves and our position as women.

Acknowledgments. This research was supported by the Carnegie Foundation as part of a larger grant to Michelle Fine, Lois Weis, and Linda Powell. Our sincere thanks to the foundation, and particularly Tony Jackson, for their continued support. Thanks also to Laura Myers-Rogerson, Director of Preventionfocus, and Michelle Fine for their comments on an earlier version of this paper.

NOTES

1. The funding source for My Bottom Line is Buffalo Adolescent Pregnancy Prevention Services, as funded by the Office of Child and Family Services (formerly Department of Social Services). My Bottom Line is under the program

auspices of Womanfocus, a program stem in the larger Preventionfocus in Buf-
falo. The larger Preventionfocus receives much of its money from the New York
State Office of Alcoholism and Substance Abuse Services, although, again, My
Bottom Line is funded by Buffalo Adolescent Pregnancy Prevention Services.

2. Data reported here are based on fieldnotes and interviews. Interviews were
audiorecorded.

REFERENCES

Bertram, C., Marusza, J., Fine, M. & Weis, L. (2000). Where the girls (women)
    are. *Journal of Community Psychology.*
Christmas, A. (1999). *An ethnographic study of an African American Pentecostal-
    Holiness church in the 1990's: An explanation of free space, empowerment, and alter-
    native education.* Unpublished doctoral dissertation, State University of New
    York at Buffalo.
Cornbleth, C. (1990). *Curriculum in context.* New York: Falmer Press.
Emihovich, C. (1998). Framing—Teen parenting. *Education and Urban Society,*
    30(2),139–156.
Evans, S., & Boyte, H. (1992). *Free spaces.* Chicago: University of Chicago Press.
Fine, M. (1988). Sexuality, schooling and adolescent females: The missing dis-
    course of desire. *Harvard Educational Review, 58,* 29–53.
Fine, M. (1993). *Framing dropouts.* Albany: State University of New York Press.
Fine, M., & Weis, L. (1998). *The unknown city: The voices of poor and working class
    young adults.* Boston: Beacon Press.
Fine, M., Weis, L., & Powell, L. (1997). Communities of difference. *Harvard Edu-
    cational Review, 67*(2), 247–284
Fraser, N. (1993). Rethinking the public sphere. In B. Robbins (Ed.), *The phantom
    public sphere* (pp. 1–32). Minneapolis: University of Minnesota Press.
Friend, R. (1993). Choices, not closets: Heterosexism and homophobia. In L. Weis
    & M. Fine (Eds.), *Beyond silenced voices: Class, race and gender in United States
    schools* (pp. 209–235). Albany: State University of New York Press.
Kirby, D. (1997). *No easy answers: Recent findings on programs to reduce teen pregnancy.*
    Washington, DC: The National Campaign to Prevent Teen Pregnancy. (cited
    in Wilcox, 1998)
Kress, H. (1997). *Bracing for diversity: A study of White, professional middle class, male
    and female student identity in a United States suburban public high school.* Unpub-
    lished doctoral dissertation, State University of New York at Buffalo.
Marusza, J. (1998). *Canaltown youth: Constructing White identities in the spaces of a
    postindustrial urban community.* Unpublished doctoral dissertation, State Uni-
    versity of New York at Buffalo.
McNeil, L. (1986). *Contradictions of control: School structure and school knowledge.* New
    York: Routledge & Kegan Paul.
My Bottom Line. (1995). Proposal for Funding. Buffalo, New York.

Oldenburg, R. (1989). *The great good place.* New York: Paragon House.

Robinson, T., and Ward, J. V. (1991). "A belief in self far greater than anyone's disbelief": Cultivating healthy resistance among African American female adolescents. In C. Gilligan, A. Rogers, & D. Tolman (Eds.), *Women, girls, and psychotherapy: Reframing resistance* (pp. 87–103). Bimington, NY: Harrington Park Press.

Trudell, B. N. (1993). *Doing sex education: Gender politics and schooling.* New York: Routledge.

Weis, L. (1990). *Working class without work: High school students in a de-industrializing economy.* New York: Routledge.

Weis, L., & Fine, M. (1996). Narrating the 1980's and 1990's: Voices of poor and working class white and African American men. *Anthropology of Education Quarterly, 27*(4), 493–516.

Weis, L., & Fine, M. (1998). What we as educators need to know about domestic violence. *The High School Journal, 81*(2), 55–68.

Weis, L., Fine, M., Bertram, C., Proweller, A., & Marusza, J. (1998). "I've slept in clothes long enough": Excavating the sounds of domestic violence among women in the White working class. *Urban Review, 30*(1), 1–27.

Weis, L., Proweller, A., & Centrié, C. (1997). Re-examining a moment in history: Loss of privilege inside White working class masculinity in the 1990's. In M. Fine, L. Weis, L. Powell, & M. Wong (Eds.), *Off White* (pp. 210–228). New York: Routledge.

Whatley, M. (1991). Raging hormones and powerful cars: The construction of men's sexuality in school sex education and popular adolescent films. In H. Giroux (Ed.), *Postmodernism feminism and cultural politics* (pp. 119–143). Albany: State University of New York Press.

Wilcox, B. (1997). *Is abstinence-only sex education effective? An evaluation of the evaluations.* Paper presented at the annual meeting of the American Psychological Association, Chicago.

Wilcox, B. (1998). Sexual obsessions: Public policy and adolescent girls. Mimeo. (to appear in N. Johnson, M. Roberts, & J. Worell (Eds.), *Beyond appearances: A new look at adolescent girls.* Washington, DC: American Psychological Association)

CHAPTER 3

Raising Resisters: The Role of Truth Telling in the Psychological Development of African American Girls

JANIE VICTORIA WARD

> When my daughter Patsy was 4, I would sit her down between my legs and every morning as I combed and braided her hair, I would have her reach up and run her hands through it. "Look," I'd say, "Look at how pretty your hair is. Feel how tight and curly it feels. Look at how pretty it can be when you style it up with ribbons, beads, and bows, or when you just let it be. Look at how different it is from your little White friends and how special that is."

Lillian's story, offered in response to questions about raising Black children, illustrates how Black mothers directly and indirectly incorporate into the daily routine of parenting powerful lessons of resistance. Like countless African American mothers before her, Lillian fashions a unique psychological script for parenting that is shaped by the socialization experiences that African Americans have accumulated as marginalized members of American society. Lillian has a foreboding sense of what her young daughter will soon encounter—the attacks on her self-esteem by those who measure her beauty against a White standard and devalue her Blackness and self-worth. In teaching Patsy to feel, play with, and cherish her naturally kinky hair, Lillian believes she will arm her young daughter with the tools necessary to resist the relentless assault of American beauty myths on the Black woman's sense of self. Lillian has had a lifetime to learn about and set in place the psychological fortifications that her daughter will need in order to develop into a competent and confident African American woman. In the safety of a homespace of care, nurturance, refuge, and truth, Black mothers have learned to skillfully weave lessons of critical consciousness into moments of intimacy between a parent and child and to cultivate resistance against beliefs, attitudes, and practices that can erode a Black child's self-confidence and impair her positive identity development.

As agents of socialization, Black families play an essential role in orienting their children to the existing social environment, teaching them what they need to know about the world and their place in it. African American parents socialize their children based on cultural and political interpretations and assumptions derived from their lived experience of being Black in White America. The parenting of a Black child is a political act. The psychological survival of a Black child largely depends on the Black family's ability to endure racial and economic discrimination and to negotiate conflicting and multiple role demands.

In this chapter I explore the intergenerational transmission of race-related resistance strategies passed down from Black parent to adolescent child. My analysis of this issue is empirically informed by the interview responses of African American adolescent girls and boys and the mothers and fathers of Black adolescents. These adolescents and parents of adolescents voluntarily participated in private, open-ended, semistructured interviews in which they were asked to interpret the nature of the socialization process in their own voices and on their own terms. Nearly 60 African American individuals from four geographic regions (Boston, Massachusetts; Philadelphia, Pennsylvania; Raleigh, North Carolina; and Albuquerque, New Mexico) were represented in this study. The mothers and fathers were 35 years of age and older; the adolescents ranged from 13 to 20 years old. In general, the parents and teens were not related to one another. Respondents were from a variety of socioeconomic groups and family configurations, including members of the middle and working classes and those of low-income status. Some were single, separated, or divorced. Levels of education ranged from respondents with doctoral degrees to those with less than a high school diploma.

The study attempted to uncover indigenous, implicit, and explicit assumptions about race that serve as guidelines for how Black parents and adolescents make sense of the world. The interview was organized by three primary themes that encompass essential elements of the experiences of African Americans: racial identity, race relations, and racial discrimination.

In investigating the intergenerational transmission of resistance as it is both constructed and transformed within Black families, I was particularly interested in the process of racial socialization during adolescence. The teenage years are often described as a period of idealism, conflict, and uncertainty. Adolescents are engaged in forming an identity, renegotiating social relations and power dynamics, and redefining the self. As the balance of parent–child power shifts in adolescence, teens frequently question their parents' values, pronouncements, and authority. In my research

I inquired into what the African American adolescents had learned as children about racism and racial matters and whether they would, in this period of experimentation and individual emancipation, reject what they had learned. Would they, in the effort to separate and individuate from their parents' knowledge of the past, renounce what they had learned and construct in its place new truths that they felt more accurately affirmed their emerging sense of identity, values, and meaning in life? The adolescents were also asked to discuss whether or not they spoke to their parents about racial matters, the content of these discussions, and how they were making sense of the information they received.

Homespace is an important socializing setting where Black children initially learn to deal with racism and prejudice and where they develop attitudes toward their own ethnicity and toward the larger social system. Parents provide their children with ways of thinking, seeing, and doing. Racial socialization includes the acquisition of the attitudes, values, and behavior appropriate to the social and political environments in which Black children are raised. Homespace is the primary site of resistance. Through relational ties African Americans pass on the knowledge needed to resist internalizing the prevailing negative images and evaluations of Blacks and to construct an identity that includes Blackness as positive and valued. This process of "self-creation" depends on Blacks' ability to invoke an "oppositional gaze" (hooks, 1992), to observe the social world critically, and to oppose ideas and ways of being that are disempowering to the self. Resistance is seen as the development of a unique cultural and political perspective—a perspective that stands against that which is perceived as unjust and oppressive. Lessons of resistance are those that instruct the Black child to determine when, where, and how to resist oppression, as well as to know when, where, and how to accommodate to it.

THE ROLE OF RESISTANCE IN THE DEVELOPMENT OF GIRLS' SELF-ESTEEM

Current research (primarily with White girls) on girls' psychological development suggests that prior to early adolescence, girls have a confidence and a clear sense of their own identity that declines as they reach the brink of adolescence. They receive powerful messages from adults and from the culture that undermine their self-confidence, suppress their self-identity, and force them to conform to limiting gender roles (Brown & Gilligan, 1992). Brown and Gilligan identify self-silencing and taking one's knowledge underground as among the costly strategies girls employ to remain accepted by others. This silence provides a frightening illustration of

women's response to and capitulation in the face of a patriarchal culture
that demands compliance to conventions of femininity. Self-silencing,
however, may have different motives and consequences for Black adolescent girls.

Fordham (1990) complicates our understanding of girls' silence in her
exploration of the use of this strategy among a group of academically successful African American girls. In her study silence was used not as a form
of acquiescence but rather as an act of defiance. These Black girls invoked
silence as a critical rejection of the low expectations of Black students held
by many school officials. Fordham's study is an example of the growing
literature addressing the unique strengths of Black girls, highlighting their
ability to be assertive, powerful, resilient, and resistant (Gibbs, 1996; Way,
1995).

The American Association of University Women's (AAUW) 1991 report,
Shortchanging Girls, Shortchanging America, provides evidence in support of
Black girls' strong sense of self. This study of self-esteem and the educational climate polled nearly 3,000 children and adolescents enrolled in
elementary, middle, and high schools across the country and identified a
gender gap in self-esteem that increases as girls get older, with boys consistently having higher self-esteem than girls. Important interactions between race and gender in self-esteem were also evident in the cross-
sectional data. Black girls in the study began with and were better able to
retain higher levels of self-esteem through adolescence than their White
and Latina counterparts. A sense of individual and personal self-worth was
important in the structure of self-esteem for Black girls.[1] Closeness to family was also central to overall self-esteem, and family and Black community reinforcement appeared to sustain high levels of self-esteem (AAUW,
1991, 1992).

This research finding was met with surprise in some circles, since it
runs counter to the stereotype that Black girls are victims of low self-
esteem. Skeptics point to the large numbers of Black girls growing up in
less than optimal conditions—single-parent, low-income families situated
in urban communities frequently beset by violence and crime. Although
such characterizations do indeed describe the living conditions of far too
many African American children today, it is inaccurate to conclude that
all Black children succumb to a fate of chronic self-doubt and low self-
esteem. Scholars of the African American family have long observed that
African American children, both male and female, are instilled with traits
of assertiveness, willfulness, and independence (Lewis, 1975). Strong values are placed on inner strength and perseverance. Moreover, African
Americans have particularly high expectations for their daughters. Historically, Black daughters have been socialized toward both traditional roles

(caring and nurturing wife and mother) and nontraditional ones (worker or employee). Parents recognize that their daughters will be at least partially, if not totally, responsible for the financial survival of their families. This orientation to the dual roles of mother and worker and the values placed on Black women's strength and perseverance are important elements of their healthy self-esteem.

Finally, it is during the process of racial socialization that Black children are taught to resist internalizing the notion that the enemy resides within the psyche of the Black individual; that is, that it is the Black individual's lack of motivation, unsuccessful identity formation, internalized self-hatred, or learned helplessness that explains his or her lack of success. Undoubtedly, most Black parents acknowledge the importance of personal effort and responsibility and do not wish to devalue their effect. However, many also recognize that a vital part of their child's socialization is to learn when to attribute lack of success to individual effort and when to attribute it to social forces. The refusal to allow oneself to become stifled by victimization or to accept an ideology of blaming the victim entails the development of a critical perspective on the world—one that is informed by the particular knowledge gained from one's social and political position. Such knowledge, in mitigating self-abnegation while fostering self-esteem, enables Blacks' resistance to oppression. It is one of the most powerful weapons African American families have had throughout U. S. history.

The AAUW data suggest that there is something positive and very powerful occurring among African American families. In shaping their daughters' understanding of racial and gender oppression, parents help them develop a healthy resistance to cultural pressures that call for maladaptive changes. Sandra Bem (1983) makes a similar argument when she encourages White parents to strengthen their daughters' resistance to traditional gender socialization and gender inequality. Parents of other ethnic and cultural groups who hope to raise strong and resistant daughters might learn from the socialization practices of African American families.

RAISING RESISTERS

Despite advances in civil rights legislation and enforcement, racial inequalities in American social, political, and economic structures continue to impact negatively the lives of African American people. Moreover, there is a widening gulf between White and Black Americans' perceptions of the effect of racism. National polls of Black and White Americans suggest that compared to Blacks, Whites see more racial progress and continue to downplay the extent of racial discrimination and the significance of race for economic success (Sigelman & Welch, 1991). Black children raised in the United States are barraged with messages proclaiming fairness and racial equality for all. According to these messages, this is a color-blind meritocracy in which upward mobility is open to all those who put forth the effort. Yet the experiences of Black parents run counter to these prevailing messages. Although the most overt signs of racism have all but disappeared, African American parents know that racism today may be more pernicious, since it is disguised in our daily course of conduct. Parents fear what can happen to a naive and unsuspecting Black child if she unquestioningly accepts the dominant culture's interpretation of her reality.

Black parents are deeply aware that "lying is done with words, but also with silence" (Rich, 1975, p. 186). They know that one does not have to look far to find Black people's lives misrepresented and distorted in the larger society, whether through overt lies perpetuated to serve the interests of others or through lies concealed by silence that marginalizes African Americans. In either case, Black parents see the misrepresentation and distortion as undermining the efforts of Blacks to gain self-determination and achieve personal and racial affirmation. Furthermore, Black parents know that silence is often the voice of complicity. The Black child who is unwilling to stand up in her own defense is vulnerable to cultural and psychological alienation. In my study, Black parents break the silence with political knowledge and self-knowledge. One parent says: "I don't teach it's an even playing field, all men are created equal, do what's right and you will be received fairly." Another puts it as follows: "If you want your children to be able to survive in this society, they'd better understand what reality is, you know, and you can never forget who you are."

These quotations from two African American fathers from New Mexico and North Carolina comment on the purposeful intent behind the child-rearing strategies they employ to prepare their offspring for the realities of racism and frequent economic discrimination that they and their children must face.

In her study of racial socialization in Black families, Peters (1985) found that Black mothers were acutely aware of the reality of racism in their own lives and that they shared their personal experiences of discrimination with their children. These parents felt it was their responsibility to tell their children the truth about the sociopolitical environment, teaching them that they would probably face discrimination in their lifetime and that they must be prepared. This preparation included presenting alternatives and instilling racial pride, self-respect, and the assurance of love as a protective buffer against the negative images a Black child might encounter (Peters, 1985).

In the current study, I asked African American adolescent girls whether they talked to their parents about race, and if so, why? April responds:

> Maybe somewhere down the line they've seen some of the same things and, of course, they got over them. Once you get out into the world, or even before you get out into the world, you're gonna hear things that you have to have the pride to back you up . . . so I won't be out there blindfolded. So many [Blacks] are fooling themselves. They say racism doesn't exist, then when it happens—shock. It's too much to handle if not forewarned.
>   (Interviewer: Is it helpful to talk about it?)
>   I don't want to say I accept it, but I don't have the hostility that might be there if I hadn't been taught about it before. I can't say I get rid of the hostility and the frustration all completely, but that always helps—to be able to talk about it.

According to April, the racial pride and self-respect that repudiates negative images and evaluations about Black folk also helps her control the range of affective reactions to frustrations associated with racial oppression. Arising from a sense of vulnerability and powerlessness, anger and rage can cause Black children to experience heightened stress. As Mrs. Grant cautions her children, "If [hate] affects you, it can bring you down, defeat and demoralize you." Black parents believe it is their task to help their children "sublimate the enduring rage and hostility in prosocial ways" (Powell, 1983, p. 67).

Lori concurs with April when asked, "Do you talk to your parents about race?" She says: "Definitely. Because they know what it was like to be Black in the last generation and they know what it's like to be Black now." Both April and Lori find strength in the intergenerational perspectives offered by their parents to make sense of the sociopolitical world. As adolescents, they do not reject what they learned as children from their parents but rather hold tight to their parents' experience and beliefs. In this study, mothers and fathers reported that they recounted to their children stories of prejudice and institutional racism in their past and in their present. In sharing their own personal, often painful, experiences, African American parents transmit to their children the knowledge that they have been there, too, and that they can see what their children see, feel their pain, and share their frustration. Through this process, Black parents communicate to their children what psychologist James Vander Zanden (1989) calls " a psychological sense oneness," an understanding that speaks to the child's assumption that her or his own inner experiences and emotional reactions are shared by others. Moreover, in the service of racial identity, communicat-

ing this sense of psychological oneness helps children to develop the awareness that they are not merely *in* the group but *of* the group (Vander Zanden,
1989). In acknowledging the unfairness of racism, as well as its capricious
nature and its lack of care, Black parents create the conditions in which
Black children feel safe in placing their confidence in parental authority.
The forthright acknowledgment of racism also helps children to trust that
the adults may know the way out of the pain.

Yvonne says that her dad tells her stories of what he had to go through
growing up: "My father has been through a lot because he just had to work
extra hard to get where he is. Maybe . . . if he was a White man, I'm sure
he would have gone up there much faster. Because of his race, he was not
given the same opportunity." She further explains that her parents don't
say, "You're Black, you need to watch out. I learn more from their actions
and just the things they do." Adolescents such as Yvonne revealed in their
interviews that information about racism can be transmitted from parents
in a number of ways. In *observing* the obstacles her father has had to overcome, Yvonne has learned much about blocked opportunities. Her story
provides an example of how, through both direct and indirect methods of
instruction, Black parents teach their children the racial realities they must
endure.

The political socialization inherent in racial socialization requires development of the ability to identify and analyze issues of power and authority embedded in relationships between Blacks and non-Blacks (Ward,
1990). Mrs. Jones, a mother in Boston, explains: "We have to be very
intentional about preparing our children for this society." Both Black parents and Black adolescents earmarked films, television, newspapers, and
magazines as deserving particular critique. According to her mother, says
16-year-old Marie, most of what White people know about Black people
is learned through observation and acceptance of what they see on TV.
Marie's mother teaches her children specific skills, including taking a critical
perspective, being able to detect racial stereotypes, and understanding how
images shape perceptions and often obscure the truth. Most importantly,
Marie's mother instills in her daughter a desire to resist both internalizing
and emulating the media's negative images and stereotypical characterizations of African American people, values, and cultural beliefs. In her
response to my question, "Why talk to your parents about race?" Erika
summarizes the political socialization of Black girls: "because I learn self-
knowledge, purpose, resistance, and how to overcome obstacles."

In this study, I heard African American mothers and fathers stating
that they believe they have an obligation to tell the truth about racism,
an obligation made morally significant by the recognition of negative consequences that could result from their silence. Black children who are not

well prepared to confront racism may fall victim to self-deception and self-hatred. Moral attitudes are mediated by social context, and undoubtedly for some Black parents there are considerable obstacles to speaking about discrimination and prejudice. Fear, embarrassment, and anger may cause some to avoid it. But many Black parents have learned that racism can be neither ignored nor denied. Some Black parents take a hard line, believing in the importance of exposing the moral and inherent contradictions of a society that professes freedom yet maintains racial and gender subjugation. Moreover, many parents fear that if children grow up in an atmosphere shrouded in deceit and illusion, not only will they be unprepared for racism but the world may suddenly be seen as chaotic, unpredictable, hostile, and rejecting when it is unveiled. Children in such a situation, feeling vulnerable and insecure, will find their perceptions about the safety and security of human relationship shaken, and they may approach larger systems with greater fear and suspicion than if they had been prepared for racism.

Black parents who successfully instill healthy psychological resistance in their children help them to cope with rather than to repress these feelings. Addressing racism and sexism in an open and forthright manner is essential to building psychological health in African American children. In explicitly acknowledging the vulnerability of their children to discrimination and oppression, Black parents hope that rather than being overwhelmed and disabled, their children will instead become empowered in the face of their condition and resist negative images. But parents' truth can also carry the seeds of betrayal and discouragement in some families.

"TONGUES-OF-FIRE" TRUTH TELLING

The poignant memoir of the late Audre Lorde (1982) provides a powerful example of the truth telling that some Black women use to prepare their children for racism. Lorde attended a small Catholic elementary school where the racism was "unadorned, unexcused and particularly painful because I wasn't prepared for it" (p. 250). When she complained about the treatment she had to endure in school, she received no help from home. Her mother bitterly complained, "What do you care what they say about you anyway? Do they put bread on your plate? You go to school to learn, so learn and leave the rest alone. You don't need friends." In her story, Lorde tells us that elections for the sixth-grade class president were scheduled. According to the teacher, winning would be based on a number of criteria; however, grades would be the most important factor. Since Audre was the smartest girl in her class, she thought she had a fair shot at winning the office. Lorde's mother was furious at the idea that she would run in the election: "What in hell are you doing getting yourself involved with so much foolishness? We send you to school to work, not to prance about with president this, election-that." Audre felt destroyed and betrayed when she learned she had lost. She was the smartest in the class, yet the teacher had chosen another student as class president. Heartbroken, Audre wondered: Was this what her mother was always talking about, that I should have won but they wouldn't let me? In the midst of her daughter's disappointment and distress, Audre's mother let loose her frustration. Slapping Audre's face she cried, "See—the bird forgets but the trap doesn't! I warned you. . . . Child why you worry your head so much over fair or not fair? Just do what is for you to do and let the rest take care of themselves" (p. 251).

Recoiling at her daughter's naive innocence, Lorde's mother raged back with "tongues of fire," a form of truth telling that bell hooks (1993, p. 32) describes as a characteristic of some Black mother–daughter relationships. The intent of the harsh critique is "to tell it like it is," to dismantle futile idealism, unmask illusions, and ultimately strengthen character. Embedded in the admonishment "The bird forgets but the trap doesn't," that Audre's mother offers is a striking image of power relations and a compelling lesson about justice and fairness. hooks (1993) argues that when Black women tell their daughters, "I would be less than a mother if I didn't tell you the truth" (p. 34), it sets in motion a survival strategy for coping with the unfairness of sexism and racism. Lorde's mother clearly did not mask her own anger, yet she refused to allow or join her daughter's feelings of disappointment and rejection. The message to young Audre was to toughen up, mask your feelings, disguise your thoughts, and whatever you do, never let them see you sweat.

This bold, unreserved, "in-your-face" truth telling in the service of racial socialization can become a point of tension. As bell hooks argues, it may be partially responsible for the high rates of emotional distress experienced by many African American women. Rather than strengthening the character of the young Black child, the harsh negative critique of the world illustrated by Mrs. Lorde may have a demoralizing effect. Uncertainty and helplessness can become ingrained in the psyche, and race-related anger can lead to self-hatred and racial resentment. Truth telling with "tongues of fire" may serve to prevent the development of a secure identity, impair a child's ability to form and sustain satisfying relationships with others, and discourage her belief in her own ability to effect change.

In raising resisters, I believe that there is a relationship between the resistance strategies that girls choose to employ (short term or long term) and the messages they receive about who they are in the world. Previously Tracy Robinson and I (Robinson & Ward, 1991) argued that not all resistance strategies are healthy. We identified two major strategies that Black adolescent females adopt in their resistance to the realities of an oppressive, demeaning, and judgmental sociopolitical environment: "resistance for survival" and "resistance for liberation." The first strategy, "resistance for survival," is oriented toward quick fixes that offer short-term solutions. They might make you feel better for a while, but in the long run they are counterproductive to the development of self-confidence and positive identity formation. "Tongues-of-fire" truth telling can lead Black girls to adopt short-term and often short-sighted resistance strategies. For example, 16-year-old Barbara says that she believes many lower-income Blacks have become disillusioned and resentful while struggling just to stay afloat. They have adopted jaded and ill-fated attitudes toward personal and collective advancement. She suggests that these Black folk should channel their energy into hard work in order to achieve their goals. Seventeen-year-old Toni says that too often Black adolescents blame everything on racism and use it as an excuse for their own inadequacies. Both of these are examples of evading personal responsibility by letting strong race-related emotions cloud one's judgment. These "quick fixes" represent adaptations to racism and will, in the long run, usually prove to be strategies that advance neither individual nor group goals.

RESISTANCE-BUILDING TRUTH TELLING

The second strategy outlined by my colleague and me (Robinson & Ward, 1991) is "resistance for liberation." This type of resistance offers solutions that serve to empower African American females through confirmation of positive self-conceptions as well as strengthening connections to the broader African American community. Truth telling that is liberating replaces negative critique with positive recognition. It helps a girl to experience constructive, critical affirmation of the individual and the collective by encouraging her to think critically about herself and her place in the world around her. Sharon provides a striking illustration of a Black woman's resistance strategy undertaken in the service of self-determination.

The setting is a university sports arena. This is the first time a soloist has been invited to sing the national anthem at the largest sports event of the season. Seventeen-year-old Sharon was initially auditioned by the athletic director, who was pleased with her rendition. About 10 minutes before Sharon was scheduled to sing, the director came down into the pit and said, "You'll do great—have fun, but just try not to sing it too . . . you know." Sharon responded:

No. I don't know. What are you talking about? And he said, "Just don't make it a jazz piece." And then he gets this very condescending tone of voice and continues, "See a couple of years ago a Black girl sang the national anthem, and she sang it to the point where no one could even understand it. It was just a bunch of frills and groans and grunts." I just looked at him. I couldn't believe he was saying this. So he walks off, and then in a few minutes he returns and asks, "Are you ready? Remember, you're going to sing it *right*, aren't you?" "I said, I'm going to sing it my way." So he says, "Well, we don't need you to sing it if you're going to sing it [that] way." Now here I am stressing—I have 30 seconds before I have to get out there and sing in front of a stadium full of people and I don't know . . . if I sing this "Black" is he gonna come and take the mike away from me?

I asked Sharon what was going through her mind during what she had described as the longest 30 seconds in her life. She explained that she prayed and then she asked herself:

Should I be Black or should I be White? Not that I could be physically, but in terms of the song. So I got up there and I [sang] the first two bars very White and then . . . then something just came over me. It was worse than what I was going to do! I wasn't going to be that Black . . . and if he hadn't said that to me, it would have been fine. But he did, and I . . .

I asked her if she thought she had done the right thing, and she explained, "I know I did, because it felt so good. Not only do I have the right to sing my own way, but if that happens to be in the Afro-American heritage that I've acquired, I'm just going to do it that way." And then Sharon lowered her voice and sat up straight in her chair and declared, "and I believe that was a stand for being Black."

Just about the same time that Sharon shared her story with me, the country was savoring the newly won Desert Storm victory and was welcoming back the returning troops with the emotional rendition of the national anthem that was sung by Whitney Houston—with her African American heritage all over it! In Sharon's narrative of racial conflict there remains, for some people, a right—read "White"—way to be. Sharon felt her artistry and her sense of herself as a Black woman was being made unwelcome. For Sharon, taking a stand against this was a transformative act of self-conscious agency.

Throughout her interview, Sharon provided evidence of stories told and lessons learned in her family about racism, race relations, and racial identity. Her parents, who themselves were strong and defiant role models of resistance, appear to have successfully nurtured Sharon's psychological growth, emotional maturity, and strong self-esteem. According to their daughter, they achieved this task by neither sugar-coating nor avoiding the truth about racism. African American parents such as Sharon's are exemplars of a parenting style that integrates a liberating truth telling into their repertoire of racial socialization strategies. They provide, over the course of a child's lifetime, plenty of opportunities within the family for meaningful discussions in a safe and supportive environment. In addition, these parents help their children to confront racism in ways that are both age-appropriate and individually appropriate. Children develop different capacities at different points in their lives, and the information parents give to their children about race begins modestly and grows more complex over time. Most importantly, Black parents who engage in truth telling that is liberating allow for strong, often painful, race-related emotions to surface. Parents, by teaching their children to cope with these emotions, refuse to allow them to equate their disappointments with psychological destruction.

In this study, Black parents and adolescents provided many examples of how liberating truth telling can be used to strengthen character and encourage healthy psychological development in Black children. This truth telling is effective in filling in the silences. As we saw in Lillian's attempt to instill in her young daughter positive messages about her beauty, it is often invoked as a corrective to those who would diminish the Black child's self-worth. Healthy psychological resistance fostered through liberating truth telling has a transformative quality. It helps children to grow strong as a resister on the individual level and to be empowered by their sense of belonging to a group whose very survival has been dependent upon the collective ability to resist. African American families, building upon their long tradition of raising resisters, continue a process of racial socialization that invites Black children into the community of resisters, transmitting to the next generation the truths they will need to know as they come to trust themselves as sources of knowledge.

NOTE

1. It is important to note that the AAUW (1991) study asked students to assess themselves in a number of different domains deemed important in children's lives, and Black girls showed evidence of a significant decline in their academic self-esteem over the course of their years in the school system. Many of

the Black girls appear not to be relying on school to give them a positive sense of self. Their academic confidence was judged as "not important." The girls showed a drop in their positive feelings about their teachers and their schoolwork. They were not feeling good about their academic performance or about the evaluations and validations received from school personnel. Such a decline in academic self-esteem has serious implications for academic achievement and may engender apathy in school, resulting in low grades and poor academic performance.

REFERENCES

American Association of University Women (AAUW). (1991). *Shortchanging girls, shortchanging America: A call to action.* Washington, DC: Author.

American Association of University Women (AAUW). (1992). *The AAUW report: How schools shortchange girls.* Washington, DC: AAUW Educational Foundation and National Educational Association.

Bem, S. L. (1983). Gender schema theory and its implications for child development: Raising gender-aschematic children in a gender schematic society. *Signs, 8,* 598–616.

Brown, L. M., & Gilligan, C. (1992). *Meeting at the crossroads: Women's psychology and girls' development.* Cambridge, MA: Harvard University Press.

Fordham, S. (1990, November). *Phantoms in the opera: Black girls' academic achievement at Capital High.* Paper presented at the annual meeting of the American Anthropological Association, New Orleans.

Gibbs, J. T. (1996). Health-compromising behaviors in urban early adolescent females: Ethnic and socioeconomic variations. In N. Way & B. J. R. Leadbeater (Eds.), *Urban girls: Resisting stereotypes, creating identities* (pp. 309–327). New York: New York University Press.

hooks, b. (1992). *Black looks: Race and representation.* Boston: South End Press.

hooks, b. (1993). *Sisters of the yam: Black women and self recovery.* Boston: South End Press.

Lewis, D. (1975). The black family: Socialization and sex roles. *Phylon, 36,* 221–237.

Lorde, A. (1982). *Zami: A new spelling of my name.* Freedom, CA: Crossing Press.

Peters, M. F. (1985). Racial socialization in young Black children. In H. P. McAdoo & J. McAdoo (Eds.), *Black children* (pp. 159–173). Beverly Hills, CA: Sage.

Powell, G. F. (1983). Coping with adversity: The psychosocial development of African American children. In G. Powell (Ed.), *The psychosocial development of minority children* (pp. 49–76). New York: Brunner/Mazel.

Rich, A. (1975). Women and honor: Some notes on lying. In A. Rich (Ed.), *On lies, secrets, and silence* (pp. 185–194). New York: Norton.

Robinson, T., & Ward, J. V. (1991). "A belief in self far greater than anyone's disbelief": Cultivating healthy resistance among African American female adolescents. In C. Gilligan, A. Rogers, & D. Tolman (Eds.), *Women, girls, and psychotherapy: Reframing resistance* (pp. 87–103). Binghamton, NY: Harrington Park Press.

Sigelman, L., & Welch, S. (1991). *Black Americans' view of racial inequality: The dream deferred.* Cambridge, UK: Cambridge University Press.

Vander Zanden, J. W. (1989). *Human Development,* 4th ed. New York: Knopf.

Ward, J. V. (1990). Racial identity formation and transformation. In C. Gilligan, N. Lyons, & T. Hamner (Eds.), *Making connections: The relational worlds of adolescent girls at Emma Willard School* (pp. 215–232). Cambridge, MA: Harvard University Press.

Way, N. (1995). "Can't you hear the courage, the strength that I have": Listening to urban adolescent girls speak about their relationships. *Psychology of Women Quarterly, 19,* 107–128.

CHAPTER 4

Free Spaces Unbound:
Families, Community, and Vietnamese
High School Students' Identities

CRAIG CENTRIE

Depending on the group, an immigrant "free space" may be viewed as a cultural/conceptual space held together by a biography of oppression, a yearning for freedom, and a commitment to the collective rearing of youth. Such spaces arise out of diasporic pain and strength, both constitutive experiences of an immigrant/refugee community, like the cultural stretches of Blackness theorized by Paul Gilroy (1993). The Vietnamese immigrant/ refugee cultural spaces analyzed here are recognized, at once, as diasporic and also (re)produced quite locally in this country, in homes and ceremonial rituals. Moving across geographic locations and institutional confines, Vietnamese, like Africans in Gilroy's *Black Atlantic*, have a double consciousness or striving to be both American and Vietnamese, as is the case with Africans of the diaspora, both Black and European.

Exploring identity production as Gilroy has theorized Blackness challenges how we think about free space. Often our explorations into spaces have been essentially neat and tidy: churches, community groups, collectives, women's spirituality meetings, or even art institutions where we can easily locate the voluntary collective spirit of a counterculture. The space I explore in this chapter floats; it is both more elusive and less bound by specific geographic locations or tangible places. In the case of the Vietnamese community of "Nickel City," cultural practices travel across generations and sites, carried with profound respect, operating primarily out of the collective and individual spirit, refusing to be colonized or swallowed.

Here I explore how this floating cultural space, carried by Vietnamese immigrant families and their community, contributes powerfully to Vietnamese high school students' construction of academic and cultural identity. The home as private sphere and community ceremonies as public sphere combine to shape student attitudes toward education and the community's collective desire to ensure that Vietnamese youth remain faithful to traditional Vietnamese values.

Since the fall of Saigon in 1975, and continuing until 1996, the United States has steadily accepted refugees from the former South Vietnam. This Vietnamese diaspora averaged 70,000 individuals a year. Over 21 years, Vietnamese immigration can be divided into first, second, and third waves. First-wave refugees (1975–1978) were primarily elites and employees of the U.S. military or the South Vietnamese government. Second-wave refugees (1979–1982) were often members of the middle class, with large numbers of Hoa (ethnic Chinese) and Catholics (Kelly, 1977). The third and final wave (1983–1996) was composed of some middle-class individuals and families, but primarily of individuals and families from the working class and the agricultural class. Since their arrival in the United States, Vietnamese students have been viewed as academic success stories (Lee, 1996) and America's most recent "model minorities" (Caplan, Whitmore, & Choy, 1989). All students and families interviewed and observed for this study are third-wave immigrants born in Vietnam.

This chapter is carved out of a larger research project that explores the totality of Vietnamese high school students' process of identity formation in one high school in a mid-size, northeastern city, Nickel City. The exploration of family and community impact on Vietnamese student identity, however, stretches beyond the bounds of the school and into the larger Vietnamese community through private and public domains of culturally embedded spaces. Participant observation was employed in Vietnamese family homes and community celebrations over a period of years, in addition to 20 in-depth interviews of parents and other family members and 15 in-depth interviews with community leaders, each 1 hour in length, which took place over a period of nine months. All interviews were conducted in English. Tapes of the interviews were transcribed, coded, and filed. Observation and participant-observation data were handwritten and labeled by location and date, later typed, coded, and analyzed for emerging themes. (Interviews with parents and community members were taped; more informal observations were not.) Data collected in Vietnamese homes are primarily descriptive and contain little actual dialogue. While employing a tape recorder during home visits would be ideal for collecting conversations accurately, I found using recording devices in the home inappropriate and obtrusive. The decision not to use a tape recorder in homes came after my first visit, because the family became guarded and conversation felt artificial when I attempted to tape, thus seriously impairing the quality of the observation.

In many ways, exploring the relationship of family, friends, and community to the construction of Vietnamese student identity was difficult. Initially, parents were guarded and frequently avoided responding directly to any of my questions. At least two parents later confided that they were concerned that I might be an FBI or CIA agent. Many of the parents were unable to speak English well and often provided truncated responses. A few were more fluent in English and provided rich accounts of their expectations, experiences, and family histories.

For the past 20 years, Nickel City, the location for this study, has experienced considerable economic decline due to the withdrawal of heavy industry (Fine & Weis, 1998). Despite some growth in the service sector, it remains a predominantly struggling, blue-collar city. The families interviewed were identified from the Vietnamese student body of West Side High School, a city neighborhood school that specializes in English as a Second Language programming. Each family lives on the west side within short walking distance of the school. Overall, the lower west side is poor or working class and is the most ethnically diversified community in the city.

The Vietnamese community, overall, remains a mobile one, disappearing from one section of the city and reappearing in another or expanding in an established location. As of the writing of this chapter, the Vietnamese community had virtually disappeared from the northern section of the city, had increased their numbers considerably on the west side, and had created an expanding neighborhood on the upper east side near African Americans and Poles. Like its west side counterpart, the east side community is considered poor and working class. Personal communications with Vietnamese families suggest that recent arrivals often choose to live in less expensive locations in order to save for buying a home or establishing a business.

In this city, the Vietnamese community (adults and children) has stabilized at approximately 2,000 individuals. The community is unlikely to increase through immigration because of the Immigration and Naturalization Service's elimination of political refugee status for Vietnamese in 1996 and the reestablishment of political relations between the United States and Vietnam. Conversations with members of the Vietnamese community indicate that growth of the Vietnamese community continues, but at a much slower pace, because of the return to Nickel City of some Vietnamese who left in the late 1980s and early 1990s for warmer destinations or larger Asian communities. The reason most cited for their return is the belief that Nickel City is easier to establish oneself in, less dangerous than other cities, and more friendly overall. Socioeconomically, the families with whom I became acquainted are considered poor or working class in the United States, with household incomes subsidized by government grants or through minimum-wage jobs; they were also never as affluent as the first-wave refugees. Nevertheless, they told of comfortable lives in Vietnam with hopes for a better future before the communist takeover of the south.

Vietnamese parents emphasize various Taoist aspects of working-class values such as respect, politeness, and adherence to traditional concepts of obedience which are also viewed as traditional American working-class values. They also emphasize higher education and upward mobility. All these values are firmly rooted in Confusionist and Taoist belief systems and are not related to the Vietnamese relationship to Western working class values.

Throughout this study I suggest that both Confucianist and Taoist beliefs contribute to Vietnamese students' identity, with its emphasis on academic success. It would be reasonable to argue that Asians work harder in school not because of traditional beliefs but rather because they understand that they are minorities and face inequality in school and the job market. While I believe this position has much merit when examining Asian Americans overall, especially those who have lived in the United States for generations, the Vietnamese are in a different position. They have only recently arrived and have no prior historical relationship with American social values. As immigrants/refugees, they would have a dual-reference framework (Gibson & Ogbu, 1991) that would permit them to view educational opportunities in the United States in a positive light. According to Ogbu's theory, voluntary minorities—the children of immigrants of color who have voluntarily come to the United States—do better in school because they view American education as an opportunity and do not have a history of being marginalized in the United States, as do Puerto Ricans or African Americans. As recent arrivals, the Vietnamese have a connection to traditional Confucianist and Taoist values, such as respect for education, teachers, and elders, as well as a drive to do well for their families and community.

Historically, traditional avenues for social mobility and advancement in Vietnam were replaced under French colonialism by education. Vietnamese children were educationally tracked through a rigorous set of exams that granted (or blocked) entrance into the university, and thus entry into the French colonial administration. The pattern of using education as a means to acquire status and upward mobility continued in South Vietnam until the communist takeover in 1975. Communism replaced the French system with college entry predicated on party membership, effectively barring almost all South Vietnamese from entering the higher education system and thus eliminating any hope of acquiring middle- or upper-level employment positions (Kibria, 1993). In *Family Tightrope*, Kibria's narrators view the communist takeover of the education system as an exceedingly traumatic experience. Individual Vietnamese families and the community as a whole clearly remember their social displacement in Vietnam and are very aware of the advantages of education in the United States as a vehicle for reestablishing prior socioeconomic status or attaining a better one than they previously had in Vietnam under the communist government.

PRIVATE SPHERES: LOCATIONS OF EDUCATIONAL VALUE REINFORCEMENT

When asked why they came to the United States, students (both males and females) and parents (both mothers and fathers) typically responded, "for freedom." Freedom was almost exclusively defined as the right to achieve, attain, acquire an education through hard work, and become "what you can." Poor Vietnamese families stress education for their children and, therefore, maintain strict control over them.

From the parents' narrations, I learned that 9 of the 10 families interviewed had enjoyed middle-class lives in Vietnam, with traditional middle-class employment for both men and women, such as teacher, secretary, or other office/clerical work. Before the takeover of the South by the North, only one family had lived in a rural farming community.

Each family reported a full reversal of family income with the communist nationalization of all property and business, along with separation of family members from one another. Many individuals stated that they were relocated by the communists to other parts of Vietnam. Often, fathers were separated from families and sent to reeducation camps to learn how to become good citizens of communist Vietnam. Some families migrated to the United States without the father. With two families in this study, the father joined the family in the United States after years in reeducation camps. Seven of the families migrated to the United States in a group, while other families waited years in Vietnam for the return of a single family member, generally the father, who later migrated alone. (None of the families I observed or interviewed had known one another before arriving in Nickel City.) Three families reunited here in the States, with some or all members spending time in countries of first asylum (an American immigration policy in the 1970s and 1980s, requiring that refugees go to another country first, where they would eventually be processed, if they chose to come to the U.S.). Each family was now struggling to regain some of its lost status by working and saving, as well as encouraging its children to work hard in school.

The following description of an evening with the Nguyen family recounts an experience typical of the families I visited during the course of this research. In the private domain of the home, in the living room and during the family dinner, I witnessed a great deal of what might be called "value work." Domestic sites are frequently unexplored by ethnographers, partly because of the difficulty in accessing this sphere and partly because of the tremendous emphasis placed on large institutional settings such as schools or the public gatherings of focus groups. In the living room or at the dinner table, family experiences and expectations are told and retold, shaping the identity of Vietnamese youth. Often, the private sphere of individual families merges with those of Vietnamese neighbors and friends, creating a collective accountability affecting every individual, moving the private space of families' expectations into shared psychological space with the community. These psychological spaces are forged in the family's shared daily lives, where expectations profoundly shape Vietnamese youths' emerging identity. Along with the Vietnamese culture and the shared experiences of the larger Vietnamese community, these spaces of dinner-table conversations, neighborhood gossip, and shared enacted expectations have a tremendous impact on identity production. All the families I interviewed and observed lived in the same west side neighborhood, forming a small, tightly knit community that supported and networked with one another in many ways.

SEPTEMBER 27, 1996

It's about 3:15 P.M. Mr. Nguyen is sitting on the porch with Dao, the youngest of the Nguyen's four children, a preschool-age girl, and two Vietnamese teenagers, one from upstairs and one from next door.[1] Mr. Nguyen sees us coming down the street and calls out a greeting to Kay (Mr. Nguyen's son, the student I am following this day) and me in Vietnamese, and another greeting in English for me. The boys yell a greeting to Kim, the neighbor boy, but the other is perplexed by my presence and asks Mr. Nguyen a question. He responds in Vietnamese. We go up the stairs and sit on two kitchen chairs; both boys shake my hand and say they are pleased to meet me.

Mr. Nguyen has been laid off from a local factory job for the past 6 months and takes care of Dao while his wife attends English classes at Catholic Charities and does an assortment of household-related tasks outside of the home. The family is sustained by Catholic Charities and government grants. The six of us remain on the porch talking. The neighbor boys are interested in what I am doing and ask a lot of questions. They are very impressed with the fact that I am doing a doctorate but don't quite understand the point of my study.

Mr. Nguyen is bothered by the hip-hop clothes Sam, the neighbor boy, is wearing, and begins to lecture him on the importance of keeping his Vietnamese culture. Mr, Nguyen begins by first asking where he got the clothes that he is wearing. Sam responds that he got them at the mall. Mr. Nguyen is clearly annoyed by this remark and then says, "I see; but where did you get the money to buy these clothes?" Sam responds that he occasionally picks up some money by doing odd jobs for the neighbors like cutting grass and raking leaves. Mr. Nguyen then asks if he gives some of his money to his mother to help with the household expenses. Sam nods in the affirmative and is now looking down at the floor. "A young man like you should be concerned only with his studies and helping his family. Because your father is not here, you should be taking your place as head of the family. Your honor comes from these two things, not trying to be fashionable." Mr. Nguyen makes a few more remarks about how these baggy clothes make him look roguish and sloppy. Shortly after, Sam leaves. Mr. Nguyen confides in me that the two neighbor boys had been seen by members of the community acting disrespectfully toward various adults. He is also concerned that some of the Vietnamese teens are absorbing too much American culture.

After about a half an hour, Mrs. Nguyen is seen coming down the street with their two girls, Xinh and Mei; Xinh, the youngest of the girls, attends elementary school nearby. Mei is a teen who goes to school at West Side High. The oldest in the family, Mei is responsible for picking Xinh up from school every day. They both walk to Catholic Charities to meet their mother and accompany her to do some grocery shopping before returning home. On their arrival, greetings are exchanged, and Mrs. Nguyen heads inside and begins delegating responsibilities. Everyone, including the boy from upstairs and myself, now heads inside.

The apartment is sparsely but adequately furnished with donations from Catholic Charities and gifts from other Vietnamese families who have been here longer and acquired new things. Mr. Nguyen explains that the Vietnamese community meets twice during the month in a downtown hotel owned by one of the community's most prominent members in order to discuss how the community is doing, who is new in town, whether they need anything or need any help. This is how, he explains, the family acquired so much stuff. There are three things rather prominent in the apartment: a Buddhist shrine to the ancestors on the mantel, a large new color TV, and a large, good-quality stereo. The stereo and TV were purchases made when Mr. Nguyen was still working at the factory.

In the living room the boys entertain themselves by playing checkers, while Mr. Nguyen and I watch TV, talking intermittently about his family's life in Vietnam. Half an hour into playing checkers, Mr. Nguyen asks the boys if they have any homework, to which they respond, "Yes." Mr. Nguyen then instructs them to begin it "now." They start with English lessons. I am frequently asked to explain something or provide the proper pronunciation to a word or a phrase. Mr. Nguyen also joins in the pronunciation tutorial. After an hour or so of English, Mrs. Nguyen announces that it is time for dinner. During the meal, everyone speaks to each other primarily in Vietnamese but occasionally in English for my benefit. A large part of the conversation centers around the children's education. Sometimes a comment is made that cold weather is coming and no one knows how they are going to handle it. Mrs. Nguyen asks all the children at the table how they are doing in school. Everyone answers, "Good." Then she asks if everyone is finished with their homework. Two children say they are not. "Right after dinner, you have to finish it." Everyone nods yes. Sung, the young Vietnamese mother from upstairs, remarks that one of her sons is not doing so well in social studies. This comment elicits disapproving sounds from the other adults. Mr. Nguyen remarks that perhaps it is his English; he seems to do well in other subjects. Perhaps, it is suggested, he should work especially hard on English and the rest would come. Mr. Nguyen suggests that Sung have a conversation with Mr. Lee (the Vietnamese teacher) at West Side High and get his opinion. "Mr. Lee should be doing his job." If he isn't, Mr. Nguyen observes, it is important that the matter be brought to his attention. Mrs. Nguyen remarks that maybe Sung's son isn't doing as bad as she thinks and that she would get a better understanding once she speaks with Mr. Lee. Sung also comments that the older boy is now making applications to college and that each college requires an application fee that she doesn't have. At this point Mr. Nguyen asks me if there is anything that can be done about this, as it would be a shame if one of Sung's boys couldn't go to school because he didn't have the fee. I was surprised at this and comment that surely this must be a problem that West Side High encounters often. I know of a couple of programs at the university that wave the fee in the event of financial hardship. I promise to call the next day and get the information to them.

Half an hour later, the women are finished with the dinner cleanup. Mei joins the boys with their homework. Sung and Mrs. Nguyen are still talking together in the kitchen. The older high school children routinely work together on all their homework assignments. The smaller elementary school children do the same. Mei is particularly adept at math and acts as the tutor for all the kids. Kim, Sung's daughter, who is also adept in math, really enjoys learning English and takes the lead there. After the older children finish their work, they spend some time with the younger ones to assist them with theirs. Mr. Nguyen and I sit talking while intermittently responding to various questions children have about their work. At one point, Mei reaches an impasse with her calculus work and asks me for help, but I am unable to give her the assistance she needs. She then sends one of the boys from upstairs to go around the corner to retrieve Joy, another Vietnamese, who is well known for her competence in math. Ten minutes later, Joy arrives. A long conversation begins, with much instruction. One hour later the math problems are solved and everyone's homework is done to the satisfaction of Mr. Nguyen.

The Vietnamese I spoke with, like the Nguyens, frequently help each other as much as possible, creating a tight network of relationships similar to a large extended family. The fathers, when present, were always the head of the household, though not always the primary breadwinner. Vietnamese children were consistently very obedient; I never saw a Vietnamese child talk back to his or her parents, or question parental or adult authority or decisions in the presence of adults, although I have observed Vietnamese children and high school students act very independently when out of adult view. When children and teens occasionally complained among themselves, it was not unusual for the oldest child, particularly a teen, to remind them of their place. Occasionally, Vietnamese students would complain that they were tired of studying and wanted to just socialize. An older Vietnamese teen would intervene and remind everyone how hard it was for their parents to come to the United States, how they lost everything in Vietnam, and that it was up to them (the students) to take advantage of school in the United States, to do well, and eventually help to make things easier for their parents. Several times, a student, when alone with me, would remark that Vietnamese adult supervision was very strict and how he or she admired the more relaxed approach Americans took toward their education. On two such occasions, the student would then recant and say "perhaps the Viet-namese way is better." Overall, Vietnamese children were respectful to all adults regardless of the relationship.

Vietnamese collective values are very pervasive. They are forged in the community and the home from traditional values and the shared ex-perience of immigration. Anywhere—on the street, in school, or at com-munity functions—the collective consciousness of Vietnamese values are reinforced wherever two or more Vietnamese gather. While individuals may feel, at one time or another, that their personal choice is minimized or even overridden by collective values and subsequent value enforcement, nearly everyone accepts this. Only an occasional disgruntled voice is heard, often relenting with a shrug of the shoulder or comment that "this is the way it is." Only on two occasions have I been aware of individuals who were completely ostracized from the community: two very effeminate Vietnamese males who live together somewhere on the west side, and a Vietnamese man in his early 20s who appeared to be completely assimi-lated into American culture and was viewed as a disgrace. Community members refused to discuss anything about them.[2] It appears that to act independently is to risk total alienation from the Vietnamese community. For example, Mr. Nguyen's comments on his young neighbor's hip-hop clothing was typical of parental or adult intervention with Vietnamese adolescents. Mr. Nguyen blamed the lack of an adult male figure in the neighboring household as the cause for their "bad behavior." Parents and community members were consistently concerned that Vietnamese youth were acquiring, in their opinion, bad American customs and ways. "Bad ways" were the Vietnamese perception that American children spent too much time watching TV and are too independent and disrespectful of adults and authority figures. African American and Latino youths were frequently singled out as examples of undesirable behavior.

It was customary for children and teens always to defer to adults; however, older Vietnamese often consulted and deferred to the opinion of the eldest high school student on issues of language and American cus-toms. On many visits, adult concerns about Vietnamese youth straying from traditional Vietnamese culture were clearly a source of tension between teens and adults. Freedom then became a double-edged sword. On the one hand, coming to the United States provides economic, educational, and some social opportunities, but it also provides the grounds for traditional Vietnamese obedience to elders to be challenged. The need for teens to "fit in"to American culture, especially in dressing habits and in the general assertion of independence, concerned Vietnam-ese adults.

An additional source of conflict, and sometimes tension, was gender relations. Again, a yearning for freedom was double-edged. Vietnamese males consistently tried to assert and reclaim their traditional dominant role, relegating wives and daughters to a secondary position. At the same time, Vietnamese adolescent females were encouraged to strive for education, often in very professional fields, and to assert themselves in ways that make them equal to men. Females were expected to balance traditional gender expectations with contradictory school messages regarding equality of the sexes and female independence. While many Vietnamese women with whom I spoke, students and adults alike, understood this conflict, many were reluctant even to discuss changes in traditional gender relationships. I was unable to explore to what extent, if any, gender tensions were discussed between mothers and daughters or males and females. Adult females and students agreed that I had located an area that was a "problem." Most women remarked that they did not know what to do about this conflict, commenting instead on the larger issues of survival. Two women explained that "for men to be the head of the Vietnamese household was traditional and is the way it should be." In the home, Vietnamese females performed the bulk of household tasks, such as cooking and cleaning, in the process participating in and enforcing gender-segregated spaces. The kitchen is always the domain of females; the living room is almost always masculine space. Even little children were not permitted to transgress established gender space for longer than was necessary. Most often, it was the women who rigorously enforced gender-segregated spaces. Interestingly, gender was not an issue in matters of learning or career choice. Here women contest the cultural dictates on gender and are encouraged to do so. Both males and females regularly studied together. The student with the most knowledge of a subject took the lead in teaching the others. The importance of studying and doing homework was evident in every household I visited. Parents always joined the students in studying and played the role of tutor to the best of their ability. If the subject was outside the ability of the parent, an older sibling or neighbor was called in to assist. Homework and studying were regarded as the children's moral responsibility in the same way adults were responsible for providing the necessities of life to the family. Household study groups were a consistent theme in all the Vietnamese households I visited, often including children from other families nearby. Recent studies on Vietnamese communities support this finding. Kibria (1993) comments:

It was not only in their conception of the goals or ends of education that Vietnamese Americans approached education as a collective family affair. This familial orientation was also expressed and promoted by the manner in which homework and other academic activities tended to be organized in Vietnamese American households. Researchers have noted how studying is organized in Vietnamese refugee households as a collective rather than individual task or activity, with children sitting down together to study and assist one another with school related problems. Rumbaut and Ima further describe the Vietnamese refugee family as a "mini-school system," with older siblings playing a major role in mentoring and tutoring their younger brothers and sisters. (p.155)

Educational stakes are perceived to be quite high and to carry important consequences. Success and failure have important implications not only for the individual but also for family members and the community in general.

PUBLIC SPHERES: COLLECTIVE RESPONSIBILITY AND ACCOUNTABILITY

The Vietnamese community, overall, exhibited a high degree of interdependence and sense of collective responsibility extending beyond the community networking that is commonplace among the urban poor and working class (Bourgois, 1995; Stack, 1974). This was especially evident in the responsibility all adults took for Vietnamese youth and the responsibility the youths themselves took for even younger members of the community in terms of discipline and education. In the previous section, we saw that Joy was expected to tutor the Nguyen children regardless of any personal plans she might have had for the evening.

While not every Vietnamese adult necessarily knows every other Vietnamese family or individual in the city personally, adults are impressively familiar with community members and collectively acknowledge their responsibility to encourage education among all children and to discipline any youngster who is seen to be out of line (as was the case with Mr. Nguyen and his neighbor's children). I never saw parents take issue with discipline enforced by a nonfamily member of the community. On at least two occasions, I witnessed minor corporal punishment inflicted by a nonfamily member with no negative response by the family; rather, other adults supported the punishment. In the Vietnamese community and elsewhere, families are very well acquainted with one another and act in ways more typical of a large extended family. The following brief notes from a Tet celebration further suggest the collective responsibility the Vietnamese community takes for the behavior of its youth.

NEW YEAR'S CELEBRATION AT THE LEXINGTON HOTEL:
THE YEAR OF THE OX, 1997

The ballroom of the Lex is filled to capacity. About 400 members
of the Vietnamese community are present. The hotel supplied most
of the food, which is traditional Vietnamese cuisine. The hotel fare
is supplemented by a great many pot-luck contributions from the
partygoers. This is an extremely noisy and celebratory affair. There
are many young families present with all their children and their
entire extended families. Occasionally a small child has broken away
from his or her parent's table and is seen doing something that is
regarded as impolite or improper. Just moments ago a small boy,
about 6 or 7 years old, was seen picking directly from a bowl of
something at the buffet table with his fingers. In mid-conversation, a
young woman, perhaps in her early 30s, spots the child picking
through the bowl and immediately jumps up and dashes to the table
and yanks the child away. This act is followed by a severe scolding
in Vietnamese and a slight slap on the hand. He is turned around
and then gently spanked on the hind quarters. As he passes several
tables, other women join in the admonitions. The small scene is
witnessed by Mrs. Kong, who is sitting next to me. Shaking her
head, she leans over and whispers to me in English that the boy's
mother is always engaged in something other than what she should
be doing: Her first duty is to see that her children are properly
disciplined. Just as expected, she points out, Quong (the boy's
mother) is chatting with some other young women in the corner.
Mrs. Kong further explains that this is becoming a regular thing and
that a group of women from the community are going to have a
talk with her.

The focus of the evening is a speaker who talks about the state
of the local Vietnamese community and the accomplishments of the
past year. The final note is a fairly long message to the Vietnamese
youth. He reminds them of the Vietnamese struggle and how their
parents have suffered to provide them with the things they need
and the difficulties encountered to keep the families together against
all odds. He reminds them to be thankful for the opportunity to live
in a free country, and especially the opportunity to go to school and
to learn. He reminds them of their duty to study, do their homework, be respectful to their elders, honor their parents, and maintain Vietnamese culture. He ends the speech with thanks and a
further reminder to the youth that it is their moral obligation to do

well in school and to go to college because it will be their responsibility to care for their parents in their golden years and to provide
the same support for their own children in the future. The end of
the speech is met with resounding applause.

The Vietnamese community uses public functions to bring the community together and to reinforce traditional culture. The group's interdependence and traditional culture fosters collective morality, as seen in
the admonition of the child eating from a common bowl or a Vietnamese
adult disciplining a neighbor on dress or demanding respect for traditional
culture and his elders. Further, the community is the sphere within which
public support for getting an education is expressed and the idea of achievement as a collective responsibility is understood. This collective emphasis
is supported in the home by parents, siblings, and neighbors.

In the school, the Vietnamese teacher and assistants support the value
of education through rigid discipline and expectations that all Vietnamese students can and will do well. Even non-Vietnamese teachers support
the expectation of Vietnamese success in school by generally viewing them
as the only serious students in the school and, as one teacher explained,
the "only bright spot" in a school full of "disappointments and lackluster
performance." The emphasis on Vietnamese traditional culture, especially
Confucianist and Taoist beliefs, along with social interdependence, have
jointly contributed to the expectation that Vietnamese children have an
obligation first to their families, and then to their communities. This effectively places the primary emphasis on collective morality and obligation, thus sublimating individual subjectivities, especially those contrary
to the group and its success. Vietnamese youth shuttle among psychological
spaces of expectations that are evident at dinner tables, in household conversations, public celebrations, schools, and home-based study groups. The
cultural spaces of importance are not simply physical, but are perhaps better
seen as embodied in the heart and minds of community members.

This space of high morals and educational expectations serves to both
comfort and contain individuals. In conversations with Vietnamese community members, I have learned that the local Vietnamese community
has very few interactions with the police. The few that have occurred are
regarded by the Vietnamese community as a result of the estrangement
of the individual from the group. The collective responsibility of the
community is to manage problems within the group rather than rely on
outside assistance, thus creating a seemingly remarkable homogeneous
ethic. American society, which places tremendous emphasis on the individual—and, by extension, encourages little or no intervention in matters of unsociable behavior by its citizenry—relies heavily on state surveil-

lance and intervention to manage breaches of its rules. The Vietnamese community, on the other hand, manages social order through rigid social or collective expectations. Sometimes social pressure is quite high, difficult, and uncomfortable. As one Vietnamese West Side High School student pointed out:

> Americans stay out of other people's business. It's not like that in the Vietnamese community. Everybody is involved in everyone else's business. If you make a mistake or do something that parents or neighbors disapprove of, it is terrible. Sometimes the pressure is really terrible. Our families and neighbors and friends keep everyone and [every] thing in order. Me, I don't know, it's different with the Vietnamese, you know. Maybe this way is better, I don't know.

The following journal entry grapples with the above point. Felixs, a West Side High junior and a resident of the west side community, was seen walking alone after school. Mr. Tran, an elderly Vietnamese man who disapproved of the youth's clothes and general demeanor, stopped Felixs and lectured him on how to be Vietnamese.

MAY 27, 1997

> This afternoon, while returning home from the supermarket, I ran into Mr. Tran, who was taking one of his slow exercise walks around the block, typically with his arms crossed behind his back. I have often seen Vietnamese elders or grandparents sitting on porches or looking out of windows, just observing the activities in the neighborhood. I am now wondering if these seemingly innocuous pastimes are really ways to keep informed about individuals and protect their families. Today, I stopped for a few minutes to talk with Mr. Tran about nothing in particular. About 5 minutes into the conversation, I spotted Felixs, a Vietnamese teen, walking down Normal Street, coming toward us. As he got closer, he saw us and crossed the street, hoping that neither Mr. Tran nor I would see him. However, Mr. Tran's keen eyes caught a glimpse of Felixs, immediately calling him over. Felixs approached slowly with his head cast down. Mr. Tran, in a stern voice, began lecturing Felixs in Vietnamese. This went on for at least 10 minutes. Occasionally Felixs would quickly glance up at me and then return his head to the downcast position. After Mr. Tran was finished, Felixs made an obligatory good-bye to us. Both Mr. Tran and I continued to watch Felixs as he quickly crossed the street and went on his way.

Mr. Tran, then speaking in English, began to complain about Felixs. He stated that his household was without an adult male. Felixs's mother, Mrs. The, continued to try to get Mr. The into the country, but the family had been here for 3 years without him. Felixs was a concern to the community because he was increasingly acting very independently and was now keeping regular company with a group of American boys who were not "serious." Felixs was known to keep late hours and was studying less. Furthermore, he was now beginning to wear clothing that was unacceptable. Mr. Tran's lecture, as he explained to me, centered on how he wanted Felixs to know that people were watching him and were concerned. He told him that these clothes suggested that he was becoming like the people with whom he was keeping company. These American teens, Mr. Tran observed, were not respectful of adults and were not serious about school. It worried him that some Vietnamese teenagers were beginning to acquire American customs that were not considered appropriate, and if the Vietnamese adults were not careful, they were going to lose these children, as he thought was the case with Felixs. I remarked that while Felixs was dressing in typical American clothes, I found him to be especially polite and commented on how respectful he acted in our presence. Mr. Tran immediately dismissed this comment by saying, "Today the clothes, who knows what tomorrow."

During several years of field work I have witnessed countless incidents similar to the one just described. These spaces of Vietnamese expectations can appear to be informal and spontaneous, crossing both the public and private spheres at one and the same time. A public context such as a street provides an opportunity for an elder to chastise a Vietnamese teen on his appearance. Such interactions were common and created heightened moments in which adults reinforced community values with lessons on how to be Vietnamese. Doing so created an extremely tight community where traditional Vietnamese ethics, values, and customs were rigidly reinforced, sometimes creating tension and making Vietnamese youth occasionally uncomfortable.

SUMMARY

Free space is most often understood as linked to a geographic location, specifically a site. As the above data suggest, it can also be conceptual, transitory, dynamic, and spontaneous.

As with Gilroy's *Black Atlantic,* diasporic free space can bridge several continents, creating, in Gilroy's case, a pan-Black experience and ethos. In a similar manner, the Vietnamese, like all peoples who have been faced with voluntary or involuntary international migration, create a dynamic pan-ethnic experience. This research explored, on a community level, how immigrants/refugees have developed survival strategies linked to their ability to create what might be called "conceptual free space," or a space of high moral and behavioral expectations, that traverses both public and private spheres. By doing so, they are able to emphasize maintenance of Vietnamese culture and language among their youth, as well as instill respect for learning and desire for success. Theoretically, these data are more compelling in light of the fact that the Vietnamese community of Nickel City is not very visible and is dispersed over a large geographic area. By living in Nickel City, the Vietnamese have forgone the benefits of the traditional large and safe immigrant community and rely on "conceptual free space" as a means to maintain cultural cohesion and safety.

The Vietnamese with whom I spoke were consistently concerned that youth maintain the native culture and language. While cultural maintenance was linked to morality and ethics, they were also concerned that young Vietnamese develop excellent English-language abilities and a good grasp of American culture. It was not lost on the adults that these skills, along with a more generalized education, were the keys to social and financial success in the United States. By extension, American culture was not viewed as being as moral or ethical as Vietnamese culture. Parents and leaders alike stressed the importance of respect for teachers, parents, and elders. They lamented what they see as the lack of morality among American children and do not want a similar attitude to be adopted by the Vietnamese.

Connection to the Vietnamese community and culture is viewed by the Vietnamese as a means to personal and group success for refugee Vietnamese youth (Seller & Weis, 1997). Refugee and immigration literature also posits that refugee and immigrant children generally do better in school and socially than those that are not connected to their communities. Although there were not many examples in my study to draw from, there were some Vietnamese teens who were consistently identified as "problems." These young men and women were more estranged from the Vietnamese community and appeared to be more assimilated into American culture than their peers.

The conceptual space created by the Vietnamese community of Nickel City is critical to the maintenance of their overall identity, but particularly important to the identity formation of the Vietnamese youth. It provides a "liminal space" from which young people can engage the challenges of

American society and receive both encouragement and structure to pursue academic and financial success.

Tracing how culture operates across time, space, and generation, in public and private corners of young people's daily life, we come to appreciate the kind of cultural blanket these immigrant youth carry around them. Such a space creates a deep generational continuity, a sense of personal grounding, and a set of academic expectations for males and females. Never quite alone as they wander through American society, they are very much between worlds, but not in a confused or torn way. Instead, this space enables them simultaneously to experience comfort and engage in adventure. While the fault lines of clashing cultural values, gender tensions, and sexuality undoubtedly complicate life for these young Vietnamese Americans, the public and private spheres of the Vietnamese community help to keep Vietnamese youth grounded rather then conflicted.

Youthful border crossers, working the hyphen of being Vietnamese and American, they bring cultural grounding and values to new opportunities and challenges. Mindful of the dangers of the new and the temptations of the novel, they carry the protection of culture as they venture forth. Margaret Gibson and John Ogbu (1991) might suggest that their armor will last only a generation before the fabric of traditional Vietnamese culture begins to unravel. W. E. B. Du Bois (1939) might be more hopeful about the enduring power of their dual consciousness. A shortcoming of ethnography is that we have only the present. But at present, the power and surrounds of cultural space are profound—at this moment, in this city, for this generation. Its endurance—in the face of American corporate commercialism, impoverished schools for poor and working-class youth, and the economic burdens shouldered by poor and working-class families—remains to be seen.

Acknowledgment. Some of these data were collected as part of Michelle Fine and Lois Weis' study of Urban Spaces, funded by the Spencer Foundation and the Carnegie Foundation.

NOTES

1. The vignettes in this chapter are adapted from my dissertation. Journal entries were almost exclusively descriptive, with little or no dialogue. The small amounts of dialogue included were reconstructed from memory and written as data after each session. My hosts were very gracious in permitting me to enter into their homes. As noted earlier, I found it especially intrusive to bring along a tape recorder that would record every comment and could cause individuals to

act in a cautious and self-conscious manner. The methods literature in sociology most often addresses how to conduct research in institutional settings and in interviews, but it does not address how such research should be conducted in very private settings over long periods. This is certainly a point for further exploration in the field.

2. It seems that there must be more such individuals. However, I made no attempt to contact these three people while doing this study. Interviewing Vietnamese who are not integrated into the general community would make an interesting separate study.

REFERENCES

Bourgois, P. (1995). *In search of respect: Selling crack in el barrio.* Cambridge, UK: Cambridge University Press.

Bowles, S., & Gintis, H. (1976). *Schooling in capitalist America: Educational reform and the contradictions of economic life.* New York: Basis Books.

Caplan, N. S., Whitmore, J. K., & Choy, M. H. (1989). *Boat people and achievement: A study of family life, hard work, and collective values.* Ann Arbor: University of Michigan Press.

Du Bois, W. E. B. (1939). *Black folk, then and now.* New York: Henry Holt.

Fine, M., & Weis, L. (1998). *The unknown city: The lives of poor and working class adults,* Boston: Beacon Press.

Gibson, M. A., & Ogbu, J. (1991). *Minority status and schooling: A comparative study of immigrant and involuntary minorities.* New York: Garland Press.

Gilroy, P. (1993). *The Black Atlantic: Modernity and double consciousness.* Cambridge, MA: Harvard University Press.

Kelly, G. P. (1977). *From Vietnam to America: A chronicle of the Vietnamese immigration to the United States.* Boulder, CO: Westview Press.

Kibria, N. (1993). *Family tightrope: The changing lives of Vietnamese Americans.* Princeton NJ: Princeton University Press.

Lee, S. (1996). *Unraveling the "model minority" stereotype: Listening to Asian American youth.* New York: Teachers College Press.

Seller, M., & Weis, L. (1997). *Beyond Black and White: New faces and voices and U.S. schools.* Albany: State University of New York Press.

Stack, C. B. (1974). *All our kin: Strategies for survival in a Black community.* New York: Harper & Row.

CHAPTER 5

Sheltered "Children":
The Self-Creation of a Safe Space by Gay, Lesbian, and Bisexual Students

RICHARD BARRY

Marginalized groups have long sought alternative venues where they could escape the presses of a dominant society, and gay men, lesbians, and bisexual men and women are no exception. From nightclubs to bars to community centers, we have carved out spaces for ourselves that are our own. These spaces have given us the opportunity to explore our "differences" from the dominant heterosexist society, to form our own notions of what society could be like, and to just relax and have fun without worrying too much about the repercussions of living in a society that is not totally our own. In urban, suburban, and even rural settings across the country, the presence of gay men, lesbians, and bisexuals can be felt as never before. Our spaces have become public, and we have become visible, changing the very face of the society that had excluded us for so long.

Evans and Boyte (1992) have called such places of resistance "free spaces." The "freedom" of free spaces, however, may be a misnomer for some groups. Although adult gay men, lesbians, and bisexuals have been fortunate in creating their own free spaces, gay, lesbian, and bisexual youth have been more constrained. Youth are just as in need of communities/localities/safe spaces as their adult gay, lesbian, and bisexual counterparts. Youth need spaces of resistance not only to formulate their place in a heterosexist and ageist society but also to formulate what types of resistance, if any, would most likely change this society. In fact, they may need such spaces even more than their adult counterparts. For unlike gay, les-

bian, and bisexual adults, gay, lesbian, and bisexual youth can be ostracized from the larger heterosexist society not only because of their sexuality but also because of their age.

Free or safe spaces are often used by adults to seek refuge from a
heterosexist society to plan political action to bring about change. For many
youth, however, planning any sort of political action is a privilege they do
not yet have. For them, the immediate need is simply to have some space
outside of the dominant heterosexual gaze, a place to recuperate before
any political action can even be considered. Further, they have to contend with an ageism that assumes that they are too young to understand
their lives or to make decisions for themselves. In addition, many gay youth
also have to contend with racism, sexism, and classism. Unlike their heterosexual counterparts, however, who presumably share their sexuality
with their parents, gay, lesbian, and bisexual youth have to contend with
heterosexism and homophobia in the home. As youth, they have little
power and often are denied basic civil rights that most adults take for
granted. Gay youth need places to gather with others like themselves,
places that they form and they control, places in which they can, for a
moment, rest, be gay and young without having to worry about heterosexism and ageism.

In spite of having little power, youth can and do formulate their own
safe spaces, as free of adult control as they can manage in a society that is
governed by adults. These spaces can be as ambiguous as the simple presence of other gay, lesbian, or bisexual youth or they can be as concrete as
a club room or a lunchroom table that, for a moment, is theirs. In this
project, I searched for such a space, an area where young gay, lesbian, and
bisexual people carved out their own space. In looking at such a space, I
wanted to see how having such spaces would affect their lives within and
beyond the space.

On a college campus in northern New Jersey, I found a group of young
gay, lesbian, and bisexual students who had created a group that met the
criteria of being a safe space separated by sexuality and age—the Gay,
Lesbian, Bisexual, and Friends Organization (GLBFO). During the 1994–
1995 school year, I attended their meetings, hung out in their club room,
and went to some of their functions. From the membership of about twenty
people, twelve to fourteen were nearly always present at meetings and in
the club room. Along with talking to all the members of the club infor-
mally and taking many fieldnotes, I interviewed twelve people, ten of
whom were members of the organization. The other two were friends of
people in the organization. They ranged in age from 18 to 29. Reflecting
the membership of the group, over half (seven) of these interviewees were
Latino and Latina, five were White, and one was Asian American. Only

two of the interviews were with women, reflecting the mostly male membership of the group. Both of these young women were Latina. These racial/ethnic categories into which I have just placed each of these young people are my own, and ones with which some of them would take exception. The ethnic self-labeled categories for the Latino students were as follows: Spanish, Venezuelan/Cuban, Mexican, Puerto Rican, Cuban, and two Hispanic. The young man who identified as Spanish said that he did not like having to choose one at all. The young man who said Mexican said he only identified as Mexican if he were in a group of Hispanics; otherwise, he would just use Hispanic. For the White students, one made the distinction of being Italian American. For the others, although White was claimed, as one person put it, "We run from being called White."

Every person interviewed identified either as gay or bisexual, but even those categories were problematic for the students when they were asked to choose one. Both of the young women interviewed identified as bisexual, although one said she had a definite female lean but did not like the word *dyke*. She preferred *ekyd*, or *dyke* spelled backwards. Two of the young men vacillated between bisexual and gay. One proposed a difference between gay and homosexual, saying that a gay person was a homosexual who knew more gay culture. No one liked the word *queer*, saying that they felt it sounded hostile and associated it with slurs like *faggot*. Additionally, people in the group also used *friendly* and *children* to signify gay, lesbian, or bisexual.

These young people used the space of GLBFO as an area of vibrant critique of the institutions around them, and this critique affected what they called themselves when asked to place themselves in a box for categorization. They resisted being put together in broad levels of categorization, such as I did by using *Latino* and even *gay* and *bisexual*. Each of these categories are contested ones that cover a broad range of people with different backgrounds and different experiences. For example, the differing backgrounds of the Latino students in the club were apparent, as these students had historical roots in Puerto Rico, Cuba, Mexico, and Venezuela. The experience gained from each of these backgrounds is different.

HISTORY OF GAY, LESBIAN, BISEXUAL, AND FRIENDS ORGANIZATION

How the members of GLBFO view their own history is important to the club's emergence as a student-run safe space. GLBFO grew out of a gay and lesbian support group that had formed following the physical assault of a gay student on campus in the late 1980s. The faculty member who started the support group was a Latina lesbian associated with the women's center. After the initial inception of GLBFO, she also became a faculty adviser to it as well.

From the beginning, there were tensions arising out of adult–youth relationships. Although the support group was created in reaction to a legitimate threat, it represented the type of organization that is often created surrounding young people. Like all youth in the United States, gay, lesbian, and bisexual youth are subject to the dictates of the adults in the society. Youth tend to be viewed as dangerous and in need of control when they do not fit in with the current zeitgeist of society (Roman, 1996). These youth can also be seen as being "in danger" from society as well as being a danger to it. Leslie Roman (1996) has written about the creation and legitimization of "youth at risk" as an agreed-upon category into which such youth are readily placed. When theorizing youth as "at risk," adults may create a moral panic encouraging other adults to take (punitive or "helpful") action. Like the moral panics surrounding dropouts described by Roman, any hint of a sexuality that is not "straight" and "normal" also encourages youth to be labeled as deviant and "at risk," spawning models of intervention that create, reproduce, and enforce institutions that are more concerned with controlling youth than helping them. In the words of Roman (1996):

> I argue that, when [educational] researchers and policy makers create youths as subjects at risk, they also become subjects of blame and pathology and, thus, are constructed as deserving particular paternalistic state interventions. Such constructions not only trivialize or silence altogether the voices of youth, they also distract from the larger structural realities of late capitalism and long-standing inequalities of distributive and social justice that are the real and complex culprits with respect to many of the problems young people face today. (p. 2)

Gay, lesbian, and bisexual adults often create organizations for gay, lesbian, and bisexual youth, just as the faculty member from the women's center did. However well meaning these institutions and the people who create them are, the unequal power caused by the age difference still exists, even if the unequal power of heterosexism does not. In the language of Roman, along with being labeled "at risk" by heterosexual adults, gay, lesbian, and bisexual youth also face being labeled "at risk" by adult gay men, lesbians, and bisexuals. Because of their own experience, the adults are aware of additional, and very real, dangers that young gay men, lesbians, and bisexuals face, dangers created from heterosexism and homophobia. A moral panic is therefore created deriving from three different assumptions: (1) Their sexuality may be seen as dangerous; (2) the heterosexuals around them may be viewed as dangerous; (3) because of internalized homophobia, the youth may be a danger to themselves. (For the dangers facing gay youth, see Gionsorek, 1988; Martin & Hetrick, 1988; Uribe & Harbeck, 1992).

According to the group members who were present at the original support group, the original group emerged out of such panic—conscious or not. The students wanted a group of their own. The faculty member wanted a support group. Although they realized that her desire to help was legitimate—she had created the support group following a physical attack on a gay person on campus—the students felt that they needed to reposition themselves. They felt that, in the support group, their needs were secondary to hers. The original group thus split into two groups—(1) a support group that was led by a faculty member and (2) GLBFO, in which faculty advisers would exercise little, if any, real power.

To the founding members of GLBFO, the word *support* implied that they needed help, that they could not handle being gay. *Support* made them seem like they were in a state of crisis, a notion from which they wished to disentangle themselves. Additionally, the group was under the auspices of the women's center, which was located off the main campus and, as such, was not considered a campus organization. The students felt that being off campus only added to the notion that they needed to be supported, that they needed to be protected. In contrast, the students wanted to be a visible force on campus, not out of the view of the heterosexual population. In the fall of 1992, they began the process to gain formal recognition of the newly named Gay, Lesbian, Bisexual, and Friends Organization as a legitimate, student-government approved organization that would meet on the main campus.

In keeping with their goal of visibility, the students wanted GLBFO to receive all the benefits and privileges that other campus groups enjoyed, including an office space in the student center and the right to reserve rooms on campus for club functions. This was not easy to obtain. As Adam (the White, gay president of GLBFO and vice president of the Student Government Association for the 1994–1995 school year) explained:

> The "legend"is that the then-president of GLBFO [an African American gay male] was run around by the student government for two semesters. Then late in the spring of 1993, the last act of the president of the Student Government Association was to approve GLBFO right before he got out of office to avoid the repercussions.

Because of the difficulty in obtaining acceptance of GLBFO as an organization on campus, the organizational structure was very formal. This formal organizational structure was put in place to insure that GLBFO would enjoy the same benefits as all other student organizations on campus. The faculty member who ran the support group became an adviser to GLBFO when it was formed. According to Adam, she wanted every action GLBFO performed approved by her. In response, GLBFO changed its bylaws so that the role of a faculty adviser became extremely clear, leaving the students to make all the decisions for the club.

Even with these limitations on the advisers in place, GLBFO continued to have trouble with their faculty advisers. As Adam explained:

> After we formed GLBFO, they kept saying, "Your functions are too social. Your functions are too social." Because we did things like bake sales and parties and movies. Our advisers said that the group had to be about something more than fun. It had to have political aims. We felt that you had to get them in the door first, have a place to hang out, and then something socially relevant could grow out of that. Even now our adviser says that he thinks that our events are too social, even though we have organized politically as well.

From early on, the students expressed concerns that the faculty were not listening to them. Even after the founder of the support group was asked to leave, the role of the faculty advisers continued to diminish until their presence was felt only during the formal organizational meetings. During the year that I was at GLBFO, the support group dwindled and eventually stopped meeting. Given a choice between a faculty-run or a student-run space, the students chose the latter.

CREATING A SAFE SPACE

The faculty advisers who created the original support group tried to construct an area of political activism for these youth. Activism implied an openness that new club members were sometimes reluctant to express. The students felt that the faculty wanted them to take part in traditionally defined overt political actions on campus such as marches, setting up information groups, and teaching the straight students about gay, lesbian, and bisexual people. But these kinds of acts would require the students to be out to everyone, putting themselves up for public scrutiny—without a space for refuge.

The students wanted and needed a simple place to gather, to work out their notions of independence on their own. Most of the young people in this group were still reliant on their families for either financial support or a place to live. Because of this reliance, much of their time was spent policing their own actions in order not to lose this support, which in turn would mean losing their chance at college. Of those who were out to their families, most spent much of their time defending themselves against verbal attacks on their sexuality. In fact, only one of the twelve students interviewed reported any kind of unqualified support from her family about her sexuality. Other students reported home environments ranging from those that were blatantly hostile to those that shifted between pockets of reluctant acceptance to open hostility to honest parental confusion about how to react. Two students had yet to come out to their parents and worried about the reactions when they decided to do so. Faced with the immediate necessity of negotiating these familial relationships, political organization seemed a far-off goal. They could not mobilize politically if they had no space in which they could relax and stop worrying about defending their sexuality against the attacks of those around them. Many felt as if they were only one person against many—a family, a society, a social network—all of whom were heterosexual. Ricky, a 19-year-old Latino who had recently joined the organization, explained it this way:

> Growing up in West New York was really hard. There is a lot of homophobic people, and in school I was always being bothered. Everyone would always say, "Oh you damn queer! You're such a faggot!" and I used to be like, "No I'm not a queer. I'm not a faggot. You're wrong" . . . and it was like a constant mocking and for a time I would constantly get into fights. I couldn't come out, even though I wanted to.

Even though they were aware that there were other gay, lesbian, and bisexual people in the world, they had no real significance in their lives. As John, one of the oldest members of the group, a 26-year-old White gay man, said, "I knew there were gay people in the world, there were just none in my world." These other gay, lesbian, and bisexual people were all adult entertainers or news figures and, for these young people, existed only in the movies and on television. They were not other young people like themselves to whom they could relate. They needed to be with people like themselves, to relax and have some fun. After spending their formative years with no place to congregate with others like themselves, having a space in which to "hang out" was important. Alejandro, a 19-year-old new Latino member who had recently come out as gay in the club, explained how the club was important to him in this way:

> I guess since I arrived at the club, I now knew there were people there that I knew felt the same way I did, so I felt more comfortable coming to them, I guess. . . . And now, I mean, since I've come out, it's changed my life. I want to do more things now that I'm

more, I guess, gay. I want to go out, I want to start, you know, having a relationship with someone. I didn't do that for the first 19 years of life, so I want to jump into that now, I guess. I want to be able to enjoy myself.

The faculty members may have failed to realize the need for a simple space to hang out. As such, the club room functioned for some members as what has been called a recuperative site (Fine, Weis, Roberts, & Centrie, 2000). Not sites of hot political action, but instead places to rest tired bodies and enjoy the company of peers, these places become spaces to negotiate collectively with peers who share a vision of what constitutes political action. Further, from the vantage of the club room, the students engaged in a kind of reversal of power. They participated in the surveillance of straight students from the window on the second floor. This window also allowed them to proclaim with the hanging of a rainbow flag that the student center was gay-, lesbian-, and bisexual-friendly. They engaged in what Pat Mann (1994) has called micro-politics.

> A micro-political analysis has several purposes. In the first place, it demonstrates that there are serious political implications in many of the everyday decisions individuals make with respect to how they will act in a given circumstance, even when these decisions are not accompanied by traditional forms of political consciousness. Second, it offers a framework for acting as intersectional agents within various institutional settings. By encouraging individuals to evaluate what sort of actions are likely to contribute to the perpetuation or, alternatively, to the erosion of complex, intersectional relations of domination within a particular situation, a micro-political analysis provides grounds for creative and unconventional forms of political organizing and struggle. (p. 31)

Tony, a 23-year-old Italian American who identifies himself as gay, recounted his reasons for joining the club in this way:

Tony: [After finding out about the club] I was like, "Wow! Great! Finally, what I've been looking for." So I just went right up to them and said I would like to join. They said, "OK, stop by the office or whatever." So I officially came out on campus on national coming-out day, so October 11th, and I've been a member since October 11th.

Richard: Of last year?

Tony: Yeah, of 1994. I wanted to do it, because, I don't know. I just wanted to somehow feel like I belong to the community somehow. That sounds funny because I could participate in something else, you know, and still be a part of the community, but I don't know, I felt that I

should somehow show, you know, that I'm one—that I'm somebody. I
feel like a somebody.

This sense of community, this sense of being with other people who are
gay, lesbian, and bisexual, became extremely important. By being in a community, the club room transcended a simple place to gather. It became,
instead, a free space in which they could work out issues that affected all
areas of their lives, a base of operations for members, a site that was transformative as well as recuperative. This transformation occurred because the
club room allowed both a critique of heterosexism and homophobia and a
site where being gay, lesbian, and bisexual was accepted as the norm. The
freedom of sexuality sometimes gave the members room to grow into critique of the other aspects of the identities they held in their lives. They could
look at the structures around them—such as family, church, school, culture—and test how safe they felt within these institutions. They could develop what James Scott (1990) has called the "hidden transcripts of resistance," critiques developed among themselves because of and outside the
gaze of the people who upheld the institutions that dominated their lives.
    Everyday actions became the bases for everyday political actions. In-
stead of big "one-event" actions, the club was visible at all times to other
students simply by being where it was on campus, thus constantly raising
awareness of gay, lesbian, and bisexual people. Adam, the president and
a longtime member, repeatedly tried to find ways to make the group more
visible not only on campus but also in the larger community. Whenever
an event was held on campus, he made sure a GLBFO table would be there.
He joined the Student Government Association and became vice-president,
becoming the first openly gay student government official. From this position, he made sure that GLBFO was in the know about every major event
on campus. He encouraged members to join local groups of gay men and
lesbians, and with John, another older member, succeeded in getting several of the male members to join a gay volleyball league, march in parades,
attend such public events as a gay business gathering, and make public
their bake sales in order to raise money and awareness on the campus.
Whenever anyone bought a brownie, they knew they were buying brown-
ies from gay, lesbian, and bisexual students.

RELATIONSHIPS WITHIN GLBFO

The older members' gaze was bidirectional: outward toward more traditional forms of political action and inward toward the younger students.

As Adam put it earlier, you had to get people in the door, you had to let them have fun, to be comfortable—then you could have political action. Tony summed it up best when he explained the reason he joined the club: "You know, to be around people. Love is the whole reason I came out in the first place. It felt good to be around people who were exactly like me and not feel pressured. So that was the way I felt here in this room." Keeping this in mind, the older members referred to other club members as family members, with the older students functioning as the "parents." Alejandro refers to this practice of calling them "children" to help in his coming out to nongay people in his life:

Alejandro: The first time I came out to the person that I told it, like that person in January, he asked if I had something to tell him and I was like yeah. And I couldn't say the word *gay. (laugh)* I couldn't say it. What they used was *children.*

Richard: Children?

Alejandro: Yeah, that's what they use in the club. That's what they call each other—children. That's what they call people that are gay. I used the word, I was like, "I'm children." And the person I was coming out to said, "No, that's not the word you should use," so like after a half an hour of me thinking what the word I should say was, I told him I was gay. Actually, now I've said that word like three times, *gay,* you know, coming out to somebody.

In setting up this notion of the younger students' being children, the members redefined the traditional power of the family by reconceptualizing it in a gay, lesbian, and bisexual way. In being a gay, lesbian, and bisexual family, the younger members did have a place in which they could escape heterosexism. This added to the recuperative nature of the club room. Family relationships are mythologized as being safe, caring, and helpful to children's becoming fully functioning members of society. This definition is the one the members of GLBFO used when naming themselves a "family." The older members would help the younger members grow into a society that included homosexuality. As John put it:

Anybody around [Alejandro's] age, between like, say 18 and 22, are new to this and this is new to them. And they are seen as almost like a neophyte—someone who can be brought into [gay and lesbian] society. Much like—almost on the same level that [the guy who helped me come out] was a mother to me. He did it in a friendly sort of way.

Families, in reality, however, often do not reflect the mythology. As Nicola Field (1995) writes:

> We are taught that to be in a family is good and natural and family ties are the most stable, loving and unselfish relationships we will have in our lives. For most of us, this lesson flies in the face of our own experience of brutality, alienation and confusion within the family. . . . The family, far from being a haven and a retreat from the outside world, is actually a very dangerous place, both physically and mentally. (p. 10)

The younger members of GLBFO experienced this dichotomy with their families of origin: dependency and love on the one hand, verbal and physical attacks due to their sexual orientation on the other. Therefore, like many gay and lesbian people, the people in the club experienced an attraction *and* a resistance to notions of family. Although the members of the club gave each other more support than did their families of origin, this familial critique spilled over into the reconceptualization of GLBFO as a family. As a result, tension sometimes arose when older members tried to mentor younger members directly, thus reproducing the unequal power structure present in traditional families. GLBFO had formed in part as an attempt to get away from the mentoring of older gays and lesbians, and the younger people in the group were just as reluctant to take the dictates of the older members as the older members had been to follow the dictates of the advisers. Tensions arose when the older members took it upon themselves to direct the younger members actively, reproducing cross-generational "paternalism." The younger members preferred that they lead by example, not by direct action. Because of this, they would often resist overt statements and acts of mentoring, as this exchange between John and Alejandro shows:

John: [Alejandro] and I fight like this back and forth because we are friends, because we have, you know, we can accept each other for who we are. I know he's gay and I know he's young, and he's going through a lot.
Alejandro: I'm friendly. *(laughing)*
John: I know he's friendly and he's young, and he can go through a tough time, and I've talked to him about experiences, that if ever needs help, he can call me. I'd want to do for him what [the person who helped me come out] did for me. He was such a positive role model that I want to be there for Alejandro. That's all.
Alejandro: Oh, how cute!

Although Alejandro resisted John's attempts at "helping" him be gay, his resistance was couched in friendly banter. John points out that part of what made this resistance to the older members "friendly" was the fact that they "can accept each other for who we are." If any overt attempt at "mentoring" were made, the younger students usually met it with this kind of resistance. Alejandro does this by saying that he is not "children," but instead "friendly." Poking fun at the authoritative air that John was adopting in talking about Alejandro, Alejandro transformed himself from one of the "children" into one of the "friends," signifying a more equal relationship.

Alejandro's attempts to put himself and John on a more equal level in the above exchange shows another important factor in the club. Whenever any signs of inequality showed themselves, the members were quick to try to reverse or play with power. John and Alejandro thus experienced different levels in comfort in how they viewed themselves and their roles. This comfort affected the ways in which they presented themselves to the outside world. John viewed himself as a teacher and thus presented himself as out regardless of the situation. Alejandro's use of self-presentation took the lines of clever reversals of power by sometimes being open about his sexuality and sometimes not. Self-presentation, however, was not the only area of inequality in the above exchange.

It could also be argued that the different positions taken by John and Alejandro could be a result of the way the outside world viewed their differences beyond sexuality. Besides being older, John was also White, while Alejandro was Latino. Although they were joined together through their sexuality, the differences of the outside world nevertheless permeated the club. There is a considerable literature documenting distinct experiences of being gay, lesbian, and bisexual for people of color compared to Whites (e.g., Chan, 1989; Espin, 1987; Loiacano, 1989). Additionally, there is a large literature on the different experiences that Latino people from different countries of origin have with being gay (e.g., Arguelles & Rich, 1984; Carrier, 1989; Hidalgo & Christensen, 1976–77; Zamora-Hernández & Patterson, 1996). When asked how their ethnicity interplayed with their sexuality, however, the students in the club categorically stated that if there were an interaction, it was a slight one. According to them, the interaction was associated with *machismo*, a value common to many Latino cultures. According to Zamora-Hernández and Patterson (1996), *machismo* requires a hypermasculine role for men, stressing dominance and aggressiveness. In comparison, women are required to be morally superior yet at the same time submissive. It therefore stresses the strength and vigor of Latino men while relegating women to an inferior position. Each of the gay Latino members of the club saw *machismo* as being a large barrier to their being out as gay men. Each of them talked of scrutiny of their actions and their mannerisms by people around them, making sure that they acted "like a man." Ricky put it this way:

> It's like really hard for me, especially coming from a Spanish family, a Cuban family, where they're so *machistic* [*sic*], and growing up was really hard because they always wanted to change my mannerisms. It was like, "No, do not scratch yourself that way. Girls scratch themselves. Do not bite your nails; that's for girls. Do not sit like that." I feel that Hispanic people—it's really hard for Hispanic people to accept someone who is gay. That's how I think. In the Spanish culture, the man is the one with the cash and the house and the man is the one with the wife. The man is, you know, and especially Hispanic, you know, where men used to control all their wives. It happened in the White culture and in the Black culture, but I think in the Hispanic culture it happened more. So there's this *machistic* thing, so growing up with this *machistic* thing, it's really hard for Hispanic. It's really hard for Hispanic parents [of gay children].

While language, culture of origin, and history varied widely, the students had primarily gathered on the basis of being young and gay/lesbian/bisexual. When any other difference was explored with them—whether race, ethnicity, or class—invariably they would turn the conversation back to the things they shared, not the ways in which they differed. Marie provides an example of this downplaying of ethnicity (a difference) and emphasis on age (a shared experience) when asked about the way that her ethnicity interacted with her sexuality:

> I don't think being Hispanic really interacts as much [with being gay]. If anything, I know a lot of people who are gay or lesbian. They're Hispanic. And the only thing I see that people who have problems with it or just don't agree with it at all are the older generation, parents if not grandparents. Those are the ones that have more problems. I see that now—people who are old generation have a problem with it. They may not act, but just comments, you know, especially my grandmother or [my] friends, their parents.

Marie said this even though she was the one person in the club who said that her own parents had reacted very well to her coming out. For Marie, and others in the club, the function of the organization was to have a shared space based on youth and sexuality. Since gay, lesbian, and bisexual sexuality is seen as a difference from the larger culture, other differences among the students could make them feel unsafe. As a result, differences based on ethnicity were downplayed. Even though many of the students took pride in their ethnicity, that was not their purpose for gathering. They gathered their sense of safety from being around other young, gay, lesbian, or bisexual people.

EXTENDING THE SAFETY OF A SAFE SPACE

Ricky described GLBFO:

> I first thought the club room was this place where you get coun-seled and it's really not that. In the club room, it's like you can like look at guys through the window as they come to the student center. And we have fun and we gossip and we mingle. It's like somewhere we can really be ourselves, really be exploded, be queens or exploded or whatever. We could do that on campus, but it's like, we don't attract negative attention from anybody here in the room. It's like everybody comes in; everybody loves us. It's like the sorority right in front of us. They love us and some of them are even in the club now. And they aren't even lesbians.

For Ricky, and others, the club room was a place to "explode," to be himself and meet people on his own terms without attracting unwanted negative attention. In that club room, even the "straight" sorority across the hall liked the club members. Although they were "not lesbians," they were not seen by Ricky to be people against whom he had to defend his sexuality. In having such a place of freedom, Ricky felt safer on campus and more accepted by everyone, even by the sorority across the hall.

Having the club room, campus visibility, and affirmative action poli-cies on campus gave the students a sense of safety. From this sense of safety, other places suddenly became safe, even if they were not perceived that way previously. The club members began to feel that they could be pro-tected against attack from other people, that they did not have to worry as much about the ramifications of the homophobia of others. John pro-vided an example of this:

> Yeah, there's a shared light switch between GLBFO and the frater-nity group next door. If you turn it off in one room, it goes off in the other room, and accidentally it goes off every once in a while. . . . Well, Adam and I were in the room one day, and we turned off the light and [they] yelled "faggot," and we got Student Services, and we had them written up on charges, which is one step

away from, I guess, taken off campus, or [the disbanding] of the group, or whatever.

The rigid area of the club room bound by the four walls became a mobile liminal "space" that the members carried with them as they moved throughout the rest of their world. In other words, from this base, safety became mobile. A place did not have to be gay, lesbian, or bisexual to be safe any longer. In fact, some people did not even feel the need to go to "gay" places outside the club as long as they had the club to come back to.

For the students the club room provided a mobile safety carried with them and their friends. This mobile safe space forced nongay environments to become gay-friendly in their eyes. According to John:

> Um, anywhere I . . . can feel comfortable being gay is a gay place, whether that's walking on the beach next to someone who also is gay. And it could be a gay beach; it could not be a gay beach. My room is definitely a gay place because I am a gay person and it is my room. . . . I belong to a gay men's volleyball league, and I feel very comfortable playing volleyball there. I never played . . . sports in high school . . . I really liked it a lot, and I still feel very, very comfortable.

This space was not a simple one, however. Although the club members came together through their similarity in sexuality, they brought with them all aspects of their identities, hidden and public, in the outside world. No space is entirely "free" and no space is entirely "safe," but by forging a space in which they could make their own rules, the club members managed to come closer to Evans and Boyte's notion of free space. A free space must be an area into which young people retreat from institutions of oppression. Ricky summed it up best:

> I feel like now, having all these gay friends and going clubbing and knowing all these gay people and how nice they treat you, that's really what's positive about being gay. They take care of you. We protect you and we're here to stick for each other. . . . They're filling in for what I didn't have at my own house, so it's like they're my family. That's why I like being here more, because I'm with them, and they're like treating me nice . . . I really feel comfortable. That's the most positive thing.

Acknowledgment. This project was funded by a grant of the Spencer Foundation, Michelle Fine and Lois Weis, Principal Investigators.

REFERENCES

Arguelles, L., & Rich, B. R. (1984). Homosexuality, homophobia, and revolution: Notes toward an understanding of the Cuban lesbian and gay male experience, Part I. *Signs, 9*(4), 683–699.

Carrier, J. M. (1989). Gay liberation and coming out in Mexico. *Journal of Homosexuality, 17*(3), 225–252.

Chan, C. S. (1989). Issues of identity develop among Asian-American lesbians and gay men. *Journal of Counseling and Development, 68,* 16–20.

Espin, O. M. (1987). Issues of identity in the psychology of Latina lesbians. In the Boston Lesbian Psychologies Collective (Eds.), *Lesbian psychologies: Exploration and challenges* (pp. 35–55). Urbana: University of Illinois Press.

Evans, S. M., & Boyte, H. C. (1992). *Free spaces: The sources of democratic change in America,* 2nd ed. Chicago: University of Chicago Press.

Field, N. (1995). *Over the rainbow: Money, class and homophobia.* London: Pluto Press.

Fine, M., Weis, L., Roberts, R., & Centrie, C. (2000). Educating beyond the borders of schooling. *Anthropology and Education Quarterly, 31*(2), 131–151.

Gionsorek, J. C. (1988). Mental health issues of gay and lesbian adolescents. *Journal of Adolescent Health Care, 9,* 114–122.

Hidalgo, H. A., & Christensen, E. H. (1976–77). The Puerto Rican lesbian and the Puerto Rican community. *Journal of Homosexuality, 2*(2), 109–121.

Loiacano, D. K. (1989). Gay identity issues among Black Americans: Racism, homophobia, and the need for validation. *Journal of Counseling and Development, 68,* 21–25.

Mann, P. (1994). *Micro-politics: Agency in a postfeminist era.* Minneapolis: University of Minnesota Press.

Martin, A. D., & Hetrick, E. S. (1988). The stigmatization of gay and lesbian adolescents. *Journal of Homosexuality, 15*(1–2), 163–183.

Roman, L. G. (1996). Spectacle in the dark: Youth as transgression, display, and repression. *Educational Theory, 46*(1), 1–22.

Scott, J. (1990). *Domination and the art of resistance.* New Haven, CT: Yale University Press.

Uribe, V., & Harbeck, K. (1992). Addressing the needs of lesbian, gay, and bisexual youth: The origins of PROJECT 10 and school-based intervention. In K. M. Harbeck (Ed.), *Coming out of the classroom closet: Gay and lesbian students, teachers, and curricula* (pp. 9–28). Binghamton, NY: Harrington Park Press.

Zamora-Hernández, C. E., & Patterson, D. G. (1996). Homosexually active Latino men: Issues for social work practice. *Journal of Gay and Lesbian Social Services, 5,* 2–3, 69–91.

CHAPTER 6

Re-Writing/-Righting Lives: Voices of Pregnant and Parenting Teenagers in an Alternative School

AMIRA PROWELLER

AP: What do you fear about your future?

Sharon: Nothing get in the way of me, my son, or my baby's daddy to make me scared or nothing. I would just rather be free.

AP: What do you mean by saying that you would just rather be free?

Sharon: You know, just let it . . . don't let nobody tell you this going to happen and that going to happen. Because if you let them tell you that, then you might as well let them tell you all [to], "Drop out of school, hang out with us, don't go to school, girls, you can do this, you can do that. You don't have to listen to your mamma, you can stay on the streets with us." Nope. I'm *not* going to do it. I'm *going* to do it. I'm *going* to go to school. I'm *going* to graduate and get a job. I'm *going* to take care of my baby. And he *going* to go to school, and he *going* to graduate, and he *going* to get him a job. And he *going* to be able to take care of whatever he have [to do].

With determination and resolve, Sharon, a 14-year-old, African American teen mom, couches the experience of teenage pregnancy less in terms of tragic destiny and more in terms of resiliency and possibility for the future. Running through a list of potential obstacles that could intervene to put her life and that of her child at risk, Sharon is fixed on carving out a future for herself and her son. Tempting discursive arrangements that have designed dismal destinies for "at-risk" mothers like herself, she projects an option-filled future for herself and her son. Michelle Fine (1995) reminds us that the category of youth "at risk" is a social construction that "serves the interests of those educators and policy makers who do not want to 'disturb' the culture of the public high school, who want to effectively keep segments of the population out, more than it serves those who are classed as at risk" (p. 88). Specious constructions of the pregnant and parenting teenager as lazy, immoral, dependent, a welfare cheat, and a drain on the national economy dominate conservative policy discourse and broadly circulate throughout the media and popular cultural forms (Kelly, 1997). As Nancy Lesko (1990, 1991, 1994, 1995), Ruth Sidel (1996), Sue Books (1996, 1998), Kelly (1996), and other critical scholars on youth culture point out, teenage pregnancy has been politically constructed as a "social problem" principally aimed at singling out poor, single mothers as convenient scapegoats for moral denigration. Echoing this sensibility, the principal of New Ventures Academy, the alternative school that Sharon attends, had this to say:

> I think when a student becomes pregnant and they are considered at risk, there is that possibility, in the minds of the public, and educators, and academicians, and social service people, [that] uh oh, they [the pregnant and parenting teenager] are either going to drop out of school and get on "welfare rolls" or they will just blindly go through life without any set purpose. But that is not necessarily the case.

Her caveat—"that this is not necessarily the case"—frames Sharon's ability to see herself as being adaptive and competent in the face of mounting public insecurity and discomfort that writes pregnant and parenting teenagers into a discourse of risk earmarked as political exploitation at its best in a struggle over how to define the Other (Swadener & Lubeck, 1995). The public anticipates their failure and targets them for blame with a rhetoric of hopelessness that denies meaning and purpose to these youth.

Sandwiched between current policy debates around the politics of sexuality and reproduction among our nation's youth, New Ventures Academy is a space where private behaviors of sexual relationships, pregnancy, and motherhood become part of the domain of public discourse. Layered over in demonizing public policies and struggling within and against the social ravages of economic disadvantage, silenced needs, desires, hopes, and fears are provided possibilities for voice in a dedicated school context. The persistent pathologization of these youth as "at risk" and "abnormal" denies them the possibility of empowering themselves and attributing educational value to life experience. New Ventures Academy provides the space for students to envision themselves in opposite terms, "at promise," leading lives that they themselves have had a hand in shaping. School space supports challenges to stereotypical notions that have foreclosed possibilities in their young lives, inviting those of us on the outside to reevaluate "dubious [mis]conceptions" (Luker, 1996) that surround the politics and practices of teenage sexuality and early parenting. Their ability to strategize effective ways of managing their lives serves to educate the broader public about resilient attitudes and behaviors that well situate urban youth to move themselves forward into the twenty-first century. Sharon and other pregnant and parenting teens enrolled at the school engage teenage pregnancy as an episode of struggle within and against existing discursive frameworks (Pillow, 1997a). At this moment, teen mothers self-present as resilient, drawing on multiple resources—self, school, family, community, and peers—to sketch the outlines of self-renewal. Pregnancy itself is recast as a site of transformation that sets the course for potentially meaningful lives to unfold.

Breaking open the ambiguous category of "at risk" by taking a close look at the narrated experiences of pregnant and parenting teenagers, this discussion purposefully disturbs the culture of vilification that surrounds young teenage mothers, who have become an icon for immorality, promiscuity, and uncontrolled sexuality (Burdell, 1995/96, 1998; Irvine, 1994; Luker, 1996; Schofield, 1994; Thompson, 1995). Inside New Ventures Academy, urban girls (re)-write/-right their lives through counterpublic narratives (Fraser, 1990) that summon a mixture of despair, desire, pleasure, and power to the surface. Pointing to the power that the narrative form holds for women's lives, Carolyn Heilbrun (1988) writes that "what matters is that lives do not serve as models; only stories do that . . . whatever their form or medium, these stories have formed us all, they are what we must use to make new fictions, new narratives" (p. 37). Through the narrative voices of pregnant and parenting teenagers, we are let into alternative cultural constructions that design the experience of eraly pregnancy and parenting differently than has largely been the case, as these youth remove themselves from the "at-risk" list and poise themselves, instead, to lead lives "at promise." Stories of reconstituted lives allow youth to see themselves in other roles, in another light. For those of us on the outside looking in, these narratives become "what we must use to make new fictions, new narratives" (Heilbrun, 1988, p. 37) that do not speak *for* but *with* others.

The data featured here were gathered as part of a study examining the production of identities as student, pregnant teenager, and mother among a cohort of middle school– and high school–aged girls attending New Ventures Academy, an alternative public school in a midwestern metropolitan area. While a wide range of school types fall under the category of alternative schools, they generally have in common curricular and support programming intended to assist youth who are likely to drop out of school to stay in and complete high school (Knutson, 1996). Alternative schools typically provide services to assist youth to remain in school and to succeed academically. Youth targeted as most likely to drop out of school tend to be those displaying poor school attendance, reluctant school engagement, low levels of academic performance, low self-esteem, and those parenting at an early age.[1] Serving approximately 500 students annually on a rotating basis, this school supports the academic and social needs of pregnant and parenting youth in grades 6–12. The student population breaks down at approximately 55% African American, 35% Hispanic, and 10% Asian, Native American, and Caucasian. Nearly 80% of enrolled students belong to families receiving public aid. New Ventures Academy is centrally located in a downtown business district, relatively free of gang and drug activity, to which most students commute from outlying neighborhoods and suburban areas, some at considerable distance from the school.

Data were gathered through interviews with select school staff and approximately twenty students between the ages of 14 and 19, all of whom had transferred to the school from local public and private schools after learning that they were pregnant. Of the twenty students interviewed, six were Latina, eleven were African American, one was Native-American, and two were White. Interviews were complemented with targeted observation data gathered from visits to classrooms and support classes on parenting and health offered by a social service agency in partnership with the school.

FRAMING LIVES "AT RISK"

For children and adolescents in our current social context, the conditions of daily life are increasingly complex, for many youth nothing short of mere survival (*The State of America's Children Yearbook*, 1998). Student anecdotes readily transform faceless statistics into the reality of home communities and neighborhoods ridden with drugs, crime, and gang activity. Their interview narratives show them troubling over a world, as one student, Tanika, describes it, "that is hell," leaving them not exactly sure of "what to think," yet quite certain that it is "nasty" and "bad." Thrust into the problematic conditions of everyday life, the students of New Ventures Academy draw clear lines between the world out there and the world inside their school, likening it to a homeplace (hooks, 1990), a safe haven removed from the immediate dangers and stresses that typify many of their lives, leaving urban youth feeling physically threatened and displaced, and rendered invisible. For pregnant teens, the relief available through an alternative school is especially significant since their pregnant bodies are often the target of critique and violence, creating an unequivocal need for alternative educational spaces. As Wanda Pillow (1997b) points out in her powerful work on reading the pregnant body as a site of reproduction, the pregnant teenager is seen as having overstepped the boundaries of appropriate reproductive practice. Not yet an adult and typically pregnant out-of-wedlock, she finds her body the focus of moral concern and the target of public outrage. Pillow identifies the paradox inherent in this construction—the pregnant teenager is fulfilling her "feminine" responsibility by bearing children, yet in a fashion that is not deemed acceptable by the public. Her vilification is morally justified on the grounds that she obstructed legitimate reproductive practice. The public appropriation of the pregnant body winds through student anecdotes of wandering eyes and offhand comments at the bus stop, on the street corner, and on the subway, as well as physical assaults in school corridors that muddle the boundaries between the public and the private. The subject/object of this type of public assault, Carmen describes her indignation over having been singled out for moral critique on a city bus:

> You know, people look at me, like when I got on the bus today—I have three buses to take here—and they look at me, and they're like, "Ugh." I can hold my own strength. I had a backpack, I had a twenty-pound baby. I got on the bus, and I had a backpack. I had a baby bag. I had my 2-year-old son, and I had my baby in front of me. . . . This lady looked at me, and she was like—"oh my God!" And I'm lookin' at her, like, and I turned around, and I said, "Is there a problem?" She goes, "You don't look no more than 18." I said, "Yes, I am 18 years old." She was like in her middle, maybe 40s. And, um, she was, like . . . I said, "I am 18 years old. I got a 2-year old son," and I said, "You look at my son right here," and I took his blanket off of him, and I said, "Look at my son right here. They are healthy, they're clean, and they don't need nothing." And she looked at me, and she's like, "That's not all that matters." I said, "All that matters is that I love my kids." I don't care if they got old jeans on, and they look like crap. But they're clean and they're fed. And I said, and I don't care. I'm a teen mom, and I know it. And I said, "And I'm doing the best I can to prove it." She looked at me, like "Ugh!" And the bus driver's [saying] "You tell her!" (laughs) I got really mad because she was like, "Ugh!" I

turned around, and I said, "Excuse me, don't look at my kids like that. You don't know my kids. Respect me. You don't know me." I just get so pissed off, you know?

Co-opting the private as the focus of moral concern and public outrage appears in a slightly different form in public school corridors, where pregnant teens often find themselves the objects of critique among their peers. Extending her analysis of the public sphere to violence against pregnant girls in school, Carmen assesses why pregnant teens might very well choose to transfer temporarily to an alternative school rather than remain in their home schools:

> Because in the home school, some people, you know, maybe some girls are gang bangers[2] you know, and they fear for their baby. They go to school and somebody's not looking, they can turn around and knock'em down the escalator. Or, you know, do whatever they do in high school. . . . They jump on girls because they didn't like'em. Their hair was long. They didn't look this way, you know what I'm saying? . . . Some . . . they, they . . . like nowadays, they'd go for your stomach. They see you with your baby, they'll go for your baby. . . . They'll go for your child, or you when you're pregnant, you know what I'm saying? Instead of going for somebody else, they're gonna go for you because they know you're pregnant. That's how they beat these days, 'cause I've seen a lot of things happen like that, you know.

COUNTERPUBLIC VOICES:
REFRAMING LIVES "AT PROMISE"

On Schooling

Research has documented that teen mothers tend to achieve fewer years of schooling than do other young women and that early childbearing is associated with increasing attrition rates among this population (Emihovich & Fromme, 1998; Furstenberg, Brooks-Gunn, & Morgan, 1987). Among girls, especially African American ones, teenage pregnancy has been cited as the leading cause of dropping out of school (Polit & Kahn, 1987). It is, however, not altogether evident that early parenthood is directly responsible for educational failure. Recent research has determined that the majority of female dropouts left school prior to becoming pregnant and that those who became pregnant while attending school were not more likely to leave school early (Upchurch & McCarthy, 1990; see also Hayes, 1987). Inconclusive findings notwithstanding, there is no question that early childbearing adds additional responsibilities to the lives of teenage girls, complicating the possibility of their graduating from high school.

Dedicated to the notion of "educated motherhood," school staff hold out the possibility of a "second chance" for these girls (Burdell, 1998).

> As one teacher put it: Nobody is there [at the school] who knew them when. They are outside their history. They do have an opportunity, and a real opportunity, motivated by the fact that they are going to be moms. And they can, they can justify—"I can change"—because no one is saying to them, "Oh, no, you are the one who did this or that." No one is quoting their past at them. It's a clean slate, and they have an opportunity to choose who they want to be from now on.

This effect contrasts with decidedly disengaged attitudes toward schooling that many of these young mothers, such as Kimberly, manifested prior to getting pregnant.

> Sometimes, my . . . me and my mother were talking, and she was like, "you know, before you got pregnant, you were failing." I was like, "I know." I wonder if I hadn't gotten pregnant, would I still be in school or not. So, sometimes I think my daughter, you know, she was [put] here for a reason—[to remind me] "Don't slack up"—you know.

The extent to which New Ventures Academy plays a direct role in shaping more positive attitudes toward school is debatable given the short period of time that students are enrolled in the school. While students showed improved grades and test scores on standardized tests since enrolling at New Ventures Academy, some admitted to a lack of challenging schoolwork, which was sufficient to pull them in the direction of early transfer back into their home schools. Although a small percentage of high-achieving students attend New Ventures Academy, most students place below national norms on standardized tests of reading and mathematics. Generally speaking, students reported supportive and caring teachers and staff who worked at creating a climate conducive to learning. Teachers told me of students who have, indeed, "turned their lives around," but they also identified an equal number of students whose histories as reluctant learners continued despite the personalized and individualized nature of instruction provided at the school. Students followed this line of thinking with their own keen distinctions between students "who want to learn" and those "who don't want to learn . . . that don't care . . . and look like the type that will go back out there and get pregnant again, probably have their second or third child." Equally important in assessing re-formed attitudes toward schooling are such key variables as family support networks and other personal strengths that motivate many of these teens to stay in school and succeed academically (Danzinger & Farber, 1990).

While the role that New Ventures Academy plays in shaping perceptions of school remains somewhat ambiguous, in an ironic twist, early pregnancy and parenting emerge here as instructive rather than destructive events. New Ventures Academy provides the space for these youth to redefine themselves as subjects of their own lives, weighting their experience as a defining moment of their educational development. As schooling moves from the periphery to the center of these students' lives, educators are inspired to rethink educational objectives and outcomes not simply in terms of achievement scores but more profoundly, perhaps, in terms of providing opportunities for urban youth to reimagine lives of promise and possibility for the future.

On Motherhood/Mothering

As a life-transforming episode, early pregnancy casts teenage girls into roles and a set of responsibilities tied to their new identity as mothers. Conflict-resolution classes and group counseling sessions with social workers under the sponsorship of the private social agency in partnership with New Ventures Academy provide seventh- and eighth-grade students supportive spaces for cultivating important survival strategies as young mothers. Group sessions dedicated to developing parenting and life skills accomplish similar curricular objectives for the high school students. Such instructional programming reflects the school's principal investment in helping students see themselves as responsible and competent parents.

Young girls are socialized early in their lives into believing that motherhood is their destiny. This role symbolically confirms their identity as women, sealing their value in terms of their capacity to reproduce (Cusick, 1989; Ruddick, 1991; Schofield, 1994). Across racial and ethnic lines, young parents constitute their lives not only within discourses of early parenting and motherhood circulating within their own cultures and communities but also against conservative discourses that stigmatize teenage mothers as "bad," "irresponsible," and potentially "abusive." While attitudes toward sex-role stereotyping and early parenting are culturally specific, manifesting differently vis-à-vis ethnic and racial groupings, the positive value attached to motherhood appears to be consistent across racial and ethnic groups represented among the students interviewed for this study. From the vantage point of the students in New Ventures Academy, early parenting and motherhood are reframed as transformational sites for crafting the private self anew (Fine & Weis, 1998). As Joyce Ladner (1971) uncovered in her ethnographic work with African American teenage girls living in a low-income housing project, motherhood has been singled out as the main standard for becoming a woman in the African American community, symbolizing the transition from adolescence to adulthood. Hill-Collins (1987, 1990) reminds us that the definition and value attached to the role of Black motherhood in the Black community is in constant flux, yet what has remained consistent is an understanding of motherhood as a site for definition and affirmation of the self. She observes that the role of the mother in the African American community has historically been a profile of matriarchal courage, strength, and determination.

Assessing how the experience of teenage pregnancy and motherhood has changed her, Lavonne, a 15-year old mom, spoke of the "courage" and "strength" that motherhood has given her, leaving her feeling that she "can just take on anything, anything that comes at me." Motherhood has created a space for her to redefine herself as competent and together, challenging public discourses that have fingered poor women of color as "bad" mothers. Working the boundaries between public and private, 18-year-old Latifa strategically resists the stereotype of the "immature" and "irresponsible" teen mother in her response to my question about what being a mother means to her:

Latifa: I think that her future lies in my hands, because if I don't show her, then she won't do it, you know? So being more responsible is very important to me.

Amira: What kind of mother would you say you are?

Latifa: I'm fair.

Amira: What does that mean to you?

Latifa: That means that I do what I have to do for her and not myself. That means that I put my wants to the side and give her her needs, you know, whatever it be, both of our needs, you know. I put our wants to the side and do the needs first. So, the wants can fall in place. I can't do everything I want to do . . . I just try to make that not important so I can do what I need to do first.

Latifa scripts herself as a mother who recognizes the weight of her new role, understanding that her ethical responsibility is to put the needs of her child first, before her own. She portrays herself as the fair mother, the moral mother, willing to sacrifice herself for her child, putting her child's concerns above personal ones. Several of the pregnant and parenting teens interviewed for this study provided remarkably similar scripts on mother-hood, arguably gleaned from the examples of women in their immediate families and communities who have consistently guided, supported, and inspired them as bloodmothers and othermothers caring for their children in their own extended family networks (Case, 1997; Cusick, 1989; Stack, 1974). Graceful portraits of strong, caring, and resourceful women thread throughout their narratives, evidencing the influence that grandmothers, mothers, sisters, and aunties have had on how they define motherhood and imagine the kinds of mothers they wish to be.

In some instances, though, images of motherhood based on examples of mothers drawn from their own families and communities are identi-fied as opposite of their vision of an ideal type. Recounting her own expe-rience as a child, Sharon, introduced earlier, is bent on becoming a mother who is *other* than what she remembers of her own mother growing up.

Amira: What kind of mother do you want to be?

Sharon: A good mother.

Amira: What does that mean to you—to be a good mother?

Sharon: A supportive mother, so I can give my son whatever he asks for.

Amira: Do you want to be the same or a different mother than your own mother was to you?

Sharon: I want to be a different mother. [In an earlier part of our conver-sation, Sharon mentioned that her mother is in and out of her life, leaving for 4 and 5 months at a time and is altogether unreliable because of her addictions to drugs and alcohol]. Because she ain't no mother. See, my sister, now that's a mother. See, she going to get off public aid because she going to get a job. She going to work. I don't know what kind of job she going to get, but I know . . . they called her, but they told her after she graduate, after she get her GED, or whenever she graduate or whatever, that she supposed to be working for the city or something . . . some part of the city, I don't know which one.

Continuing our conversation, she names other mothers, in addition to her sister, that she draws on to inform her understanding of what a "good" mother is.

Sharon: I look at my baby's grandma.

Amira: What is it about her?

Sharon: She got a job. She supported her kids. And she doing all she could for them when she could. So, I want to be that type and get a job.

> That's what I want to do. I want to get a job (*laughs*) so I can buy my baby a lot of stuff.

Shaping her own perception of motherhood against the backdrop of her own experience, Sharon paints a portrait of her own mother reminiscent of the mothers of color typically labeled and portrayed in the mass media as welfare matrons and irresponsible caretakers (Cook & Fine, 1995; Polakow, 1993). In the shadow of her own growing up, she projects herself a "different" kind of mother in the image of her sister and her baby's grandmother instead, each of whom represent the "good" and "supportive" *morally deserving* mother. In her desire "to be that type," Sharon defines herself as different from other single, African American mothers, whom she perceives as less deserving or worse than she is (Phoenix, 1991). Young motherhood is recast as a site of social critique where the young mother, as "self," is located in opposition to an "other" situated within her own experience, within her home community. Projecting the mother *she* wishes to become, Sharon draws a clear dividing line between herself and those "other" mothers who are the designated target of conservative moral outrage dominating current discourse around teenage motherhood.

Carmen, the single mother of two young children introduced earlier, had the opportunity to participate in a student-written and -directed cable television program intended to provide teen mothers with a public forum for addressing a range of issues relevant to their lives, among them welfare reform, domestic violence, responsible parenting, and child care. She spoke of an incident during the taping of one show where a caller had phoned into the station, complaining that her tax dollars were going toward support of welfare for teen moms who, she noted, are "laid up and having sex constantly." Coming up short in her benign response—"I don't know"—Carmen ideally wanted to answer this way:

> I wanted to tell her, there are teen parents that do the best they can. It's a last resort of going on welfare. I'm not on welfare. I get the Medicare card. And if I have to work for it, I will work for it. I thought—I go to school full time. You know, I wanted to tell her so much stuff, but I . . . I just was afraid I was gonna blow, and I just sat there.

Despite the fact that repeated studies have established no correlation between welfare provision and out-of-wedlock births, poor, single, African American and Latina mothers remain mired in public debate about welfare and the distribution of national resources (Lesko, 1994;

Luker, 1996; Phoenix, 1991). As they narrate it, their pregnant bodies and acquired parenting roles are the focus of public castigation and wandering looks on the streets, on the subway, and at the bus stop—all places where the boundaries between the public and the private are elided. Unwilling to abide misrepresentations of pregnant and parenting teenagers, Adrian rejects prevalent portrayals of teen mothers like herself as culturally deficient, deprived, and depraved, picking up where Carmen left off.

> The media. That's how they think of us [the pregnant teenager]. They, you know, they, ahm ... OK, there is a lot, there is a lot of pregnant girls that have dropped out of school. They never say anything about pregnant girls that do things, who go on for their education, and other people that didn't even have kids, you know. They ... they list the bad, you know, things about it, and they never say anything about the good things. What about the people that don't even have kids and drop out of school. What's their excuse? In the suburbs, what about all the Caucasian people that had abortions? There are so many girls out there that just ... they got money like that, you know. Money that comes that fast, or, I mean, or I need $300. For what? Oh, just to buy something, and they can hide it and cover it up. It's not that easy for minorities. Yeah, people that stay in, you know, urban communities, it's not easy. They ... I mean, they put things in the paper and on the news like a teenage girl abandoning her baby or, you know, things like that. And they don't ever say [anything] about the teenage girl that's going to school, or just graduated high school, or just graduated college that was a teenage mom. They never say anything like that. They always put the bad news on television.

Adrian's commentary reflects the incisive observations of her peers who read the condemning signifiers of teenage practice, drawing clear divisions between "good" and "bad" teenagers and "good" and "bad" teen mothers within their own communities. The experience of becoming teenage mothers has thrust them into the spotlight of public critique, yet these students do not choose to sit idly by in the wings as they are repeatedly blamed for rending the social and moral fabric of the nation. Instead, they align themselves differently than they have been positioned by outsiders and marshal a critique of their own in response to the exploitive and dismissive messages of the welfare state. As they re-write/ -right the lives of urban youth like themselves who have been culturally framed as "bad," they work to dislodge the weight of public discourse and cast the net of social responsibility more widely. As these girls position themselves as mothers within and against socially sanctioned examples of the "good" mother, we should not forget that cultural constructions of the responsible parent emphasized in schools like New Ventures Academy cannot be read apart from the social realities of low-income, African American and Latino communities in peril in urban centers (Fine & Weis, 1998). The very survival of these communities is at stake, so it stands to reason that family and community members would support young mothers' becoming competent and responsible caretakers to their children.[3] In this light, it is worth speculating that student identity formation processes in school reflect broader social interests within their host communities, reminding us that school commitments to outfitting young mothers with skills for effective parenting need to be contextualized and read against the backdrop of struggles within family and community spaces as well.

To the Future and Back

Teen mothers' stories of how they became pregnant are varied. A small number of teens admitted to wanting a child at this early age. Most found themselves with an unplanned pregnancy as a result of unprotected sex or unsolicited violence on their bodies. Whatever the circumstances, teen mothers widely profess that early pregnancy and parenting has awakened them to the reality of not being able to trust in the fundamental right to being treated with human decency and respect, and they weave this life lesson into descriptions of how they will parent their own children. Projecting into the future, Tanika is concerned that her son understand the importance of treating others, particularly girls and women, with care, integrity and respect.

> I would tell him to treat them with the utmost respect, to never put them down. I would tell him to find somebody; I would tell him to be wise upon his choice, and to not get her pregnant, and not to go out there and get all these girls, all these different girls pregnant, then catch a disease, and then be all these babies out in the world that doesn't even have a father. If you're gonna have sex, have sex with someone you're gonna make sure that you want to be with for the rest of your life, and that you'll want to have . . . that they're gonna have your child or whatever. And don't go out there, you know, using or abusing a girl, hating her or beating her, or anything, 'cause I wouldn't tolerate it. I wouldn't at all.

Building on this line of thinking, Julie, a White teen mother in the eighth grade, weaves similar calls for girls to be treated respectfully into her parenting role:

Julie: I cannot stand disrespectful men. And since my baby's a boy, when he gets older, he is not going to disrespect women. I can't stand that. So, I'm going to teach him, I'm going to be like, "You treat women with respect. Treat them like you would treat your mother. That's how you treat ladies. Don't call them out of their name either."

Amira: Meaning what?

Julie: You don't call them "bitch," you don't call them "cunt," nothing like that.

Steeped in the understanding that girls' voices have moved underground as a result of personal trauma and damaging discourses that weigh on the backs of urban youth, particularly girls, New Ventures Academy allows for spaces that support girls' gender work as they hash through less-than-promising experiences with men in their lives that have mainly taught them fear and mistrust but, ironically, have also armed them with critical lessons in what they must ask of men in the future and, perhaps more important, of themselves and their children. During one parenting group session led by a social worker devoted to discussion of gender roles in the family, students discussed and pointed to examples in their own experience of perceived differences in roles and behaviors expected of men and women. Recognizing how firmly entrenched double standards are in social consciousness, they agreed as a group that things "need to be changed." Several students chimed in that roles are more equal between men and women now than had been the case in the past but that there are still strong expectations that girls will cook, clean, have sex, have babies, and stay at home. Talking excitedly over each other as they waved their fingers in the air, they concurred as a group that they will not stand for any man "telling them what they should or should not do." Collectively, they move into a discussion of how becoming a teen mother has reshaped their expectations in relationships with men, conceding that it has made them "stronger" and "more determined to teach their children that men and women need to treat each other with respect." Follow-up conversations with several of the students in group elicited a strong plea for respect from the men—fathers, brothers, boyfriends, husbands—in their lives. Repeated accounts of being talked to "out of my name" and physically and verbally abused by their boyfriends wind through their perspectives, along with anecdotal accounts of violence between men and women in their immediate and extended family networks. With insights far beyond her years, 14-year-old Tanika comments in response to my lead-in question to her whether she had ever seen men try to put women down:

Tanika: Yeah, I've seen that. Oh, I've seen that a lot in my life. Like, they'll try and get . . . like, you know, the head of, they consider themselves the head of the house 'cause they have to bring home the bills and everything. So they expect for you to kneel down whenever they say so, or . . . that's why there's not so much independency between a woman and a man. And the man always try . . . is the dominant, and they always try and put you down 'cause they say—"well, I can do this, and I can do that." It's influenced me to let no one pull me down, including a man.

Amira: So what does that mean for you in the future?

Tanika: Just for me to stand my ground.

Amira: What does that mean for the kind of woman you see yourself becoming in the future?

Tanika: An independent Black woman . . . raising her child and going on with her life and becoming someone successful other than what people have told me. Because some people will be like, "well, she's not gonna make it. She has a baby. The baby's gonna hold her back."

Having sustained multiple levels of pain, teen mothers like Tanika channel betrayal into resiliency as an antidote to their pain, telling of newfound self-respect as a consequence of having gone through pregnancy and now raising a child. Teen mothers borrow aspects of self from strong women around them who pass on valuable lessons about who they should become and others whose contrasting lives become pivot points for their own decision making as parents. Building on the small yet growing body of ethnographic data on the identity constructions of African American teen mothers, Kaplan (1997) characterizes motherhood as it has been framed for her by parenting teens as a "resistance strategy," where pregnancy and parenting substitute for the absence of intimate relationships, in effect allowing them to gain control and restore meaning lost on them up to this point in their lives. They remind us that lives braid together school, family, community, and culture and that social constructions of self grow because of and in spite of what external structures have designed for them. They have learned the importance of being responsible to themselves, meaning that they need to be able to rely on themselves as resources of strength first and foremost. In a context of relative instability in which they have either ceded control to parents, boyfriends, or the state or had it unwittingly taken from them by any of these agents, they put a premium on reinventing themselves as self-reliant. As one teen mother testifies, independence becomes a prized commodity.

Amira: What do you plan to tell your daughter about being independent?

Lucy: That she always should do for her own, you know. Just think about, you know, herself and whoever else that she has [in her life]. Like if she ever has babies, you know, she can, you know, worry about her and her children. But, I mean, I feel the woman should never depend on men whether or not, you know, they are married. You shouldn't because he's not always gonna be there, regardless if you have a ring around your finger or not. He's not always gonna be there for you. So you always make sure that you can be independent, and you know you can be independent if anything happens.

The experience of teen pregnancy has developed in Lucy, among other teen mothers, a keen awareness of potential disruptions to the paths that their respective lives are now on. The value they attach to financial and emotional independence in their own lives resonates with conservative policies that mandate cuts in welfare policies, arguing in veiled language for these women to take personal responsibility for their own behaviors. Introducing their own spin on conservative discourse, pregnant and parenting teenagers show themselves more acutely aware of their surrounding environment then those of us on the outside mistakenly assume them to be. Countervoices of recast needs, desires, and projections for the future force those of us on the outside to revisit teenage pregnancy through critical and honest examination of the construction of youth "at risk," looking *to* pregnant teens, rather than *at* them, for direction in shaping young lives "at promise." Independent behavior and reliance on themselves as resources of strength and vision leads to their re-writing the discourse of teen pregnancy through an inversion of the dominant, conservative script. Challenging the prevailing discourse on teenage pregnancy and setting it right, they braid responsibility, independence, and self-determination into motherhood and caretaking, in radical opposition to what the public at large has chosen to see and what teen mothers have been led to believe about themselves.

CONCLUSION

Teen mothers' narratives remind us that identities crafted at school are constituted in the nexus of family, community, and the broader society. Critical scholarship on teenage pregnancy submits that school-based redemption depends on contextualizing the "problem of teenage pregnancy" at the intersection of these domains. By casting the net more broadly, the responsibility for the problems that youth navigate on a daily basis are distributed over a wider spectrum of institutions and structures that are arguably responsible for putting youth, especially urban girls, "at risk."

The voices of pregnant and parenting teenagers re-writing/-righting their lives suggests to educators and policy makers a profound need to introduce youths' telling narratives *on their own terms* directly into debates and discourses around teenage pregnancy. Given the space to challenge prescriptive discourses, teen mothers have begun the difficult work of reeducating the broader public from within the particular confines of school space.[4] Constructive identity work going on in segregated school space has the potential to seep into the broader public arena and interrupt misconceptions that have long taken hold in the public imagination. Private matters are thrust back into the public arena in terms that bear the imprint of teenage girls hard at work reimagining themselves as participatory members of the larger social collective. In the process, the public cannot escape having to confront their own complicity in and responsibility for fostering the conditions for teenage pregnancy. Rather than managing pregnant girls' lives in ways that are often more about the conservative alignment of public attitudes than responding to the needs of young mothers as "subject" (Victor, 1995), educators and policy makers are being called on to listen to and hear the voices of teen mothers as they adeptly manage their own lives as their own personal constructions.

Institutionally, New Ventures Academy is committed first and foremost to the intellectual and psychosocial development of a group of students among those most "at risk" for school failure and dropping out. As such, it aims to provide girls the necessary academic skills to support positive learning experiences and future academic potential. Private matters of teenage sexuality and reproduction are literally thrust out into the open. Having translated teen pregnancy—what many of them have heard described as a "mistake"—into a resourceful site of resiliency, New Ventures Academy provides legitimating space for girls to mobilize themselves, albeit for the most part individually, as they take their place inside and stand against prevailing discourses and material constraints that limit and foreclose alternative lives for them. In this space, pregnant and parenting mothers and school officials sketch the outlines of a *pedagogy of resiliency*, which challenges the pedagogy of deficiency that has conventionally constructed teenage mothers "at risk," "deviant," and, at worst, "abnormal" (Adams, 1997; Berliner & Benard, 1995). A pedagogy of resiliency recognizes experience itself as a site for self-exploration and self-understanding. Calling for educators to reappropriate teenage pregnancy as a life-affirming event, a pedagogy of resiliency supports decoding work among pregnant and parenting teens in particular and youth in general focused on gender roles and expectations young women face daily that introduce competing pressures into their adolescent lives (Pillow, 1997a, 1997b; see also Irvine, 1994, 1995; Taylor & Ward, 1991; Tolman, 1996). Attributing to pregnant and parenting teenagers competency, resourcefulness, insight, and vision, a *pedagogy of resiliency* writes/rights lives that have been underwritten as wrong, in terms articulated by teen mothers themselves.

Student narratives illustrate young women shaping school space in ways that align with the twists and turns that their lives have taken. In her desire to be free, Sharon, introduced at the beginning of this chapter, projects a future for herself and her child unfettered by elements bent on holding her back. While she faces a barrage of challenges as a teen mother looking toward the future, she holds out the promise of more for herself and her child. Her resiliency poses a threatening challenge to the educational and policy community that can no longer avoid asking itself what it is about the "at-risk" population that unsettles them/us, as Valerie Polakow (1993) pointedly puts it, "less out of outrage and compassion than because their condition threatens our security and comfort" (p. 43). Having lived this social construction, youth have suffered at great cost. For those of us on the outside looking in, we must ask what we risk by continuing to deny adolescent youth, namely pregnant and parenting teens, the possibility of lives lived "at promise." And finally, we must ask ourselves what we ultimately have lost and stand to lose by continuing to ignore our complicity in social injustice on this scale.

Acknowledgment. This research was supported by the Spencer Foundation in a grant to Michelle Fine and Lois Weis to study "spaces" in urban America and through a Competitive Research Grant from the University Research Council of DePaul University. I gratefully acknowledge the students, teachers, and staff of New Ventures Academy who gave generously of their time and helped to shepherd this research through, and I extend special thanks to Michelle Fine, Lois Weis, and Carole Mitchener for helpful comments on earlier drafts of this chapter.

NOTES

1. For further discussion of the profile of youth "at risk," see Wehlage, Rutter, Smith, Lesko, and Fernandez (1989). See also Kelly and Gaskell (1996).

2. Gang bangers refer to youth who are members of gangs who commit acts of violence against rival gang members and others outside of gangs. This activity solidifies gang affiliation.

3. I am indebted to Lois Weis for pointing this subtle connection out to me.
4. My thanks to Michelle Fine for bringing this point to my attention.

REFERENCES

Adams, N. (1997). Toward a curriculum of resiliency: Gender, race, adolescence and schooling. In C. Marshall (Ed.), *Feminist critical policy analysis: A perspective from primary and secondary schooling* (pp. 153–164). London: Falmer Press.

Berliner, B., & Benard, B. (1995). *More than a message of hope: A district-level policy-maker's guide to understanding resiliency.* Portland, OR: Western Regional Center for Drug-Free Schools and Communities.

Books, S. (1996). Fear and loathing: The moral dimensions of the politicization of teen pregnancy. *Journal of Thought, 31*(1), 9–24.

Books, S. (Ed.). (1998). *Invisible children in the society and its schools.* Mahwah, NJ: Erlbaum.

Burdell, P. (1995–1996). Teen mothers in high school: Tracking their curriculum. *Review of Research in Education, 21,* 163–208.

Burdell, P. (1998). Young mothers as high school students: Moving toward a new century. *Education and Urban Society, 30*(2), 207–223.

Case, K. (1997). African American othermothering in the urban elementary school. *The Urban Review, 29*(1), 25–39.

Cook, D., & Fine, M. (1995). "Motherwit": Childrearing lessons from African American mothers of low income. In B. Swadener & S. Lubeck (Eds.), *Children and families "at promise": Deconstructing the discourse of risk* (pp. 118–142). Albany: State University of New York Press.

Cusick, T. (1989). Sexism and early parenting: Cause and effect? *Peabody Journal of Education, 64*(4), 113–131.

Danzinger, S., & Farber, N. (1990). *Keeping inner-city youth in school: Critical experiences of black young women.* Discussion Paper No. 931-90. Madison: University of Wisconsin–Madison, Institute for Research on Poverty.

Emihovich, C., & Fromme, R. (1998). Framing teen parenting: Cultural and social contexts. *Education and Urban Society, 30*(2), 139–156.

Fine, M. (1995). The politics of who's "at risk." In B. Swadener & S. Lubeck (Eds.), *Children and families "at promise": Deconstructing the discourse of risk* (pp. 76–94). Albany: State University of New York Press.

Fine, M., & Weis, L. (1998). *The unknown city: Lives of poor and working-class young adults.* Boston, MA: Beacon Press.

Fraser, N. (1990). Rethinking the public sphere: A contribution to the critique of actually existing democracy. *Social Text: Theory/Culture/Ideology, 25/26,* 56–80.

Furstenberg, F., Brooks-Gunn, J., & Morgan, S. (1987). *Adolescent mothers in later life.* Cambridge, UK: Cambridge University Press.

Hayes, C. D. (1987). *Risking the future: Adolescent sexuality, pregnancy, and childbearing.* Washington, DC: National Academy Press.

Heilbrun, C. G. (1988). *Writing a woman's life.* New York: Ballantine.

Hill-Collins, P. (1987). The meaning of motherhood in Black culture and Black mother/daughter relationships. *Sage, 4*(2), 3–10.

Hill-Collins, P. (1990). *Black feminist thought: Knowledge, consciousness and the politics of empowerment.* New York: Routledge.

hooks, b. (1990). *Yearning: Race, gender, and cultural politics.* Boston: South End Press.

Irvine, J. (1994). Cultural differences and adolescent sexualities. In J. Irvine (Ed.), *Sexual cultures and the construction of adolescent identities* (pp. 3–28). Philadelphia: Temple University Press.

Irvine, J. (1995). *Sexuality education across cultures: Working with differences.* San Franciso: Jossey-Bass.

Kaplan, E. (1997). *Not our kind of girl: Unraveling the myths of Black teenage motherhood.* Berkeley: University of California Press.

Kelly, D. (1996). Stigma stories: Four discourses about teen mothers, welfare, and poverty. *Youth & Society, 27*(4), 421–449.

Kelly, D. (1997). Warning labels: Stigma and the popularizing of teen mothers' stories. *Curriculum Inquiry, 27*(2), 165–186.

Kelly, D., & Gaskell, J. (Eds.). (1996). *Debating dropouts: Critical policy and research perspectives on school leaving.* New York: Teachers College Press.

Knutson, G. (1996, December/January). Alternative high schools: Models for the future? *The High School Journal,* pp. 119–124.

Ladner, J. (1971). *Tomorrow's tomorrow.* Lincoln: University of Nebraska Press.

Lesko, N. (1990). Curriculum differentiation as social redemption: The case of school-aged mothers. In R. Page & L. Valli (Eds.), *Curriculum differentiation: Interpretive studies in US secondary schools* (pp. 113–136). Albany: State University of New York Press.

Lesko, N. (1991). Implausible endings: Teenage mothers and fictions of school success. In N. Wyner (Ed.), *Current perspectives on the culture of schools* (pp. 45–63). Brookline, MA: Brookline Books.

Lesko, N. (1994). The social construction of "the problem of teenage pregnancy." In R. Martusewicz & W. Reynolds (Eds.), *Inside/out: Contemporary critical perspectives in education* (pp. 139–150). New York: St. Martin's Press.

Lesko, N. (1995). The "leaky needs" of school-aged mothers: An examination of US programs and policies. *Curriculum Inquiry, 25*(2), 177–205.

Luker, K. (1996). *Dubious conceptions: The politics of teenage pregnancy.* Cambridge, MA: Harvard University Press.

Phoenix, A. (1991). Mothers under twenty: Outsider and insider views. In A. Phoenix, A. Woollett, & E. Lloyd (Eds.), *Motherhood: Meanings, practices and ideologies* (pp. 86–102). London: Sage.

Pillow, W. (1997a). Decentering silences/troubling irony: Teen pregnancy's challenge to policy analysis. In C. Marshall (Ed.), *Feminist critical policy analysis: A perspective from primary and secondary schooling* (pp. 134–152). London: Falmer Press.

Pillow, W. (1997b). Exposed methodology: The body as a deconstructive practice. *Qualitative Studies in Education, 10*(3), 349–363.

Polakow, V. (1993). *Lives on the edge: Single mothers and their children in the other America.* Chicago: University of Chicago Press.

Polit, D., & Kahn, J. (1987). Teenage pregnancy and the role of the schools. *Urban Education, 22*(2), 131–153.

Ruddick, S. (1991). Educating for procreative choice: The "case" of adolescent women. *Women's Studies Quarterly, 1*(2), 102–120.

Schofield, G. (1994). *The youngest mothers: The experience of pregnancy and motherhood among young women of school age.* Brookfield, VT: Avebury Ashgate Publishing.

Sidel, R. (1996). *Keeping women and children last: America's war on the poor.* New York: Penguin.

Stack, C. (1974). *All our kin.* New York: Harper & Row.

The State of America's Children yearbook. (1998). Washington, D.C.: Children's Defense Fund.

Swadener, B., & Lubeck, S. (1995). The social construction of children and families "at risk": An introduction. In B. Swadener & S. Lubeck (Eds.), *Children and families "at promise": Deconstructing the discourse of risk* (pp. 1–14). Albany: State University of New York Press.

Taylor, J., & Ward, J. (1991). Culture, sexuality, and school: Perspectives from focus groups in six different cultural communities. *Women's Studies Quarterly, 1/2,* 121–137.

Thompson, S. (1995). *Going all the way: Teenage girls' tales of sex, romance, and pregnancy.* New York: Hill & Wang.

Tolman, D. (1996). Adolescent girls' sexuality: Debunking the myth of the urban girl. In B. Ross Leadbeater & N. Way (Eds.), *Urban girls: Resisting stereotypes, creating identities* (pp. 255–271). New York: New York University Press.

Upchurch, D. M., & McCarthy, J. (1990). The timing of a first birth and high school completion. *American Sociological Review, 55,* 224–234.

Victor, K. (1995). Becoming the good mother: The emergent curriculum of adolescent mothers. In J. Jipson, P. Munro, S. Victor, K. Fourde Jones, & G. Freed-Rowland (Eds.), *Repositioning feminism & education* (pp. 37–60). Westport, CT: Bergin & Garvey.

Wehlage, G., Rutter, R., Smith, G., Lesko, N., & Fernandez, R. (1989). *Reducing the risk: Schools as communities of support.* New York: Falmer Press.

CHAPTER 7

Body Work on Ice:
The Ironies of Femininity and Sport

SARAH K. CARNEY

December 1996: A 6-year-old beauty pageant veteran was found murdered in her home in Colorado, and, though it is more than 3 years later, the headlines have yet to die down. Was she sexually abused? Had she been starved? Was she beaten? Was her blond hair dyed? And what exactly was she doing performing in so obviously a sexually suggestive manner? Public interest in the 6-year-old body of JonBenet Ramsey seems as yet unabated, and if magazine sales or tabloid television ratings are any indication, there is hefty profit to be made sensationalizing the murder of little girls—at least for those who report it.

At the 1996 Olympic games in Atlanta, the eyes of the United States were riveted on the bodies of seven American adolescent gymnasts, scrutinizing their every gesture: their smiles, their tears, their youthfulness, and, most of all, their weight—or lack thereof. As music played during the opening credits, the nightly voice-over to this demanding athletic competition promised that the viewers would see "little girls dancing."

During the summer of 1997, the *New York Times Magazine* devoted a cover picture and multiple pages to the story of a 16-year-old "self-mutilator" who, when she reached adolescence, picked up a razor and began cutting—slicing—into her arms. The *Times* called self-mutilation (or "carving," as it has been labeled in clinical psychological circles) the "latest expression of adolescent self-loathing" (Egan, 1997, p. 21).

The psychology of girls/young women and, in particular, the psychology of girls' bodies, has moved out of academic and clinical journals and onto popular, mainstream bookstore shelves. A glance in a local Barnes & Noble psychology section or a search through academic journals reveals the multiple and nearly all-encompassing ways in which U.S. culture surveils and, indeed, obsesses on the psychological and physical selves of young people—young girls especially . Anorexia,[1] teenage pregnancy and abortion,[2] drug and alcohol abuse,[3] suicide,[4] AIDS,[5] obesity,[6] low self-esteem and poor body image,[7] sexual abuse,[8] bulimia,[9] cutting,[10] burning[11]—these and other topics make up a dizzying array, and they result in a frightening cacophony of titles, all of which suggest that the adult scrutiny that has surrounded girls throughout history has never been stronger or more persistent. Indeed, though it has recently been suggested that adolescent girls are ignored by both U.S. culture and psychology as a field (Pipher, 1994), I believe that the reverse is true; I would argue that there exists in our social system a guarded watchfulness—and a fascination—that never really goes away. The eyes of the world seem to follow the bodies of adolescent girls everywhere, and the appraisals and evaluations that follow appear inevitable and unending.

A POSTMODERN SHIFT
IN FEMALE BODY DISCOURSE

Although cultural interest in the physicality and physicalness of girls has been continuous throughout history—more so than ever in recent decades (Bordo, 1993b)—scientific scrutiny of the bodies of girls is a relatively new and specific phenomenon. As members of the social and medical sciences become interested in the bodies of girls and young women, they often direct their attention to body problems and pathologies (both social and physical). Conceptions and explanations of girls' bodies are framed through a medicalized, individualistic gaze (Pipher, 1994), and much attention has been devoted to creating a system of accurate diagnosis for the body as well as developing a treatment/cure. Thus, for example, a bodily condition such as excessive thinness is first named—anorexia—and is then explained causally—as the young woman's assertion of control during the turbulent period of adolescent development (Paxton, 1993) or as a reflection of a fear of womanhood (Cross, 1993). These explanations lead naturally to recommendations for cure, through the specification of treatments (individual/family therapy, drug related, or behavioral) designed to help bring the victim of what is now termed an "eating disorder" back to health.

This internal, individualistic perspective, with its attendant worry about the bodies of young women, is consistent with a particular Western medicalized gaze, and it makes up the bulk of the literature on the bodies of adolescents. It is a gaze, furthermore, that is understandable; the "diseases" (physical and psychological) of adolescence are dangerous and life threatening. More recently, however, a shift in researchers' conceptions regarding the causes of social and physical symptoms/problems is occurring. In postmodern literature in particular, the social/physical problems of teenagers are being reconsidered. The bodies of adolescents and their attendant "problems" (eating disorders, pregnancy, drug use, etc.) have come to be framed as symptomatic of an ailing culture rather than viewed through a traditional medical lens of individual pathology (Pipher, 1994). Thus, individually directed diagnoses and treatments are now being challenged by theories of environmental, structural/institutional causation (McKie, Wood, & Gregory, 1993; Smith & Cogswell, 1994; Taylor et al., 1998; Wertheim, Paxton, Schultz, & Muir, 1997). Under this gaze, the psychological and physical bodies of girls are seen as cultural indicators; they mark particular social, political, economic, and historical moments. The effects of current social and political arrangements have become visible, these researchers argue, in the emaciated, bulimic, drug-using, pregnant, suicidal, carved bodies of today's young women (Bordo, 1993b). This shift in perspective does nothing to change the pathologizing that surrounds our images of girls' bodies, however; it merely refocuses the diagnosis and alters established recommendations for cure. The aura of deficit and "illness" remains essentially unquestioned (Fraser, 1998; Freedman, 1984; Gillies, 1989; Pipher, 1994; Ryan,1996; Tiggemann & Pickering, 1996). Teenage pregnancy, drug addiction, eating disorders, and the like are still constructed as problems; they are positioned, however, as symptomatic of what Pipher (1994) calls our current "girl poisoning culture" (p. 12).

WHICH "GIRLS" ARE SURVEILLED WHEN?

Before considering how the current conception of adolescence as a state of crisis and girls' bodies as pathological affects the languages and experiences of the girls themselves, we must reflect more closely on who we are including under the generalization "girls." For truly, although all girls are surveilled, not all girls' bodies are of concern all the time. In fact, who is being watched—who is the object—and at what time have very much to do with which body "problems" of childhood and adolescence are being considered. Drug addiction, pregnancy, AIDS, and abortion are constructed primarily as problems of the poor and of girls of color, despite much documentation of high rates among White, middle-class adolescents. Thus, the bodies of girls of color and working-class girls are very much on display if the topic under consideration is crime, teenage pregnancy, alcohol abuse, or abortion prevention. Eating disorders, self-mutilation, self-esteem issues, and suicide, on the other hand, are assumed to affect White, middle- to upper-class, heterosexual young women most often, despite the increasing documentation of their impact on girls of color and girls living in poverty (Thompson, 1994; Walkerdine, 1997). These assumptions play out and get perpetuated as truth or fact when published research on eating disorders focuses exclusively on elite, White girls, while explorations of such topics as pregnancy prevention efforts focus on inner-city youth. In effect, this focus erases the "sordid" problems of drug abuse, addiction, battery, and so forth from White, mainstream consciousness and replaces it with an image—and a particular discourse—of elite White girls silently vomiting in suburban bathrooms. White girls, so goes the literature, are body-obsessed. They are typically constructed as trivial, silly, and neurotic—they are to be protected rather than punished. They are (cultural) Ophelias in need of saving (Pipher, 1994)—they are little girls in pretty boxes (Ryan, 1996). These are negative images surely, but they are not, in fact, discourses that are devoid of glamour (Bordo, 1993b). No such glamour or protective language exists in current conceptions of teenage mothers addicted to cocaine. Instead, the operating discourse is one of punishment, of management, and of control.

In fact, if race is considered at all in relation to anorexia/bulimia/self-mutilation, it is most often treated as a factor that mitigates *against* body-image disorders; much of the work on race and body "problems" demonstrates that girls of color do not have the same body-image disorders as their White counterparts (Lee & Lee, 1996; Loda, Speizer, Martin, Skatrud, & Bennett, 1997; Smith & Cogswell, 1994) . These findings are most often explained as either reflecting differences in cultural values and standards for beauty among African American and Hispanic subcultures, or as supporting the notion that conditions of hunger and poverty preclude the development of eating disorders (the hunger of girls in poverty is not seen as self-imposed). Despite the occasional comparative study, however, for the most part current psychological literature avoids talking about race or class as important factors in the discussion of eating disorders or self-harming behaviors, erasing or "Whiting out" (Fine, 1997) the effects of oppression and poverty on the bodies and body images of young women.

The racist and classist theory that women and girls of color, as well as working-class and poor girls, are unaffected and untroubled by cultural standards of beauty or femininity remains a fairly strong one. Murmurs of dissent are now appearing, though, that call into question this stereotypical assumption. Thompson (1994), for example, suggests that the standard profile of sufferers of anorexia, bulimia, or obesity (as White, wealthy, image-obsessed perfectionists) is the result of oversimplified assumptions about the

causes of eating disorders. She argues that, among women of color and lesbians, eating disorders are frequent responses to injustices such as racism,
sexism, homophobia, classism, the stress of acculturation, and emotional,
physical, and sexual abuse. She underscores the traumatic origin of eating
disorders rather than the generally accepted version of gender socialization,
thus making it clear that their invisibility within populations of women of
color reveals who is in the limelight in the field of psychology rather than
who actually suffers. Walkerdine's (1997) recently published work complicates social scientific considerations of cultural standards and pressures for
femininity as she examines our current assumptions about girls, their bodies, and cultural conceptions of "innocence," demonstrating that these views
are, in fact, "gendered, classed, and ethnically specific" (p. 5).

Perhaps we are about to enter an era when these singular discourses—
that White girls' bodies are silently inscribed with cultural pressures for
femininity that need to be alleviated, while Black girls' bodies symbolize
willful anger and innate appetites in need of external control—will be
reconsidered and complicated. Thompson's and Walkerdine's recent work
provides some hope for this shift. It is my intention to follow their lead.
With the goal of discourse complication in mind, I chose to target a site
where one particular singular discourse is presumed. I elected to explore
whether a certain type of space—in this case an athletic space—allows for
a doubled, even tripled, discourse to occur. I began my work with two
assumptions: First, that elite White girls are more than suffering anorexics
or trivial, self-absorbed neurotics, and second, that the various "spaces"
in their lives both stifle and encourage alternative ways of looking at their
bodies. I wondered if within the space of athletics I might see a more
culturally critical and embodied view of self than in the singular discourse
that so dominates popular culture. I hoped that the discourse of psychology and culture that has so interlinked the female [adolescent] body with
deficit or illness had not created conditions in which the girls themselves
no longer see their bodies in any other way but diseased—either psycho-
logically or physically. My intent was to raise the question of whether, by
limiting its perspective on girls' bodies to one of problems or illnesses to
be cured, social science also closes itself off to the possibility that girls may
conceive of their bodies as sites of freedom, of expressiveness, and of
beauty. Does athletic participation in fact, not just in theory (Cross, 1993;
Fraser, 1998; Freedman, 1984; Thompson, 1994; Tiggemann & Pickering,
1996), enable girls to reimagine and rework their physical selves as functioning, beautiful, and strong? Does the "safe" space of athletics provide a
moment in the lives of today's girls where they can express themselves
physically? Furthermore, is that same physicality then embraced with a
sense of pride and possibility? What is it about the specific space of sports—

their physical and psychological locations in the minds of the girls who participate—that allows this sense of expansion, this broadening, this brief defiance of cultural expectations, and this freedom?

DISCOURSE OF AN ATHLETIC SPACE— FIGURE SKATERS ON BODIES AND FEMININITY

Because I am a figure-skating coach, I spend early mornings, evenings, and weekends with young athletes. We ride for hours in cars, eat meals, share hotel rooms, hang out, talk on the phone, play cards between practice sessions, and listen to music together; we are *in* each other's lives. I am old enough to be a mother to some and young enough to be an older sister to others, and given this status of "in between mother and sister," I hear things. The girls talk about themselves in front of me, and they discuss their lives with me. We talk about problems with friends, fights with parents, worries about geometry, deaths of relatives, soccer games, hassles (and the lack of hassles) from boys at school, swim meets, the pressures to fit in with other kids, the pros and cons of painting one's toenails, movies, the best locations for tattoos, baseball (Derek Jeter!), cross-country races, college options, the meaning of the words "democrat" and "republican," what we want to be when we "grow up," the possibility of biking across the country some day, if (in a pinch) lip liner may be used around the eyes, whether the energy food Powerbar tastes like dirt, and, of course, skating. Our conversations range from the important to the ridiculous—from deep to shallow. The girls are frequently silly, sometimes fearful, occasionally mean, regularly cynical and pessimistic, sometimes serious, often surprisingly insightful, and, once in a while, even generous. Given that these girls are the same ones so frequently depicted as neurotically obsessed with their bodies—their weight, in particular—I decided to study these skaters (ages 7–16) to examine the space of sport/athletics and its potential for opening up bodily possibilities for preadolescent and adolescent girls.

My specific questions were about whether sport can provide a safe place for girls to explore the aspects of their physical selves so frequently pathologized in popular and academic literature today. As a result of my interviews and focus-group discussions (the 31 girls I studied are privileged—upper-middle-class, suburban daughters of professionals, predominantly White) there is some cause to be nervous about answers to my questions, but also some room for hope and cautious optimism. Clearly, given these data, and in agreement with much of the current research on and with adolescent girls, young women are saturated with limiting media images, and they are extremely adept at using a pathology discourse to describe their bodies as well as the bodies of others. However, peeking out from behind the sometimes overwhelmingly negative, disordered, diseased discourses, these girls did struggle with me to conceptualize their bodies in terms other than issues of body weight or appearance—and their visible efforts in describing bodily possibilities or physical triumphs indicate the lack of a cultural language for imagining girls' bodies in different ways. They also mark the importance of and the need for places where youth—in this case White girls, but indeed I believe that the importance cuts across race, class, and gender—can reexamine and reinvent themselves, play with notions such as femininity/masculinity, create new discourses, and perform/enact new versions of self and embodiment.

What is it about the athletic space that allows for this doubled, sometimes tripled discourse? How is the "place" of an ice rink perhaps contributing to a larger sense of bodily possibility for these girls? It should be stated at the outset that the data make clear that, in this case, the ice arena is not some protected, safe, other-worldly place that supports and allows for skaters to imagine unlimited potentials. In fact, if anything, my work supports the often expressed criticisms that the world of figure skating, and girl-culture in general, is conspicuously rigid—and often blatantly exclusionary based on appearance and size as well as race and class (Brooks-Gunn, Burrow, & Warren, 1988; Cross, 1993; Freedman, 1984). The athletic space generally, and the ice arena in particular, is *not* a self-consciously political or revolutionary place. Often the opposite is true—conservativism, conformity, and assimilation of standardized, homogenized norms of beauty and behavior are the rule. For instance, Sharon, a 15-year-old competitive skater, states, "Like, if you show up and you're wearing leggings and everyone else is wearing a skirt, you feel stupid. And you show up and everyone else's hair is in a pony tail and your hair is in a braid, you feel stupid."[12] Later, she adds, "Most skaters that I've seen are really like . . . skinny . . . like have really skinny legs or . . . they have really muscular legs. Like, you can't be a little out of shape . . . because . . . you don't look right. I don't know." And later still, "I'm always . . . I'm always umm . . . at home . . . worrying about like, what I'm eating and stuff . . . like 'Oh no . . . is this going to make my butt big?' (*laughs*)." Lara, age 13, says that skaters "have to be thin, you know, and beautiful. The judges mark you down . . . for . . . if you're fat or like, scary looking." Mallory, age 14, states at the outset of her interview, "I'm too tall for a skater . . . and my legs are too big."

Reproducing Traditional Discourse

Traditional femininity goes almost unquestioned in the sport of figure skating just as it does in the culture at large—upper-middle-class culture in particular. Makeup, skating dresses, elaborately styled hair and jewelry are considered not only desirable but almost mandatory. These skaters (and girls in general) are expected to be seen and not heard, to be respectful to adults, to be obedient to coaches, to be modest about their accomplishments, not to display disappointment or anger, and not to flaunt their successes. They embody, then, the "good girl" wishes of the upper-middle class to a marked degree.

In addition, the girls I interviewed accept—even buy into—cultural expectations about successful femininity. They actively reproduce patriarchy and the cultural oppression of their own bodies within the space of the ice arena as well as in their everyday lives. They pine for, obsess about, and vigorously construct thin, toned, and socially desirable bodies. They decry "athleticism" and embrace delicacy and fragility. (For example, Helen, age 14, worries that she is too athletic: "I don't want to always be the strong one . . . why can't I be the graceful one?") They try not to laugh too loud, eat too much, or show when they hurt. They retreat to locked bathrooms to cry out of sight in frustration or pain. They apologize first. They cover bruises with makeup. They give the male skaters the right of way. They try to take up as little space as possible. They rush to help when needed. They are unfailingly polite, at least to the adults in their lives. Much of what goes on in an ice rink, therefore, seems to reinforce and re-create mainstream, White, middle-class values and patriarchal notions of femininity. It is a limiting place; in so many ways it is a frustrating, conforming, nonfeminist world.

Indeed, the girls I interviewed had noticeable difficulty even framing our conversation in any way other than one that was focused on body weight. They provided me, as if by rote at times, the views of the dominant culture; namely, that [White] girls worry about their weight and that the sport of figure skating contains within it some of the most weight- and physical-appearance-obsessed adolescents on the planet. I tried to redirect them and explained that I was just as interested in what they *liked* about their bodies as I was in what they did not; however, the girls I was interviewing gave, for the most part, only short, clear answers about what they had eaten the day of the interview, how they felt about their size, and how much they wished to be smaller, thinner, prettier, and so forth. When I asked them about their positive feelings about their bodies or about the ways in which the physical activity of skating made them feel beautiful, their sidelong glances and confused silences betrayed the reality that there was no such language in their formulations about their bodies. I probed, often not subtly, for a resistant, defiant language—I was received with silence and bewilderment. This silence is, I believe, testimony to the fact that, once a psychological language (in this case, a language of body pathology) has become mainstream, it becomes, for all of us, a powerful way of making sense of our experience, and thus it finds its way into our stories about ourselves, our families, our relationships, and our friends. It becomes a way of talking about our lives—of framing interviews in other words. In the case of my own work on girls and body experience—at least for White, upper-middle-class girls—the dominant language seems to be anorexia and bulimia, a discourse of body deficit rather than physical possibility.

In acknowledging the influence of dominant cultural discourses on the ways in which people make sense of their lives, we as researchers are forced to confront questions about the data we collect by qualitative interview methods, just as we were forced to question experimental, statistical, and survey techniques. Perhaps these questions become most salient for those of us who wish to become researchers who seek to uncover previously untold, suppressed, or ignored realities. We are interested in questioning/ overturning dominant cultural ideologies, but, when we collect data from participants whom we know are victimized by these discourses of domination, we find that they themselves use the same languages, the same constructions, and follow the same strict and limited guidelines for "normalcy" that have oppressed them. We expect and search for languages of resistance—we find languages of what looks like reproduction. This was certainly the case in my early interviews of figure skaters. I looked for signs of body appreciation and joy, but found at first only confirmation that the dominant discourse is frustratingly enduring.

Expressing a Language of Possibility

As the girls got more comfortable with questions about things they had never been asked before, however, they began sidling back up to me to tell me more. I found that my conceptions about interview "parameters" had to change to include the second, third, and even fourth "interviews" with the girls. Hours, days, even weeks could go by between the formal interview and their approaching me again, but slowly, haltingly, my participants began speaking in a language that was not the reproductive, clear, concise version of reality they had given me before. "Remember when you asked me," one girl starts out. "I should have remembered to tell you," another says, stopping me on the ice. "I've been thinking a lot about," begins another. And what would come next would be amazing, beautiful, gentle, forgiving, funny, playful, creative, and surprising thoughts about the use of their bodies, their participation in physical activity, and the joy they took in their bodies and in expressing themselves through the figure skating. These were not fluent, seamless stories. They were told on the run: in parking lots, while holding doors, between skating sessions, in hotels late at night, during lessons, in cars, or as we said good-bye.

Regardless of where these stories were told, however, it seemed clear to me that they were *data*—just as legitimate as the data I had collected in the formal interviews. Though no tape recorder was running, I was determined to honor the complex, double messages offered by my participants, who were so willing to engage themselves and think deeply about the questions I had asked.

Slowly, haltingly, a hesitating language of possibility did emerge, offering a glimpse of an alternative discourse constructed by the girls who participate. Despite the acknowledged stringent rules and pressures toward conformity, the girls often spoke with great feeling about their relationship with the "space" of the ice rink and the sport of figure skating. In their informal comments they made clear that they feel a certain level of ownership over this particular athletic space—they have a sense that the arena is a nonparental space and in some ways their time is their own. Thus, the space of the rink, at least for some, appears to act as a place of refuge from outside pressures and parental and peer surveillance, perhaps contributing to their ability to begin to construct a discourse about their bodies that runs counter to existing cultural (and psychological) conceptions. For instance, Erin says, "Oh, the rink? When I come here it's like 'ahhhhhhhhhh' (*sighs*)." Hannah, age 14, says similarly, "I'm here . . . alone kind of. I mean, my mom can't skate and my sister doesn't either so I get time to myself. I turn off my he- . . . my brain I mean. Just glide." Sharon says: "It's up to me, you know . . . skating. It's my thing . . . my place . . . you know . . . umm. I'm not sure . . . it's dumb but I feel at home here." Amy smiles when I ask her how she feels about the rink itself: "This is my favorite . . . favorite place in the world." Clearly operating here is the girls' sense of the rink as a place in which they have some personal control, despite their acknowledgments that they are also controlled by the space itself. Perhaps then, one might suggest that a space for reimagining—a space that encourages a doubling of the dominant discourse—must belong, at least in part, to the girls themselves. Though some argued that they felt watched all the time (on and off the ice), many of the girls said that they felt a measure of privacy, even in the "goldfish" bowl of the ice rink.

The rigidity and discipline of skating—its rules and limitations—are also noted by some of the girls as strangely freeing. Sharon, who struggles repeatedly to get this difficult idea across, finally states:

> It's hard . . . I mean . . . you have to do everything . . . *just so.*
> There's rules for how you hold your hands . . . how you . . . how
> you wear your hair . . . how . . . every step is, you know, written
> down. But there's . . . there's freedom, too. When you learn
> everything the right way you can kind of push the edges . . . see,

you can say . . . where can I go next? To take . . . once I know
how to do [the footwork pattern] I can change it by playing with
the speed, and . . . stretching out you know?

Catherine, age 17, also attempts to describe what she sees as an ironic sense
of "freedom": "I like the discipline of skating. I like it. (*laughs*) I don't know.
(*pause*) It makes me feel sure of . . . I know what I'm doing . . . I practice and
I get better. Today . . . always . . . you . . . I know what my days are going to
be like. I get up . . . I skate . . . I try not to look at my feet. (*laughs*) I try to do
a better job. It's fun to skate well." Karen says she wants to be a coach some
day: "I would like to teach kids how to skate. I think it's a lot of fun and you
know, . . . it teaches discipline." I ask why that's a good thing. She answers:
"Discipline? Well, you need it . . . I mean, all the time. In life. You have to
learn to be . . . focused. And it can be fun to be really, really good at something." Cait, 16, speaks most eloquently: "I love the edge of skating . . . I
mean the curves, the glides. I like that you have to find the perfect spot on
your blade . . . you train and train so that you can find that spot. But when
you find it, you can do anything . . . you . . . can do *everything*!"

These young women are struggling with a sophisticated concept—the
idea that rules can be both confining and freeing at the same time. They
say that the boundaries, the rules, of the skating space actually enhance,
at times, their experience of possibility and freedom. Arthur (1993) argues that this seemingly irreconcilable dichotomy is actually a normal part
of everyday experience, not reducible or simplifiable. Archer (1988) states
similarly that it is normal to "feel both free and enchained, capable of
shaping our own future and yet confronted by towering, seemingly impersonal constraints" (p. 67). Discipline, and a space typified by discipline,
is felt as both limiting and exhilarating according to these girls. Their
understanding of the double meaning of terms such as *limitation* or *regulation* allows them to reinvent a discourse that takes into consideration all
of their experiences rather than just the negative side of the rule-oriented,
rigid world of athletics.

Recognizing a Doubled Discourse

The girls did acknowledge and critique the feminized nature of the space—
as one skater notes, "It's like Barbies on ice sometimes." Their discourse
doubles again, however, when they note (almost simultaneously) that they
enjoy having a place in their lives where they can be unapologetically
feminine. The girls I interviewed seem sometimes poignantly protective
of their desire to dress up and be "girls"—thus, they end up vacillating
between defensiveness and apology.

Clearly, they have been taught not to make the feminine side of themselves too visible; they know they are viewed as superficial by outsiders. "Oh yes . . . that's us," states one skater sarcastically, "we're the little *princess* girls. We only wear dresses and we paint our nails during our time off!" They frequently belittle themselves for their interest in makeup or in other things feminine—perhaps to guard against outside imposition of stereotypes they feel are denigrating or simplistic. They call themselves "silly" or "stupid" when they stray into "girly" talk. Kristen, age 13, for example, begins excitedly: "Oh wait til you see . . . oh *here I go again* . . . I got a new dress for competition and that's all I can think to tell you!" While discussing the strict guidelines for thinness and femininity typical of figure skating, and after a short silence, Carrie, age 12, reveals her contradictory feelings: "But is it bad to want to be a princess for an hour?"

Not all the girls I interviewed apologized for their femininity. Some were vocal in their belief that the space of figure skating is one that is misunderstood and underappreciated by outsiders. They stress that the appearance of the sport is deceiving. "It's girly-girly, yeah," says Lara, "but that's OK. I *am* a girl, too, you know." Erin, age 12, says similarly, "I swim. I play soccer. I skate. There's room for all my personalities here!" Sharon notes during her interview, "Well, I'm a girl *here* I guess (*laughs*) but you have to be strong, too. I mean . . . skating's not for wussies! (*laughs*) We look all . . . you know . . . like whatever . . . all girly. But we're tough, too. We're tough girls." When asked about the feminine nature of skating, Lara says, "OK, but I can skate faster than *any* hockey player I know." Beth, age 14, states succinctly, "Perfect dress . . . perfect hair . . . but you know what? Perfect double jumps."

Clearly, the space of figure skating—and the space of athletics—makes a doubled discourse possible for these girls. As their interviews demonstrate, they have a more complicated sense of their own body possibility as well as a more complex relationship with their own femininity than is currently discussed in the literature on girls. These girls *know* they are strong, they *know* they are "tough"—they live that strength every day in the rink. Regardless of how they are perceived by outsiders, they are determined to acknowledge both parts of skating—the feminine side as well as the athlete side. Discourses of potential, of freedom, and of body expression begin to appear, offering evidence that there is more going on in the minds, hearts, and bodies of adolescent girls than may be commonly found in psychology journals and in the popular press. While my interviews provide ample evidence that a cultural discourse of adolescent body pathology is alive and well, data also suggest that girls do struggle to create new languages of physicalness, beauty, and femininity—and that they do have other conceptions of "body" that include notions other than illness or deficit.

Frequently, those alternative discourses contain within them a note of playfulness, and even of joy. Sharon, for instance, reflects, "I think skating . . . I think a good adjective for skating is thrilling . . . because . . . you get to . . . you get to flow along with the wind in your face . . . and you get to be up in the air . . . and . . . you get to be spinning around . . . and . . . I don't know." When I ask Amy, a younger beginning skater, what she likes about figure skating, she says, "I like . . . like . . . when you walk you really can't glide [she imitates stumbling on the ground] . . . and I like to glide on the ice and spin around." Erin says, "When I'm out on the ice and no one is there . . . it's so . . . quiet you know . . . quiet and . . . ummm . . . peaceful. Like I'm resting . . . just gliding around." Later she adds: (*laughing*) "I feel like a fish . . . like I'm slipping and sliding between people . . . in and out . . . I'm quick and fast and (*laughing*) . . . this sounds dumb." ("No," I say.) "You can't catch me . . . I'm slippery and cold and . . ." She can't finish because she starts laughing and shrugs her shoulders. Christine, age 16, stops me after a skating session saying she "finally" thought of something good about her body and about skating: "I like it that my legs can skate fast," she says, "and I love to rip across the ice and terrify the ice dancers." Amy says that she reminds herself to jump quickly through her combinations: "I think (*high voice*) *happy toes . . . happy toes . . . happy toes!*" Similarly, Sharon tells me that she talks to herself while practicing the long, and sometimes tedious, required footwork patterns: "I say *you are a graceful swan . . . you are a swan.*" Finally, when I ask Kristen, age 13, what her favorite skating move is, she says, with a brief hesitation and a shy smile, that she loves to do layback spins. She explains, "Because . . . while I'm upside down . . . I . . . like to watch the people go by. I let my head go back further and further . . . and I think about . . . like. . . . look at all those people skating upside down on the ceiling." Clearly these girls are describing and embracing a view of their bodies (and of figure skating) that is rarely described in psychology, in education, or in the popular media.

CONCLUDING THOUGHTS AND (PERHAPS) LESSONS LEARNED

In this seemingly rigid space of figure skating, then, the dominant discourse breaks open to reveal these girls' complicated perspectives on surveillance, on discipline, on femininity, and on the oppositional definitions of work and play. Their narratives disrupt current popular as well as clinical assumptions about the relationship between adolescent girls and their bodies. These girls struggle to invent a language that takes into account both their dissatisfaction with as well as their love and appreciation for their own physicalness. They speak with conviction about the presence of multiple rather than singular discourses.

I take seriously Bordo's (1993a, 1993b) warnings about the implications of some postmodern work. She cautions us that researchers and social scientists must be careful in their postmodern analyses not simply to embrace counterexamples and particularities in their rush to deuniversalize social science. If their goal is actually to do something to help people, she states, researchers must recognize the real limits and oppressions sustained in and sustaining culture. If all they do is demonstrate freedom and resistance within groups, they end up perpetuating and reproducing gender, race, and class oppression, since there is no clear impetus for change or revolution. Postmodern research, she warns, may glorify the spirit of people who are the victims of racist, classist, sexist cultures—it may give in to the temptation to romanticize these resilient people. But researchers then may end up doing nothing to stop the oppression or to change the dominant cultural arrangements.

In my work with skaters and their feelings about their bodies, I have tried to walk this very thin line between acknowledging the ways in which these particular girls are struggling with current cultural conceptions of femininity and beauty, and how they actively search within fairly stringent borders for some freedom and room to express themselves and reinvent their bodies. In a society that so inundates us with images of young women in crisis, it seems to serve both the culture and the girls themselves to begin to imagine an alternative language to the limited one they have with which to describe their physical lives. I cannot, however, and do not wish to, erase the problems and pain that the girls have internalized. Clearly, there is reason for concern.

But perhaps there is also some reason for hope. The girls I spoke with were neither "dupes" nor "resisters"—they were both. They play within cultural rules and they break them. They both see and don't see the ways in which they are oppressed. They buy into cultural expectations and they push the boundaries. They speak the language of patriarchy and they defy it. They regulate each other and at the same time they cheer for each other. They carve out spaces for themselves in some of the most restrictive locations in the world. They learn to use limits to experience freedom. They use discourses that place them in the role of agents (Brodkey & Fine, 1988) even as they reproduce the languages that threaten their fragile agency. It is my hope that this postmodern analysis can stand alongside a cultural critique as simultaneously as the girls themselves express their feelings of freedom and restriction. There is more than one language for describing the bodies of girls; and the language is more complicated than either pathology or resistance—more complex than "either/or."

I would like to end this chapter with two overriding conclusions that I have drawn from my study. First, it is clear that "spaces" are not all they seem and that researchers must be willing to look deeply (and over the long term) into particular spaces in order to begin to find evidence of alternative discourses—especially if they are looking for languages that run counter to deeply held cultural views. Clearly, in the case of my work, the world of figure skating appears on the outside to be a profoundly feminine, patriarchical, reproductive site, a place with little visible potential for reconceptualizing female embodiment. Spaces that serve as sites for reimagining and reinventing languages may be hidden behind conservative facades; they may be guarded closely, and they may not reveal themselves to researchers instantaneously but only over time.

Second, adults have a responsibility to create spaces in which young people can shed the dominant "discursive skins" (M. Fine, personal communication, June 1998) that have been culturally attached to them and can explore alternative ways of viewing themselves. If it is true that there exist various spaces with the power to challenge dominant cultural languages (and dominant cultural arrangements), it is up to adults to construct places where young people across gender, race, and class boundaries can try on other ways of being in the world. If girls are in fact performing the roles that we have assigned them culturally (Barbie for these girls, gangsta for others) while yearning for places to explore new ways of being in their bodies, performing, taking up space, and so on, it is clear that job of creating such spaces rests with the adults in their lives. We are the ones that need to create/encourage/nurture spaces that question dominant cultural arrangements. The continued presence of these spaces is a promise adults must make to young people today.

If we can do work that demonstrates the oppressive power of the dominant discourse—as Bordo (1993b) makes clear that we must—as well as do work that makes visible the murmering, reluctant, shy existence of other possible languages, we may demonstrate a more complicated version of reality than we had once envisioned. Among and between the often contradictory languages of pathology and deprivation currently dominating the field of psychology as well as the media, girls do struggle to speak in ways that celebrate their physicalness—ways that embrace their strength, their playfulness, their power, their beauty, their grace, and their pleasure in what their bodies can do. What does such a language look like? It's a language of fits and starts, pauses, hesitations, and nervous laughter. It's a whisper. It's just a start, a beginning. The language of body possibility, and its attendant call for spaces for reimagining offered by these girls, reminds us—psychologists, researchers, family members, and so forth—that our cultural conceptions of what is "real" are always more interesting when they are complicated by the experiences, thoughts, hopes, dreams, and performances of those who are frequently overlooked or, in the case of priviledged White girls, those who are often *seen* but rarely heard.

Acknowledgments. I want to thank Hillary Felton-Reid, Emma Hennessey, Kara Lamb, Emily Pease, and Ashley Wells.

NOTES

1. See Bordo (1993); Fraser (1998); Lee & Lee (1996); Paxton (1993); Pipher (1994); Taylor et al. (1998); Thompson (1994); Wertheim, Paxton, Schultz, & Muir (1997).

2. See Donoghue (1992); Griffen-Carison & Schwanenflugel (1998); Loda, Speizer, Martin, Skatrud, & Bennett (1997); Morgan, Chapar, & Fisher (1995); Pipher (1994); Trad (1994).

3. See Diem, McKay, & Jamison (1994); Garnefski & deWilde (1998); Miller (1997); Pipher (1994); Sutherland & Willner (1998); Windle & Windle (1997).

4. See Christoffel (1998); Pipher (1994); Potter, Rosenberg, & Hammond (1998); Reder, Lucey, & Fredman (1991).

5. See Barling & Moore (1990); Eiser, Eiser, & Lang (1989); Pipher (1994).

6. See Bordo (1993b); Pipher (1994); Thompson (1994).

7. See Bordo (1993b); Fraser (1998); Pipher (1994); Smith & Cogswell (1994); Tiggemann & Pickering (1996).

8. See Ackerman, Newton, McPherson, Jones, & Dykman (1998); Hazzard, King, & Webb (1986); Pipher (1994).

9. See Bordo (1993b); Dacey, Nelson, Clark, & Aikman (1991); Pipher (1994); Thompson (1994).

10. See Pipher (1994); Schwartz, Cohen, Hoffman, & Meeks (1989).

11. See Cross (1993).

12. The names of all of the skaters interviewed have been changed to protect their privacy.

REFERENCES

Ackerman, P., Newton, J, McPherson, W., Jones, J., & Dykman, R.(1998). Prevalence of post traumatic stress disorder and other psychiatric diagnoses in three groups of abused children (sexual, physical, and both). *Child Abuse and Neglect*, 22, 759–774.

Archer, M. (1988). *Culture and agency: The place of culture in social theory*. Cambridge, UK: Cambridge University Press.

Arthur, L. B. (1993). Clothing, control, and women's agency: The mitigation of patriarchal power. In S. Fisher & K. Davis (Eds.), *Negotiating at the margins: The gendered discourses of power and resistance* (pp. 66–84). New Brunswick, NJ: Rutgers University Press.

Barling, N., & Moore, S. (1990). Adolescent's attitudes towards precautions and intention to use condoms. *Psychological Reports, 67,* 883–890.

Bordo, S. (1993a). "Material girl": The effacements of postmodern culture. In S. Fisher & K. Davis (Eds.), *Negotiating at the margins: The gendered discourses of power and resistance* (pp. 295–315). New Brunswick, NJ: Rutgers University Press.

Bordo, S. (1993b). *Unbearable weight: Feminism, Western culture, and the body.* Berkeley: University of California Press.

Brodkey, L., & Fine, M. (1988). Presence of mind in the absence of body. *Journal of Education, 170,* 84–99.

Brooks-Gunn, J., Burrow, C. & Warren, M. (1988). Attitudes toward eating and body weight in different groups of female adolescent athletes. *International Journal of Eating Disorders, 7,* 749–759.

Christoffel, K. (1998). Psychiatric and injury prevention approaches to youth suicide: Questions, answers, and lethal means. *Journal of the American Academy of Child and Adolescent Psychiatry, 37,* 481–484.

Cross, L. (1993). Body and self in feminine development: Implications for eating disorders and delicate self-mutilation. *Bulletin of the Menninger Clinic, 57,* 41–68.

Dacey, C., Nelson, W., Clark, V., & Aikman, K. (1991). Bulimia and body image dissatisfaction in adolescence. *Child Psychiatry and Human Development, 21,* 179–184.

Diem, E., McKay, L., & Jamison, J. (1994). Female adolescent alcohol, cigarette, and marijuana use: Similarities and differences in patterns of use. *The International Journal of Addictions, 29,* 987–997.

Donoghue, E. (1992). Sociopolitical correlates of teen—age pregnancy in the United States Virgin Islands. *International Journal of Mental Health, 21,* 39–49.

Egan, J. (1997, July 27). The thin red line. *The New York Times Magazine,* 20–26.

Eiser, C., Eiser, J., & Lang, J. (1989). Adolescent beliefs about AIDS prevention. *Psychology and Health, 3,* 287–296.

Fine, M. (1997). Witnessing Whiteness. In M. Fine, L. Weis, L. Powell, & L. M. Wong (Eds.), *Off White: Readings on race, power, and society* (pp. 57–65). New York: Routledge.

Fraser, L. (1998, October). Body love, body hate. *Glamour Magazine,* pp. 280–283, 330, 332–333.

Freedman, R. (1984). Reflections on beauty as it relates to health in adolescent females. *Women and Health, 9,* 29–45.

Garnefski, N., & deWilde, E. (1998). Addiction-risk behaviors and suicide attempts in adolescence. *Journal of Addictions, 21,* 135–142.

Gillies, P. (1989). A longitudinal study of the hopes and worries of adolescents. *Journal of Adolescence, 12,* 69–81.

Griffen-Carison, M., & Schwanenflugel, P. (1998). Adolescent abortion and parental notification: Evidence for the importance of family functioning on the perceived quality of parental involvement in U.S. families. *Journal of Child Psychology and Psychiatry, 39*, 543–553.

Hazzard, A., King, H., & Webb, C. (1986). Group therapy with sexually abused girls. *American Journal of Psychotherapy, 15*, 213–223.

Lee, A., & Lee, S. (1996). Disordered eating and its psychosocial correlates among Chinese adolescent females in Hong Kong. *International Journal of Eating Disorders, 20*, 177–183.

Loda, F., Speizer, I., Martin, K., Skatrud, J., & Bennett, T. (1997). Programs and services to prevent pregnancy, childbearing, and poor birth outcomes among adolescents in rural areas of the southeastern United States. *Journal of Adolescent Health, 21*, 157–166.

McKie, L., Wood, R., & Gregory, S. (1993). Women defining health: Food, diet, and body image. *Health Education Research, 8*, 35–41.

Miller, P. (1997) . Family structure, personality, drinking, smoking, and illicit drug use: A study of UK teenagers. *Drug and Alcohol Dependence, 45*, 121–129.

Morgan, C., Chapar, G., & Fisher, M. (1995). Psychosocial variables associated with teenage pregnancy. *Adolescence, 30*, 277–289.

Paxton, S. (1993). A prevention program for disturbed eating and body dissatisfaction in adolescent girls: A one year follow-up. *Health Education Research, 8*, 43–51.

Pipher, M. (1994). *Reviving Ophelia: Saving the lives of adolescent girls.* New York: Ballentine.

Potter, L., Rosenberg, M., & Hammond, W. (1998). Suicide in youth: A public health framework. *Journal of the American Academy of Child and Adolescent Psychology, 37*, 484–487.

Reder, P., Lucey, C., & Fredman, G. (1991). The challenge of deliberate self harm by young adolescents. *Journal of Adolescence, 14*, 135–148.

Ryan, J. (1996). *Little girls in pretty boxes: The making and breaking of elite gymnasts and figure skaters.* New York: Warner Books.

Schwartz, R., Cohen, P., Hoffman, N., & Meeks, J. (1989). Self harm behaviors (carving) in female adolescent drug abusers. *Clinical Pediatrics, 28*, 340–346.

Smith, P., & Cogswell, C. (1994). A cross-cultural perspective on adolescent girl's body perception. *Perceptual and Motor Skills, 78*, 744–746.

Sutherland, J., & Willner, P. (1998). Patterns of alcohol, cigarette, and illicit drug use in English adolescents. *Addiction, 93*, 1199–1208.

Taylor, C., Sharpe, T., Shisslak, C., Bryson, S., Estes, L., Gray, N., McKnight, K., Crago, M., Kraemer, H., & Killen, J. (1998). Factors associated with weight concerns in girls. *International Journal of Eating Disorders, 24*, 21–42.

Thompson, B. (1994). *A hunger so wide and so deep: A multicultural view of women's eating problems.* Minneapolis: University of Minnesota Press.

Tiggemann, M., & Pickering, A. (1996). Role of television in adolescent women's body dissatisfaction and drive for thinness. *International Journal of Eating Disorders, 20*, 199–203.

Trad, P. (1994). Teenage pregnancy: Seeking patterns that promote family harmony. *The American Journal of Family Therapy, 22*, 42–56.

Walkerdine, V. (1997). *Daddy's girl: Young girls and popular culture*. Cambridge, MA: Harvard University Press.

Wertheim, E., Paxton, S., Maude, D., Szmukler, G., Gibbons, K., & Hiller, L. (1992). Psychosocial predictors of weight loss behaviors and binge eating in adolescent girls and boys. *International Journal of Eating Disorders, 12,* 151–160.

Wertheim, E., Paxton, S., Schultz, H., & Muir, S. (1997). Why do adolescent girls watch their weight? An interview study examining sociocultural pressures to be thin. *Journal of Psychosomatic Research, 42,* 345–355.

Windle, R., & Windle, M. (1997). An investigation of adolescent substance abuse behaviors, depressed affect, and suicidal behaviors. *Journal of Child Psychology and Psychiatry, 38,* 921–929.

CHAPTER 8

The House That Race Built:
Some Observations on the Use of
the Word *Nigga*, Popular Culture,
and Urban Adolescent Behavior

A. A. AKOM

Niggers are scared of revolution but niggers shouldn't be scared of revolution
because revolution is nothing but change, and all niggers do is change. Niggers
come in from work and change into pimping clothes to hit the street and make some
quick change. Niggers change their hair from black to red to blond and hope like
hell their looks will change. Niggers kill others just because one didn't receive the
correct change. Niggers always going through bullshit changes. But when it comes
for a real change Niggers are scared of revolution.
　　　　　　　—"Niggers are scared of revolution," The Last Poets (1970)

And being that we use it as a term of endearment . . .
Now the little shorties say it all over town
And a whole bunch of Niggaz throw the word around
Yo I start to flinch as I try not to say it
But my lips are like ohh I betta starts to spray it . . .
Hey Sucka Nigga who ever you are . . .
　　　　　　　—"Sucka Nigga," Tribe Called Quest (1993)

What is the political and social significance of the word *Nigga*—on the playground, in the street, on the corner, and in educational and public spaces?
Is the word *Nigga* part of the pleasures and politics of Black working-class
culture? Is the word *Nigger* part of the pain and patriarchy of working-

class White culture? What is the trajectory of the word *Nigger/Nigga* and its relationship to other communities usually not defined as Black or working-class? Too often language is approached from the angle of how people use it rather than why. By shifting our attention to the strategic moves behind language, the memories that propel it, and the motivations that give it a certain visibility and social mobility, we can begin to understand the cultural and power relationships involved in the construction of language—that directly and indirectly influence people's living standard, life chances, and command over resources.

In what follows I use a symbolic interactionist approach, as well as cultural and historical sociology, to trace the development of the word *Nigger* as it has grown from a linguistic method of social control designed by White supremacists to regulate human behavior, to a distinctive Black radical tradition found mainly in working-class populations, to a word currently endorsed by popular culture—extensively used in public and educational spaces—as well as in the entertainment arena.[1]

The goal of this chapter is to illuminate the linguistic world that many urban youth travel on a daily basis. Not much is known about life "beneath the veil," as Du Bois (1899) termed it, and even less is known about the language urban youth use to sojourn in deteriorating public parks, increasingly militarized city streets, and sociopsychological dreamscapes produced by the formulaic music and narratives of rap.

Consequently, in trying to make sense of how discursive spaces help young urbanites identify and reconstitute themselves as social beings, it is important to look critically into sets of spaces where urban youth play, spend time, and just hang out (Kelley, 1997). This chapter does exactly that. Each scene examines a set of conversations involving the use of the word *Nigger* that occurred outside of school yet well within imagined or territorial community boundaries where youth develop, resist, try on, and re-create political and social identities.[2]

In order for this research to be representative, I conducted 60 interviews with African American, European American, Puerto Rican, and Asian American youth throughout the United States in places such as Philadelphia, Oakland, Berkeley, and New York.[3] The young men and women who have given their time to this project varied in terms of social background, education, regional history, and shade of skin; however, all shared one thing in common—they have either been called *Nigger/Nigga* or participated in calling other people *Nigger/Niggaz*. As a result, determining the social and political character of the N-word is essential, not only because the word is full of definitional ambiguity but also because language plays a critical role in the formation of individual and collective identities and, as a result, in one's personal politics.

HISTORICAL OVERVIEW: EXAMINING THE SHIFTING
LINGUISTIC TERRAIN FROM *NIGGER* TO *NIGGA*

For the past five centuries or more, perhaps the most hotly contested word in the English language has been the racial and spatial designation of the term *Nigger* (Boyd, 1997). At its most degenerative level the term connotes the racial stratification and class hierarchy that have been defining characteristics of the English cultural landscape since its inception (Drake, 1987). In the United States, where race is an important calculus of social identity, the word *Nigger* reflects a particular way of looking at and interpreting human differences—both biophysical and cultural. Historically, as a way of imposing order and asserting dominance over others, Europeans used the word to transform their own social identities (irrespective of class), as well as to ascribe social inferiority to those populations encountered and exploited in the New World, Asia, and Africa. As a result, the word *Nigger* in the archives of the American historical imagination is not only a word but also an idea—an idea expressing the centrality of race and racial reasoning in American cultural politics, as well as the lingering legacy of slavery and the world emerging in its aftermath (Smedley, 1993).

The current debate over the word *Nigga*, as it relates to historical consciousness, has its roots in the Black power movement of the 1960s, shifts in the culture industry, and underground discourses on authenticity and the meaning of "Blackness." During the 1960s, when debates about the Black aesthetic were at an all-time high, it seemed unthinkable to certain segments of the Black community that a word like *Nigga* could be separated from the White supremacist boundaries responsible for bringing its linguistic cousin—*Nigger*—into existence in the first place. *Nigga*, for many Black folks of that era, not only was a derogatory term but also represented the old-fashioned notion that a Negro was expected to endure White insult, accommodate to oppressive working conditions, and accept comparatively poor treatment in wages, education, and housing (Brown, 1972). The word *Nigga*, for that generation, also signified an explicit rejection of the Black power ethos, which, according to social historian Harvard Sitkoff (1994), galvanized the civil rights movement and changed static notions of Black identity.

Not surprisingly then, the term *Nigga* for many Black folks who occupied the industrial ghettos of the 1960s and 1970s, was not viewed as the friendly appellation that it is in some communities today. Nor was the word used as a synonym for *Black* or as just another way to talk about Black cultural products without reference to skin color—which speaks to the way individuals from other ethnic groups have incorporated the word *Nigga* into their own cultural repertoire. On the contrary, *Nigga* for many Black urban residents of the past was a word that was to be tolerated, depending on the context of the situation, age and hue of the messenger, and tone and texture of the message being sent. Further still, *Nigga* for the two extremities in the Black spectrum—the conservative and the militant—was not a word that evoked any deep-rooted sense of community, common destiny, or collective understanding that there was indeed an authentic "Black" way of doing things (Brown, 1972). Rather, *Nigga*, regardless of spelling or enunciation, was a word with a particular recipe and a particular cook. In other words, *Nigga* was a term linked to the world of White supremacy and, as a result, laden with derogatory meaning.

The pleasure industry changed all that. It changed the way Black images were created, enhanced, distributed, and maintained within and outside of the Black community. It also magnified and narrowed the success narrative for many Black working-class youth by suggesting that the realm of sports and entertainment was probably the most realistic and economically viable option for a kid who was looking to avoid dead-end jobs and low-wage labor. Consequently, during a time when there were few employment opportunities for Blacks outside of the color-coded environment of ghetto communities, the White consumer market remained poised and eager to be entertained by the exotic Other. A classic example of this is the Black comedy of the 1960s, 1970s, and early 1980s, in particular that of Richard Pryor, Red Foxx, Flip Wilson, Moms Mabley, Dick Gregory, Steppin Fetchit, Nipsy Russell, and Eddie Murphy, to name a few. These comedians specialized in turning pain into profit by racializing and eroticizing Black bodies that historically had been sites of White exploitation and embodiments of the "darker side" of sexuality, criminality, and transgressiveness (a good example of this today would be Chris Rock) (Brown, 1972).

Black comedy—whether it was about sexual interludes, Black and White discrimination, or the hidden codes of public and private behavior—is a very complicated issue to think about in relation to the linguistic transformation of the terms *Nigger* and *Nigga*, especially when we consider that most Black comedy was not created or experienced in the pursuit of pleasure alone. Besides being about pleasure and expression, much of the Black comedy of the past three decades carried with it the potential to heal deep emotional scars, soothe the trials and tribulations associated with second-class citizenship, and push issues of power, expression, and aesthetic value into the forefront of American public and cultural consciousness (Kelley, 1998).

As a result, when we examine Black comedy, in relation to our argument about the shifting linguistic terrain of *Nigger* to *Nigga*, the commercialization of language as a form of creative, expressive, pleasurable, and paid labor becomes paramount to the discussion. Because the truth of the matter is, whether you called it *capping, sounding, bagging, dissin'*, or *the dozens*, these discourses, offered mostly by Black male comedians, powerfully reproduced hierarchies of gender (often while deconstructing hierarchies of racial and class exploitation) in a profession where being able to get a laugh ultimately increased the value of man's sexuality while devaluing the sexual appeal of a woman (Kelley, 1998). And yet, even though Black comedy represents an important link between the commercialization of language and the changing meanings and practices of the word *Nigga* for African American youth, few Black urban residents of the past—who rarely owned, controlled, and distributed their own images—envisioned that in just a decade or two, *Nigga*, as word and concept, would be commercially appropriated by the culturel industry and thus deeply implicated in the burgeoning marketplace of creating a new Black cultural aesthetic mainly through a musical form called "rap."

THE ADVENT OF THE MODERN-DAY *NIGGA*

It is quite clear that, for many Black folks, the civil rights movement developed critical consciousness about the politics of race (hooks, 1990; Sitkoff, 1994). Passive consumption of images designed to promote and reinforce domination were challenged or replaced by the active production of images whose central emphasis was on decolonization. As a result, the advent of the modern day *Nigga* is fairly new to the African American lexicon and reflects a visible split between those forces that seek to call attention to the fluid, hybrid, and multinational aspects of Black cultural identity and those that maintain that the word *Nigga* romanticizes and reproduces race relations rooted in domination. According to social historian Robin Kelley (1994), the defining characteristic of the modern day *Nigga* is class as opposed to race:

> The construction of the ghetto as a Living nightmare and gangstas as products of that nightmare has given rise to what I call a new Ghettocentric identity in which the specific class, race, and gendered experiences in late capitalist urban centers coalesce to create a new identity—Nigga. (p. 210)

Kelley goes on to say that Niggaz link "their identity to the hood instead of simply skin color" (i.e., geography, socioeconomic status, and experience matter more than race/ethnicity) and that the use of the word *Nigga* acknowledges "the limitations of racial politics, including black middle class reformism as well as black nationalism" (p. 210). However, my research suggests that it is more complicated than this. For example, in interviews I conducted with Puerto Rican youth, many discussed using the term *Nigga* among themselves as well as with Blacks as a term of endearment. However, when asked specific questions about confrontations with law enforcement agencies or struggles over scarce community resources, many of my informants (Puerto Rican as well as African American) reverted back to the age-old "race rule" that you protect your own first and think about why later (Dyson, 1996). As a result, in order to truly investigate the relationship between "ghettocentric" identity and the use of the word *Nigga* by diverse populations, we must first understand the role that gangsta rap, the mass media, social scientists, and multiracial political and religious leaders have played in defining "Blackness" and exporting Black cultural images to the world outside of the ghetto.

Beginning with Du Bois' (1899) *Philadelphia Negro*, progressing with the "culture of poverty" of Oscar Lewis (1965), continuing through talk shows such as those of Rush Limbaugh or Howard Stern, and ending with descriptive lyrics of Ice Cube or Ice-T, problems of inner-city communities have been disproportionately identified as the pathological problems of poor urban residents. Even as interpretations and opinions have differed, the adjectives used to describe Black urban physical, cultural, and social space have remained the same—culturally *defective, nihilistic*, and *dysfunctional*. These terms suggest that the causes of racial inequity and poverty are to be found not in economic decline or inefficient government structures but rather in the pathologies and cultural values of inner-city residents themselves.

Unfortunately, very little of the cultural production and monologues produced by sociologists, cultural critics, social commentators, and rap singers provide an adequate understanding of the richness and textured variety of people's lives and cultures in inner-city neighborhoods. Much of the problem can be attributed to the fact that rarely do the residents speak for themselves. Consequently, what cultural forms mean from the standpoint of the practitioner is largely ignored in social science research. My purpose, then, is to offer some observations as to why some Black (and non-Black) working-class youth have chosen to adopt a nuanced version of the word *Nigger* as an intricate part of their cultural identity. In order to accomplish this task, it will be important to examine several different cultural venues where the word has come to prominence—including the basketball court, the barbershop, and rap music, as both physical and/or cultural spaces and as places central to the construction of young people's social identity.

THE ETHNOGRAPHIC REPORT

The first scene of this ethnography opens at a basketball court in South Philadelphia. My involvement at this court is one of both participant and observer. What I am participating in, to an outsider, may appear to be just a simple game of basketball. However, what I am observing is that basketball in my neighborhood is not only a platform for cultural expression, stylistic innovation, and racial, gender, and class construction; less formally speaking, especially from the standpoint of the practitioners, the court is simply a leisure spot, a place of play, a community space, a place to build (or destroy) an opponent's self-esteem and work ethic amid the abandoned buildings, concrete walls, and disembodied dreams that characterize the modern-day ghetto.

Each time a player steps onto the court, the game itself generates enormous kinds of possibilities, while at the same time imposing different sorts of limitations. One of the most obvious limitations is the language of the game—the way Black males (of all classes who play the game) talk to, about, and around each other. Some call it "trash talkin'," others call it "talkin' shit," still others call it "talkin' head" or just plain "smack." Whatever you want to call it, it is clear that the policing of boundaries on the basketball court, the competition to see "who got game and who don't," and the construction of masculinity for young boys and men is expressed as much through the language of the game as the game itself. In other words, language is a place of struggle on the basketball court—a place to fence in, hold down, bind in, and check your opponent, as well as a place to recover, renew, and refine lost or undiscovered parts or yourself.

Dante is a 17-year-old Black male whom I have seen and talked with before on and off the court. When I approach, he first comments on my shoes.

D: Yo Nigga . . . where'd u get them shoes?
AA: Wha-chu talkin' about man (*as I look down*) . . . these are the shoes I always be wearin'.
D: I know, Nigga . . . that's the point . . . why don't you spend the cold hard cash . . . and get yourself some real sneaks . . . made out of real leather and shit?
(*The fellas on the sidelines start laughin' and Fella 1 jumps in*)
Fella 1: Dem new Iverson's boy . . . Dem shits is tight . . . I'd drop dime on them if . . . (*I interrupt him*)
AA: Muthafucka . . . whether I be wearin' Converse All stars . . . or the Muthafuckin' new Jordans . . . I still got enough game to dunk on your sorry ass. [I'm talking to Dante.]

D: Nigga please . . . you ain't never dunked on me. . . . Maybe you schoolin' them college niggaz . . . but here Nigga . . . this is my hood . . . and my court.

AA: Who got next anyway?

D: I do Nigga . . . you want to run?

AA: Yeah . . .

D: What about him? Who he?

AA: That's my boy . . . he cool

D: Do he got game?

AA: Why don't you ask him?

D: Where you from?

Friend: Iowa.

D: Damn I didn't know there were Niggaz in Iowa.

(The fellas on the sidelines start laughin')

Friend: Yeah, there are a few of us running around up there.

Fella 2: Nigga even sound like he from Iowa.

D: Hey yo . . . [Dante's talking to me] . . . I only got room for you . . .

AA: Why you dissin' my boy like that?

D: Nigga . . . I ain't dissin' him. . . . The Nigga just sound like he from Iowa . . .

Fella 2: Nigga probably play like it too . . .

D: Shit . . . I'm tryin' to hold the court all day . . . last week we got our asses kicked by them hollywood Niggaz . . .

AA: Whatever man. . . . I'll wait and run with my boy . . . Yo. . . . We got next . . .

Like most racialized minority youth who negotiate the demilitarized space of the ghetto, marked by chainlink fences, garbage-strewn streets, bent and rusted basketball rims, and graffiti-filled walls (and I mean bad graffiti, not good graffiti), Dante's use of the word *Nigga* does not necessarily signal immaturity, false consciousness, or some form of linguistic rebellion. Rather, if we are to understand his use of the word *Nigga* as simultaneously more and less than a mere pronouncement of exploitation, victimization, stigmatization, and racism, then we must ask: Why does Black communication work? And how and why does it fail? These question suggest that we should consider the nuances involved in Black intracultural communication.

Black intracultural differences have largely been ignored in educational and social science research. One reason for this is that cultural differences play a covert role in the communication process. When Black folks from different social backgrounds, educational levels, and regions of the country interact in public space, there is generally little or no discussion about the ways in which they are interpreting one another's behavior, the reasons they are interpreting it as they do, or the way they are expecting the interaction to evolve (Heath, 1983; Kochman, 1981).

As a result, Blacks often assume that they are operating according to identical speech and cultural conventions that were formed in opposition to, or in accordance with, standards that the socially dominant White group has established for itself (Fordham, 1996; Ogbu, 1991). This assumption speaks to the general public failure to recognize the notion of a core Black culture—which, according to social historian Robin Kelley (1997), "incorporates a diverse and contradictory range of practices, attitudes, and relationships that are dynamic, historically situated, and ethnically hybrid" (p. 27).

While Kelley's definition of a core Black culture may be viewed by some as oxymoronic—essentialist because it suggests that there is a core Black culture, yet anti-essentialist because the core Black culture it suggests is composed of diverse and contradictory elements—it does speak to the ways in which class mobility has altered the collective Black experience so that racism no longer has the same impact on all of our lives that it once did (hooks, 1990; Oliver & Shapiro, 1995). Add to this generational, intercultural, and gender specificity, and one begins to understand that a great deal of what the word *Nigga* means, how it is received, and its social conventions have to do with the social spaces that one occupies when using the word—be it work, leisure, or community—and one's position vis-à-vis existing racial and class hierarchies.

As a result, in the case above, Dante and the other ballplayers made the fallacious assumption that there were "no Niggaz in Iowa." Furthermore, they assumed that even if there were Niggaz in Iowa, the few there don't know how to play basketball. Assertions such as these, which seek to confine Black folks to a universal, homogenized, and singular notion of Black identity, fail to capture the complex and variegated experience of Black people's everyday lives. This process of social excommunication extends far beyond the basketball court and serves to promote the notion of an "authentic" Black experience by identifying as unnatural those expressions of Black life that do not conform to preexisting patterns or stereotypes (hooks, 1990).

The Power of the Blade

Historically, the barbershop in the Black community has performed a function very similar to that of the Black church; that is, it has been a place of belonging and togetherness (Anderson, 1999). A place where people who were collectively experiencing racism in similar ways could come together and feel a stronger sense of group solidarity. A place to rebuild communal feelings and acknowledge each other in daily life. A place to undo years of racist teachings that had denied Black folks the power to recognize themselves. The looks and conversations in the barbershop were affirmations of our struggle, our Blackness, our wounded spirits, and the alienation that was dehumanizing us. Another important practice in the barbershop was that of sharing stories, family gossip, and facts about African-American life.

Today, the conversations in the barbershop have changed a great deal. As overt racial discrimination and violence have diminished—and more Blacks have been incorporated into the mainstream—the Black imagination has been commodified as never before. At this historical moment Black folks are divided. Many of us do not live in Black neighborhoods, and most of us work for White people. Large numbers of us are socialized and educated in historically White institutions or through a historically White controlled mass media (hooks, 1990). Interracial relations are on the rise, and looking back we can see that the racial solidarity born of the 1960s and 1970s will be very different from the racial solidarity that may (or may not) emerge in the twenty-first century. As a result, people young and old must rearticulate the basis for collective bonding.

Accordingly, this scene opens up at a barbershop in Oakland. Two men (one in his mid to late 30s, the other well over 40) and two boys (juniors and seniors in high school) are in chairs getting their hair cut. The conversation on this day is about the situation of being a Black man in America.

Barber 1: So how was your day today, Leonard?

30-yr-old: Rough day today, Mr. Jones . . . I mean . . . being a Black man in America sure is hard . . . I mean . . . White people think you're acting paranoid when you tell them about it. . . . But I'd like to see them try to live in a Black man's skin just one time . . . I mean just one time . . . and see how they like it . . .

Barber 1: I know . . . the White mans got the badge, the power, the law . . .

High school student 1: The money . . .

Barber 1: So anyway you look at it the Black man loses . . .

30-yr-old: That's what I'm talkin' about. . . . Unless you're a celebrity . . .

40-yr-old: It don't matter if you're a celebrity . . . even movie stars and athletes get harassed by the cops. . . . I can't remember exactly where I was . . . but I saw this boy who plays for the Raiders [football team] get completely disrespected by the cops. . . . And he kept saying . . . do you know who I am . . . do you know who I am . . . and they were like . . . Yeah, we know who you are. . . . We know who you are . . . and these were Black cops, too . . .

High school student 1: Who was he?

40-yr-old: I don't remember.

High school student 1: Was he doin' anything wrong?

40-yr-old: He wasn't doin' a damn thing wrong . . . I remember that.

High school student 2: That's right . . . it don't matter what you do if you're
    Black . . . because Black cops are *Niggers*, too.

Barber 2: That's true, *Nigga* . . . that's true . . . Black cops will make a
    spectacle out of you . . . if you don't "yessem" and "noem" to death . . .
    Sell-outs, man . . . they're nothin' but sell-outs.

30-yr-old: I disagree. . . . White cops are much worse than Black cops. . . .
    Man, I remember this time when a White cop stopped me for some
    bullshit . . . and I was in the middle of nowhere . . . And the cop was
    like . . . *Nigger* . . . I'll put a bullet in your ass if you don't do exactly
    what I say. . . . And that shit was crazy . . . 'cause I was out in the
    middle of nowhere.

Barber 1: And you did exactly what he said, didn't you?

30-yr-old: Sure as hell did.

Barber 3: I hear cops make good money though.

40-yr-old: Yeah, they do.

Barber 1: And we need some good cops in Oakland . . . the police force
    here smells like turpentine.

30-yr-old: Taste like it, too . . . [the conversation sort of dies out after this].

The criminalization, surveillance, and incarceration of Black men and
young adults in the heart of Oakland speaks to the larger social issue of
disproportionately placing more Black men, especially poor Black men,
in prison or on probation than any other group in relation to the proportion of the total population. For the men in the barbershop, and Black
urban youth in general, the police are a major part of an oppressive criminal justice system, which in 1995 placed 24% of Black males between the
ages of 20 and 29 behind bars or on parole. As a result, in the streets of
Oakland as well as in other cities across the United States, calling cops
"Niggers" or "Nigga killaz" is one way Black urban youth challenge the
status quo and attempt to move police brutality into the discursive arena.
As Foucault (1977) explains, "when prisoners began to speak, they possessed an individual theory of prisons, the penal system, and justice. It's
this form of discourse which ultimately matters, a discourse against power,
the counter-discourse of prisoners and those we call delinquents—and not
a theory about delinquency" (p. 209).

Most Black urban youth, like the high school student 2 in the scene
above, use *Nigger* as a word-weapon of choice, not only to name the op-
pressor but, perhaps more significantly, to name the oppression. Thus,
regardless of the color of the perpetrator, *Nigger* in this context is meant to

suggest that the experiences of inner-city Black men are not universal to all Black people and, further, that some African Americans play a key role in perpetuating intraracial oppression (Drake, 1987). In other words, "Niggers" as well as "Niggaz" are not only victims but also agents of racial and class oppression (Kelley, 1994).

"Niggers," according to the men and young boys in the barbershop, perpetuate racial and class oppression by concerning themselves with racism solely to the extent that it limits their upward social mobility. This sort of analysis is aimed particularly at the Black cops who harassed the football player. That is, the Black cops were "Niggers" because they lacked a complete understanding of the link among racism, poverty, unemployment, youth culture, and police repression—as it relates to overcrowded, poorly funded schools, urban decay, the growth of privatized public spaces at the expense and exclusion of young Blacks and Latinos, and the erosion of youth programs and recreational facilities. Consequently, the Black cops, whether they were conscious of it or not, ended up reproducing racial stratification by equating Black skin and youth culture with the categorical meanings of crime and delinquency. hooks (1991) explains it like this: "Work is not necessarily oppositional because it is created by a black person" (p. 8).

Equally revealing is how the Niggaz in the barbershop (here I am referring to barber 2 and the two high school students as *Niggaz* because of their relatively youthful age) did not realize how they, too, were perpetuating racial and class divisions: first, by socially labeling individuals in the Black middle class as assimilationists, "tokens," or "sell-outs," and, second, according to psychoanalytic anthropologist Signithia Fordham (1996), by mockingly addressing those affiliated with predominantly White institutions as "not Black enough" or labeling those educated in institutions of higher learning as "not Black-identified" (Fordham, p. 14).

In concluding this section, it is important to remember that there is a visible split within the Black community between those forces who call themselves integrationists and those forces who consider themselves self-deterministic (Brown, 1972; Cayton & Drake, 1944; hooks, 1990). However, even this simplistic dichotomy is filled with gaps and fissures, precisely because there are many Black folks who fit into neither category or into both at the same time. Add to this how the corporate imagination undermines not only Black solidarity but also various other forms of solidarity by promoting personal choice and individual rights, "in a way which suggests 'freedom' for a Black person can be measured by the degree to which we can base all decisions in life on individualistic concerns, what feels good or satisfies desire" (hooks 1990, p. 37; see also Gregory, 1992).[4] And it becomes clear how the culture industry provides not only information or entertainment but also "'pockets of consciousness'—frameworks for interpreting and reacting to social and political reality" (Hallin, 1986, p. 22). In the next section I examine the pocket of consciousness where the word *Nigga* is most commonly used in the public sphere today, that is, in the world of gangsta rap.

Music as Space

Rap and hip-hop are the common literacy of urban and suburban youth today. The aesthetics, style, and sonic pleasure of the cultural form cuts across boundaries of race, class, gender, and sexual orientation. However, while studies of rap and hip hop have been useful in terms of recognizing the critical voice of contemporary Black urban youth, they have done little to advance our understanding of the role gangsta rap plays in extending *Nigga* into the realm of popular culture (George, 1998). As a result, in this scene I talk to urban youth about the use of the word *Nigga* as it relates to gangsta rap. In this first account, Tanya, a Puerto Rican high school student, discusses hypersexuality, violence, and power issues as they relate to gangsta rap:

T: To me, what I love about rap and hip-hop is the videos . . . I love them Niggaz with them nice clothes, cars, and shit. . . . They be drivin' around lookin' all fly. . . . Me and my Niggaz watch that shit all the time. . . . Dem Niggaz is hard . . . and fine too . . .

AA: Who do you watch the videos with?

T: My girlfriends.

AA: Black or Puerto Rican?

T: Puerto Rican, man. . . . But I'll tell you one thing I don't like . . . I'm not sure I like those little kids tryin' to act like gangstaz. . . . Now that really bothers me . . .

AA: What do you mean?

T: I mean . . . I don't like little kids feeling on each other and shit. . . . tryin' to look all hard . . . bumpin' and grindin' . . . that's too much for me. . . . But dem other Niggaz . . . they like it . . .

AA: Who do you mean . . . them other Niggaz?

T: I'm talkin' about my friends and my brothers . . . especially my brothers . . . they don't care . . . all they care about is cars, pussy, and ass . . .

Wayne, a 24-year-old Vietnamese male, had this narrative to offer.

W: Man, I used to use the word *Nigga* all the time . . . I mean I'm a DJ and that's how those of us in the rap game used to talk to each other. . . . You kno' . . . Nigga please . . . or Nigga, fuck you . . . or who the fuck does this Nigga think he is. . . . You kno' how it is . . . You kno' how it is . . .

AA: And do you think gangsta rap had anything to do with how y'all talked to one another?

W: With what?

AA: With y'all calling each other *Nigga*?

W: I don't know man . . . I've never thought about it like that before. . . . *Nigga* is just a word that we all used to say "wassup" to each other . . . I mean, there's no harm in it . . . but I never thought about it much before you started to ask me all these questions . . .

AA: OK . . . well, let me ask you one more question . . .

W: Shoot.

AA: Why don't you use the word anymore?

W: I don't know . . . I guess I've just out grown it . . .

Jim, a 17-year-old White male, added this:

J: When I'm around my close close friends . . . I say Nigga all the time . . . and when I'm listening to my music . . . I can't help but say Nigga. . . . But on the street . . . around people I don't know . . . I never use the word . . . too political, man . . . too political. . . . Using *Nigga* the wrong way is a good way to get your ass kicked around here [Berkeley] . . . and I ain't tryin' to start nothin' like that . . . that's not my style . . .

The reconfiguration of Black identity through the medium of rap indicates that generational shifts have rearranged established boundaries between the old image of "Nigger" and "new jacks" who may, or may not, be Black in color, culture, or consciousness but still identify with the contemporary usage of the term *Nigga*. Those who make up this new generation have been raised during a time when overt racial discrimination in the form of Jim Crow laws or separate facilities has been outlawed, allowing more access to institutional resources and privileges than previous generations had. As a result, this new generation has the added advantage of being as Black as they want to be and still occupying a significant position in the cultural marketplace. A good example of this can be found in the lyrics of Ice T and Ice Cube:

I'm a nigger, not a colored man or a black
or a Negro or an Afro-American—I'm all that
Yes I was born in America too.
But does South Central look like America to you?
—Ice T, "Straight Up Nigga"

Niggaz always gotta show they teeth
Now I'mo be brief
Be true to the game
    —Ice Cube, "True to the Game"

Discourses such as these demonstrate that in today's cultural marketplace one can be both "true to the game"—that is, true to their own cultural identity—while at the same time having a great deal of crossover
appeal. However, it is also important to note that as cultural identity becomes a marketable commodity, easily projected into mainstream society,
it loses some of its sociopolitical impact. For example, Ice Cube and Ice T
are certainly not the threatening phenomena today that they were when
they first burst on to the cultural scene. Todd Boyd (1997) describes the
fluid nature and political complexity of cultural boundaries:

> It is interesting how one audience can perceive this move to the mainstream
> as becoming part of the establishment, while another sees it as a threat to-
> ward losing power. Thus it is not uncommon to find individuals who are
> criticized by mainstream audiences as being "too Black," or at least pushing
> a Black agenda, and at the same time criticized by another Black audience as
> having sold out. (p. 29)

Like Boyd, I found in my own research with young people that audience perception of the word *Nigga* oscillates with respect to race, class,
geography, and age differentiation. It seemed that young people of different
races and classes seemed to be comfortable with using the word *Nigga*, or
even being called the word *Nigga*, depending on individual musical taste,
neighborhood context and social background, social networks, and degree
of interest in those spaces within the culture industry where the word *Nigga*
is most often used.

As a result, I concluded that social environment was a necessary, but
not sufficient, factor in being able to negotiate the shifting linguistic terrain
of *Nigger* and *Nigga*. I say necessary, but not sufficient, because there were
individuals such as Darnice in Philadelphia, who attended a segregated high
school, who stated very clearly that "I just don't like the word *Nigger* or *Nigga*
. . . I don't like the way it sounds . . . or the way it makes me feel. . . . Plus
my momma told me I shouldn't talk like that anyway. . . . She says it's backwards actin' . . ."

CONCLUSION

These scenes, taken together, suggest that the word *Nigga* is still a contentious term in the lexicon of American popular culture. Though it is con-

sidered improper in formal public conversation, and *African American* seems to be the politically correct choice, the word still obviously holds a great deal of currency in the private sector and increasingly so in much of the public sector (Boyd, 1997).

Finally, proper terms of identification change as society changes. Shifting linguistic terms, such as *colored, Negro,* and, most recently, *Black,* can be linked to changes in the cultural industry, the economy, grassroots movements, individuals' daily struggles, and legal apparatuses that serve to classify and perpetuate popular beliefs about human difference. Additionally, the persistence of the word should be a reminder of youth's enduring ability to map its own cultural terrain. In *Freedom Charter,* a work which captures the historical struggles and strategies of the resistance movement in South Africa, the phrase "our struggle is also a struggle of memory against forgetting" is continually repeated (hooks, 1990, p. 40). In many ways this captures the complexity and confusing lines of demarcation involved in using the words *Nigger* or *Nigga.* To use them, or even to hear them, given their tumultuous history, is truly a struggle of memory against forgetting.

NOTES

1. In the tradition of symbolic interactionism, I adhere to Blumer's (1969) classic three premises of symbolic interaction: that we know things by their meanings, that meanings are created through social interaction, and that meanings change through interaction.

2. The three discursive spaces analyzed in this chapter are the basketball court, the barbershop, and rap music. These discursive spaces were selected because they represent key sources of identity and security for individuals as well as groups of youth and, consequently, are important locations in which to witness the dialectical interplay among experience, perception, and imagination as they relate to the shaping and reshaping of young people's identities, the claiming and reclaiming of public spaces, and the political contradictions involved when language is delivered as social critique.

3. The interviews, as well as the participant observation in this report, were collected through a comparative urban ethnography project of the University of Pennsylvania and the University of California at Berkeley. The Coca Cola project (University of Pennsylvania) and the Diversity Project (University of California at Berkeley) are linked through my dissertation, examining factors that contribute to disparities in academic achievement, as well as factors responsible for the racial separation of students within and outside of school. Both projects were started in the summer of 1996.

4. By various forms of solidarity I am referring to racial, ethnic, religious, and gendered forms of solidarity. And by *undermine* I am referring to the erosion

of collective solidarity. For a more detailed discussion of the ways in which the corporate imagination erodes various forms of solidarity, see hooks (1990).

REFERENCES

Anderson. E. (1999). *Code of the street*. New York: Norton.

Boyd, T. (1997). *Am I Black enough for you? Popular culture from the 'hood and beyond*. Bloomington: Indiana University Press.

Blumer, H. (1969). *Symbolic interpretationism*. Englewood Cliffs, NJ: Prentice-Hall.

Brown, C. (1972). The language of soul. In T. Kochman (Ed.), *Rappin' and stylin' out: Communication in urban black America* (p. 134). Urbana: University of Illinois Press.

Cayton, H., & Drake S. (1944). *Black metropolis: A social study of a northern city*. Chicago: University of Chicago Press.

Drake, S. (1987). *Black folk here and there*. Los Angeles: University of California Press.

Du Bois, W. E. B. (1899). *The Philadelphia Negro*. Philadelphia: University of Pennsylvania Press.

Dyson, M. (1996). *Race rules: Navigating the color line*. New York: Addison-Wesley.

Fordham, S. (1996). *Blacked out: Dilemmas of race, identity, and success at Capital High*. Chicago: University of Chicago Press.

Foucault, M. (1977). *Discipline and punish: The birth of prison* (A. Sheridan, Trans.). New York: Pantheon.

George, N. (1998). *Hip hop America*. New York: Viking.

Gregory, S. (1992). The changing sign of race and class. *American Anthologists, 19*, 272.

Hallin, D. (1986). We keep America on top of the world. In T. Gitlin (Ed.), *Watching television* (p. 125). New York: Pantheon.

Heath, S. B. (1983). *Ways with words*. London: Cambridge University Press.

hooks, b. (1990). *Yearning: Race, gender, and cultural politics*. Boston: South End Press.

Kelley, R. (1994). *Race rebels*. New York: Free Press.

Kelley, R. (1997). Playing for keeps. In W. Lubiano (Ed.), *The house that race built* (p. 219). New York: Random House.

Kelley, R. (1998). *Yo' mama's disfunktional: Fighting the cultural wars in urban America*. Boston: Beacon Press.

Kochman, T. (1981). *Black and White styles in conflict*. Chicago: University of Chicago Press.

Lewis, O. (1965). *La vida; A Puerto Rican family in the culture of poverty—San Juan and New York*. New York: Random House.

Ogbu, J. U. (1991). Immigrant and involuntary minorities in comparative perspective. In M. Gibson & J. U. Ogbu, *Minority status and schooling: A comparative study of immigrant and involuntary minorities* (pp. 3–33). New York: Garland Press.

Oliver, M., & Shapiro, T. (1995). *Black wealth/White wealth: A new perspective on racial inequality.* New York: Routledge.

Sitkoff, H. (1994). *The struggle for Black equality, 1954–1980.* Cambridge, MA: Harvard University Press.

Smedley, A. (1993). *Race in North America: Origin and evolution of a world view.* Boulder, CO: Westview Press.

PART II

SPACES FOR BORDER CROSSING

Across communities and schools, youth are not only engaged with questions of their own identities but are also exploring commitments and relations across the chasms of class, race, ethnicity, gender, sexuality, nationality, and neighborhood. Indeed, it is compelling to watch youth stretch in ways that are both awkward and far more relaxed than those of our generation. In this section, we encounter young people self-consciously carrying themselves, or allowing themselves to be carried, across social borders of "difference." Interrogating their many identities, they take up ethical, spiritual, athletic, intellectual, and political projects larger than self. In these spaces, educators, activists, families, and youths carve corners in which young people come together to critically construct communities of difference. Here, youth discover and invent poetic, intellectual, athletic, cultural, and spiritual relations that reveal the many strands of self, weave colorful threads of community, and reconfigure projects for collective social justice. In these essays you will hear the struggles of learning to work through—rather than ignore—difference, to challenge personal experience as the sole source of authority, to challenge dominant cultural discourses, to rewrite biographies and cultures, and to (re)create poetry, friendship, and conversation from the wreckage of poverty, racism, and gendered subordination.

In this section you will encounter spaces, largely in schools, where youth are invited to travel into unknown social relations with strangers they are about to meet. We begin this section with an essay by Michelle Fine and three high school/middle school educators—Bernadette Anand, Carlton Jordan, and Dana Sherman—as they analyze the dynamics of a World Literatures classroom in which students of different racial, ethnic, social-class, and academic backgrounds engage texts from around the world and produce rigorous work as a community of intellectuals. Jennifer McCormick takes us into a very different school—a large urban comprehensive high school, filled with metal detectors, security guards, old books, and the most updated of surveillance technologies. She then escorts us into a profound and sacred little corner in which youth create poetry. McCormick juxtaposes the tight bodies who walk through the metal detectors and are searched by the guards with the flowing minds released in the poetry workshops.

With her college students, Nancy Barnes navigates across teaching locations to try to discern how it is that privileged youth, new to college, come to see themselves in relation with poor and working-class urban high school youth. Barnes offers a close analysis of what educators must do if we are to create spaces in which youth and young adults can situate themselves in surprising community across class and race lines. Like Anand, Jordan, and Sherman, Barnes details the micropractices that must be established by adults in order for youth to dare to cross borders long considered a "No Trespassing" zone. Colette Daiute tracks a group of young writers in urban schools, elementary through early adolescence, over a year, as they write and rewrite narratives on conflict, freedom, love, discrimination, and justice. Daiute positions writing as a space for critique and engagement across difference. By so doing, she reveals a pedagogy of transformation and critical intellect from youth whom many assume to be too young, immature, poor, or developmentally unready to confront crucial issues of social significance. Constance Webster, who studies with high school students, allows us to witness the shifting subjectivities of those youth active in sports, visual arts, and the performing arts. As Daiute argues that writing creates a labor in which consciousness and social action can be engaged, so, too, Webster documents the social sense that students develop when they undertake projects of aesthetic and/or athletic significance. Webster finds that in the small spaces of sports and the arts, young women are able to develop a robust sense of connection to process and product, persistence and performance, self and others; to cultivate a sense of social justice for those unseen and unheard; and to practice a set of responses to the well-rehearsed sexism, racism, and homophobia that fill the halls of the American high school. For Webster, these spots are not merely extracurricular. They are spaces for challenge, creativity, and possibility. Yet these are the very spaces that are threatened by budget cuts in public education.

In these essays, we witness the strength and capacity of youth in the 1990s, eager to resist binary essentialisms, challenge the narrow constraints of identity politics, and forge connections beyond shallow commonalities. These are essays of hope, insofar as they reflect youth raised in the Reagan–Bush–Clinton years of a shrinking public sphere and shriveling sense of the common good, who nevertheless flourish when challenged to engage a sense of possibility and justice beyond self.

CHAPTER 9

Before the Bleach Gets Us All

MICHELLE FINE, BERNADETTE ANAND, CARLTON JORDAN, AND DANA SHERMAN

> To sum up this: theoretically, the Negro needs neither separate nor mixed schools. What he needs is Education. What he must remember is that there is no magic either in mixed schools or segregated schools. A mixed school with poor unsympathetic teachers, with hostile public opinion, and no teaching of the truth concerning black folks is bad. A segregated school with ignorant placeholders, inadequate equipment, and poor salaries is equally bad. Other things being equal, the mixed school is the broader, more natural basis for the education of all youth. It gives wider contacts; it inspires greater self-confidence, and suppresses the inferiority complex. But other things seldom are equal, and in that case, Sympathy, Knowledge, and the Truth outweigh all that the mixed school can offer. (Du Bois, 1935, pp. 334–335)

As W. E. B. Du Bois challenged his peers in the 1930s to consider the profound and contradictory consequences of "mixed schools," so, today, the nation writhes in a moment of painful reflection on desegregation. Since 1960, public schools in the United States have become substantially less integrated by both race and class (Orfield, Easton, & The Harvard Project, 1996; see Taylor, Piche, & Trent, 1997). The notion of K–12 integration has become passe, unrealistic, or undesirable for many. Instead, as Gary Orfield and colleagues (1996) argue, too many communities are rushing toward neighborhood schools. Du Bois is rapidly becoming a prophet into the twenty-first century.

Over the past few years, Denver, Seattle, Kansas City, Buffalo, Little Rock, and scores of other communities around the country have been released from their desegregation agreements. It was too hard, not effective, or not enforced. There may be few communities still willing to try to make real the dream of *Brown v. Board of Education* and Martin Luther King, Jr.

So, too, national opinion shifts, refracted by race. A 1998 Public Agenda survey found that

> African-American and white parents see great value in having their children attend integrated schools. About 8 in 10 black parents and 66% of white parents say it is very or somewhat important to them that *their own child's* school be racially integrated. . . . [But] despite widespread support for the concept, there is a distinctive lack of energy and passion for integration among both black and white parents. Only a slim majority of black parents (52%) say the nation should do more to integrate schools. It is even harder to detect an appetite among whites for invigorating integration efforts: Only 27% want the U.S. to do more. (p. 11; emphasis in original)

The ambivalence about K–12 integration is palatable. In higher education, the retreat from integration is far more explicitly mean-spirited. In the 1990s, public universities on both coasts began to lock their doors to poor and working-class students, especially students of color. In the West, California's public universities radically rolled back on affirmative action, substantially reducing the numbers of African American, Latina/o, and Native American applicants and students accepted. In the East, the trustees of the City University of New York have waged a battle to restrict open admissions and withdraw remediation at 4-year colleges, thereby denying educational access to thousands of poor and working-class students of all racial and ethnic groups (for evidence in support of affirmative action higher education, see Bowen & Bok, 1998). At this contentious moment in history, we write with the gall, the desire, and the sense of obligation to insist on public educational spaces that promise integration, offer democracy, and assure racial and class justice—before the bleach gets us all.

Over 2 years, we have had an opportunity, generously supported by the Spencer and Carnegie Foundations, to collaborate on a study of high school de-tracking in northern New Jersey, the fourth most segregated state in the nation. This is a district in which students, primarily Whites and Blacks, range from extremely poor to extremely wealthy; a district in which all schools are "integrated" by court order, but where the high school tracking system of high honors, honors, and regular tends to resegregate. High school students across race and across social-class lines rarely mingle during their academic periods.

Montclair, New Jersey, is one of the few communities nationwide that has worked to keep the dream of integration alive, not without troubles, not without disappointments, not without a court order. But the town has struggled to provide both excellent and equitable education to all its students—poor, working class, middle class, and rich; White, African American, biracial, Latino, Asian American.

In this high school, in 1993, educators took it upon themselves to challenge the school's (and district's) structure of tracking. Educators in the English Department, inspired (and then chaired) by Bernadette Anand, argued that ninth-grade English be de-tracked for all students, offered at the level of high honors (for a review of tracking research, see Oakes, Wells, Yonezawa, & Ray, 1997). A World Literatures course, with high standards for all, would be taken by all.

Predictably, as Wells and Serna (1996) have written, the town blew up and, as predictably, it eventually settled down (for a history, see Fine, Weis, & Powell, 1997; Karp, 1993; Manners, 1998). Since that time, the current mayor has run on a platform to do away with the course, on which the school board is deeply split. Some Whites protested publicly that their children's chances of admission to Ivy League colleges would be jeopardized, and a number pulled their children out of the public schools. A small subset of the Black and White middle-class/elite families were concerned but remained publicly quiet. Yet a powerful multiracial and cross-class coalition of educators, parents, and community activists organized and prevailed. The ninth-grade World Literatures course has celebrated its fifth birthday in 1998. Still treated officially like a family secret, many in the community recognize it as a family jewel ("No Racism Found . . . ," 1998).

With this brief history, we now wander into this course to understand how a space for youth can be designed within a public school both to produce "smarts" in all and to model racial/class democracy. Drawing on 2 years of Michelle's participant observation (2 days per week, sitting in on five classes per day) and more than 50 years of combined public education experience for Bernadette, Carlton, and Dana, we write this chapter from our very different standpoints. For 2 years, Michelle observed a series of ninth-grade World Literature classes that embody the best of this town. In this course, students reading on a third-grade level converse, write, argue, and finish projects with students who have been reading the likes of Morrison, Whitman, Homer, and Cisneros since they were quite young. In this class, the chasms of race and, more precisely, of class are bridged by the talent of educators, the rigor of the curriculum, and the elasticity of youth. Everyone has been reading *Of Mice and Men* (Steinbeck, 1937), the *Gilgamesh* epic (1992), *Nectar in a Sieve* (Markandaya, 1954), *Antigone* (Sophocles, 1984), and *Two Old Women* (Wallis, 1994). Everyone is writing critical essays, literary reviews, creative works, and character analyses. Students who have been educated, to date, within relatively segregated gifted classes are hearing voices they had never before heard. Students who had been in segregated special education classes are learning they have things to say, poetry to write, critical analyses that deserve public audience. The choreography of the teaching is breathtaking—and exhausting.

On Monday and Friday mornings, in chairs too hard for my aging body, I (Michelle) am the delighted, intellectual voyeur to this work of integrated education. High-quality courses, rigorous standards, and heterogeneous groups of students engage together to produce new forms of knowledge, discovering how narrowly we have circumscribed what counts as "smart," inviting buried treasures to speak, creating at once a community of intellectuals and citizens.

But this work has a price tag. To educate all thoroughly, efficiently, and in sprawling multiracial communities means that a community must take seriously the costs of busing, early education, multicultural curriculum, professional development for teachers, even summer courses for those who are falling behind. The price will not be extravagant, but high-quality education costs.

Throughout this chapter, we reflect critically on 2 years' worth of data, and present the patterns of two cohorts of students, each moving through the course of 1 year. We consider how a space within public school, marked by race and class integration, stretches to create an intellectually engaging context for all. At one and the same time, these three teachers work to inspire and support those students who enter the course biographically assured of their (assumed natural) academic advantages *and* those students who have long been convinced of their (assumed natural) *in*ability to work through challenging texts. While inviting new voices to speak, they also insist on an ethic of respectful listening. This is a space that constructs what Jana Sawicki (1991) calls "radical pluralism," that enables a re-vision of social possibilities for and by youth. We trace the bumpy road of this space—contradiction-filled, if thoroughly integrated—recognizing how increasingly rare such spaces are today in U.S. public schools. Drawn from Michelle's participant observation and grounded in interactions in and beyond Carlton's and Dana's classrooms, we collectively write a biography of a public space for intentional interruption, a space for rigorous democracy, grown among youth and adults across "differences."

The text carries the powerful legacy of Bernadette Anand, evident in her words throughout, as we examine classrooms constructed by Carlton and Dana. No longer at the high school, Bernadette is the principal of a highly respected, very rigorous, extremely diverse middle school in Montclair. In this story, we are self-conscious that the text moves across an academic year as if September through June represented a "true" line of progress. Instead, as any educator will attest, a school year is punctuated by loops, surprises, backslides, and rewinds. September to June does, however, capture a flow of the class, a set of collective moves over time. Indeed, some incidents and relations that happen in June could not have occurred in September.

I (Michelle) delight in this narrative journey because these three educators have enabled and invited us all to look closely at a space in which racial, gendered, and economic power are self-consciously analyzed and interrupted; a space in which re-vision is insisted upon; a space orchestrated and negotiated by educators who dare to challenge *The Bell Curve* (Hernstein & Murray, 1996), refuse to hide behind the illusion of "neutrality," demand high standards for all, and well up with tears when most students rise to the occasion.

The educational project cultivated here necessitates that educators and youth create a space of intentional interruption in which young people can think through World Literature and the complex relations of class, race, gender, and sexuality around the globe. This is a space in which all ninth-graders are included: those delighted, those appalled, and those terrified.

A space in which youth, across race and class, engage with vigor will never occur by chance, by accident, or without leadership. Nor will it be applauded by our colleagues, supervisors, parents, or students in unison. And yet, we assume in this chapter, and in our work, that this is precisely our public responsibility—to create just such classrooms for and with youth.

(SEPTEMBER–NOVEMBER)
THE VICTIM-BLAMING MANTRA

With texts, students, anxieties, memories, colleagues, budget crises, faculty cuts, and wild anticipation, the year opens. It's September and we bend the spines of new books, launch new lives, try novel identities, and sneak toward new relationships among these 14- and 15-year-old bodies filled with delight, dread, hormones, excitement, premature boredom. For some, the room is filled with friends. For all, the room is also filled with strangers.

Today, they're discussing *Of Mice and Men* (Steinbeck, 1937), in particular George and Lennie's relationship at the end of the book. Carlton Jordan asks his students to form what he calls a value line: "Stand on my right if you think it was right for George to kill Lennie. Stand on my left if you don't. Stand in the middle if you are of both minds."

Much to my (Michelle) surprise (and dismay?), the room tips to the right. The crowd moves in those loud clumsy teenage feet over toward the "it's OK to kill" side. I look for patterns by gender, race. Nothing. To the left wander three boys, a bit surprised and embarrassed, two White and one Black, feeling like they are going to lose. "But it's never OK to kill a friend," insists Joshua.

Carlton, momentarily stunned but never stumped by his "pedagogical failure" to get equally distributed groups, undermining his "plan" to set up pairs to discuss their positions, invites them to sit in groups and discuss.

The "it's OK to kill a friend" group gets loud, animated, vile. "Lennie's stupid." "He's the biggest retard in the world. He likes to pet dead rabbits. He don't need to live," shouts Kizzy—Muslim, brass, wonderful, noisy, always the voice that provokes Darren, an African American boy, to respond with emotion. Sofia continues, "He should have killed Lennie long ago; he's a burden." Kizzy continues: "He's stupid. He murdered cold-blooded. We got to make him bad if we're gonna get George off." Eli joins, "By killing him, it was like saving a life."

Carlton and I exchange glances. I'm thrown by the raw but vicious analyses of these young adolescents and their endless creativity. The screams of "stupid, useless, dumb" are rusting my soul.

Carlton is as visibly shaken as I am. A strong, bold African American educator, he begins to teach, to preach, to speak with his heart, his eyes, his arms, and his mouth. "Let me say something about Lennie, because, as I walk around, I am disturbed. What are the characteristics of Lennie?"

The class volunteers: "Stupid, slow, dumb!"

Carlton continues. "Dumb. Retarded. When you use language like that, I have to speak. You may say it was right for George to kill Lennie because Lennie killed someone else or Lennie would have been killed. There are many reasons. But because [he] is stupid, slow, no. Some of you have learning disabilities. Some of you have persons with autism or retardation in your family. And none of us knows what's coming next. It is important to see Lennie as a man, as a human being, not as something that should be destroyed."

Kizzy: "But he stupid. You are coming down on our group."

My mind wanders. Remembering the calls [from some White parents] to the superintendent about "them," remembering talk at the school board about how "those students" will hold back "the motivated ones," I am brought back to the room by Carlton's voice. "Some of you have been called stupid by others. You have to think about what it's like to be in a world where everyone seems to be getting it right, and you don't even know what you don't know. Some of you sit in lunchroom and won't eat tuna sandwiches because you're going to save the dolphins, but you'd laugh at Lennie in our school. Some of you will send money to Rwanda and Bosnia to save children over there. But you would make fun of Lennie, throw stones or shun Lennie over here." The students have reproduced the discourse being narrated about them. "George should not be burdened by Lennie." That is just what some at the school board meeting were implying.

Carlton: "Let me say, I take this personally. If you can't walk with Lennie, if you can't see Lennie as a human, as a brother, what future is there for our community? What possibilities are there for us as a whole?"

Class is over. I'm feeling exhausted and depleted, and amazed at the strength of a teacher willing to speak, interrupt, listen, and educate. After a weekend of worries and exchanged phone messages with Carlton, I returned to class on Monday to re-find "community," orchestrated by Carlton, already at play.

The lecture opens with a discussion of first-person and third-person narratives. Carlton asks students to "turn to a page of *Of Mice and Men* where George and Lennie are interacting. I want you to rewrite the passage as Lennie. In first person narrative. To see how Lennie's wheels turn."

"What wheels?" snipes Paul.

The students clip through the text, muttering, but writing eagerly. Carlton waits patiently for volunteers. Hands shoot up. "I am just a happy man, likin' my rabbits." "Why George callin' me a stupid so and so." Hands of all hues fill the air. The room is alive with Lennies.

"How do you feel?" asks Carlton. "Stupid?" The point was made. Carlton was crafting a community not yet owned by students, but the students were growing extensions with which to connect in the room and beyond.

A parallel exchange occurs in Dana's classroom, early in October. Note how powerfully the character of George is relentlessly protected by the students, while Lennie is ruthlessly discarded as if disposable.

Charles: George is trying and Lennie is holding him back.

Erika: Lennie died happily. George did what he had to do. He gave a final request about rabbits. It's not right to kill, though.

Ben: It's not George's fault.

Dana: Why not?

Ben: If he had known what Lennie was thinking, maybe. But George is off the hook.

Dana: Who is solely responsible for ending the life of Lennie?

Angela: I still feel exactly the way I did before what you said. Lennie couldn't live.

.

.

.

Shana: George wanted Lennie to die. It's not fair for Lennie. Maybe George, in the back of his mind, Lennie was such a burden.
Mikel: I'm not sure, Curley was going to do something. George protected himself.
Liza: Lennie is a nothing. He's a *sausage!*
Dana: Is it hard to hang out from Lennie's point of view?
(Dana and Carlton insist, but don't yet prevail. The students in September and October refuse to view social relations from the bottom.)

Across the five classes, we hear a ringing, shared, often painfully victim-blaming consensus—in September and October—in which most *who speak* agree that Lennie is a "loser," a "leech," a "sausage," and that social relations are inherently and fundamentally hierarchical, competitive, and back-biting. These are the Reagan–Bush and now Clinton children of the 1990s. These are the children who have been raised on policies that are anti-immigrant, antiwelfare, anti–public sector, pro–death penalty, anti–affirmative action, "national/maternal" ideological milk. And many seemingly swallowed. If I (Michelle) were to report on only what I heard from September through November, the Right could relax. These preadolescent youths have been well trained by a nation armed with victim-blaming rhetoric. In the beginning of the year, while there are pockets of silence and some raised eyebrows, moments of "Wait a minute . . .," we hear mostly that "murder and crime can keep the population down," that George was "entitled" and Lennie "dispensable." And so, too, we witness fatigued teachers, still standing in the front of the room, trying to create a space that provides a view from the bottom, a moment of empathy, a peek from another angle. In the interim, victim-blaming analyses, a longstanding tradition in the United States—in a kind of White and Black hegemony—can be (and were) a horror to progressive educators standing in front or sitting in the back of the room. Yet in this class, over time, many students are encouraged to produce kaleidoscopic understandings of social issues, to engage standpoints that are shifting, and to reject victim blaming.

By mid-October, having finished *Of Mice and Men* (Steinbeck, 1937), Dana's class has moved on to *Two Old Women* by Velma Wallis (1994), a Native American woman from Alaska who retells a story told to her by her mother. The story tells the tale of two old women left to die, abandoned by their community.

Dana: In the book *Two Old Women*, where two Alaskan women are left to
   die by their tribes, should the two old women have forgiven the tribe?
Ben: Maybe they should. It was their time to go. It was their survival.
Dana: I heard that for George [protection of the powerful].
Michael: I don't think they should forgive because they weren't helpless or
   lame. Just old. It wasn't right. They shouldn't forgive.
Angela: I was raised to believe old are wiser and keep heritage alive. From
   old you get new experiences, but young have little to offer. Even
   though they were old they were strongest in the book. Like Lennie.
Ben: If they didn't forgive, they couldn't last long. If we saved all old, we'd
   be overpopulated. Murder and crime may keep this earth's population in
   balance.
Dana: Do we bear *no responsibility* in the taking care of?

   In the beginning of the school year, there are typically few who will
publicly annotate a perspective from the bottom. And yet, by November
students like Michael [Black boy] and Angela [White girl] are beginning
to chance another point of view, beginning to notice that something is
different. Their teacher is not simply a carrier of dominant views, rein-
forcing only the view from above. Dana and Carlton are offering many
lines of vision and insisting that challenging whispers get a hearing when
they are voiced.
   It is toward the end of this season of victim-blaming chill, when parental calls to the superintendent start to come in, demanding to know
why Candace didn't get an A on the first draft, why Dana is "bending over
backward for *some* students," why Carlton is having "political" and not
"literary" discussions. These are the days when "everyone has a choice" is
declared as truth by some students, when victims are blamed and those
who challenge social arrangements grow suspect—students and teachers
alike. But work is yet to be done. And at this point in the class, all students suspect that something is up. The dominant conversation prevails,
but on its last legs for this year.

(DECEMBER–FEBRUARY) THE MELTING,
AND THEN PARTIAL RESTORATION, OF PRIVILEGE

Creating an intentionally interruptive space that is also safe for all means
breaking down the invisible walls that segregate those historically privileged from those historically silenced, that separate traditionally "smart"
from traditionally "slow," that challenge the categories and "right" answers
that worked so well in the past. Forcing students to "come out" from be-

hind their performances of nerd, athlete, scholar, clown, or dummy, we invite them to reveal and develop deeper, more complex performances of themselves. We model, chance, and push the very categories that they (and we) have taken for granted—categories that have celebrated some while suffocating others. And then, at moments in our classrooms, our attempts at social justice step right on the toes of academic traditions. Ruptures occur. Breaks and fractures explode. Crises boil over. Conflicts erupt. That's when we know we have done our work and that the most serious work of education is ahead of us.

Alas, by December, it is clear that the teachers invest in what might be called standpoint theory, an understanding that people think, feel, see, express, resist, comply, and are silent in accordance with their social power and that a view from the "bottom" may diverge dramatically, critically, and brilliantly from a view from the "top."

Even if a view from the "top" has been the standard, accepted as "best," assured an A+ to date, those standards, oddly, are no longer operating. Equally rigorous, new standards are emerging. We turn now to a discussion of the book *Nectar in a Sieve* (Markandaya, 1954), an analysis of dharma, fate, and hope, to notice the early awkward stages of trying to get all voices heard, without privileging elite or dominant perspectives that have long passed as the only form of "smart."

Seri (mixed-race boy): People *live* based on hope.

Alison (White girl): I think that's *sad*. If it's just based on hope, you need to study.

Pam (White girl): You need not just *hope* but *goals*.

Cecil (Black boy): My *hopes* are to do the best that I can, be a musician and NBA player.

Danielle (White girl): I think it's true. Everybody has *one dream* and they have to accomplish the dream.

Carlton: What keeps you in school?

Chris (White boy): I think about school, it's the future. College and further, career, family, and support.

James (White boy): Work hard.

Sara (White girl): My *goals* are based on education, not McDonald's.

Cecil: I would rather have McDonald's.

Sara (White girl): I don't want to *depend* on a husband or taxpayers or my parents.

Alison: Most people only have *hope*. That's sad.

Kareem (Black boy): Animals don't have hope, only people. Animals have instinct.

MF [*Fieldnotes*]: It's polarizing: Blacks defend hope and Whites defend
    ambition/goals as if hope were silly, as if this dichotomy made sense!
Hannah (*White girl*): Lennie doesn't know what hope means but he hopes to
    be as smart as George.
Qwuinette (*Black girl*): He does have hope.
Alison: Maybe ignorant people have more hope and smarter people are more
    cynical.
Cecil: You've got to be kidding!

Cecil carries the momentum here. The room spins, the conversation
stops and then begins again, changed. These critical turns, upon which our
pedagogy relies, are as necessary as they are unpredictable. We yearn to
understand how we can nurture, cultivate, fertilize our rooms so that critical turns get a voice—and eventually get a hearing.

At this point, "smarts" are popping out of unsuspected mouths, bodies buried into oversized jackets. At the same time, perhaps in response,
there is a parallel move, a polarizing performance. So, for instance, Blacks
defend hope and Whites defend ambition/goal as though these were sepa-
rable. As previously unheard voices sing, there is a subtle polarizing, a
freezing of positions. Now that the voices are up, there is nothing automatic about creating a community of differences in this space.

It's becoming clear that student identities ranging from "smart" to
"disengaged" to "at-risk" are unraveling—not so predictable. In integrated
schools, as Du Bois worried, sorting typically means that a small core of
students, usually White and/or middle-class students, rise like cream to
the top and blossom as institutional signifiers of merit, smarts, advanced
achievement (Bowles & Gintis, 1976; Moore & Davenport, 1989; Ryan,
1971). It is their loss most profoundly dreaded by public education. Today
urban and suburban school boards live in terror of losing White and middle-
class students across races and do all they can to keep them—even if that
means holding other students hostage (Kohn, 1997; Sapon-Shevin, 1994).
And yet this splitting is, as Eve Sedgwick (1990) would argue, fundamentally parasitic. The structural splitting elevates one group while it *requires*
that others (Blacks, working-class/poor, disabled students) be seen as lacking. Funneled through a lens of hierarchy and limited goods, standards,
achievements, and excellence demand exclusivity. Michel Foucault (1977),
Erika Apfelbaum (1979), and, most recently, Jean Anyon (1998) have
argued in very different contexts that power is always in and around classrooms. No classroom is Teflon-resistant to the winds of racialized, gendered,
classed, and homophobic elements in America. The splitting into "good
students" and "remedial students," which characterizes high schools and

is interrupted in this classroom, reveals the workings of power. The ethnographic work in this classroom renders visible how power and privilege are ruthlessly enacted in integrated classrooms, evident particularly when educators seek to interrupt racialized and classed hierarchies.

Power operates as a set of social relations both inside and beyond the room. Outside the room, power is assured by the watchful surveillance of a resistant mayor and some school board members who threaten to "shut down" the course for fear of White/middle-class exodus from the public school and by the few educators and colleagues annoyed that these teachers dare to educate all to high standards, trivializing their work as "frills—more politics than rigor."

Within the room, as new voices emerge, mostly heretofore unheard Black voices, a kind of polarizing occurs. Again a small group of White students may decide to sit together, to reinforce each other's points, synchronize eye rolls when a student of color speaks. In ironic similarity to the oft-repeated "Why do all the Black students sit together?" at this point in the semester, there is a consolidation of a White-resistant position— not all, just a few, but enough to chill the room. The days of listening to "them" are over. It's important to note that most White and most Black students don't glacialize. But most are at a loss for how to engage this conversation outside the polarities.

Then I have a frightening thought: Is it possible that Whites work "optimally," that is, uninterrupted, when we *don't* have to discuss race and ethnicity and that students of color can only be engaged and most unburdened when race and ethnicity are squarely on the table? (See Billig, 1995; Fraser, 1990.)

As Linda Powell (1997) argues, it seems likely that students of color are "stuck" until "race" is discussed, while White students are "stuck" once race is discussed. Teachers (or students) who speak through race, ethnicity, and class in the curriculum get accused of dwelling on race—again! And a few outspoken White parents "save" the White students (through phone calls) from the conversation.

By January, midterm grades are in, and the old stratification system is not layered like it used to be—no longer a two-tiered White and Black cake. Carlton and Dana have been reading aloud to the class some of the writings of students who sound like poets, like journalists, like creative writers. Sometimes a White kid raises an embarrassed hand when Carlton asks "Whose paper is this?" As often an African American boy from the back of the room will lift a reluctant finger, or an African American girl will hide her giggle as she sashays up to the front of the room to reclaim her text. This moment is one of both racialized melting and desperate consolidation of racial privilege. The contrast sails through the room. Stakes are growing clear, as the educators are riding broncos of resistance. This is a crucial moment in a space designed to interrupt, a moment in which many give up. But listen and you'll hear that these educators are relentless—over Starbucks—in their commitments to re-vision.

Bernadette: When you publicly state to the community, when you're only one course in the sea of all the other courses, that you truly believe in multiculturalism, and then you make the literature, the part, the actual content to open up those issues and the students begin to see the connections. And I think, even if they don't at the beginning, all of a sudden the other voices that never got heard someplace down below, they may have had these people in the classroom with them, all of a sudden these voices come and somebody turns around and says, "Whoa!" And they'll say that to you. They'll say, "I didn't know so-and-so was so smart." And then, someone else's voice is honored, is sort of affirmed through that one student, and through yours. And everybody starts, the classroom is never the same after that.

Dana: That's when the phone calls, that's when you start getting calls. When you start, when other voices start to be heard and the kids start to see that you're actually giving validity to other writers, and then they see that when certain kids, the kids who are always there at the center of the room, start to see that they're not any longer the center of the room, all of this subversive activity starts. And the challenging, the constant challenging of your ethics and of your teaching ability. . . .

Carlton: It's like a disability of privilege. What are they holding onto? But the only way they can make the connection is to co-opt it, that it has to become *their* hurricane. They have to define how the winds move and whether they go from north to south. If it's not mine, how do I conquer it? I know it better than everyone else and will make people listen to me. This is a problem of privilege that needs remediation in our course.

At this point, a small set of relatively well-off White students (not all, but a few in particular and in full voice) search to reclaim status by displaying their family treasures, what Pierre Bourdieu (1991) would call cultural capital: "My mother is a literary agent, and she said *Two Old Women* never would have been published if the author wasn't a Native woman." "Have you read any of Sigmund Freud? My father is a psychoanalyst, and he would contest your interpretation." "My mother is the chair of the board of _____ and she said that Camden is lucky that outsiders have invested money because there was *nothing* there before." Some, at this point, less decorated with biographic merit badges, simply assert that "Today, in this country, we *all* have choices." Oppression and history are deemed largely irrelevant. A few gracefully sneer or turn away when students of color talk about race (not again!). I (Michelle) time the conversations that address race: The average conversation lasts 30 seconds. The record conversation lasted 45 seconds before someone shifted to, "But I don't think it's race, it's class." "It's age." "What about Whites in basketball?" "What about sexism?" "How about when you say faggot?" "But the Holocaust was . . ." And we're off . . .

Old lines are being redrawn, gentrification in academic blood. A sharpened White line of demarcation is being drawn. Interestingly, most White students refuse to employ these displays or barricade themselves, but they don't know what else to do. They can't yet invent another discourse of Whiteness. And so they retreat to a kind of silence, sometimes wonder, sometimes embarrassment. A few seem delighted that those who have always "won"—from prekindergarten to eighth grade—are not the automatic victors in this class. Like a fight in a hockey game, it is part of the work—not an interruption and not a failure. Re-vision. There is more to learn on the other end of this struggle.

(MARCH–APRIL) PLAYING WITH POWER, SHIFTING AND REVERSALS

It's been a long stretch, but some of those students who never expected to be seen as smart, never expected to get a hearing from teachers or peers, are now opening their mouths, challenging myths and stereotypes, rejecting lines of vision from the top represented as if "natural" or "what everyone believes." And these challenges are getting a hearing.

There is a long conversation about the story *The Legend of La Llorana*, by Rudolpho Anaya (1991), a literary giant of a text about Cortez and Malintzin, about the conquest of Mexico. In the final scene, Cortez is invited to return to his homeland in Spain. Cortez insists upon taking his sons to Spain, lest they become "savages" and "uncivilized." In response, Malintzin, their mother, a native unwilling (and uninvited) to go to Spain, ultimately kills the boys in the belief that their death will liberate the people of Mexico. Dana has invited the students to prepare a mock trial of Malintzin.

"Is she guilty for having killed her children?" The pros and cons polarize almost immediately. The most vocal White students form a chorus, "You should never kill your children." "She must have been crazy." The most vocal African American students circle around another question, "What do you have to do in order to survive oppression?" Four Black boys refuse to take sides, "You never kill *and* it was a time of incredible oppression."

Aziz, an African American boy, breaks the stalemate, reversing the power and insisting that the trial of Malintzin is itself contained within colonialism. He queries, "Why is Malintzin on trial? Why isn't the Captain [Cortez] on trial?" At once the air thins, the fog lifts, the fists of power are sitting in the center of the room. The debate is not about Malintzin's innocence or guilt but rather about who decides what is the crime—colonialism of a race or murder of two children? Now, three-quarters the way through the term, questions of power are engaged, often, but not always, by African American males like Aziz.

The theater is alive. Girls, for the most part, are carrying on the debate about social injustice. Some African American girls assert their position in a discourse of power and inequality. In response, some White girls displace a discourse of power with a discourse of psychology, motivation, and equal opportunity. Trying to be sympathetic and inclusive, they may offer up universals such as "everyone loves their children" or "we were all raised to try to achieve," while African American girls, equally insistent, are more likely to draw attention to power, difference, and inequality. Typically an African American girl is pressing a question of race, class, and gender alone, and yet she stands sturdy, bold, and alone, often without support in the room. The room coalesces around its desire for her just to stop. The end of the year is riddled with a series of power eruptions. The dominant hold is cracking and freeing everyone. Splinters fly.

(MAY–JUNE) COALITIONS, STANDPOINTS, SPEAKING TRUTH TO POWER— PREPARING FOR THE "REAL WORLD"

This course is messy. Little can be said that is linear, developmental, moving forward in a predictable line. And yet, with strong pedagogical commitments and the reading of great literatures these educators invite young minds to travel, to tackle the perspective of others, to review their perspectives of self. In this context, there are sometimes fleeting and sometimes sustained moments of coming together across "differences."

Students stretch, as a collective, to cross borders of race, class, gender, and "difference" and meet each other in a June Jordan poem, mourning for Rukmani, angry at Cortez, re-citing what Lennie in *Of Mice and Men* (Steinbeck, 1937) might have really been thinking. These moments of coming together are, for us, the hope, the point, the real metaphor for America as it could be. For in these moments of coming together, students and faculty embody their differences in a chorus of voices, in a tapestry of cloth, in a fruit stand of delicious points of view. Very smart and bold, not

compromising, not "Whiting out" differences, not "not noticing" but standing together, even if for a moment, challenging the separations that we
adults—the "other" America—try to impose on them. Coming together
to build knowledge, community, and serious intellectual work through
and across race, ethnicity, class, and gender.

From May through the end of the term, students have learned to
engage in this space, for 45 minutes a day, with power, "differences," and
a capacity to re-vision. Some with delight and some still disturbed. Everyone will get a chance to speak and be heard. They will be surprised, still,
to learn that "*she* said something so smart" or "*he* plays golf?" By now
(finally), it is no longer rare to hear White students refer to, grow a conversation off of, interrupt with praise, or even disagree with students of
color, or to observe African American students challenging, extending, or
asking a question of a White student. These may sound like minor accomplishments, but in a sea of parallel lives stratified by geography, class, color,
friends, language, dress, music, and structures of tracking around them,
the moments of working together, not always friendly or easy but engaged
across, are worth comment. For these are moments that, once strung together, weave a frayed tapestry of cross-racial/class practice inside and
outside of schooling. It is at this point in the semester when students assert positions from a standpoint. And they shift. They may risk a statement
that will get little support from peers; they may dare to not support a lifelong ally/neighbor/friend; they may wander into a more treacherous alli-
ance with someone previously unknown; they may challenge a comment
that sounds, on the face, racist or homophobic even if a Black person, or
a White person, uttered it. They may opt for a co-authored poem, a joint
extension project. It is in this moment that the tears of the ethnographer
fall too easily, when after a protracted conversation about race and power,
John, a young man I had "coded" as middle-class and Black, offered, "These
conversations are very hard for me. I understand both points of view. You
all think I'm Black, but actually my mom is White and I could take either
position in the room. But I don't talk much because I don't think anyone
will catch my back." His eyes fill with tears as do those of many others in
the room. There is a stunning silence. "I just felt confused." At which point,
from across the room, on the diagonal, Eddie has begun the pulse of clap-
ping that waves across the 24 young men and women. The writing has
changed, sometimes dramatically.

At this point in the year, the end, at the just-arrived-at point of fragile, transitory, fleeting cross-race and -class alliances, students "choose"
what level of courses they will pursue in the tenth grade. This school is as
hyperbolically organized as most integrated schools: The three tenth-grade
tracks are high honors, honors, and regular. High honors is the level at

which ninth-grade English is offered, doubling in tenth grade as Advanced Placement. Regular is the more remedial level of English.

One day in the spring, I was shadowing a young White ninth-grader, Zach. It was the day he had to "choose" the level for his tenth-grade social studies. He and two African American ninth-grade male students opted for high honors. I noted to myself how unusual it was for two African American boys, in this system, to self-select into high honors. The town is filled with scuttlebutt that "the reason so few African Americans are in high honors is that they don't *choose*. Peer pressure, wanting to be with their friends, low self/teacher expectations keep them out." Now, the threesome approached the social studies teacher's desk and requested high honors. To my surprise, loud enough for us all to hear, the teacher responded, "High honors? You three are not mature enough to be in high honors. Honors will do."

Zach, humiliated, visibly hurt and shaken, began pounding desks and lockers, insisting he would call his parents and appeal the teacher's decision (all quite admissible in this "choice" system). I approached the two other young men, the African American students, and explained that they, too, could appeal. I would be glad to call home and suggest that their mother, father, or guardian elect high honors. They both "independently" responded, "No, that's OK. I can be in honors. That will be fine." And therein lies the perverse consequences of tracking, the limits of a "space" designed to interrupt hierarchy. As Franz Fanon (1967) predicted, Zach, the White boy, will appeal with an appropriate sense of outrage and entitlement. And he will prevail. The African American boys didn't, couldn't, didn't believe it was worth it, didn't believe they deserved it. No matter what the interior dialogue, the micropolitics of race and class operate through the bodies, the minds, the resistances, the assumptions, and the resignations of youth.

On good days, I (Michelle) am simply thrilled with the possibilities released in this course, this classroom, the intellectual, political, and relational opportunities launched from within this space. On bad days, when state and local budgets are so obviously and grossly cut with the blades of racism and classism, I despair. I despair that this course is a simple wrinkle in an otherwise fundamentally stratified national school system. Those with too much privilege fear so much their loss of privilege. And those with so little privilege are too delighted to not be in Newark. I despair that this course is not a free space at all, but an illusion of democratic access and engagement within a sedimented racial hierarchy, a number-by-color meritocracy, a cosmetic fissure in an otherwise fixed race/class formation. On really bad days, I worry it may be a con for students, a ploy, a tease, a contradiction. And at these moments, over something stronger than coffee, I turn to my colleagues, and we remember the power of the space in freeing an imagination for racial justice. We yearn for more such spaces but also recognize the power of the interruption. While we shiver over the ruthless onward march of systemic racism, we find comfort in the fissure within hierarchy and the gift these teachers have shared in this space with their students. We end this essay as we often end our coffee-based professional development, with the teachings of Maxine Greene (1995):

> We all learn to become human, as is well known, within a community of some kind or by means of some kind of social medium. The more fully engaged we are, the more we can look through other's eyes, the more richly individual we become. The activities that compose learning not only engage us in our own quests for answers and for meanings; they also serve to initiate us into the communities of scholarship and (if our perspectives widen sufficiently) into the human community, in its largest and richest sense. (p. 3)

Acknowledgement: We wish to thank the Spencer Foundation, the Carnegie Foundation, and Teachers College Press for their support, and Jenni Hoffman and Steven Fine for their fine assistance.

REFERENCES

Anaya, R. A. (1991). *The legend of La Llorona: A short novel.* Berkeley, CA: TQS Publications.

Anyon, J. (1998). *Ghetto schooling.* New York: Teachers College Press.

Apfelbaum, E. (1979). Relations of domination and movement for liberation: An analysis of power between groups. In W.G. Austin & S. Worchel (Eds.), *The social psychology of intergroup relations* (pp. 188–204). Belmont, CA: Wadsworth.

Billig, M. (1995). *Banal nationalism.* London: Sage.

Bourdieu, P. (1991). *Symbolic power.* Cambridge, MA: Harvard University Press.

Bowen, W. G., & Bok, D. C. (1998). *The shape of the river: Long-term consequences of considering race in college and university admissions.* Princeton, NJ: Princeton University Press.

Bowles, S., & Gintis, H. (1976). *Schooling in capitalist America: Educational reform and the contradictions of economic life.* New York: Basic Books.

Du Bois, W. E. B. (1935). Does the Negro need separate schools? *Journal of Negro Education, 4,* 328–335.

Fanon, F. (1967). *Black skin, White masks.* New York: Grove Press.

Fine, M., Weis, L. & Powell, L. (1997). Communities of difference. *Harvard Educational Review, 67,* 270–284.

Foucault, M. (1977). *Discipline and punish: The birth of the prison.* New York: Pantheon.

Fraser, N. (1990). Rethinking the public sphere: A contribution to the critique of actually existing democracy. *Social Text, 8–9*, 56–80.

Gilgamesh: A new rendering in English verse. (1992). New York: Farrar Straus & Giroux.

Greene, M. (1995). *Releasing the imagination.* San Francisco: Jossey-Bass.

Hernstein, R. J., & Murray, C. A. (1996). *The bell curve: Intelligence and class structure in American life.* New York: Simon & Schuster.

Karp, S. (1993). Many pieces to the detracking puzzle. *Rethinking Schools, 8,* 16–17.

Kohn, A. (1997). How not to teach values: A critical look at character education. *Phi-Delta-Kappan, 78,* 429–39.

Manners, J. (1998). Repackaging segregation? A history of the magnet school system in Montclair, New Jersey. *Race Traitor, 8,* 51–97.

Markandaya, K. (1954). *Nectar in a sieve.* New York: J. Day Company.

Moore, D. R., & Davenport, S. (1989). *The new improved sorting machine.* Chicago: Designs for Change.

No racism found in Teaneck schools. (1998, June 24). *The Record,* p. B2. Bergen County, NJ.

Oakes, J., Wells, A., Yonezawa, S., & Ray, K. (1997). Equity lessons from detracking schools. In A. Hargreaves (Ed.), *Rethinking educational change with heart and mind* (pp. 43–72). Alexandria, VA: Association for Supervision and Curriculum Development.

Orfield, G., Easton, S., & The Harvard Project. (1996). *Dismantling desegregation.* New York: New Press.

Powell, L. (1997). The achievement knot. In M. Fine, L. Weis, L. Powell, & M. Wong (Eds.), *Off White* (pp. 3–12). New York: Routledge.

Public Agenda. (1998). *Time to move on: African American and White parents set an agenda for public schools.*

Ryan, W. (1971). *Blaming the victim.* New York: Vintage.

Sapon-Shevin, M. (1994). *Playing favorites: Gifted education and the disruption of community.* Albany: State University of New York Press.

Sawicki, J. (1991). *Disciplining Foucault.* New York: Routledge.

Sedgwick, E. (1990). *Epistemology of the closet.* Berkeley: University of California Press.

Sophocles. (1984). *The three Theban plays* (R. Fagles & B. M. W. Knox, Trans.). New York: Penguin.

Steinbeck, J. (1937). *Of mice and men.* New York: Modern Library.

Taylor, W. L., Piche, D., & Trent, W. (Eds.). (1997). The role of social science in school desegregation efforts: The St. Louis example. *Journal of Negro Education, 66,* 153–161.

Wallis, V. (1994). *Two old women.* New York: HarperCollins

Wells, A., & Serna, I. (1996). The politics of culture: Understanding local political resistance to detracking in racially mixed schools. *Harvard Educational Review, 66,* 93–118.

CHAPTER 10

Aesthetic Safety Zones: Surveillance and Sanctuary in Poetry by Young Women

JENNIFER McCORMICK

You look at me
because you want to know.
If I speak, I am to be quieted.
If I move, I am to be stopped.

—"My Abstract Life," Tanzania, age 16

The security apparatus in overcrowded, and New York City high schools consist of guards and machines: approximately 18 to 20 officers per school and technical equipment that includes walk-through metal detectors, x-ray machines, and portable scanners. At Urban High School, 2,500 students wait to be checked for weapons on a daily basis. The body assumes a particular position when one waits. I remember a young woman sitting on the stairs in a foyer area. She is inside the building yet remains outside a main hallway, outside the linear space that enables people to flow between two points. The area functions like a subway platform—those who wait anticipate the passage of time. The girl's shoulders hunch forward. Her head rests in her hands. She stares directly in front of her, mouth pressed in a thin line.

As the student enters the school's front door, she inserts an identification card into an "access" machine. It responds "good morning." It indicates whether she has arrived "early" or "late." It displays a time. If she has committed a violation, a red light blinks on. A yellow light signals her birthday, accompanied by a text that reads "Happy Birthday." We see in the greeting an institution's attempt to anthropomorphize the machine(Richard Blot, personal communication, October, 1997).

Once past the machine, the student places her bookbag on an x-ray conveyor belt. She may then be asked to spread her legs and stretch her hands out in front of her so a security guard can wave a portable metal detector over her body. The demeaning effects of assuming a criminal stance are evident in the following dialogue:

Jennifer: Were you ever scanned?
Tanzania: Yeah, I hated it.
Jennifer: Why did you hate it?
Tanzania: I have to put myself down. I have to put my hands out *(she places her hand on the table in front of us, fingers stretched apart)*. I have to stand straight for a few minutes, legs apart, my hands outstretched in front of me. I have to take my bracelets off, take everything out of my pockets. It's very uncomfortable; I feel embarrassed among everybody else. It's not good. It's not a productive way to start off school. I hate it. I don't feel right. I feel out of my element. (January 1994)

Before beginning her day, Tanzania must take everything out of her pockets and then put her hands out. We begin to see, in her physical submission, traces of Goffman's (1961) "total institution," a central feature of which is the loss of "identity equipment" that made previous conceptions of the self possible. This loss is achieved, in part, when an "inmate" is forced to assume postures that conflict with societal notions of propriety. "Any regulation, command, or task that forces the individual to adopt these movements or postures may mortify [her]self" (p. 22). Outside such "asylums," we control our bodily stances, but with a school's routinized search for potential criminality, the boundary that Tanzania places between "[her] being and [her] environment" is invaded and "the embodiment of the self profaned"(p. 23).

Guards and x-ray scanning machines are now fixtures in schools located in the most highly segregated, most deteriorating neighborhoods of New York City (Devine, 1996). Alongside these interventions exist conditions of overcrowding, inadequate academic preparation, and insufficient access to high-quality curricula. Students move through school doors as a mass. In the classroom they remain largely undifferentiated, and in corridors and the cafeteria they are watched by police and a uniformed security force. These tactics separate teens, who are primarily Black and Latino, into criminal and noncriminal categories

In this dehumanizing atmosphere, I found that poetry provided a means through which four young women gained control over self-representation.

I contend, moreover, that by writing poetry these women constructed a space within, a kind of creative colony that was a haven for individual expression (Fine, Weis, & Powell, 1997). School was thus a contradictory site that both limited and expanded self-perception. "Here was an arena where I could be free—a place where I had the freedom to express myself. Poetry was a small world within the larger world of school" (Tanzania, December 10, 1997). My argument grows out of an analysis of student texts and ethnographic documentation. During 3 years of research in a comprehensive urban high school (1991–1993), I observed students, teachers, guidance counselors, and security guards as they interacted in the hallway, classroom, counselor's office, and student cafeteria. I also conducted poetry workshops. At this time I established contact with four young women—Nikki, Nessa, Jhoy, and Tanzania—and for 2 additional years, I spent time with them in my home, in their homes, in community centers, in local theaters, and while walking through their Brooklyn neighborhood. For 5 years, I listened to their stories, and I read their poetry. Ensuing reflective conversations with Tanzie, Nessa, Nikki, and Jhoy informed the conceptualization of my work.

THE CHAOS WITHIN US

In 1992, I had the good fortune to work with Hermine Meinhard, a poet and a teacher. For an hour every Wednesday, we planned class assignments. Then we walked down crowded corridors, and I watched her elicit poems from groups of students in classrooms that never seemed to have enough desks. Outside these workshops, guards walked the corridors with walkie-talkies. Occasionally they entered classrooms to remove students—interrupting a space that, for some, "still holds out the promise of dialogue . . . and the possibility of narrative " (Devine, 1996, p. 2). In *Maximum Security*, John Devine details the social and economic inequities that render large comprehensive city schools hostile places, institutions that few students choose to attend. He then suggests that the presence of security guards in urban high schools reifies a mind–body split by relegating discipline to a pseudo–police force and leaving instruction to teachers.

Despite the interruptions of the guards, Hermine solicited fragments of experience and urged students to weave an aesthetic whole. By privileging both literal and metaphorical references, the real, the remembered, and the imagined, she helped students seal the images of childhood. Her small voice rose and fell in classrooms that became perfectly still: How do identities affect storytelling? Are stories from home told, or are they left behind? Who keeps the old stories alive? Are identities at war with each other? Do you feel like you have to throw everything away? Your language? Your stories? Tell a story from where you grew up. Tell the stories your grandmother told you.

Hermine believed that "place" generates writing and talked about "the place where I learned to follow whatever obsession was inside of me." Place began as a literal reference and grew into a metaphorical sanctuary inside her mind. Her assignments constructed a refuge for dreams and the flow of memory, allowing teens to access that place where writing occurs. With guidance, students shaped the past: "Take us back to the place you remember. Close your eyes. Does it take you back? What do you see, taste, feel?" Tenth-graders captured the events they witnessed in school, at home, and on the street in spiral notebooks.

These notebooks, decorated with thick markers, became "the place" to record and reflect on lived experience.

> I remember walking around with a notebook, ready to write down what I had seen. I remember being with my father, after church. He was bringing me home in a taxi. We stopped in front of a club, and waited for the light to turn green. I saw a huge group of people outside that club and I thought they were waiting to get in, until I heard the sound of the gunfire. The shots didn't sound real to me; I have defined TV as reality and TV sounds different than gunfire in my face. I wanted to get home and write about how Black men are killing each other; I wanted to tell on people. (Tanzania, December 1997)

Railing against atrocities, bearing witness to them, reveals Tanzie's belief that writing affects social change; at the very least, it implies the hope that someone in the world cares enough about Tanzania to listen to her. That hope was sustained by a poet who read and valued the distinct voices of her students.

Assignments that asked teens to capture the language of the street and record daily events occurred alongside permission to speak through another's body. Hermine brought in newspaper photos of characters that were both provocative and ambiguous and asked the students to write: "Are you male or female? Young or old? Look at that face—its eyes, its mouth. Now see through those eyes, and speak through that mouth" (Hermine, spring 1993). This experimentation with persona may have blurred the distinction between reality and imagination, allowing writers to discard meanings that are seemingly fixed and try on new ways of being. In response to Hermine's request that she wear a mask, Tanzania construed various possibilities for her identity:

> When Miss Meinhard asked us to write through a mask, I was I
> always thought about how many masks I present to the world able
> to write through many masks. I remember asking who do I want to
> show. I remember drawing a happy and a sad face alongside my
> poem. Here were the doors I'd been dying for. By presenting the
> mask, Miss Meinhard allowed me to recognize that I have masks,
> that everyone has masks. She was the only one who asked me to
> do what I wanted. Finally, some adult gave me what I wanted.
> (Tanzania, December 27, 1997)

Doors leading to the embodiment of multiple roles offer powerful alternatives to the criminal and noncriminal categories imposed through high-tech surveillance. They open an imaginative space that is always flexible and often contradictory. Through metaphor, surrealist fantasy, and personification, students rendered temporary constructions of themselves and often subverted all simple pronouncements regarding individuality.

I used Hermine's classes as models for group workshops, reading Nikki Giovanni (1970) to demonstrate how writers express the images in their minds, reading Kincaid (1992) to capture a mother's voice: "On Sundays try to walk like a lady and not like the slut you're so bent on becoming" (p. 4).

Jhoy: My grandmother would never use the word "slut," never.
Jennifer: What word would she use?
Jhoy: She would say, "don't care woman."

Jhoy's poetic language, "don't care woman," spins off multiple meanings and possibilities for identity, while resisting rigidly prescribed norms.

In my workshops, students wrote in small groups, taking turns, speaking, scribbling lines. They would face each other, bodies erect, stopping often to read aloud and laugh. A few came to recognize that within the enabling constraints of a poem, segregated voices (private/public, real/fictitious) can be integrated, and sentiments, often veiled, can be safely revealed.

> Poems are harder to write than stories. You can't ramble in a
> poem. You have to get somewhere quickly. I write to get feeling
> out. My poems don't have story—I want the feeling. I'm not giving
> the story. I'm giving you anger. (Tanzania, December 27, 1997)

Paul Ricoeur (1974) claims that poetic language can subsume a writer, generating a text seeped in its surroundings. Poetry as a direct genre—one that is largely unmediated by self-censorship—serves as a particularly appropriate vehicle through which to perceive the effects of schooling routines. Yet writing it also enables four young women to creatively reconstruct many selves. The flexibility of poetry invited confusion, vulnerability, and anger; through figurative language, Nikki, Nessa, Jhoy, and Tanzania write themselves in opposition to harmless/dangerous labels of "distinction."

> I sit and yell back
> not with words
> but with feelings.
> (Nikki, age 15)

By constructing a space "to yell with feelings," they reach what Audre Lorde (1984) calls the "chaos within us," a chaos that expands their identities despite the reductive practices of an institution.

THE THING AROUND/THE THING WITHIN: IMAGES OF VICTIMIZATION AND ARMOR

The students at Urban High School wait to be checked for weapons, then "stand straight for a few minutes, legs apart hands outstretched" (Interview with Tanzania, January 1994). When logged, they wait again, as a guard takes their names, the date, their ID numbers. Technology—the handheld scanner, the x-ray's conveyor belt, a guard's pen—is mobile; students are not. While poetry is a liberating form, the personae in the poems below never transcend the limits placed upon body and self by reductive routines of surveillance. The subject of every poem is fixed, objectified. At times, she is completely immobile, holding a position that parallels the one she is assigned during intrusive schooling routines. In the following text, Nessa speaks of *the thing around*, an all-consuming object that will eventually "get her." This construal of outside forces that subject or dominate the individual replicates Foucault's contention that we are objects—imprinted, regulated, and surveilled to the point of entrapment (Foucault, 1979). Paradoxically, the poem effectively denies the creative, interactive self that articulates it.

THE THING AROUND

> I'm scared of the thing around
> They're going to get me.

I'm scared of what people say
about me. They don't like me.
Why? because I'm different
from them. I come from a poor
family. Clothes I have to wear
everyday holes in my sneakers.
I'm scared of what's going to
happen to me.

"I" is repeated. It is nearly encircled in the first line: "I'm scared of the thing around." This language echoes a clause in another narrative. During a poetry reading in the school's library, students heard gunfire. Nikki described the event as follows: "We were reading our poetry in the library and we heard shots. They sounded so loud. When I heard those shots, I jumped under the table. Everyone was looking for me." Jhoy added: "Then we heard screeches and the police cars because they're always around the school sometimes." The police surround; they enclose like "the thing around."

Nessa becomes the object of others, of their pronouncements, of their actions. Poverty defines her. In doing so, it seems to construct a fearful passivity. "I'm scared of what people [peers, classmates] say about me. They don't like me. Why? . . . because I come from a poor family." With the fifth line, the sentence structure changes. The "why" indicates that Nessa expects a response. She is conscious of an audience; she approximates dialogue, posing a question and providing the rationale. Through this structure, she places herself within a social context and actively interprets everyday experience. The last line returns to a previous sentence structure; Nessa is the recipient of possible action.

In "The Thing Around," Nessa's agency is never clearly or assertively represented. Yet in "The Troll Is Loose," inspired by an assignment to imagine a physical metamorphosis, the character of the writer/subject changes. She is no longer passive. Transformation invokes a creative freedom that allows Nessa to rename herself and the world around her. However, the ultimate image she constructs is a reflection of immobilization. The author has devised a poetic sanctuary, but she remains frozen within it.

THE TROLL IS LOOSE

I was jumping rope and something weird happened.
I was jumping real fast and it happened.
I turned into a troll.

I had big ugly eyes a big flat nose,
my hair was sticken up. My skin was all bumpy.
I was the worst creature alive.
Everybody was just standing there
in total shock of what happened.
And I don't know what happened to me.
I started chasing them.
Everybody was yelling help help the troll is loose.
I started making a face
and then I turned into a moving tree.
I started knocking people over.
And yelling please make it stop
please. And then I turned into a sculpture
and everybody else went back to a normal life.

But now Nessa is violent, "the worst creature alive." She doesn't want this new form, nor does she get to keep it: "I started knocking people over. And yelling please make it stop please. And then I turned into a sculpture." With each transformation, the writer becomes increasingly stationary until, finally, she is a sculpture—cold, hard and immobile.

Throughout the text, Nessa is subject to her own body, subject to its violence and then to its petrification. Each physical manifestation becomes "the thing around"—not poverty, not the police, and not those who "jump" her. External threats have permeated her consciousness, her physical existence. In a discussion of women's poetry, Alicia Ostriker (1986) states: "Women do not really want to be secure, hard dispassionate objects. They hate it. The flat inflections of their voices say they hate it"(p. 87). If Nessa despises petrification, other students accept its normality. One 14-year-old told me: "My eyes are open at all times because students jump at you for nothing. You can be minding your own business and they hit on you, just to get a rep." Perhaps teens expect images of fortification in a school where people "hit on you" for "every little thing." Yet Nessa moves away from an aggressive persona. She is protected, but immobile. Her exterior can only be defensive. The price of such armor may be self entrapment— "a prison sanctuary which prevents us from entering another's mind" (Ostriker, 1986, p. 171). Nessa wrote "The Troll Is Loose" in response to a teacher/poet's prompt, and she wrote it in a classroom where student poetry was often read to an audience. Even though she is entrapping herself in the text of the poem, the poem provokes connections; by writing it, she increases the likelihood that others will know her. Impermeable imagery seems to contradict creative reproduction, once again revealing the irony of writing a passive self.

Police surveillance, poverty, violence, and the defensive pose clamped on Nessa's body lead to passivity and alienation; these states become "the thing around." Her struggle against this object/thing occurs, in part, through poetry. In the next section, watchfulness, not armor, protects the self, and unlike images of petrification, it interacts.

WATCHFULNESS/SURVIVAL/INDEPENDENCE

> In a way they are trying to take my shield away because with the scanning, they are looking for something I may have concealed. (Tanzania, 17 years old)

In a school where the seemingly contradictory "criminal" and "vulnerable" subject are continually and simultaneously represented, a shield enables students to regain some control over presentations of the self. Shielding often entails watching. By watching others, students guard themselves. By watching out for others, they split the need to protect the self and guard others.

> I'll watch out for Sam [a shy, unassuming student]. I like to look at him. I like to watch him walk, and do stuff and speak. Did you ever see him get happy or bold about something? I like it. I like when he gets out of his shell. I like to see him smile. (Tanzania, January 23, 1994)

Tanzania performs a watchfulness that enables her to put aside her shell and see Sam emerge from his own. With this kind of watching comes a will to construct anecdotes, to shape a narrative out of experience, and to weave broken pieces into a whole. By recording, Tanzie further develops habits of observation and narration that allows her to rework atrocities. The poetry that follows reveals how watching enables self-possession despite objectification. In the next piece, Tanzania urges a victim to become a subject, by watching herself.

CHRISTINE!

Small girl
quiet girl
with a small
and quiet
voice.

You scare me,
my dear.
I never
knew you
or
cared of you,
until the day I met your mother.
Nice lady.
Concerned
for her small and
quiet daughter.
Christine!
I am so sorry I spoke
too soon.
Telling her I knew not
of
your whereabouts.
I thought she was just concerned.
but I knew
it was more than concern
when I saw
your red bruised face
the next day.
She's followed
you to where
she is not
and watched.
She's just making sure you stay the way
she wants you.
Do you see it too?

Watching leads to three very different effects. In one instance it accompanies violence: "She's followed you to where she is not and watched." The image of the daughter's red bruised face rips perceptions of home as a safe space. In another refrain, watching fosters Tanzania's desire to protect Christine. After writing the poem, she said: "I have always thought I could do more than I actually could. I thought I was the protector and that by watching, I could stop whatever was happening, watching was like doing something physical." The author's active role as public witness in the text implies concern. But it is a concern that begs the protagonist for self-recognition: "Do you see it too?" The last line suggests an imprisoning relationship that can be disrupted when Christine realizes that her mother is "just making sure you stay the way she wants you," young and dependent. Self-perception would raise the girl's consciousness, enabling her to resist control.

In the following poem, concern shifts. It is no longer a suffocating watchfulness of the mother. No one watches "making sure you stay the way she wants you." Nessa wrote "Subbie" after her uncle died. She came to the tutoring room sad and preoccupied. I told her to write what was on her mind.

SUBBIE

Subbie, what's happening to me?
I think I'm falling apart.
No? You're just going through a rough time
now with your mother dying,
grandfather, grandmother, uncle.
You are known to be a strong, willing person
to get behind your troubles.
Subbie you're right I'm strong
and I will put this behind me.
Because that's what they would want,
I think it is best for me too.
Good for you Nessa. Because
I'm here and I will take the place of all
of them and love you even more NOW.

The object position, repeated throughout "The Thing Around," begins with the first line of this poem. Semantically we see a reappearance of fear and uncertainty. However, with the poet's shift into an active role, this text differs in both context and form. Dialogue reveals a definite conversation between two clearly defined subjects. The last six lines of the piece divide equally between two speakers, Nessa and her aunt Subbie. The convention conveys an equality, or the give-and-take of relationship. Within the dialogue, Subbie defines why Nessa is "falling apart." She defines loss, and she defines Nessa: "You are known to be a strong, willing person." Although the writer is again explained, interpreted from outside, this time the definition imposed is empowering. Nessa becomes an actor, someone who gets behind her troubles, someone with a *will*. Subbie's redefinition generates a resolve. "I *will* put this behind me." Subject to someone who watches over her and with her, the writer gains the subjectivity of a woman who is unafraid. Such relations of belonging can provide a space for a positive sense of self, a space that activates.

Reading back and forth between "Subbie" and "The Troll Is Loose," we see a vacillating self, one that moves between desire for and dread of human contact, and we see contradictory conceptions of sanctuary. At first, sanctuary is protected within the stone walls of a statue; threats never enter Nessa's body; she remains safe inside her own skin. But later in the poetic dialogue of Subbie and Nessa, safety entails "entering into another's mind to know what it is like for you there" (Ostriker, 1986, p. 171). Sanctuary rests with Nessa's knowledge that Subbie *sees* her and listens to her.

SEARCH/SAFETY/REFUGE

Our feelings are sanctuaries, safe houses for dreams and frightening ideas, but within structures defined by institutional dehumanization, they do not survive easily (Lorde, 1986). The texts below are emotional preserves, expressions of what could be. They interrupt the unequivocal criminalizing categories and suspicious silences that characterize school, and perhaps home and the streets.

Rape, the controlling metaphor in "Don't Hurt Me Anymore," uncovers the twin abuses—sexual and racial—that Tanzania encounters in school surveillance. That ripping metaphor creates an aesthetic safety zone, a sanctuary that allows her to speak and demands that we listen.

Don't Hurt Me Anymore

Don't hurt me anymore
Don't follow me
like a rapist stalks his prey
Don't quiet the words I have to say
like a rapist covers the mouth of his victim to hold back what she
must say
Don't rip savagely apart my dreams
as a rapist rips the clothes off his victim
Don't throw me down when I try to get up
like a rapist throws down his victim
when she tries to escape
Don't hit me and beat me
when I struggle to learn and survive
like a rapist beats his victim
when she struggles to break free
Don't threaten me to keep my mouth quiet

Don't pin my thoughts down
like a rapist pins the arms of his victim
on the cold concrete
Don't heave your hateful thoughts down on me
like a rapist heaves his body down on his victim
Don't thrust anymore of your sick ideas into my head
like a rapist thrusts his body into his screaming victim
Don't force me to say what you want
like a rapist forces his victim
to perform debasing sexual acts
Don't leave me crying without a shred of confidence to go on
like a rapist leaves his victim feeling cold,
in a dark secluded place
without a shred of dignity to continue living
Don't make me second guess myself
when I know I have the right to speak
like the rape victim second guesses
if she deserves what happened to her
You've left me with the hate
I never asked for
Rapist. Racist. They look almost the same.
Rapist. Racist. They are the same.

Tanzania knows she is defined by an outsider who "thrust[s] . . . sick ideas into my head." She knows she has been marginalized in a dark, secluded place. She knows she has been stripped of her confidence through the imposition of a debasing sexuality. Yet she has the power to command control. She speaks through the imperative: "Don't rip savagely apart my dreams . . . Don't make me second guess myself when I know I have the right to speak." Rape as a metaphor allows Tanzie to speak of her own experience. First indirectly: "Don't pin my thoughts down like the rapist pins the arms of his victim." Then directly: "Rapist. Racist. They are the same."

As I read Tanzania's poem, I was reminded of her narration of the bodily stance that young women assume as they enter the doors of their high school. Teenage girls are asked to stand, legs apart and hands outstretched, positioned both as sexual objects and as suspects. For many young women, this routinized pose separates the self that emerged from the cultural norms engaged and enacted at home from the girl who walks through a metal detector. "We were reared as girls; we were told to keep our legs closed." The conflict that arose when cultural expectations clashed with institutional practice often led to self-denial. Years after attending high school, Tanzania surmised: "I was asked to see the scanning as normal, nothing more. By bringing the girl who said let it be nothing into existence, I pushed the self that was hurt away." Conversely, poetry's open-ended and indeterminate nature lets Tanzania speak of invasive oppressions without self-censorship. Listen repeatedly to the lines of poetry, excerpted from "Don't Hurt Me Anymore," and they will become a resistant response to Tanzania's description of the criminalized searches prevalent in urban high schools:

> I have to put myself down.
> I struggle to learn and survive
> I have to take my bracelets off. Take everything out of my pocket.
> Don't heave your hateful thoughts down on me
>
> I feel embarrassed among everybody else.
> Don't make me second guess myself

Ricoeur (1974) tells us that the poet resigns herself to meaning, gives herself over to it. Her obedience resides, in "this following, this letting be" (p. 93). When Tanzie explains why rapist and racist are the same, she hesitates: "When I first started writing I was just writing about a rapist. Then I realized a rapist and a racist are the same and I don't know. I don't think anybody ever looked at it that way." Paradoxically, the poetic resistance in the lines above and the writer's submersion in language allow fresh insights into experience, such as the connection between sexual and racial oppression. But in a conversation about the effects of scanning, Tanzie retracts her insights and inverts her critique against herself. Stripped of metaphor, she now denies that the stance objectifies her.

Jennifer: What were you thinking of when you said: "I feel like they're trying to get to know my body"?
Tanzania: You know, I feel like I'm hearing the words of a paranoid person. I listen and say am I really paranoid about sex? A lot of people tell me that's a phobia for me. (May 1994)

She is simply "paranoid." The self-assurance evident in poetry disappears. While the black-and-white of a story line inside conversation leaves little room to hide, poetry opens a space for social commentary, public displays, and witnessing. The poetic "I" is always a persona. It enables a writer to turn around and say "that's not me" without repudiating her feelings, her knowledge, her experience. Student poets use this understanding to reveal multiple selves and to subvert institutional practices of criminal surveillance that otherwise reduce them to a single, dehumanizing identity.

Although violent labels and simplistic categories are inscribed in student writing, poetry enables young women to construct themselves in sanctuary, free from the censure of others. In Nessa's poem below, safety, or home, is never simply a metaphor. After reading "I See the World as Water," I began to see that for Nessa home is not a stationary place but a quality within oneself, evoking dialogue and connection with God and others.

I See the World as Water

I see the world as water.
Nice and blue and clean.
The world should be like waves
one after the other. My house
is surrounded by water
nobody to bother me. I live on
an Island with God but nobody knows.
It's in Jamaica.
God is a black man who lives
in Water. The Door to his house
is always open for people who want
help. That's the World
Me and God live in.

The image of water conveys security, a place where one will not be hurt, alien yet home. When I told Nessa I loved it, she said, "Water is true to me, it is clean, it is pure." Water, pure and clean, surrounds home like a protective shield. In the last line, it becomes home, and Nessa lives in a shield, with God, in safety. The space where young women feel safe enough to sit back and yell with feelings was both physical and aesthetic, carved out, in part, by a poet/teacher who helped her students see the world through metaphor. Invited into a space for imagination, Nessa, Nikki, Jhoy, and Tanzania creatively fashioned and projected their interior lives; and, like water, these lives were in constant flux, refusing stillness.

PUBLIC SPACE

Poetry is a sanctuary within, a place to play out conflict and imagine multiple possibilities for identity. Through it, teens become the subjects rather than the objects of their own experience. Evidence shows that when students perceive themselves as the victims of individual or institutional violence, but see no way of effecting change, their perceptions simply fold into a heap of hopelessness, cynicism, or alienation (Pastor, McCormick, & Fine, 1996). Writing may be a route to an expressive self-confidence that alters the writer's perception of self and the outer world. The poetry workshops that Hermine initiated opened up public places where human beings came together in their freedom and entered into dialogue with one another as *who*, not *what*, they are (Greene, 1998). Tanzania has continued to open *public* places where students revisit their lives and interact as *who* they are. After returning to her former junior high school to teach poetry, she told me the following story:

> I did a Meinhard exercise. Something you told me to do. I asked the class to tell me what they felt, what they saw. DeMille, a student in the class, was known as a bad, crazy girl. She wrote about Trinidad, put herself right there, told me how the sun felt on her skin, described the color of her drink. I was proud of her Toward the end of the month, we had a party. I brought Jamaican patties. We sewed Japanese books and ate. DeMille didn't show up but came later on. We talked for a long time. She was no longer the bad, crazy girl. She could write, and speak to me.

REFERENCES

Devine, J. (1996). *Maximum security: The culture of violence in inner-city schools.* Chicago: University of Chicago Press.

Fine, M., Weis, L., & Powell, L. (1997). Communities of difference: A critical look at desegregated spaces created for and by youth. *Harvard Educational Review, 67*(2): 247–284.

Foucault, M. (1979). *Discipline and punish.* New York: Vintage.

Giovanni, N. (1970). *Black feeling, Black talk.* Detroit: Broadside Press.

Goffman, E. (1961). *Asylums: Essays on the social situation of mental patients and other inmates.* Chicago: Aldine.

Greene, M. (1998, July). *Imagination and perception.* Paper presented at the Lincoln Center Institute, New York.

Kincaid, J. (1992). *At the bottom of the river.* New York: Plume.

Lorde, A. (1984). *Sister outsider.* Trumansburg, NY: Crossing Press.

Lorde, A. (1986). *Our dead behind us.* New York: Norton.

Ostriker, A. S. (1986). *Stealing the language: The emergence of women's poetry in America.* Boston: Beacon Press.

Pastor, J., McCormick, J., & Fine, M. (1996). Makin' homes: An urban girl thing. In B. Leadbeater & N. Way (Eds.), *Urban girls: Resisting stereotypes, creating identities* (pp. 15–34). New York: New York University Press.

Ricoeur, P. (1974). Violence and language. In D. Stewart & J. Bien (Eds.), *Political and social essays* (pp. 88–101). Athens: Ohio University Press.

CHAPTER 11

Teaching Locations

NANCY BARNES

Understanding how people become good teachers is surprisingly and peculiarly difficult. This is true in part because we have all spent so much time as students, as Sarason (1993) explains: "Understanding is hard to attain, *especially in regard to a setting that influenced you in diverse ways and toward which you have attitudes you absorbed, not attitudes you thought through*" (p.114, emphasis in original).

This chapter reflects my efforts to construct a new teaching location, a site that compels college students to think hard about what it would mean to become public school teachers—and whether or not they want to do that. As an anthropologist whose teaching and research converge on the study of schooling in American culture, I find that it is no longer enough to unpack the layers of social reproduction, inequality, and constraint that fill much of the best theoretical work on education. Instead, I want students to unearth the buried contradictions of urban public schooling, the life-changing possibilities as well as the relentless, devastating injustices. This desire has led me to create a course called the Practicum in Urban Education.

The original questions guiding the design of the practicum were: What would it be useful for undergraduates in the liberal arts to think about as they contemplate becoming public school teachers? What do they need to know? And, I must now add, *where* can they possibly do this kind of thinking? The practicum asks college students to become involved with a number of the distinctive small high schools that have been spawned by the recent period of progressive school reform in New York City. Each week, they traverse physical and ideological spaces and spend time at locations, or what Sarason calls "settings," that are astonishingly far from the classrooms where most of the college students have "absorbed" their "attitudes" about teaching and learning. The distinctive power of the practicum grows from its linking of sites, people, and politics that are usually separated by well-guarded borders.

The academic part of the seminar is designed to weave in and out of the "practice" dimension, generating the complex questions that theory and experience always pose for each other. The year-long syllabus bridges and interrogates the disjunctive locations by exploring how selected theoretical perspectives illuminate various issues in urban education; for example, tracking, heterogeneous grouping, and the teaching of academic skills to what Mike Rose (1989) calls "underprepared students." The particular readings for any given semester matter much less than the thinking that practice-based inquiry characteristically demands.

Elizabeth Minnich (1990) articulates why thinking that moves among sites of learning can be politically as well as intellectually powerful. The practicum's sites include lived experiences in a student's own schooling, field observations in a high school, and selected theories that are applied and critiqued in the contexts of the student's autobiography, the high school classroom, and the syllabus itself. As Minnich argues:

> Change comes when *thinking* [emphasis added] is released from old tangles of errors that have locked it into the past *and* [emphasis in original] when we learn to analyze the potential for real change in our very specific contexts. In that movement from the conceptual to the concrete, and from the concrete to the conceptual, is one of the most important conversations of all, the one that returns thinking to the world it helps illuminate, and, in turn, challenges that thinking to take account of particulars, individuals, specific situations. (p. 190)

The college students themselves are the critical agents in this project, weaving between and linking worlds. The students I teach are undergraduates, age 17 to 22, who attend a private liberal arts college in Manhattan. The practicum has been made up of a majority of White students with a few students of color; one year the class was half students of color, which yielded predictably different discussions. The student bodies in the participating high schools are predominantly students of color, some of them as much as 95% African American, others more mixed in terms of race, language, and cultural backgrounds, all of which are diverse in the small new public schools in New York City. The college students I work with are middle and upper middle class as a group, although there are significant numbers of working-class students. The high school populations include a high proportion of young men and women from poor, working-class, and immigrant families.

The disparate locations spanned by the practicum require students shuttling between them to think about the high school classrooms, their own experiences, and the readings. For example, they write on their relations to privilege in their families and schools, and they reflect on the concept of privilege in relation to Delpit's (1995) idea of a "culture of power" that governs academic life yet is profoundly unfamiliar to many students when they first arrive at the university. The college students then consider what privilege might mean in the life of the high school student that each member of the practicum follows throughout the year.

Clearly, the possibilities generated by moving across teaching sites extend far beyond this seminar to all kinds of conversations among teachers and those who are becoming teachers. Clandinin, Davis, Hogan, and Kennard (1993) speak to the need for fresh narratives of teachers' experiences composed in newly invented spaces: "Teacher education programs cannot be conceived at the university and implemented in the schools. Rather, teacher education programs *must be situated in a middle ground created by [the] conversations"* (p. 219, emphasis added).

The practicum is emphatically not "student teaching" in any conventional sense; the college where I work does not have an education major or a teacher certification program. Rather, each person who takes the course is responsible for joining the conversation, negotiating a useful role he or she can play in a specific classroom. This is a tough assignment. A number of the new high schools have opened their doors very recently; the settings make enormous demands. The tumult of school reform, especially in schools situated in poor communities that are dealing with drastically reduced social services, calls for serious commitments to social change.

The work feels political, which is exciting and also raises haunting questions about exactly what kind of teaching location the practicum is. Maxine Greene's (1995) essay "Choosing a Past and Inventing a Future: The Becoming of a Teacher" speaks to these questions. My past was the civil rights and antiwar movements of the 1960s when I was in high school and then in college, actively forming myself as a political adult. Because I "choose" the 1960s for my past, and because I've spent many years talking with young people as a college teacher, I'm acutely conscious that politics as I knew it is seldom available to my students. In these bleak times, when the possibilities for change in the public culture seem so diminished, many college students find meaning in identity politics.

The point of the comparison is not that the power of identity was insignificant when I worked in a welfare rights organization or opposed the war in Vietnam, or when I became a feminist. Rather, the context was different. My friends and I discussed into the night where to place our energies and why, but we also knew that we were joining huge, historic struggles, social movements that were transforming not just the United States but also the world. These revolutionary changes existed totally independent of who "we" were.

Today, identity politics prevail in campus struggles that center on aspects of who individuals "are"—lesbian and gay, African American, Latino. Initiatives for rights and equality and issue-based campaigns do, of course, emerge from this kind of organizing, which is exhilarating and important. But the sense that politics is embodied in one's own "self" (and that such a politics highlights a single significant "self," the same self that "has" what my students call their "personal experience") is a shaky foundation from which to engage the incredibly diverse and complex other "selves" going about their everyday business in urban public schools. As a teaching location, the practicum grapples with this dilemma all the time. I'm uncertain about how identity politics helps us to "invent a future," as Maxine Greene puts it, and I'm increasingly persuaded that it doesn't help very much in "the becoming of a teacher."

It is spectacularly good news, nevertheless, that so many undergraduates think they want to teach and are attracted to school reform as an overtly political site. Since we have weathered the 1980s, young people are again moved to political action, public service, and all kinds of projects that speak to the creation of a better world. Maxine Greene (1995) celebrates this intentionality as "a mode of thought and action that reaches beyond the private sphere" (p. 70).

Now that I have been shuttling between these sites with my students for several years, I want to explore two of what Minnich (1990) might call the "old tangles" that have revealed themselves as the college students encounter, observe, participate, analyze, and generally begin to imagine their possible work lives in this (to them) novel location, the classrooms of the small progressive public high schools in New York City. The first tangle represents how complicated it is for young people who have always been students to position themselves as teachers. The second tangle addresses how relentlessly college-age Americans rely on "personal experience" to understand and explain the complex "other" realities they encounter in urban classrooms.

These two themes lie at the heart of this practice-based project. They are, however, elusive, emerging as they do from the multiple teaching locations that they also interpret. They speak to each of us who is engaged in "the becoming of a teacher," not just to these young people. This chapter frames these themes by borrowing George Marcus's (1994) notion of "messy texts," which he discusses with reference to contemporary ethnography:

Messy texts are messy because they insist on an open-endedness, an incompleteness, and an uncertainty about how to draw a text/analysis to a close. . . . I find them interesting as *symptoms* of struggle . . . to produce unexpected connections and thus new descriptions of old realities. (p. 568; emphasis in original)

In the case of the practicum, messy texts are unsettling, provocative stories about teaching and learning; they embody the rich, often contradictory thinking that occurs in the seminar precisely because it spans a number of distinct locations. I now believe that such thinking is what permits people to grasp the meanings of "the becoming of a teacher." This can, in turn, help them make choices and decisions about their own commitments to public education.

POSITIONING YOURSELF AS A TEACHER IS NOT EASY

Undergraduates in America come at virtually everything from a lifetime of being positioned as students. Analyzing the contradictions we all face because we enter teaching after having been students for many years, Deborah Britzman (1991) writes:

But what occurs as well is the startling idea that the taking up of an identity means suppressing aspects of the self. So at first glance, becoming a teacher may mean becoming someone you are not. It is this dual struggle that works to construct the student teacher as the site of conflict. (p. 4)

The practicum asks students to reposition themselves as teachers. This entails a number of complex shifts including Britzman's "suppressing aspects of the self" in order to take responsibility for other young people. I had no inkling, when I began to develop the practicum, of how extremely problematic this would prove to be. Students' travels between locations do indeed initiate a reexamination of the selves they bring with them from their families, home communities, and prior schooling, which they understand for the most part through their experiences. This way of understanding also becomes a site of conflict.

Shirley is a rural White woman from a tiny town in the Texas panhandle, a student in the practicum who found herself in an eighth grade at one of the high schools where all the students were African American or Latino, many of them poor, all city dwellers. At the end of her second week there she wrote:

> Oh boy, what an incredible day! I'm in the street walking up to the building and I hear "Miss! Miss!" being screamed really loud. I look up and see Shaniqua and another brown face peering down at me. I broke out into a full grin, laughed, and called up to them "Whassup?" I remember when I lived in the dorm at Union Square I used to try and get people to acknowledge my screaming "Good Morning!" from the eighth floor! (It never happened.) I sometimes wonder if the kids ever look out the window and see me walking away. It's really a strange thought—another side effect of my longing to know if and how the kids think of or view me.

Shirley continues, in the double-entry journal that she used to reflect on her fieldnotes from the school: "But I can't ever find out how the kids see me—and I shouldn't. They have every right to decide my place in their lives—and most likely it's a very small place."

These ruminations suggest Shirley's ambivalent feelings about "suppressing aspects of the self" as an apprentice teacher. Other students were more self-knowing as they approached the high school kids. Frank is a young man who grew up in a lower-middle-class household in the suburbs in Westchester. One of my favorites, Frank had had a bad time in high school; he identified strongly with underprepared students. He delineates a nuanced position even as he, a White man who wears jeans and T-shirts, obsesses about his appearance.

> I decided not to alter my dress because, as insignificant as it may seem, I think it might make me more approachable; I do not want to represent the myth that I subscribed to as a high school student—that college students are "nerds" and only "nerds" become college students. The color barrier, I am sure, will present many tangible and intangible obstacles. Why try and separate myself from the students even further by pretending to be something I am not? Besides, I don't really have any "nice" clothes.

Here is a third glimpse of how "messy" it is when undergraduates first attempt to shift locations, to adjust their preconceptions and convictions as students to their new positions in the high schools. A White woman in the class named Thelma, a creative, libertarian thinker, recounts her day in a ninth-grade classroom. She was angry because the African American teacher had taken her aside and expressed concern that she, Thelma, might find the teenagers (all of whom were African American) "stupid." "Does she think I'm a racist?" Thelma yelled at the rest of us in the seminar.

Thelma explained that she had been sitting under a table in the classroom, talking with one of the boys, LeRoy, because "he felt safer there." Reasonably enough, the teacher had asked LeRoy *and* Thelma to get up off the floor. Later, the teacher explained her request to Thelma, saying "You have to be an authority with the children—you can't just be yourself!"

Young people who are thinking seriously about teaching need to comprehend that they are no longer at the center, even though as students they have been. There have been wonderful moments when practicum students revealed their awareness of this, shifting positions to see how funny a situation looks through the eyes of the teenagers. Consider Ben's fieldnotes from his first day. The tenth-grade teacher asked everyone to introduce themselves:

> I said, "Hi, my name is Ben. I am interested in becoming a teacher and if there is anything I can do to help, just let me know." One of the boys remarked that I looked like I wanted to be in the army. (Ben had a shaved head at the time.) The first girl to my right introduced herself as Egypt. I believe that this was her name. Then the next two girls also introduced themselves as Egypt. This set a precedent. One of the boys said his name was Thomas, the next said his name was Jefferson, the next Washington. I think the first girl may have been the only one to give me her real name.

Perhaps the high school students were consciously resisting Ben's presence or disrespecting their regular teacher's instructions. Or maybe they were just goofing around. In any case, Ben definitely understood that he had to figure out how to position himself, now that he was an apprentice teacher.

It seems as though narratives of teacher authority almost inevitably produce messy, unfinished texts, an outcome that is not limited to undergraduates. At one point in the semester, a famous White educator came to speak with us in the practicum. Coincidentally, the educator was friends with an administrator at one of the schools in which members of the class were working. The administrator, a person of color, had been a member of a militant political party in the 1960s and 1970s. To make a long agonizing story short, the educator "outed" the administrator to my students as having been a revolutionary.

I knew that the administrator did not like to have people discuss his political past. Yet the educator spilled the beans in a way that was friendly, even comradely. He indicated that he, too, had been involved in radical politics during those years. But then he became anxious and told the 19- and 20-year-olds that he probably shouldn't be saying these things so *they* oughtn't to repeat them—thereby making all of us complicit as he put the administrator back in the closet. This was disturbing. The famous educator was clearly uncertain about his position, much as the students were when they entered the high schools. Was he telling stories, sharing his 1960s' experiences, or was he teaching, claiming authority and taking responsibility in the practicum that day? And if he was teaching, what was the lesson?

In this messy text, the disclosure of the administrator's radical past could have had practical consequences: Someone we knew could have been hurt, and the person who actually "owned" that experience was silenced by someone else's need to speak it. (It seemed to me the educator had "outed" the administrator in order to claim his own political heritage.) Of course, the educator didn't mean to put so much at risk. But there is an even further "unexpected connection" (Marcus, 1994) in this messy text. Because he reversed himself in my class, the educator *was* teaching my students that the world of school reform depends on silence and makes use of the closet. The practicum students weren't the only ones for whom becoming a teacher constructed a "site of conflict" (Britzman, 1991); positioning was giving the famous educator trouble, too.

Robert Coles (1997) points to the dilemma that I call "positioning yourself as a teacher" in his writing about documentary work: "Once more, the issue is that of location—how a particular writer or researcher [or teacher] decides to commit himself or herself with respect to those others being studied, watched, heard, [taught], made the subject" (p. 32). The idea that a certain location can require us to *commit* ourselves is central to my argument about what happens to students who seek to position themselves as public school teachers for the first time.

As a site, the practicum establishes relationships that make intense demands on the college kids. Struggling with their commitments, some individuals reach crucial, if negative, conclusions. "I have figured out that I don't want to be a teacher," one of them reported after her return to the high school with a black eye she had gotten in a car accident the weekend before.

> I knew that the students would question me about my eye, but I really wasn't prepared for Luis's response. It was almost as though this was what was supposed to happen. He told me that he and his friends were playing around throwing eggs and then "bang-bang," he got shot.
>
> The hardest thing for me was that I could not separate my experience at the school from the rest of my life. The school managed to inspire and paralyze me all at the same time. The

school system can't solve the problems of the world. Why *should* students care about their school work when they're busy staying alive? I know I wouldn't.

Coles's language illuminates what the young men and women in the practicum wrestle with: They have to "decide to commit" themselves to teaching "with respect to those others." Their decisions about how (and whether) to make a place for themselves as teachers are especially difficult because they have always been students. Positioning yourself as a teacher is not easy.

PERSONAL EXPERIENCE IS *NOT* A PRIVILEGED WAY OF KNOWING

The practicum students almost always speak about what they are learning at the high schools in terms of their "personal experience," the most fundamental source of knowledge they feel they have. For them, using personal experiences to think about specific issues in education means identifying as someone who loves children, or who was classified "learning-disabled" in elementary school, or who grew up as a White person in an integrated neighborhood. Importantly, "personal experience" grounds the systems of meaning that the college students believe they share with the kids and teachers in the high schools. Over and over again, these young Americans valorize their experiences as sufficient, even ample resources for them to draw on as neophyte teachers.

The second theme or "old tangle" (Minnich, 1990) that has emerged from the practicum is thus epistemological; it concerns how the college students know or understand what happens at the various teaching locations. Teaching, like knowledge, always presumes relationships: between teacher and student; among the students in a given class; between the individual and a cherished text, or a daunting skill, or a life-changing theory. Teaching is also embedded in relations of identification and difference that are less easily named: between the teacher's background (race and class and gender are only a start) and fields of intellectual interest and dreams and fears and ambitions—and similarly for the students.

Viewed in this light, teaching relationships evidently consist of both shared and divergent experiences and meanings. The young people in the practicum, however, always gravitate toward *shared* meanings. They search for commonalities and yearn for connections, as when Frank reasoned out his decision about how to dress in the school by how he had felt about "nerds" when he was a ninth-grader. Hillary, a self-dramatizing

White woman, a fiction writer with dyed green hair, expressed an extreme version of this when she responded to my beginning-of-the-year question about what the practicum students thought they would bring to teaching:

> Relation. I am not such a far distance away. I do not feel there is such a separation between the "adult" and "child." I have been alive longer. Period. Age is a number. Experience is everything that makes the blocks we build with. I am *with* the children. Their minds are very close to mine.

The work of the practicum is, however, laced with divergent and contested meanings; the web of teaching locations is constituted by experiences that are not shared. The college students bring this realization back to our classroom from their time in the schools. What do you do, for example, as an apprentice teacher in a history class that is studying the uses of Scripture by both slaveholders and abolitionists when a high school senior insists that the Bible is the word of God?

Feminist historian Joan Scott (1992) frames the dilemmas that experience poses whenever it is, as she says, "the bedrock of evidence upon which explanation is built" (p. 25). She continues, "Experience is at once always already an interpretation *and* is in need of interpretation. What counts as experience is neither self-evident nor straightforward; it is always contested, always therefore political" (p. 37; emphasis in original). Nothing is more consequential in the process of becoming a teacher than how one thinks about one's own "experience."

The vastly disparate historical and cultural circumstances represented in public school classrooms are not exactly news to those of us who spend time in urban schools. Yet little attention is paid to how problematic it is to use one's "personal experience" (whatever counts for that) as though its meanings are obvious and obviously applicable. Once again, the shuttling between sites of learning in the practicum (the seminar discussions and the high school classrooms), and between differently located experiences and interpretations, poses generative "problems" in Freire's (1970) sense.

Sara, a self-involved White student who was surprisingly attuned to socioeconomic class, divulged how she was thinking about the high school site in relation to her personal experience:

> Not being part of the majority culture at [the school] is very difficult for me. I am not Latina and, unlike many of the students and community members, my family has a lot of money. I wonder, then, what can I learn from this out of place feeling? Why am I working

here? How can I possibly ever fit in? *What can I as a White woman possibly contribute to a tight-knit community that does not validate me, or my culture, at all?* This recognition shows me that I need to look deep into my own racism, my own fears, and my own assumptions.

It didn't occur to me that I had a culture to impose on anyone. When I tried to see my own culture, it looked "transparent" to me. I had never thought about how it feels to exist within an unfamiliar culture, to be asked to learn within (and from) an unfamiliar culture. . . . Somehow my own self could get erased by the out-of-place feeling I get when I am at the school.

Sometimes the college students achieve breathtaking insights in this unfamiliar terrain. One White woman told about an African American teenager who was sick of hearing (in her high school's progressive curriculum) about the oppression of Blacks by Whites because, the girl said, there was more to her people's experience than that. The practicum student's observation to us was that "in an attempt to be Afro-centric, Whiteness can still occupy the center. Obviously, when the material is tied so closely to identity, identity itself is at stake."

Understanding or knowing how to think about issues of difference in public school classrooms, clearly a critical dimension of the practicum's work, overlaps with what Lisa Delpit (1995) calls teaching "other people's children." Delpit refers primarily to White teachers working with children of color. But the debate she sparks is paradigmatic for the conflicts that arise whenever we are honest about divergent meanings, often attributed to people whose cultural experiences are unlike our own. Delpit offers sharp tools for understanding how schooling looks to "other" students and for ethnographic research into "other" systems of meaning. Despite the tremendous importance of Delpit's analyses of these relationships of power and difference, however, *where* teaching relationships take place—take "place"—is still largely unexplored territory, as is *how* we know whatever we learn at various teaching locations.

It often appears as though the practicum students' liberal arts educations have not touched their adolescent certainty that the most compelling epistemology is that which is based on their personal experience. Consequently, the practicum must construct not only a network of teaching locations but also an analytical scaffolding that is simultaneously subtler and more expansive than the students' self-referenced, experience-based view of the world.

Even as I reached this understanding, I failed to appreciate the contradictory force the practicum as a teaching location was exerting on me. The following messy text interrogates a situation in which I used one aspect of my experience or, as the students would say, my identity—that I am a lesbian—to explain and teach something with reference to the high schools. Striving to keep my balance as the teacher, I resorted to exactly the same strategy the students so often employ: I privileged my "personal experience" as a pedagogical device, a way of knowing.

Weird things had happened in the practicum that particular spring. An "out" lesbian student, a White woman who is often mistaken for a Latina (a misunderstanding she does not correct), and a straight African American man got involved with a social issues club that met in the afternoon at one of the schools. These were strong-minded, politically active, somewhat immature students, also good friends with each other. A rape crisis counselor came to speak to the club; during the discussion the man from my class took on a seventh-grade boy who was insisting girls and women "want it." Among other inappropriate comments, the male practicum student said that the boy was "an embarrassment to the race." All of this was reported to me in agitated phone calls that night.

Within the week, the lesbian student extended herself to an eighth-grade boy, also in the club, whose sister may—or may not—have been being abused at home. The practicum student not only gave the boy her phone number; she said that he and his sister should get out of their house and invited them to stay with her anytime, day or night.

This was pretty bad. One of the reasons I love teaching at the college level is because the young people behave like grown-ups—most of the time. I've never wanted to be a parent, and I didn't like having to be as an explicit authority with my students as these events demanded. I spent many hours talking with these two and eventually had to ask one of them not to return to the high school because we couldn't agree about what constituted acceptable behavior. The students in question had violated many boundaries, not the least of which were mine, in their entanglements at the high school.

The only way I could find to teach the practicum from inside this messy text, to explain limits and help the students respect the fragile relationships that our involvement in the high school communities entailed, was to center my identity, incongruous as that sounds now. I told them that *as a lesbian* I understand that gay public school teachers face great pressures and that, as a consequence, many of them stay in the closet. I hated doing this, especially since I often "come out" in teaching, albeit for much less convoluted reasons.

This troublesome class followed New York City's debacle over the Rainbow Curriculum, which had led many to acknowledge that feminists and those of us on the Left must find effective ways to address sexuality in public education (Lee, Murphy, & North, 1994). Faced with competing political allegiances, to myself as a gay person and to the new public schools I so strongly believe in, I told the practicum students that I really didn't know whether I would be openly gay if I were a high school teacher. I wanted them to understand that the practices and the politics of the new high schools mandate that much more than *my* identity is at stake at these locations. I thought my example would impress upon them that they were not the center of what happens at the school sites. The students, however, insisted on asserting their particular identities in the incidents in the after-school club. Because the practicum compels both the students and the teacher to scrutinize our practice in these multiple sites, I was profoundly implicated.

What does this messy text mean? And what does it say about a practice-based course in which the undergraduates travel between teaching locations? I had self-consciously come out of the closet and then, in effect, put myself back in—not unlike what happened in the messy text about the famous educator. I strategically and naively used my own experience to send a message of caution to the practicum, to explain the safety of my location at the university in contrast to the contested sites where gay public school teachers work. Distressed by how directly the people in my seminar read from their experiences as students to the classrooms in which they were assisting as teachers, I (the teacher) read equally directly from my story to "teach" them to exercise care in the high schools.

In the name of pedagogy, I privileged my personal experience. Claiming my identity as a lesbian in order to think about the problem of the two practicum students who were overly involved with the teenagers meant centering myself. Centering personal experience meant claiming identity as the grounds for thinking.

This tension is extremely important and, as the messy texts reveal, always problematic. Identity politics has a feverish quality on college campuses these days; undergraduates caught up in this climate view coming out (like the urgent assertion of other identities) as perhaps *the* most meaningful political act. I was saying that their personal experience (like mine) was simply not the most significant, given what was happening at the high schools. If they wanted to think like teachers, they had to commit themselves with respect to a larger project, to "those others" who were being taught (Coles, 1997).

The power of the practicum is that it compels college students to think hard about what it means to be a public school teacher as they travel between the various teaching locations that construct the course. Because it is practice-based, the practicum spins a delicate, sticky cobweb of connections between the formal academic inquiry in the seminar and the fieldwork that takes place when young people who are thinking about becoming teachers apprentice themselves in other people's classrooms for many months.

Practice-based education underscores the complex significance of differences at the sites; for example, how predominantly White college students at a private college come to think about the "others" with whom they work, teenagers of color attending urban schools. The two messy texts illuminate just how conflicted college students are as they reposition themselves as teachers and how tenaciously they privilege personal experience as they seek to explain what they encounter at the school locations. Because it is practice-based, a course like the practicum also requires the teacher (me) to think hard about positioning, and differences, and the privileging of experience, as dimensions of pedagogy that construct the conversation I can have with the college students.

The practicum is often exhausting and sometimes confusing, for the students and for me. But I find I can't turn away from it; the stakes are too high. It is too easy to feel, during this barren time in public life, that concerns like coming out can reasonably be seen as purely personal; that individual students' decisions about the work they want to do after graduation are simply individual; or that attention to teaching as a locus of change is somehow too local. Yet the web of teaching locations described in this chapter brings me to just the opposite conclusions. We all need to grapple with the "messy texts" that are being written at diverse sites of teaching and learning. We all need to recognize the fears and choices college students confront as they search out their futures and decide whether or not to make a commitment to public education. We all need to construct conversations that cross the boundaries between educational sites, so that we can think together about teaching and change.

REFERENCES

Britzman, D. (1991). *Practice makes practice: A critical study of learning to teach*. Albany: State University of New York Press.

Clandinin, J., Davis, A., Hogan, P., & Kennard, B. (Eds.). (1993). *Learning to teach, teaching to learn: Stories of collaboration in teacher education*. New York: Teachers College Press.

Coles, R. (1997). *Doing documentary work*. New York: Oxford University Press.

Delpit, L. (1995). *Other people's children: Cultural conflict in the classroom*. New York: New Press.

Freire, P. (1970). *Pedagogy of the oppressed*. New York: Herder & Herder.

Greene, M. (1995). Choosing a past and inventing a future: The becoming of a teacher. In W. Ayers (Ed.), *To become a teacher: Making a difference in children's lives* (pp. 65–77). New York: Teachers College Press.

Lee, N., Murphy, D., & North, L. (1994, Winter). Sexuality, multicultural education, and the New York City Public Schools. *Radical Teacher*, pp. 12–16.

Marcus, G. (1994). What comes (just)after "post"? The case of ethnography. In
    N. Denzin & Y. Lincoln (Eds.), *Handbook of Qualitative Research* (pp. 563–574).
    Thousand Oaks, CA: Sage.
Minnich, E. (1990). *Transforming knowledge*. Philadelphia: Temple University Press.
Rose, M. (1989). *Lives on the boundary*. New York: Free Press.
Sarason, S. (1993). *The case for change: Rethinking the preparation of educators*. San
    Francisco: Jossey-Bass.
Scott, J. (1992). Experience. In J. Butler & J. Scott (Eds.), *Feminists theorize the
    political* (pp. 22–40). New York: Routledge.

CHAPTER 12

Narrative Sites for Youths' Construction of Social Consciousness

COLETTE DAIUTE

Text by John in October, fifth grade:

> *My conflict is when me and my best friend Robert and I was*
> *fight because i didn't want to be on his team so and we soloved it*
> *later that day no body got herti. and that is when we became best*
> *friends.*

Text by John in April, fifth grade:

> *One day I was walk in the croner store and manni [manager/clerk]*
> *said get out for no resana at all so I walked out of the store and*
> *maget was walking right behind me and he tryed to hit me so he hit me*
> *and I truned a round and I punched him in the face and he stared to cry.*
> *He was feeling bad and I was not so happy me self becaues I [k]now that*
> *I could have talked it out and not punched him. He walked away crying.*

This chapter argues that young authors' narrative writing serves to develop social consciousness rather than being a passive reflection of social capacity or risk. In the context of discussing social issues, such as discrimination, children as young as 10 can write to engage, juxtapose, and contradict story lines from different aspects of their lives. According to this view, we read the narrative texts above as experiments in social positioning, in this case, a 10-year-old African American boy exploring a range of social issues—from the intimate realm of best-friendship to encounters with strangers that are rife with discrimination and violence. Of interest in this examination of such texts is not so much whether they are "true" or what they reveal about the author, but how young authors use narrative contexts as "construction sites" (Weis & Fine, Introduction, this volume) for their analysis of self in society. In addition to completing school assignments, young authors narrate to interpret history in the light of personal experience, play out fantasies, and orient themselves for future action.

John wrote the two narratives presented above in the context of a year-long study of twelve third- through fifth-grade urban pubic school classrooms where children and teachers used literary narratives and children's own stories as bridges between their classrooms, their lives outside of school, and their imagined worlds (Daiute, 1997). The context was one that introduced issues of racial and ethnic discrimination as a theme, with high-quality children's literature as the point of departure for class discussions, peer group activities, and children's writing around social conflict (Walker, 1998). For example, in the fall, the fifth-grade classes each spent several weeks reading, discussing, and extending the novel *Felita* (Mohr, 1979), about a Puerto Rican girl in the 1960s in New York City. In this novel, Felita and her family suffer many explicit and implicit discriminatory assaults by neighbors, family, friends, and community representatives, and the characters deal with these issues in diverse ways. Every day for several weeks in the spring, the fifth-grade classes encountered the world of *Mayfield Crossing* (Nelson, 1993), in which the main characters are a group of African Americans in the 1960s South. In the novel, the small, predominantly Black middle school closes and the Mayfield kids must go to a mostly White school in another community. The story is about how these youth learn about, experience, and react to the racial discrimination they find in the world beyond "the Crossing."

Interspersed with sessions devoted to reading and discussing these novels, the young people participated in a range of collaboratively and individually written narrative experiences designed to extend the social conflict themes in literature to their own real and imagined lives. About halfway through each book, students were asked to work with a partner on a "literary re-construction" task, which explicitly foregrounded issues of discrimination in a quote from the novel and asked the author teams to write their own endings after discussing different options. The reality-based "personal conflict story" was designed to extend the work classes had been doing around social conflict literature to events in their own lives. These tasks differed in whether and how they specified character(s), voice (first- or third-person narrative), fiction/nonfiction, social themes (discrimination or social conflict more generally), and composing contexts. Since social critique in the stories resulting from these tasks is implicit as well as explicit, reading them requires theory about discourse, development, and social relations.

FROM NARRATIVE COHERENCE
TO NARRATIVE CONSEQUENCE

Narratives are cultural shapings of values, expectations, and practices (Bruner, 1986; Tannen, 1991). This enculturation perspective has been important in overcoming assumptions that narrative is transparent—a window on youth's capacities, secrets, and problems—but this view implies a cultural consistency that is far from the case for many children. Young people from mainstream backgrounds may experience discursive consistency across home, school, community, and personal experience that can account for their relative success in institutions such as school (Ball, 1998; Cazden, 1988; Heath, 1983; Lee, 1993; Michaels, 1991). In contrast, young people with multicultural experiences face the challenge of recognizing, mastering, and integrating scripts from the diverse ethnic, class, and educational cultures in which they live. Since differences in the organizations, implicit values, and purposes of narratives used across contexts are sometimes extreme, the development of youths' social understanding may be obscured by an emphasis on coherence. Mainstream narrative coherence is defined in terms of structure and content, such as conforming to chronological order, creating a clearly marked beginning–middle–end structure, or grounding narrative events in an initiating action that progresses through a problem to a resolution, if not always a happy ending. Reading narratives by urban youth involves resisting the assumption of such coherence because, I argue here, their stories call on other histories and logics.

Developmental theory provides the basis for narrative coherence, such as using standard orthography and chronological sequence before juxtaposing multiple story lines. In terms of such developmental norms, the narratives by John conform to many conventions of standard written English, but the April story in particular challenges notions of a culturally coherent script. While John's October narrative can be interpreted as coherent because it conforms to a mainstream narrative structure, including conflict development and resolution, the April narrative merges two story lines as it implicitly shifts across event and intention. This story is, however, successful in identifying conflicting realms of interpersonal and intergroup relations.

Reading John's texts for dissonant cultural scripts opens up at least two story lines—reporting and social commentary—and the April narrative, in particular, evokes contradictory social orders. The young author, for example, tells one story of intergroup conflict interwoven with an interpersonal drama of empathetic discovery. In the intergroup conflict story line, a person in a position of power played out a discriminatory social scenario—"manni [manager/clerk] said get out for no resana at all . . . was walking right behind me . . . tryed to hit me so he hit me." The author described his retaliation: "I truned a round and I punched him in the face." Then he described the complex emotional consequences of this conflict from the point of view of the perpetrator—the other: "he stared to cry. He was feeling bad. . . . He walked away crying," as well as from his own point of view: "and I was not so happy me self becaues I [k]now that I could have talked it out and not punched him." The author underscores the distance between the injustice and empathy story lines by their juxtaposition, some self-critique, and the lack of resolution, in spite of the emphasis on conflict resolution in the curriculum and classroom discussion. From a perspective where diversity is the norm, John's April story can thus be viewed as a meaningfully disjointed narrative that juxtaposes a discourse of discrimination with a discourse of caring. This move toward cultural complexity requires serious consideration as development rather than as incoherence.

Viewed this way, such recognition, albeit subtle, of conflicting life scripts is a major social and cognitive move accomplished by youth through discursive work. John exploited literary tension and multiple voicing in April to tell a coming-of-age story in which social recognition and personal pain are embodied in narrative structure. The lack of resolution in the April story is consistent with an explanation that coordinating different perspectives requires developmental maturity that a 10-year-old is not likely to possess, but this 10-year-old's recognition of the conflict, his shifting across conflicting perspectives, and the story's lack of resolution suggest that social consciousness work may interact with developmental limits. Writing as the study of social issues thus involves examining the consequences of living in complex and contradictory worlds, in particular when youth use their own real and imagined experiences as the basis for community awareness and participation across cultures.

Conceptualizing social consciousness as tension around social issues has a history in theory about self–group relations in oppressed groups. Multiple awareness has been noted in social theory as a "double consciousness" (Du Bois, 1903) with which African Americans have interpreted their affective experience as indicating an ongoing struggle against institutionalized oppression and discrimination. The similar notion of "two consciousnesses" has been proposed to characterize how the poor struggle to survive in political/economic contexts in which others survive

(Gramsci, 1971). *Conciencizacion* is a process among groups who transform tools of oppression such as literacy into tools for their liberation (Freire, 1989), and contemporary theory posits resistance (Ward, 1996) and the multiple moral discourses of adolescents struggling for independence, identity, and connection (Lightfoot, 1997) as critical stances. As a socially symbolic act, narrative is social action (Jameson, 1981), but the constructive role of narrative social action and struggle has previously been reserved for those with the privilege of age (having achieved at least adolescence), skill (having basic writing skills), audience (being a published author), and objectivity (knowing how to distinguish fact from fiction, truth from lies). Common across these perspectives is the recognition that thought is situated in critical social action and reflection, based at least in part on being able to engage multiple realities.

Such multiple consciousness occurs most obviously in John's story as compassion in the face of injustice. The young narrator recognizes aggression toward him but also recognizes the impact of his retaliation on the aggressor. In addition to the implication that the author was unhappy because he made the manager cry, the author's unhappiness could have been compounded by his assuming the responsibility to talk things over, even though, as he reported the events, he had not initiated the violence. In this way, the mix of fantasy and reflection reveals another plight of a reflective powerless person—the paradox of having to walk away after suffering aggression or dealing with the consequences of hurting someone else. Another interpretation of the split between reported action and responsibility for having to "talk it out" is a history of accepting responsibility and blame in youth and other relatively powerless people—an explanation that belies the multiple voices in the telling.

Thus, the development of narrative social consciousness is one of tension, disruption, and invention, in which a child's push to make sense of the world in terms of his or her own experience provides coherence—as incoherent as it may seem from outsiders' perspectives. Rather than conforming to the structures of any one dominant narrative script, young people living across cultures seem to address contradictions head-on as they create narratives with details that clash. Paying attention to the clash and gaining insights about it is a major focus of this chapter. Rather than assuming that these moments are incoherent, I am looking for the complex arguments these youth are posing. This chapter is a reading of content and consequence in youth's social critique.

Narratives in response to different writing prompts raised issues of intergroup and interpersonal relations, but the nature and explicitness of social consciousness varied across the corpuses for each task. Written narratives and transcripts of teacher-led class discussions from two fifth grades whose literature and writing classes were audiotaped are the basis for this discussion. Examination of 116 narratives by 43 fifth-graders indicated that the young authors used narrative writing for social work. Dynamics within, across, and around the narratives offer insights about how these young people used narrative writing to construct social consciousness.

Identifying conflict issues, developments, outcomes, character perspectives, and character interactions provided the basis for examining narrative social consciousness. Narrative social consciousness is marked by multiple discourses in a text, which occur in a variety of ways, including as (1) explicit reflection on social issues or relationships; (2) the co-occurrence of diverse cultural scripts; (3) dissonance within story lines, such as between story means and ends or between story lines and themes; and (4) resistances to narrative structure or social relations scripts, such as not resolving a story. Examinations of two narrative tasks began in the same way, but as distinct patterns emerged, I described those varying patterns. I was also interested in variations across narrative social consciousness representations, in relation to the writers' classroom membership, sociocultural backgrounds, and changes within and across narrative tasks over the year.

Writing by children and adolescents is often used as a window into their minds and hearts, yet even though beginning writers may not have much control over the writing process, they use written language as a medium for social positioning. Although the focus in this chapter is not spelling and phrasing, original wordings provide important grounding in the authors' material circumstances as youth from a range of racial, ethnic, and socioeconomic groups attending urban public schools. Spontaneous spellings, oral phrasing, and diverse structural organizations in the texts by young writers in this study poignantly voice serious, mature psychosocial engagements.

RETICENCE AND HOPE ABOUT PERSONAL AND POWER RELATIONS

A truly remarkable aspect of social consciousness in personal conflict stories by people this young is their tendency to portray others' opinions of themselves and their ability to distinguish between social roadblocks they can remove and those that are more intransigent. These social sensitivities are often expressed implicitly through characters' interactions and reactions in mundane as well as dramatic scenarios around issues of intimate friendship, possessions, power struggles, play, and collaboration.

In October, as the culmination of the class study of *Felita*, the fifth-graders were asked to write about a personal conflict:

Write a story about a time when you or someone you know had a conflict or disagreement with someone your age. What happened? How did the people involved feel? How did it all turn out?

Maria Tierra, a girl describing herself as "Latina," wrote the following story:

Unfair

I've had a disagreement with my friend next door. Every time we play outside she always get the most jumps then everyone playing with her. I ask her why are you not playing fairly? She says yes I am. Then my other firends tell her the same. She says you are just jelious of me. We say why should we be jelious of you? We are all playing together just asking if you play fairly. She gets five jumps and then everybody else gets only four jumps. We all stop playing and she gets mad I tell her you want us to turn for you but you never let anybody else get there jumps, and you never turn for us. So if you want to continue to play with us you must be fair and we'll all have a lot of fun together.

As in the story "Unfair," personal conflict stories raised issues of fairness, typically addressing issues among friends, siblings, cousins, or neighbors as interpersonal conflicts or intergroup conflicts of one against many. The story "Unfair" is introduced by the "I" character as an interpersonal conflict—"I've had a disagreement with my friend next door"—but winds up as a conflict between a group of girls unhappy with another girl who takes the most jumps and doesn't "turn for us." This one-against-many conflict is developed with the narrator voicing most of the queries to the girl who is "not playing fairly": "I ask her why are you not playing fairly? She says yes I am. Then my other firends tell her the same." Then the voice shifts to "we" as persuasion and judgment are introduced: "We are all playing together just asking if you play fairly . . . We all stop playing," statements that occur in response to the girl's offense—"She gets five jumps and then everybody else gets only four jumps." The narrator recounts from a position of power, treating the jumping offender distantly, offering specific rules on behalf of her group, and keeping tabs on the "friend's" violations of the rules. The "I" character is bolstered by "everyone" else who plays, the "we." The author ends the story with conditions rather than a resolution.

The story Maria wrote in April (in response to the prompt used in October) is also framed as a conflict of one against many, but this time she situates herself outside the group.

The Disagreement

One day when I went in the hall to play with my friends from my building they got angry at me because I wouldn't bring out my nail salon. I told them that maybe next time I would bring it out. But they still kept on fussing and mubiling under there breath. What happen was that I tried to slove the problem. They felt angry because I didn't bring it out. So I promised them when I went to there house I would bring it with me downstairs. So they were still alittle made so I just started dealing my cards out. We were going to play I de clare war. I asked if they still wanted to play cards they thought about it for a few muintes then they said ok we'll play so we played. There was silence through the game. Then I said are we friends they said friends then for the rest of the time we played and played.

In this story, interactions occur between the "I" character and the group: "my friends," "they." The narrator's shift from object ("they got angry at me") to her taking personal responsibility to address the conflict ("I told them that maybe next time I would bring it—so I just started dealing my cards out"—"I asked"—"I said . . .") is characteristic of stories written in the spring, as it was in John's story discussed at the beginning of the chapter.

The spring story also presents diverse sides of "The Disagreement" more fully than the author had in the fall. The April story includes a variety of evaluative techniques, expressing reticence, reserve, and suspicion of the author's friends in the building. The "I" character's approach to the conflict is also a subtle nonconfrontational one in which she deflects the issue of her nail salon by starting to play cards. Rather than issues of fairness within groups, this is a story about an individual's need for personal/social resources, inventiveness, and persistence when facing a group with an opposing perspective. Seeming at times powerless and at other times in control, this narrating character describes an astutely observed progression of softening in her adversaries' position from "they got angry at me" to "But they still kept on fussing and mubiling under there breath"—"they were still alittle made"—"they said ok we'll play"—"There was silence through the game" and finally "they said friends" in response to the author's well-placed "Then I said are we friends" after she had moved the others to a point of minimal anger.

Reading for social relational issues such as power and discrimination also reveals differences of narrative social consciousness across the fall and spring personal conflict stories, in particular in terms of a shift in the social organization of conflicts. A notable critical consciousness theme across the conflict stories is the "I" character's, narrator's, or other major character's suspicion or reticence about social relationships, concerns about fairness, and trust in his or her abilities to work out problems. At the same time, characters were portrayed increasingly over the year as representing diverse perspectives on disagreements and strategies to address them. Whether these stories were or were not based on actual experiences, as the task requested, the young authors used the task to examine power plays from different perspectives and to examine the nature of social conflict itself by increasingly representing conflicts as embedded in social systems. The fall stories tended to describe conflicts as oppositions and fights, with others doing something unpleasant, unfair, or aggressive toward the author, such as someone not letting them play with a toy or saying something mean. In contrast, the spring stories tended to be framed as "we're all in this together," with conflicts described as mutual involvement in situations. This interaction was represented in diverse ways—sometimes by the use of "we" or "both" as a plural, mutual point of view around an issue; sometimes by a sequence of actions and/or perspectives portraying a complex conflict situation rather than two opposed points of view.

Another difference was that many stories written in the fall described interpersonal conflicts over possessions, desires, social control, and so forth, while in the spring stories there was an increasing tendency to describe social systems beyond those of friendship, as in John's example of an altercation with a store employee and Maria's facing an angry group with which she gradually united—albeit still somewhat suspiciously. In this move toward intergroup conflicts, groups tended to be described subtly as "they" or "are we friends" rather than named explicitly in terms of race, ethnicity, gender, or gang.

Representing social systems is consistent with elaboration of character perspectives—thoughts, feelings, intentions, perceptions, and speech. Character perspectives in fall stories tended to be mostly from the narrator's point of view, while the spring stories also portrayed points of view of adversaries and other characters involved more peripherally in the conflict. In terms of the overall social organization of conflict representations, narratives at the end of the year tended to involve compromises and coordination among the characters' needs, desires, fears, and intentions, meaning that conflict resolutions moved increasingly toward ones that involved new ways of relating and acting as well as addressing conflicting character perspectives. Although there were also a few instances in which social representations remained the same across the year, most personal conflict stories expressed increasingly consequential social relations, even if structural coherence appeared to suffer in this development.

Thus, from jumping rope to fist-fighting, youths' stories of conflict are tales of social strife, connection, and survival. In contrast to the relatively subtle social consciousness work in personal conflict stories, stories written in response to literary re-construction tasks involved explicit social critique, which is not surprising since this task directly addressed issues of discrimination.

SOCIAL INJUSTICE IS NOT A FICTION

Halfway through the study of social conflict in the context of the novels *Felita* (in the fall) and *Mayfield Crossing* (in the spring), young people worked with partners to write original endings to each novel, as framed in the Literary Re-construction task.

LITERARY RE-CONSTRUCTION TASK

Tensions between the Mayfield and Parkview kids come out on the baseball field one day, as described in the beginning of Chapter 7 (page 39):

> "I'm the pitcher! Get off my mound!" Clayton Reed shouted to Billie.
> We had started a pick-up game after lunch a couple of days later, just like we planned. We had been hanging around the swings, watching the Parkview kids play ball long enough. Today was our turn.
> "You deaf or something, tar baby?" Clayton said as he marched across the field with about twenty kids following him.

What happens next? Working with your partner, continue the story from here. First discuss a good (peaceful) ending with your partner. Then write your story together in the space below. Take turns doing the writing. As you write, keep discussing with your partner.

The idea behind this task was to engage young people with the characters and discriminatory conflict plots of novels they were reading by providing the opportunity to transform a story scenario. Given the highly charged nature of the quoted event, the characters in the story and the young authors in control of these characters' futures had myriad options from escalating the conflict to resolving it. The peer writing context was designed, in particular, to provide the young people with a social situation in which they could consider issues on their own terms more than they might have in the full-class discussions, where teachers conveyed their representations of social conflict, as we have seen occur in other studies (Daiute et al., 1998). Partner literary creations such as this one are also consistent with the approach of addressing racially explicit conflicts through role-playing activities that engage children in strategies for dealing with verbal and physical assaults. Since children enact stories as they compose them together, peer writing activities are social action as well as imagination.

Exploring issues of discrimination in narrative contexts provides a vicarious social context and safe distance from actual events, yet the richness of narrative makes this more than an exercise. Writing their own endings to the story from the high point of the conflict where Clayton was poised as a racist bully, yelling "You deaf or something, tar baby?" involved the young authors in a conflict that they had not begun but that they would have the opportunity to respond to or to rewrite, as if rewriting the course of history.

Stories resulting from this task strikingly engaged social consciousness, as captured in several patterns, including (1) confronting social injustice; (2) appealing to agents of power in power struggles; (3) appealing to rules, conditions, and the American Dream; and (4) talking things through, person-to-person.

Confronting Social Injustice

Many of the partner stories depicted characters' explicit confrontation of social injustice in Clayton's racist name-calling and the Parkview kids' unfair attempt to exclude the Mayfielders from playing on the field because of their race or any other reason. The following story by Dinna and Leshauna is an example of the explicit confrontation of social injustice.

BASEBALL

Alice started yelling, "This is'nt ony your field" Thats right Luke said. And me my brother and the rest of the gang nodded.

"I don't know who you think you are but I agree with Alice" Luke siad"

"Get out of here colored" one of the Parkview kids siad.

"That's not Right, We might be a different color but we are still PEOPLE" I siad. At that moment I felt spiecal cause the whole gang was chiering for me. Then billie got in the front of the Parkview kids and siad "What are you doing to do" The Parkview said let them play because we are to tought for them." So the Mayfield kids played ball.

The stories that directly confronted social injustice usually identified a specific injustice and offered a basis for this claim, but stories differed in the character that voiced the confrontation, the specific injustice they identified, and the basis for retribution. All the stories by boys voiced the objection through Billie, the young man that Clayton singled out. Some female partners also had Billie respond to Clayton, and some had Clayton apologize immediately. Some of female–female partners, as in the above example in which Alice took charge, and female–male partners positioned other female characters as the activists, including Meg and Ivy Scott, a Parkview girl who gradually befriended the Mayfielders. The range of responses included "It's not fair"; "No!"; "That wasn't very nice"; "Why can't we play?"; and "Stop!" These conversational responses were followed by specific claims of injustice, including "This is'nt ony your field" as in Dinna and Leshauna's story, "What does color have to do with it?"; "You get to play every day, and we don't"; "I'm not only Black"; "They called you Tar Baby!"; and "What's wrong with you people?!" In addition, each of the stories in this group offered a basis for their complaint, such as "We're all people"; "We're all human"; "We're part of the school, too"; and "it's our field, too."

Appealing to Agents of Power in Power Struggles

Injustice was also addressed by a third party in a number of stories, such as a teacher, the principal, an older kid, or the character Ole Hairy, who facilitated or forced a resolution. Such resolutions sometimes involved issues of fairness but most often established the social order of "this is how it is." This story written by Tamara and a partner (who was not named on the text) is an example of such a direct appeal to authority.

THE MAYFIELDERS AND THE PARKVIEW KID

Billie felt sad and mad at Clayton from what he had said to him.

Then a teacher came to the kids and said "Hey what's the problem."

Then Billie said to the teacher "The Parkview kids are alway's playing baseball now it's our turn to play".

"Why don't all of you share the baseball field, the teacher said.

Then Clayton said to the teacher "Me and my friends don't whant to play with those trashy Mayfielders."

Then the teacher say's to Clayton "Well you are going to have to learn to play with them."

So the teacher stood there watching them play.

> Then Clayton said to Billie "I'm sorry I said that nasty word to you," and Billie said to Clayton "It's O.K." Then the Parkview kid's said to the Mayfield kids that they will be their friends and they are.

This story by Tamara and a partner challenged Clayton's injustice by writing in the teacher, who at first suggested that the children share the field. When the Parkview kids hurled another offense—not wanting to play with the trashy Mayfielders (a spontaneously selected quote from the book)—the teacher in the story took an authoritarian approach, "You are going to have to learn to play with them." Across stories where they were included, such arbiters operated in a variety of ways, including ordering Clayton or the entire Parkview group to "lay off" ("You leave these kids alone you hear me! Now run along and play"), scaring them as only scary Ole Hairy could do, introducing a problem-solving or conflict negotiation approach where the arbiter says, "Hey what's the problem," or inviting both groups to a party the next week, as did a slightly older boy called in for help.

Appeal to Rules, Conditions, and the American Dream

Another kind of intervention in the conflict was a utilitarian one in which characters set conditions, set up a competition or bet to establish who had rights to the baseball field, or brought in a game of chance, such as flipping a coin. While this strategy addresses the conflict, it does not confront the issue that discrimination is wrong. The following example was written by Donald and his partner:

> Billie said "Hey lets not fight. How about we play, a game against each other.
> Clayton said "Yes but if my team win we can play here any time." What if we win" said Billie. "Then you can play here any time" said Clayton.
> The next day was the day they played. Billie's team was hitting first. Claytons team playing out field. The game was 20 points to win. The first hitter was Billie he hit a home run.
> Two hours has past the game was tied Billie's team was up. Meg shouted out "it's only 19 to 19 just make a home run." Billie hit the ball he didn't hit a home run bit it stayed in the park. Billie ran as fast as he could and made the home run. Billie's team screamed ina happy way.
> Clayton walked slowly to Billie and said "I'm sorry about all that I said about you." Billie said, "It's OK" "So you can play ny time Billie" Clayton said. "Well I guess so" Billie said.

Stories like this one seemed to be based on the assumption that someone could earn the right to the field, but the stories in this group differed in the specific procedure they proposed, ranging from playing a game to determine who would use the field, as in the story above, to flipping a coin or dividing the week into days when one or the other team would play. While most of these approaches were also built implicitly around an assumption that the groups would remain divided, one story concluded that they would play together at least one day of the week—on Fridays.

Talking It Through, Person-to-Person

Another group of stories involved the more interpersonal strategy of addressing the conflict with apologies, usually initiated by Clayton or other Parkview kids. As in the following story by Rosanna and her partner, the social mechanism seems to be one of respect, since apologies were often quickly accepted:

> Clayton and the other kids behind him started to walk across second base but they turned back. They come back to apologys. "I'm sorry for everything that I done wrong or what I said to you, to make it up to you, how about a game of baseball, You and you could be the captains of the teams." It was Mos and Luke that were the captains. All of them where choosen. To play frist we needed to do hand-over-hand. After the good game they all went to Meg and Billie's house, They stayed for dinner and the parents go to now them better and they met Old Hairy they all became good friends and every weekends the Parkview kids would come to play with the Mayfield Kids and Old Hairy told them that the hachet with the blood and hair on it was from a chicken to make Owen's cosin a vegetable soup.

In this story, the authors portrayed second thoughts by Clayton and the other kids who came to apologize, presumably to the Mayfielders. Clayton then was allowed the power to decide which Mayfielders would be captains, although it is not clear who decided to establish order with the hand-over-hand method. In this relatively unusual approach, the groups came together in a "good game" and they actually socialized at Meg and Billie's house in Mayfield Crossing, becoming "good friends," even with Old Hairy, whom they had all feared or suspected as a murderer. Even this most interpersonal of the literary re-construction stories addressed social issues more explicitly than personal conflict stories by the same young people. This diversity across tasks illustrates youth's sensitivity to narrative as well as interactional contexts, which provide forms for diverse social positioning.

SOCIAL CONSCIOUSNESS IN CONTEXT

Links between the curriculum context and young people's sociocultural backgrounds are relevant to how they identified injustices around conflicts. While recognition of injustice differed across narrative tasks, differences also occurred across classrooms, with all the stories that explicitly confronted social injustice coming from one class, and most of the stories with intimate, interpersonal scenes such as the "talking it out person-to-person" style above coming from another class. Sensitivity to social injustice is an aspect of young people's home preparation for interacting in the world, especially when they come from groups that have faced discrimination (Garcia & Hurtado, 1995; Hill-Collins, 1993; Ward, 1996) and when they live in multicultural settings. The children in the schools and classes in this study labeled themselves as African American, Black, White, Latina, Latino, Puerto Rican, Domincan, or other recent immigrant groups (and this information is noted with the examples quoted when available), so living and working in culturally heterogeneous cities may have made them especially prepared for the discussions of social issues they had with their teachers and classmates.

Insights about differences in young people's approaches to the narrative writing tasks come from examining transcripts of class discussions. For example, one of the fifth-grade teachers had emphasized interpersonal approaches, linking literary to real-life conflicts. This experienced teacher from a European American background sometimes pointed out racial discrimination as taught in society and families, and much of her detailed discussions with her students extended such issues to interpersonal interactions, such as talking things out as a way to resolve conflicts and the emotional consequences of these interactions.

The following excerpt from a class discussion about taking the perspective of someone with whom one disagrees engaged children in thinking about a time when they had considered and acted to respect another person's point of view, as in their sensitivity to Chu and his limited English and a time when they should have worked toward perspective-taking—the time when several members of the class had thrown water balloons as retaliation for an aggressive act.

Teacher: You know there is that old expression about putting yourself in someone else's shoes, and we've had to do that recently since Chu came into our class with a handful of English words, and we've had to think a lot about how difficult it is for him, not understanding our ways. We look so different from the kids who were in his class a couple of weeks ago, lots of new experiences. All right, we've been talking a lot about this and it is difficult to constantly be explaining what this means and what that means. Sure it's difficult but after seeing how ugly things can escalate to, do you ever think now that you might . . . do something about trying to communicate better with friends that, it sounds to me that in this balloon incident you just were having a lot of fun in between there too. . . . It sounds like an easy situation that could have turned into a fun thing instead of a battle, doesn't it? Especially in the summertime when we welcome getting smashed with a water balloon.

Student: And Sofia got mad . . . she run because they kicked Lana off the bike cause she got mad, that . . . water balloons.

Teacher: Hmmm, do you think that the water balloons was the best solution. Did you hear why she brought the water balloons to start? Carola, did you hear, I think you need to listen a bit more carefully, she brought the water balloons because one of them knocked her friend off the bike, knocked her cousin off the bike. Do you think water balloons was the best solution to, what do you think they could have done?

Student 2: Talk to them.

Teacher: Talk to them and if that was too different, too difficult because of language what else could they have done, Elise?

Student 1: Told their father.

Teacher: Their father's on the corner 24 hours a day, one of their dad's there . . .

Student 1: Actually uncle.

Teacher: Uncle, father, there's a few relations there.

Student 1: And, umm, I think Elise got mad because they did something to ah, I mean his sister, to their sister.

Teacher: Well that upsets us, that's the way conflicts escalate, they might not attack you, but they might attack somebody in your family, or you may do the same thing. . . . I can understand your anger. I can understand your anger.

Student 1: It's that they always start fighting.

Teacher: They, they, they, they. . . . Do you ever think that maybe sometimes they are trying to get your attention and say "Hi, I'm here, be my friend."

Student: Yeah.

Teacher: Do you think that's possible?

Student 3: We let them play basketball every day.

Student 4: Every day.

Teacher: We let them play basketball. . . .We let. I'm hearing this literature now. I'm hearing the Parkview ballfield now. We let them play basketball, where is the basketball court?

Young authors in this class overwhelmingly crafted stories consistent with the value of talking through conflicts. The young people in the class also constructed stories honed to their teacher's desire for students to use writing as a way of enacting nonviolent outcomes to potentially violent situations, as expressed in the excerpt of classroom interaction above. One day, for example, after becoming alarmed at a number of violent stories written by children in her class, the teacher changed the task prompt from "good story ending" (intended to engage partners in discussing what they thought an appropriate—"good"—ending would be) to "peaceful story ending." Apparently as a result, few literary re-constructions written in this class escalated into violence, while many of the stories conformed to the request for a peaceful ending, even in some cases in which characters' interactions did not lead smoothly to happily-ever-after conclusions. Empathy and perspective-coordination were notable as themes in the stories by children in this class as the school year progressed.

Another fifth-grade teacher, a White woman in her first year of teaching, allowed children to write stories with physical conflicts, while urging them to identify racism, reflect on the causes of conflicts, and struggle through considering "what is right" in such situations. The following excerpts illustrate this teacher's approach to exploring issues in these books. First, she directs a considerable discussion to getting the children to focus on "Tar Baby" as a bad, insulting word.

Teacher: Open your books . . . to the start of the chapter, who wants to give a retell? . . .
Boy from Asian background: In Chapter 7, umm, Billie and Meg and them, the Mayfield kids wanted to play baseball, and they went to the baseball field and they were playing half, half the game, and then the Parkview kids came and said, get off the field, they want to play.
Teacher: Did they say, " get off the field, we want to play"?
Student 1 [boy from European background]: No.
Teacher: What did they say?
Student 1: Get off the field, and he called him "Tar baby."
Teacher: Right. . . . That's the big problem.
Student 2 [boy from Asian background]: Right here, he said, I'm the pitcher, get off my mound.
Teacher: Clayton said something else after he said, "I'm the pitcher, get off my mound."

Student 1: He said, you deaf or something?

Teacher: You deaf of something, Tar Baby? Do you know what that word means? Let's see.

Student 2: Tar is something you cover the roof with.

Teacher: Tar is what you cover the roof with. . . . Is that a nice word or not?

Student 3: It's a nice word, but not like. . . .

Teacher: Tar is not a bad word, but. . . .

(Several students give comments at once.)

Teacher: . . . (*admonishing the talking at once*) because it's impossible for me to listen to you both of you at once, so why don't you put your hands up and . . . then you can share your thoughts.

Student 4: I think tar means, like if someone's Black and, and someone's been raised saying tar baby, like call it black.

Teacher: What were you going to say? . . .

Student 5 [boy from African American background]: Like umm, if somebody, like they say something bad, like somebody else's skin, they say . . . like in a bad way, like tar, that's what they mean in a bad way.

When the conversation veered from the intergroup conflict, this teacher repeatedly directed children's attention back to it.

Student 6 [girl from African American background]: And then she's really upset.

Teacher: And she's really upset about those words, but why? Leshauna.

Student 6: Because in the beginning of Chapter 7, nobody cares in Mayfield who's White and who's Black, and the Shermans are from Mayfield, and she was surprised . . .

Teacher: Yeah, she, her, the whole emphasis, at the very beginning of the book, Papa said, "Mayfield's different, Mayfield's not like other towns," and what we understood from that was that it didn't matter in Mayfield what color skin you had, whether you had Black skin or White skin or whatever, and now all of a sudden one of her friends is using words like, White kid . . .

Teacher: And why didn't the boy who had only one spelling word wrong didn't want his name up on the board with Owen's name who had no spelling words wrong?

Student 6: Because he was Black.

Teacher: Because he didn't want to be associated.

Such focus on intergroup conflicts and discussion of the discriminatory meaning behind interactions create a safe space for explicit confrontation of social injustice by young authors in this class. In addition, while a number of literary re-constructions written in this class escalated verbal and physical conflicts, the stories also included characters' mutual sharing of points of view, reasoned agreements about how to address differing points of view, and their need to live together, even if they might not become best friends.

THE SIGNIFICANCE OF NARRATIVE WRITING
FOR SOCIAL CONSCIOUSNESS

Differences in social consciousness themes across the personal conflict stories and literary re-constructions are important for several reasons. The diversity in how young authors worked each narrative task is a remarkable testimony to their ability to "read" cultural scripts, work with them, and embed them in their own sense-making processes. Requests for social participation, such as narrative task prompts, play a role in constructing young people's engagement with social issues, make a difference in the nature of social issues examination, and provide the basis for subsequent class discussion of different approaches to each task and what they imply about issues facing youth.

Brief prompts put in motion narrating processes that are often sophisticated reflections on discrimination. Varying the nature and explicitness of social conflict themes, varying voice, and varying the amount of background in the writing prompts provided common material for diverse and uncommon social critique. The explicit confrontations of social injustice, appeal to authorities, and appeal to rules in the literary re-construction tasks—as compared to the more implicit engagement of intergroup conflicts in the personal conflict stories—indicate that asking children to deal directly with social issues involves them in complex analysis of injustice and the need to address it from positions of power and powerlessness. Other aspects of the literary re-construction task may also have contributed to the writers' critical approaches on that task, including how the novel had laid out characters and events leading up to the discriminatory event. Being able to build on a poignant story fragment may have facilitated an explicitly analytic stance. Nevertheless, working with a story already in progress also required the youngsters to recall and deal with a range of details that had been conveyed in the novel. The third-person perspective of the literary re-construction task may also have removed stigma, embarrassment, or other factors that minimize directly addressing the charged issues of discrimination. Having some distance from actual events may also make it more possible to experiment with hopefulness. Thus fictional contexts that explicitly address issues are fruitful for developing imaginative approaches to social analysis, while more open, reality-based tasks provide opportunities for personal integration of these issues, as has been suggested in research on relationships between education and action around substance abuse (Levitt & Selman, 1996).

Thus we have seen that inviting young people to narrate in particular ways involves them in social reflection that might otherwise go unexplored. Such content-based invitations to write, however, are somewhat inconsistent with prevailing views about classroom-based narrative writing that emphasize authenticity and spontaneity rather than imagination, invention, and focus on specific issues. While these two approaches could co-occur, the preferred approach in writing-process classrooms has been to encourage children to write only from personal experience about topics of immediate importance to them rather than to respond to assigned tasks (Calkins, 1984; Graves, 1983). There is much to be said for spontaneously generated writing, but school also needs to develop an agenda for examining social issues that youth may be unlikely to address on their own. When under the tutelage of open, sensitive teachers such as those described above, discourse about social issues can occur with literary and documentary forms of writing.

This chapter suggests that discursive work around challenging life issues is important for social as well as literacy development. The examples here illustrate how young people's engagement of social issues in narrative contexts can grow in complexity, and the diversity of responses to narrative task prompts indicates that prescribing social topics for conversation opens up reflection rather than closing it off. The value of varied narrative engagements as well as the realization that no writing activity occurs outside cultural construction underscore previous arguments about the need to reconsider "naturalistic" approaches. The notion that knowledge evolves naturally has been increasingly questioned because of the socioculturally specific nature of all written language structures and processes. Those who have observed children from minority backgrounds working in writing-process classrooms, for example, have argued that culture and teaching shape writing even when children write without reference to specifically stated prompts (Delpit, 1988; Heath, 1983).

FROM STORY TO ACADEMIC ACHIEVEMENT

Invitations to narrate create anomalous spaces in schools. While much school discourse involves decontextualizing in its tendency to isolate concepts through defining and categorizing, narrative sites are context-rich opportunities for reconstructing self, other, conflict, and action. Similarly, while much of the focus on content in schools aims toward objective truth, narratives are interpretive in their portrayal of characters and events from specific points of view. This interpretive aspect of narrative thus engages children and adults in drawing on contexts they know well, including places, relationships, and meanings in their homes, neighborhoods, and imaginations. At the same time, school values shape young people's writing toward common meanings and modes. This case study illustrates how young people interpret and alter such meanings in narratives, where institutions may be personified in characters that interact, combat, change, and deal with consequences of their actions and beliefs.

Much of the previous research on narrative development has been done with children living in homogeneous settings where addressing issues of diversity may be abstract if it occurs at all. In such settings, progress toward conflict resolution may appear direct and linear, but when young people who have observed and experienced discrimination read and discuss literature about discrimination, they do not accept the same causal interpretations or resolutions. Instead, given the opportunity to discuss and probe, children can examine experience critically and, for the most part, generously construct a range of interpretations and social strategies. Even though urban youth may have more direct experience with people of different races and classes than do their counterparts from more culturally homogeneous settings, the ways in which they bring these experiences into play in narrative sites is unpredictable and may be subject to painful realities as well. The flexible, subjective representations in the texts discussed here underscore the creative, cathartic, and critical use of narrating.

While functioning successfully in U.S. educational and other mainstream institutions requires using standard narrative frames for communication, multiple voicing may occur especially in minority-group discourses because youth need to address issues of power from culturally specific points of view and critical insights (Gates, 1989). Adults who work with children need to deal with what may seem like contradictions in their narratives as opportunities for cultural interaction and social development, such as in the stories cited here. The pressure for singular forms of narrative coherence in school-based writing is a microcosm of the tremendous political pressure for a unified society, as in English-only movements. Teachers can help students from all backgrounds participate in social discourse by considering students' multiple and complex story lines.

FROM STORY TO STREET

Education and policy interests always raise questions about how cognitive and social work leads to action. The argument in this chapter is that given certain stances, pedagogies, and projects, young people can discursively address problems in society and in their lives, even though these issues may be controversial. The stories cited here illustrate transformations of social representations across a school year, in particular changes from polarization to social engagement and from walking away to talking it through. Young authors qualify their hopes for social connection with wisdom that seems beyond their years, as others have found with teenagers (Burton, Obeidallah, & Allison, 1996). Writing is an active process as young authors work with the social and physical realities around them through fiction and fantasy to imagine lives of connection and consequence. It is a significant achievement for any of us to practice strategies for thinking and talking through angry moments by writing stories. The most important aspect of this practice is that it helps young people acknowledge the diversity and mutability of power struggles, rights, and responsibilities. These discursive activities provide orientations for future action, where young people can feel agency to interact, analyze, defend, walk away, or rewrite history.

Young people need support in their efforts at trying on different ways of being in the world. Narratives that do not seem to follow cultural scripts may well be young authors' committed, personal interpretations of the cultures in which they live—even when these narratives are nonconforming or critical. Support should not be withdrawn when virtual lives in narratives do not progress directly to a standard pattern. Room to explore in the narrative realm, of course, may challenge notions of conventional morality, as occurs when young people write violent stories and stories that do not end happily. Such narrating is a context for meaningful discussion of social issues that are bypassed when stories are censored, scripted, or left to spontaneous generation. Variability in narrative positioning could be the most productive occurrence, but much more practice-based research by interdisciplinary teams is needed to examine how narrative social positioning occurs over time and how youth interpret connections between narrating and acting in the world. If adult fiction serves cathartic functions, then why not children's? Certainly, experienced adult authors recognize that coming to know via writing is often a struggle among public and private voices, if not clashing cultural mores.

The value of narrative social consciousness work is that it engages young people and adults who listen to them in thinking complexly—recognizing and cultivating abilities to see the world in diverse ways at the same time. Literature of social justice is thus a narrative genre that can have an impact on young people's development of social consciousness as well as on their literacy skills. We have much to learn from young people in U.S. cities—about social understanding, reality, action, tolerance, and hope—if we provide them with spaces, support, leadership, and assessments in which re-construction is encouraged and celebrated.

Acknowledgments. The research reported on in this chapter was supported in part by the William T. Grant Foundation. I thank the following research assistants for their work, especially with data collection: H. Jones, C. Rawlins, R. Stern.

REFERENCES

Ball, A. (1998). The value of recounting narratives: Memorable learning experiences in the lives of inner-city students and teachers. *Narrative Inquiry, 8,* 151–180.

Bruner, J. (1986). *Actual minds, possible worlds.* Cambridge, MA: Harvard University Press.

Burton, L. M., Obeidallah, D. A., & Allison, K. (1996). Ethnographic insights on social context and adolescent development among inner-city African-American teens. In R. Jessor, A. Colby, & R. A. Shweder (Eds.), *Ethnography and human development: Context and meaning in social inquiry* (pp. 395–418). Chicago: University of Chicago Press.

Calkins, L. (1984). *The art of teaching writing.* Portsmouth, NH: Heinemann.

Cazden, C. B. (1988). *Classroom discourse: The language of teaching and learning.* Portsmouth, NH: Heinemann.

Daiute, C. (1997). *Discourse and action around social conflict* (Research proposal). New York: City University of New York Graduate School.

Daiute, C. (1998, February). Points of view in children's writing. *Language Arts,* pp. 138–149.

Delpit, L. (1988). The silenced dialogue: Power and pedagogy in educating other people's children. *Harvard Educational Review, 58,* 280–298.

Du Bois, W. E. B. (1903). *Souls of Black folk.* Chicago: A. C. McClurg.

Freire, P. (1989). *Pedagogy of the oppressed.* New York: Continuum Press.

Garcia, E. E., & Hurtado, A. (1995). Becoming American: A review of current research on the development of racial and ethnic identity in children. In W. D. Hawley & A. W. Jackson (Eds.), *Toward a common destiny: Improving race and ethnic relations in America* (pp. 163–184). San Francisco: Jossey-Bass.

Gates, H. L. (1989). *Loose canons: Notes on the culture wars.* New York: Oxford University Press.

Gramsci, A. (1971). *Selections from the prison notebooks.* London: Lawrence & Wishart.

Graves, D. (1983). *Writing: Teachers and children at work.* Portsmouth, NH: Heinemann.

Heath, S. B. (1983). *Ways with words: Language and life in a southern community.* New York: Cambridge University Press.

Hill-Collins, P. (1993). *Black feminist thought: Knowledge, consciousness, and the politics of empowerment.* New York: Routledge.

Jameson, F. (1981). *The political unconscious: Narrative as socially symbolic act.* Ithaca, NY: Cornell University Press.

Lee, C. D. (1993). *Signifying as a scaffold for literacy interpretation: The pedagogical implications of an African-American discourse genre.* Urbana, IL: National Council of Teachers of English.

Levitt, M. Z., & Selman, R. L. (1996). Personal meaning in risk and prevention. In A. A. Noam & K. W. Fisher (Eds.), *Cognition, evolution, and development.* Mahwah, NJ: Erlbaum.

Lightfoot, C. (1997). *The culture of adolescent risk-taking.* New York: Guilford.

Michaels, S. (1991). The dismantling of narrative. In A. McCabe & C.Peterson (Eds.), *Developing narrative structure* (pp. 303–351). Hillsdale, NJ: Erlbaum.

Mohr, N. (1979). *Felita.* New York: Bantam.

Nelson, V. M. (1993). *Mayfield Crossing.* New York: Avon.

Tannen, D. (1991). *Framing.* New York: Oxford University Press.

Walker, P. (1998). *Voices of love and freedom.* Logan, IA: Perfection Learning Corporation.

Ward, J. V. (1996). Raising resisters: The role of truth telling in the psychological development of African-American girls. In B. Leadbeater & N. Way (Eds.), *Urban girls* (pp. 85–99). New York: New York University Press.

CHAPTER 13

Pitching, Dancing, and Budget Cuts

CONSTANCE WEBSTER

When I think about it . . . even in the middle of the worst game, the most pressure, I still really love pitching. I just love standing there and being in the center of everything. I don't know . . . it's like my chance to show people what I can do. (Barb, athlete)

I love dancing . . . it's like total escape. Like I can leave all the problems of school and homework . . . and I dance and move around and that's why I like it, because I can leave everything behind. Before I did it for dancing; now, since life has gotten more complicated, I like it to escape. (Linda, performing artist)

The prolific literature on concerns about girls' identity development (Fine, 1993; Gilligan, 1982; Lesko, 1988; McRobbie, 1978; National Council for Research on Women, 1998; Pipher, 1994; Wellesley College Center for Research on Women, 1992) has yet to be linked to the reporting of accelerated budget crises in educational settings. With a particular eye to the relation of extracurricular activities and girls' healthy identity development, this chapter looks inside one school to document how girls produce and challenge traditional identities through their participation in sports and the arts. In these two spaces, within a school, girls discover and invent ways of thinking about gender that assist them in challenging the stereotypical image of what it means to be "popular" and female in the halls of their high school.

The President's Council on Physical Fitness and Sports (1997) and the National Council for Research on Women (1991, 1998) list the benefits that occur when girls "come together in solidarity" (National Council for

Research on Women, 1998, p. 10): improving self-esteem, developing positive feelings about body image, increasing self-confidence, increasing opportunities for experiences of competency and success, and increasing willingness to take risks and try new experiences. Sports and the arts represent two spaces in schools, both under budget attacks nationally, where girls can come together and may take advantage of these developmental opportunities.

Dorothy Smith (1988) reminds us that "women aren't just passive products of socialization, they are active; they create themselves" (p. 39). Girls' identity construction occurs both on their bodies, through appearance work, and by actions they take in school. For the purposes of this chapter, athletics and the arts are identified as counterhegemonic spaces in the school where girls' identities are influenced by messages that challenge the common image of what it means to be female. In these spaces, traditional masculine constructs such as "achievement, toughness, endurance, aggressiveness, and competitiveness" (Adler, Kless, & Adler, 1992, p.170) are appropriated by and for girls. Involvement in athletics and the arts provides the girls with opportunities to lead, experience personal success, be self-motivated, and be involved with varied aspects of school life and the student body. Without such spaces, these opportunities are lost, with potentially dramatic impact on girls.

The opportunities realized from participation in athletics and the arts are presented in this chapter by eight White, middle-class, 16-year-old girls attending Rockland West High School, an average-size school located in a primarily White working-class neighborhood with small pockets of more affluent neighborhoods.

The girls in the sports peer group are members of at least two varsity athletic teams sponsored by the school in addition to club teams outside the school. Donna plays for the volleyball and basketball teams, Bridget is on the basketball and softball teams, Colleen is co-captain of the softball team and a member of the swim team, and Barb is captain of the softball and basketball teams. Beyond sports, all are involved with other school activities, including the National Honor Society, the student council, and the string quartet. Three of the girls are enrolled in academic honors and advanced placement classes.

I met each of the girls in the arts peer group from observing drama and visual arts classes during the schoolday and the after-school drama club. Karen and Linda are active in the school musical and the school theater club and include both acting and visual arts as part of their academic schedule. In addition, both girls are enrolled in private dance and acting classes outside of school. Sue is very active in the visual arts programs at the school. She also takes an acting class as part of her school curriculum and performs with a local acting company outside of school. Peg is enrolled in an advanced visual arts class and is very active in a music subculture outside of school. All are enrolled in academic honors and advanced placement classes.

I begin this discussion by presenting the athletic girls and their identity development. I then move to the arts girls before concluding with a summary of the overall influence that involvement in athletics and the arts has on these girls' identity development.

GIRLS' PARTICIPATION IN SPORTS

An important message, received and carried by the girls in the sports peer group, is the motivation to succeed through their bodies and minds. When the girls talk about their personal successes on their respective athletic teams, they do so with a sense of excitement and power. Individual successes are something to be proud of, not downplayed in the company of peers. Barb's quote at the beginning of the chapter illustrates this point. Bridget, too, talks about her successes on the athletic field: "Motivation basically: it's like excelling to a higher level. It's like you achieve something and you just want to get better because you know you have made it to that level, and you want to get even higher. It's a rush . . . it's great."

Resisting Stereotypes

These personal successes provide the girls emotional tools to carry into challenging situations off the field. Bridget and Barb both reported incidents in which they were confronted with sexist remarks regarding women athletes. Each taps into energy experienced on the field, which is then re-"pitched" to "shut up" those making the remarks.

> There is a foreign-language volleyball tournament next week, and some of the guys are like, "Oh, well, we shouldn't have any girls on our team because they aren't good enough to play at our level." It's like OK. So it's kind of frustrating, but it's like as long as you know what you can do and prove yourself, it shuts them up. It does; they don't have much to say. (Bridget)

Barb shares a similar story of dealing with male students' perceptions of female athletes:

> A lot of people, especially men, tend not to like women who play sports . . . or who have strong opinions and who are not like, "OK,

whatever you say," like the ditzy cheerleader type . . . like freshman year, I think it was, some guys would get jealous and pissed because my name would be on the announcements and they would be like, "Oh, you're such a brute" and stuff like that. I hated that. I mean just 'cause I play sports and I'm a girl. And because I'm not a little twig or cheerleader or something.

When I asked Barb how she handles situations such as the one above, she replied: "I don't care, 'cause most of those people are losers anyway. I mean, it bothered me more then than it does now; I think it like hardened me, which is good."

Negative reaction to her success in a male-dominated field doesn't deter Barb from pursuing her athletic goals. She frames these reactions as jealousy, identifies herself as "hardened," and sees those students who react negatively as "losers." In a quick turn against girls, she then juxtaposes her identity as an athlete against the "ditzy cheerleader type." Representing an unfortunate splitting among girls, cheerleaders get derisively positioned as the "traditional" group of females, in part because they are accepted by males in the domain of athletics.

Both Bridget and Barb take on female stereotypes as they challenge the negative image of the "inadequate" or "brutish" female athlete. They choose to prove themselves on a coed athletic team and refuse male taunting. By doing so, they incrementally refocus athletics as a space for both male and female students, although traditionally occupied by male students. They model for other female students the strength of women as athletes in the face of male critique. These girls are slowly prying open a space within schools for future generations of female athletes to enjoy.

Attention in Athletics and Academics

The pride that the girls gain from their personal successes is encouraged by the positive recognition they receive for their efforts. At the softball games I attended, there were often 50 or more spectators. During the playoffs, these numbers increased to upwards of 100. I would often hear mothers and fathers talking about taking off work to get to a game on time. Attention experienced on the field carries over into the school. The school has institutionalized ways to recognize the girls' athletic efforts. Barb's successes were frequently broadcasted on the morning announcements. The girls wear their jerseys to school on game day. Barb comments, "When we wear our uniforms to school, I really like that kind of stuff." Eder and Parker (1987), referring to male athletes, state that "wearing uniforms was a major source of pride for team members. It was a reward coaches granted team members for exceptional effort and performance" (p. 203). Barb echoes this sense of pride.

For many adolescent girls, being the center of attention is often achieved through physical appearance or membership in a popular clique. For Barb, it's done through pitching. Barb and the other female athletes attract attention to themselves in ways that are in stark contrast to what much of the literature suggests girls find important (Eder, 1985; Eder & Kinney, 1995; Eder & Parker, 1987). Eder (1985) suggests that "adolescent females are more concerned with popularity than with achievement or success" (p. 154). Yet for Barb, aspects of the attention she receives in school derive from athletic achievements. When schools enable girls to thrive in "nontraditional" spaces, they rise to the occasion.

Experiences with success on the field carry into academics. Colleen transfers her "field" competitiveness into her academic work. Referring to the classroom, Colleen comments: "I pick someone out just to get me going if I feel like I'm slacking. And that's what I do in sports also. I'll find someone who is as good as me or better than me, and that just makes me work that much harder to where I want to be." By picking out students who excel, Colleen sets up an internal competition.

Bridget also talks about her academic placement. She, too, equates achievement with high standards, not necessarily popularity. The only girl in the study who is not in academic honors classes, Bridget relates her feelings about her placement within the academic hierarchy. She states:

> I want to be in honors classes. I have the ability to be in honors big time. I know I have the ability; I just want the challenge. I feel like I'm surrounded by people who don't have the same goals as I do . . . they don't do their homework, they don't want to learn, and it's frustrating because I want to get somewhere and that bothers me. They're mostly kids who don't want a challenge, and it's boring.

Barb also links her academics and athletic success:

> Grades are the most important thing to me—probably more than sports . . . or at least up there with them; it's probably half and half. When we went to Florida with the softball team during spring break, I did some homework and they [other players] were all like, "Barb is doing homework!" You know, like they don't understand that when you take advanced placement classes you get like hours and hours of homework. And what am I supposed to do, just not

do my homework and fail? I mean, what's the point of taking the classes, you know?

For Barb, grades and athletics are equally important. "I want to get a softball scholarship. . . . I know I want to go to college and hopefully get a scholarship for softball so I can play."

Emphasis on success and its expression in the classroom challenges the traditional image of the complacent, nonaggressive female. Sadker and Sadker (1994) found in their research that "the classroom consists of two worlds: one of boys in action, the other of girls' inaction" (p. 42). The girls' experiences with athletics influence their interactions in the classroom, reclaiming at least one, and maybe more, spaces traditionally occupied by males.

Attitude Toward Appearance

In today's society, with its never-ending barrage of culturally defined concepts of "beauty," it is not surprising that many young girls take their external appearance very seriously. Lesko (1988) writes that "the body is the primary site of identity construction; style and appearance signify consciousness in relation to social environments and institutions as well as in relation to peers" (p. 123). For these young athletes, successful construction of their outward appearance moves beyond fashion. The girls view appearance as power, an opportunity to demonstrate self-respect and to command respect from others. Donna states, "Your first judgment about people is really what they look like and how they carry themselves." They like being tall, find comfort in looking "like dad," and take some delight in their muscle. When asked, "How would you describe your body image?" they responded:

> Well . . . being tall, I'm 5'9", it's kind of, I don't think of it as anything. It's definitely not curvy, it's definitely not like a womanly body or anything, but it's not like a boy body. It's a cross between athletic. Like I have huge upper arms . . . and I hate that. But then I like my legs because they are thin and muscular . . . I'm built like my dad. I have thin legs and I have kind of a belly and big arms. (Barb)

> Umm, I don't consider myself fat, but I think I could work on a lot, like tone. I'm very conscious about that. Donna and I, we are not like toothpick figures because we run a lot and do a lot of extra

activities. I don't know; we have bigger bones than other people. (Bridget)

I have an athletic build, I think. I have a lot of muscle and, umm, I'm a strong person. So basically that's what I perceive. I exercise frequently; I play sports. It's just better for you, I feel better about myself when I'm doing stuff like that. I feel better when I'm in shape, but I'm not compulsive like, ohhh, I have to build my muscles. (Donna)

When Donna states "I just feel better about myself," she makes a profound comment regarding the positive effects exercise can have on a girl's body image. The girls describe their body image as athletic, big-boned, and strong. Considering the growing numbers of White girls their age who have a negative body image (National Council for Research on Women, 1998; Pipher, 1994), it is significant that these girls have cultivated a positive self-image through athletics.

Being athletic and looking physically fit are aspects of the girls' identity that they work to create and maintain. Watson (1987) writes: "The simultaneous production of a feminine identity and the relational identity of athlete is characterized by dilemmas and contradictions" (p. 435). Never outside the hegemony of "thin and feminine," and yet contesting this as the only image, for these girls the dilemma is illustrated by the attempt to keep the development of their athletic physique in check. Having muscles on one's arms and legs is a consequence of frequent exercising. Yet being too "bulked up" equates to looking "boyish." If the physical development crosses the line between "muscular and thin and bulked up and boyish," the girls become dissatisfied with the results. While they see themselves as athletic, "athletic" is carefully mitigated by an avoidance of appearing masculine. Although each of the girls expresses a personal investment in being physically fit, building up "too much muscle" is not welcomed. Barb likes her legs because they are "thin and muscular," but she worries that her arms are "huge, like bulked up all this muscle . . . it looks so boyish." As the starting pitcher for the girls' varsity fast-pitch softball team, it makes sense that she would develop strong arm muscles. But this is a consequence she would like to avoid. Yet, from the same physical work, her legs become thin and muscular. Thin, muscular legs are acceptable for Barb, but she draws the line with muscular arms. She sees them as too boyish.

Girls' identities develop within and across athletic sites, permeating other spaces where identity development takes place. The attention, encouragement, motivation, and competitiveness experienced by being on a team carry over into other experiences in school.

GIRLS' INVOLVEMENT IN THE ARTS

Interesting similarities cut across the arts and athletic peer groups. Both groups of girls express a willingness to confront stereotypes, take on challenging situations in the classroom, and appreciate the attention received from peers and adults. Similar to the "sports girls," the "arts girls" have discovered an institutionally recognized space within the school where the fanning out of female identity development is encouraged, not thwarted or constrained.

On Self-Reflection

When using the term *art*, one often thinks of an end product—a finished painting, drawing, song, or sculpture. For these girls, artistic expression unravels in a process of performance and creation. The art space enables reflection and relaxation, as well as allowing them to revise their work.

When the girls talk about the space where their artistic expression takes place, they all do so with an appreciation for how the experience grounds their personal growth and launches a sense of freedom. Sue captures the clear air of art when she states, "It's . . . it's breathing as far as I'm concerned." She goes on to say: "Even in classes and stuff, I'm able to think clearer. It [drawing] helps me to focus. It keeps me . . . I don't know how to describe it; basically it just keeps me going. It's something I really can't live without." With a similar lightness, Linda talks about dancing in the quote that opened this chapter. Karen states: "I've been taking drama classes since I was 11, and so it's like . . . it's a nice part of the day to just relax." Peg explains, "After I go to a really good show I feel like, Oh, I could conquer the world now! And I don't care about those stupid girls in school! For that bit, I'm like, yeah!" While many adolescents find it difficult to step back from their social life and reflect on the pressures they are experiencing (Pipher, 1994), these girls are able to take that step back and utilize the artistic space as one means of gaining release from these stresses.

Receiving Recognition

Girls' artistic skills, and the products, do not go unrecognized within the school. The time and energy the girls invest in the musical or the art show is acknowledged by peers, school personnel, and family. Sue and Linda delight in the positive attention they receive.

> Like, some of the teachers are really nice. They wrote me congratulation letters after the musical. They care about you a lot. (Linda)

> Encouragement? From teachers, yes, definitely; from my friends, yes, definitely . . . my friends say basically anything I do is good. I'll do stuff, like I'm playing around, and they will be like, "Oh, that's so good, you shouldn't be throwing that out." Like they kind of encourage me when they look at my stuff and go "wow," they seem really impressed. That means a lot to me; it's nice to hear. At my old school I had a really close bond with a teacher, and we would go out after school and weekends and stuff to go paint and things like that. That really encouraged me a lot. Just the thought that I was worth spending time with a teacher. She thought that I was a good enough artist to want to go do these things with . . . to take an interest in me. (Sue)

Getting a card, spending after-school time doing artwork, and positive accolades from peers are some examples of support Linda and Sue receive by sharing their artistic skills with others. Additionally, photographs of Karen and Linda hang in the front office's kiosk, and Sue's and Peg's artwork decorates the halls of the school.

Appreciation of Learning and Diversity

The "arts girls" connect their performances and creations to academics and also to a sense of moral inclusion:

> It's more important that I learn something [other] than whether I did good on a test. If I'm in a really fascinating subject . . . Like social studies is a good example—there are parts of history that fascinate me. Like dates, I'm really bad with, but I like stories—the whole Russian Revolution, the Anastasia story, Rasputin—they're really great, really great. And I'm really getting into it and loving it, then I take the test and I don't do so well. I'm not upset, because I know I picked up a lot that I'm going to remember. I don't just learn facts then regurgitate them and throw them out. The whole point of the thing is to understand people more, understand life more, understand the world we live in more, what happened before us, what's happening now. (Sue)

Grades are more important but are not important like other things. They are not like overly important, and like I get good grades and like, I'm an overachiever in things that I like. Like our *Macbeth* project for English, we worked so hard, and there was no need to work that hard. Like, other people did whatever, but we loved doing it. (Linda)

Linda's work on *Macbeth* resulted in an elaborate staging of the witches' interaction with Macbeth. She included other students in the project, as well as costumes and props; she even manipulated the atmosphere of the room to enhance the staging. Her love of the subject, coupled with her creativity, resulted in a performance far outdistancing the basic assignment. The girls are committed to producing results from their exquisite attention to content.

The girls' artistic involvement also influences their identity construction vis-à-vis their engagement with "differences":

Linda: The art world is more discriminatory toward men ... men are more inclined to math and women are better at art and English things. Like I know a lot of guys who are into art. And I know that at least by some jock people, they say, "Oh, yeah, he's such a fag" and everything like that.

CW: Are you saying that jocks call males that are into the arts "fags"?

Linda: Oh yeah ... they're queer and everything because they're not big jock manly men. Artists are expected to be real sensitive and appreciate things. And traditionally women are supposed to have that aptitude. Personally, I think it's really cool when a guy can appreciate and be sensitive and feel things. I think that every person in this world is bisexual in some way or another and just doesn't recognize that. In every person there is a little male and female, the yin and yang.

Karen states:

One of my best friends, that's a guy, is gay. We were in the musical together. And a lot of my mom's students are gay, and I've known a lot of gay people in my life and it's never been an issue with me. Like in my acting classes, my teachers are all like very artistic. And like, my last years instructor, he was openly gay ... which I respect so much.

The art world is a space where diversity is sought and invited to flourish (Fine, Weis, Centrie & Roberts, 2000). Through their involvement in the arts, these girls provide themselves an opportunity to experience the broad varieties of the human experience. In response, Karen and Sue have little tolerance for students who express homophobic remarks:

> I've known a lot of gay people in my life, and it's never been an issue with me. Like I've never been like, "Oh, you faggot." Like oh! That makes me so mad! If people are like knocking homosexuals, I like go through the roof. Even if they are not my friends. I just like get so upset, you know. If people ask me questions, of course I'm gonna tell them, because I want people to understand it and not be afraid of it. I just don't want people to be ignorant. (Karen)

> There is a great deal of homophobia in this school. There are some people who are like, "OK, whatever," and then there are some people who, if they don't like someone, they will say, "Oh, yeah, you're such a fucking faggot man!" I hate that phrase. Every time I hear it, I basically have to walk out of the room. It just affects me. Like they make it so cheap, the same way they make sex cheap and love cheap. It's like no, no. (Sue)

Karen's and Sue's appreciation and understanding of "difference," fostered within their artistic spaces, inspires them to risk challenging homophobia within the school. By articulating their acceptance of gays and lesbians and by challenging homophobic remarks, the girls expose themselves to potential harassment from other students (Fine, 1993; Friend, 1993; Rofes, 1989). Yet the positive experiences they have had both educate them and inspire confidence in them to challenge homophobia expressed by others. The safe space of the arts spills over into the moral fabric of the school.

Appearance as Performance

The art girls' appearance work, combined with their creativity and intellect, culminates in performances. Each young woman uses her body to communicate an identity that she marks as being different from that of the overall student body. Involvement in the arts, coupled with their interest in popular culture, influences their appearance work. Just as they perform on stage, they also perform with their bodies, constructing appearances that deviate from the "typical teenager." Karen states:

> I don't go with the flow like the people in school. If I want to wear something, I'll wear it and I don't care. Well, I care, but I'm willing to get looked at or whatever. It gives me more fuel for the fire. I

just want to do it more if people look at me. I'm just like different with a sense of style. . . . Like I can tell when I walk down the hall and people look at me or whatever . . . like some of the stuff I wear just happens to catch people's eye and rub them the wrong way. . . . So I think they [other students] might be jealous of me and that might be why they call me names and make fun of me; that's their problem if they're that insecure.

Similar to the way Barb from the sports peer group identifies male students who pick on female athletes as "losers," Karen identifies students who call her names because of her appearance as "insecure." Karen typically wears platform shoes, short skirts, and small form-fitting shirts. Rather than internalize negative comments, both girls maintain their identity and resist conforming to social critique expressed by other students.

I dress different than the normal, like, typical teenager. I like anyone who has their own sense of style. I like people who are not afraid to be original because of the clothes they wear. It's just been my experience that people who dress differently are different. They aren't the basic everyday person. They have something to offer . . . like I can love something Carol [a friend] wears and hate something she wears, but I love that she does it. And not just Carol—any people, like the Guidos [associated with baggy pants, gold chains, and rap music]. Like they love their chains and their pants and I give them prop. (Linda)

"Giving prop" means that she supports, or props up, expressions of individuality. An example of this is Peg's style of dress, which includes very baggy pants with wide bell-bottoms, small shirts (usually T-shirts), and sneakers. In addition, Peg sometimes wears small miniskirts with short tops and platform shoes. Peg's dress marks her involvement in her music subculture, which provides social support to dress in the manner that she does.

Of all the girls in the arts group, Sue is the only one who, when asked what type of image she wants to convey, links her "look" to intelligence:

I don't want to appear to be like, stupid . . . I don't want to appear that I can't think for myself. That above anything else . . . and being smart is kind of coming back in more. Like Jim Morrison of the Doors, he was obviously very intelligent. He screwed up his life big time but he was intelligent. I like that sort of like . . . that poetic thing . . . that philosophizing . . . that kind of thing. It's respected in some circles.

The girls offer the student body ways to be involved within "safe" and more public, that is vulnerable, spaces of the school and use this involvement as an opportunity for self-reflection within a culture demanding conformity.

CONCLUSION

The "sports girls" and the "arts girls" remind us that spaces for athleticism and creativity enable diverse expressions of gender. These spaces are not fluff or extra. They are fundamental to identity and academic work. It is important that support be provided to girls as they invest and commit time and energy to academics and extracurricular activities.

Schools need to consider equitable funding of girls' athletics and school art programs (National Council for Research on Women, 1998). With the never ending emphasis on funding and budget crises within educational settings, there must be continuous surveillance of and advocacy for the maintenance of programs which provide young girls tools for positive identity development. If school personnel, parents, and other stakeholders can offer girls opportunities in the public sphere (not only for those who can afford private lessons) to develop bodies and creativity, young women will indeed rise to the occasion.

Acknowledgments. Special thanks to Lois Weis for her support in the completion of this work and to Michelle Fine for her very helpful comments in the refinement of this chapter.

REFERENCES

Adler, P., Kless, S., & Adler, P. (1992). Socialization to gender activities on peer-group culture. *Sociology of Education, 65,* 169–187.

Eder, D. (1985). The cycle of popularity: Interpersonal relations among female adolescents. *Sociology of Education, 58,* 154–165.

Eder, D., & Kinney, D. (1995). The effect of middle school extracurricular activities on adolescents' popularity and peer status. *Youth & Society, 26,* 298–323.

Eder, D., & Parker, S. (1987). The cultural production and reproduction of gender: The effects of extracurricular roles: Popularity among elementary school boys and girls. *Sociology of Education, 60,* 200–213.

Fine, M. (1993). Sexuality, schooling, and adolescent females: The missing discourse of desire. In L. Weis & M. Fine (Eds.), *Beyond silenced voices* (pp. 75–99). Albany: State University of New York Press.

Fine, M., Weis, L., Centrie, C., & Roberts, R. (2000). Educating beyond the borders of schooling. *Anthropology and Education Quarterly, 31*(2), 131–151.

Friend, R. (1993). Choices not closets: Heterosexism and homophobia in schools. In L. Weis & M. Fine (Eds.), *Beyond silenced voices* (pp. 209–235). Albany: State University of New York Press.

Gilligan, C. (1982). *In a different voice: Psychological theory of women's development.* Cambridge, MA: Harvard University Press.

Lesko, N. (1988). *The curriculum of the body: Lessons from a Catholic high school.* In L. Roman, L. K. Christian-Smith, & E. Ellsworth (Eds.), *Becoming feminine* (pp. 123–142). Philadelphia: Falmer Press.

McRobbie, A. (1978). Working class girls and the culture of femininity. In Women's Studies Group, Center for Contemporary Cultural Studies (Eds.), *Women take issue* (pp. 96–108). London: Hutchinson.

National Council for Research on Women. (1991). *Risk, resiliency, and resistance: Current research on adolescent girls.* New York: Author.

National Council for Research on Women. (1998). *The girls report: What we know and need to know about growing up female.* New York: Lynn Phillips.

Pipher, M. (1994). *Reviving Ophelia.* New York: Ballantine.

President's Council on Physical Fitness and Sports. (1997). *Physical activity and sport in the lives of girls: Physical and mental health dimensions from an interdisciplinary approach.* Minneapolis: Center for Research on Girls and Women in Sport.

Rofes, E. (1989). Opening up the classroom closet: Responding to the educational needs of gay and lesbian youth. *Harvard Educational Review, 59,* 444–453.

Sadker, M., & Sadker, D. (1994). *Failing at fairness.* New York: Simon & Schuster.

Smith, D. (1988). Femininity as discourse. In L. Roman, L. K. Christian-Smith, & E. Ellsworth (Eds.), *Becoming feminine: The politics of popular culture* (pp. 39–59). Philadelphia: Falmer Press.

Watson, T. (1987). Women atheletes and athletic women: The dilemmas and contradictions of managing incongruent identities. *Sociological Inquiry, 57,* 431–446.

Wellesley College Center for Research on Women. (1992). *How schools shortchange girls: The AAUW Report.* Washington, DC: American Association of University Women Educational Foundation.

PART III

SPACES OF PRIVILEGE
AND RESISTANCE

We turn, finally, to spaces in which a few historically marginalized and excluded youth are today invited—relatively privileged settings that may invite but then refuse to analyze (much less revise) their internal dynamics of oppression. These are the spaces of opportunity—at a cost. Steeped in the contradictory dynamics of inclusion and silencing, these sites are included in this volume because they tell rarely told, typically smothered stories about youth struggle, mobility, resistance, and the everyday battles of what looks like "good news." They are sites of political struggle, and sometimes victory. These are stories of youth entering spaces of some privilege that remain staunchly unwilling to reflect on their internal practices of exclusion: The working-class boy "allowed" to attend a private school on scholarship, the Black girl who "wins" the right to a desegregated education by attending an angry all-White school, the young Chicanas who are "welcomed" into cultural theater only as long as they portray the most stereotypic of roles and perform gratefully. With a sense of moral responsibility, we include these cautionary tales to shed light on stories from the bottom of three relatively privileged (or unreconstructed) settings. Listening to what are usually framed as the "good news" stories of integration, assimilation, or opportunity, the chapters in this section reveal the price.

Mindy Fullilove, now a psychiatrist, writes through autobiography about a terrified Black girl raised in the 1950s and 1960s, given the opportunity to integrate an all-White school, facing many teachers who "didn't love me" and peers who chose to ignore rather than engage her. Fullilove demands that we attend to the price paid by African American children who were pioneers, who today are the veterans of the desegregation battles. In a similar spirit, Michael Reichart writes on the plight of working-class boys who have won scholarships, thereby enabling their entry into an elite, private, all-male school. Reichart, a clinician and researcher, reveals the pain, struggle, loyalty oaths, and scars of marginality endured by those few working-class boys who survive. This section ends with an essay by Aida Hurtado in which she problematizes at the intersection of cultural performances and gender, documenting the struggles of girls and women invited into a male-dominated, culturally rich and compelling Chicano theater group. These essays may sound self-consciously critical and perhaps ungrateful, particularly at a moment in history in which desegregation, affirmative action, and all forms of "equal opportunity" are under siege. And yet we include these essays because they force our attention onto the unacknowledged—but dear—price of admission into privileged settings and on the very mixed blessing that policies of unreflective inclusion have foisted upon those invited into the exclusive—and often revengeful—club.

These essays reveal the resilience of youth, their ability to traverse settings of delight and danger with humor, humility, and sometimes horror. Each of these stories is actually a story of success, resistance, and tenacity. But it shouldn't take a hero to graduate from high school, go to a neighborhood elementary school, or to join a theater club. These essays are testimony to the strength of youth, their ability to shed and grow many skins in many spaces on the spot, their capacity to critique and see possibility despite what is often educators' collusion in not seeing what Nell Painter (1995) might call "soul murder." The implications of these essays, for educators, activists, community organizers and youth, are enormous—if we decide to listen.

REFERENCE

Painter, N. I. (1995). Soul murder and slavery: Toward a fully loaded cost accounting. In L. Kerber, A. Kessler-Harris, & K. Sklar (Eds.), *U.S. history as women's history* (pp. 125–146). Chapel Hill: University of North Carolina.

CHAPTER 14

Waylaid

MINDY THOMPSON FULLILOVE

Once upon a time there lived a turkey named Tom. One day Tom the turkey went for a walk. He walked and walked til he could walk no longer. Then he saw some food but it was only a nut. Then O how he wished he was safe on the farm with the other turkeys. Then he saw something moving along the road and then he saw a little girl her name was Betty and she was picking flowers for her mother. She was very poor.

Today was Thanksgiving. When the girl saw the turkey she ran after it and the turkey ran away from her too! But at last she had him and that was the end of Tom the Turkey.

—Mindy Thompson, "Tom the Turkey" (1959)

By gradual steps, children come to know place beginning with the discovery of their own toes and extending through time and space into the wide, wide world. In infancy the world is linked tightly to Mother. In early childhood it lies within sight of the house. In middle childhood it extends into the near fields and woods and playgrounds, often centered on a self-made home, like a fort or a den. In adolescence it opens wide, as far as one can go and return in a day, preparing the young person for the day when she will leave and make a new home in a new place.

The spiral of movement from the first home to the world develops outward in an orderly fashion. At each step of the way, the growing child learns new skills for managing the world: new skills in navigation, in being with friends, in meeting strangers, in learning new customs and languages. As with all developmental tasks, the timely completion of each stage is a prerequisite to good progress in the next. My spiral to the world was knocked off kilter because I lost my school when I was 7.

The first part of my childhood was nearly all nice. The first place I remember is my crib, which was located under a window in the back bedroom of our first-floor apartment. I remember a moment of great pride as I drank from a cup. Then I lay down and tried to drink again. The water felt cold as it spilled over my face and pajamas, and I was filled with acute embarrassment. It was at that moment I understood the difference between a cup and a bottle. In those days, 1 liked to wear my mother's high heels (and nothing else, my mother points out) and walk up and down the sidewalk in front of our house.

My world enlarged to include school, and I have many memories of the Community Chest Nursery School that I attended for a couple of years. I had a friend, Raymond. We thought of ourselves as Roy Rogers and Dale Evans, and we coveted guns and boots and bullets. We were deeply envious of a classmate who had a bandana full of bullets. One day, Raymond and I were the last ones at school. We found our friend's bullets and decided to keep them. Raymond took the silver ones. He said, as he was Roy Rogers, that he deserved them. As Dale Evans, I had to be content with the red wooden ones. I count that day as the birth of feminism in my life.

Another fine day we fulfilled a lifetime dream. We loved making crumbs of graham crackers and longed to have a whole package to break up into pieces. One day we found a neglected package at school and learned that indeed it made a remarkably tall pile. We were quite proud. Imagine our surprise when the teacher came along grumbling and annoyed, and threw our crumbs in the garbage.

My mother came to school one day with her Rolleiflex and took photographs of us painting, washing our dolls, climbing, and sitting around. I was very proud of her pictures and glad to have her document our world. The photographs lifted us out of the ordinary. We were, after that visit, preserved in black-and-white for future generations to learn how to go to nursery school.

Each year there were more places in the repertoire of my memory. I was shy but happy. I liked the world. I liked frogs and swimming. I liked barbecues in the backyard. I liked thunderstorms in the summer and snow in the winter. I liked school.

I liked *my* school, Oakwood Avenue School in Orange, New Jersey. I remember hopping to school, remember school as something to hop to. Hopping because you had to jump over the cracks in order not to break your mother's back. Hopping because some paving stones had crosses in them and those stones you had to jump over entirely: the crosses seemed to carry some very special message, as if we could read runic letters and communicate with the ancients who had carved the news for us in silky gray slate. Hopping because at school we played hopscotch with passion and intensity, searching for the right stone to throw, one that would fly through the air, landing surely, not glancing off the number, but resting soundly and reliably, and then hopping to retrieve that stone and keep it in your pocket for a day or a week or until it was lost and you had to find another one. Hopping because going up stairs to class was a passage in which we converted giggling brown selves into quiet studiousness, a passage strewn with betraying laughs under the sharp eyes of the teachers and the hallway monitors who could disgrace you if the giggles hopped out. Hopping like the facts that were jumping into my mind as if they couldn't wait to be learned and then hopping out quite unpredictably, like trying to remember Frosty the Snowman had a very shiny nose and and and. . . . The facts always seemed to hop out just when you thought you could most depend on them to be there.

I didn't know or care about the silly map that made my mother so furious. I know that she went to the board of education to get the map. My mother is a mild-looking woman who inspires trust, so of course they gave it to her. I imagine that she brought it home to my father. "Ernie," she said, "you have to do something."

My mother means it when she says that. You can argue with her if you want to, but you might just as well give up. Aside from Dad's anger at Jim Crow, I bet he was just nagged to death. I have experienced my mother's fervor when she gets what he used to call "a bee in her bonnet." So Dad took on the Orange School Board and crushed them. Out of the joy over that victory arose a campaign for John Alexander, my pediatrician, to be mayor. For the first time in Orange history, a Black candidate chosen by the people was running for that office.

My life had been filled with hopping before, but I was even more joyous when the campaign headquarters opened. Suddenly, as if it had always been there, the headquarters appeared at the corner just as you came out of the shadow into the sunlight. The campaign headquarters was very shiny. The paper was shiny, the buttons were shiny, the people laughed and guffawed in a delicious, embracing way. And no one said "no" when you went back every day and got another shiny button. No one said "you took one yesterday"; they just laughed and guffawed. Every part of the campaign was shinier and more exciting than the part before. The ice cream, the barbecue, the motorcade. I sat in an immense convertible, feeling very satisfied that, as we drove through town honking and calling, everyone would look proudly at me in the car and I would look proudly at them from the broadness of the cool leather where I sat.

That was a wonderful, joyous period. We were doing something grand, I knew, from the smiles on the faces of the adults around me. I did grand things, too, from time to time. I wrote a leaflet. I left flyers at my neighbors' houses. I was happy to be a part of what I knew to be a moment in history.

But I had no wish to do more than that.

I was shocked to learn that my parents wanted me—expected me—to be part of the school desegregation they had fought to win. They wanted me to give up my world, my warm segregated school, to go to a new school on the *hill*, where the *White* people lived. It was not in our neighborhood. It was high and big, not our kind of place. It was far. Someone who clocked the distance on his car odometer said the schools were equidistant from our home, but never in all the years I walked back and forth was I ever convinced of that. It was *much* farther to Heywood Avenue School than it was to my Oakwood Avenue School. I did not want to go.

The itching came in the summer. In the summer there was no hopping. Life seemed too big and too hot. Too itchy. At day camp it seemed hard to keep up with people. When the itching came I would feel overwhelmed, as though I would have to claw my skin off to find peace. Finally I learned that by supreme will I could ignore it and it would run its course and pass, yet be the only existing experience of the world as it swept my body. One day, after the itching passed, I fainted, feeling the blood rush from my head, leaving it empty and floating as my stomach rushed up to fill the hollowness.

But the headaches were yet again worse. I knew that they followed the rage, a screaming, impotent rage that I would hurl at the world. And the rage was followed by tears of such force that I felt I would lose myself in them. The headaches would not come the day of the rage, however, but the next day. I wondered whether I couldn't bring on the headache sooner by taking a nap. That way I could get it over with and be well the next day. I don't remember why I needed to be well, but I do remember that my plan didn't work. The headache was there in the morning as it always was the day after the rage. It tore at my eyeballs and drained weak and feeble tears. It engulfed my stomach. Motion was intolerable. Light was intolerable. Time was intolerable.

The day before I started my new school, I cried. For once, the headache didn't come the day after rage, but the second day after the rage. I was sick for several days. I did not feel like hopping to school anymore. School was strange. The only other Black person in my class was Stevie from around the corner. But Stevie had little to say; he rather searched the world from behind the protective plate of thick glasses. I felt very lonely.

My teacher had a device for teaching us good habits. It was a big "apartment" house made out of cardboard, very like the graphic at the beginning of the *Late Movie*, with a window cut in it for each student. At the beginning of the year she had us each bring in a picture and put it in a window. Then we had to carry out a number of good behaviors, including brushing teeth, eating citrus, and going to bed by eight o'clock. Every morning you had to report. If you had not done all those things, your window was closed for the day.

I became fanatical about this. I once ate a lemon because it was the only citrus in the house. One time my mother took me with her to collect money for the Mothers' March of Dimes. It became clear that we were not going to get home on time. I made my mother flag down a police car so I could get to bed by eight. On at least one occasion I was forced (as I saw it) to lie. But the gravity of lying mattered little compared to the fear of having my window closed: Then I felt terrible shame and loss. It was all too much.

The new school was a strange place for me, and I couldn't get a foothold. I had had a plan for fitting in at Oakwood, but at Heywood I never knew what to do. The pain of dislocation was so intense that I gradually retreated more and more into a world of my own creation. Robert Coles (1967), in his writings on children who desegregated schools in the South, has tried to understand how they were able to withstand the awful indignities to which they were subjected by White mobs. I experience those stories with nearly the same wonder he felt. How *did* they do it? I was deflated by loss and overwhelmed by the challenge to adapt. I focused on surviving. I constantly told myself that there would be a happy ending some day. In the interim, I became the hero of my own story, a figure-skating star or great actress, in a tale that started in the morning before I even opened my eyes and ended only after I went to sleep.

The story of my alternate life as an ice-skating star was largely a device for moving through space. Waking up, brushing my hair, walking to school (especially), being in gym class with no one to talk to: Those were the times that I slipped into my own universe, away from the awful awkwardness and ineptness that my isolation engendered. When I could sit, I read. My mother had collected a rich and varied library that introduced me to the classics. When I was old enough, I went to the Orange Public Library, whose cool, quiet presence was a balm. I fell even more in love with the Newark Public Library, which introduced me to the augustness of learning. There, the long reading tables and high ceilings created in me the sense that I had room to think and need not fantasize. Books and dreams, then, became my world.

Lincoln Steffens, in his autobiography, makes the point that getting a horse shaped his childhood. Instead of joining in games with other boys, he started a more independent life of adventure and exploration.[1] For me, the abrupt shift in my world turned me inward and away from social interaction. Going places was largely intolerable, meeting people burdensome. Thinking was my most accessible pleasure.

Around age 12, this alternate universe seemed to dissipate, as if a fog had lifted. Probably this occurred because I was given a small bit of life that I wanted to live: the world of The Theater. Roz Wilder, who directed the Pied Piper Teen Theater Workshop, took me into her world of improvisation and production even though I was a little too young for her classes. She might have guessed how desperate I was. The theater was an amazing discovery. Until then, alternate worlds had only been in my head. Now I could actually be *in* them, at least for moments at a time. I had no great gift for acting. I could barely be myself, much less someone else. I was awed by performers, though, especially when it came to expressing loud, transporting emotions. The 5 years I had lived in my head had left me with a social disability: I was clueless about real life. The theater provided a bridge back. Through our work in improvisation, Roz taught us what people did. Most of her students were learning to act. I was learning to be.

Much as it helped, it nevertheless failed. I couldn't find a place in the theater. I was a tall, plain, tan girl with short hair, hence I spent my early adolescence as the understudy for the male lead. Around the age of 15, I went to see *Oliver!* on Broadway. At the end the cast sings a rousing conclusion, "Consider yourself one of us! Consider yourself part of the family!" I wept to myself that the only part of the theater family I would ever be in was the seats, watching, and that was not enough.

I knew that I was a child of crisis, a tender warrior. I had done the right thing; I was the pride of my race. My early showing as a race hero gave me inflated hopes for what I would achieve in life. I didn't want to be in a place like the theater, where race would so define my opportunities. I didn't want to watch: I wanted to be grand. One day my high school biology teacher, Mr. Amen, said to one of my classmates, "You should study biology because you're really good at it." He didn't say it to me. I wanted to be welcomed like that.

But it was never so simple as someone saying "Come with me." While in college at Bryn Mawr, I had a wonderful Spanish professor, Mrs. Paucker, who was so impressed with my quick mastery of the language that she invited me to spend the summer with her in Spain. I couldn't understand the invitation, and so I didn't go. The real toll of the 5 lonely years was an enduring suspicion that no one else's place could be mine.

Ambition and suspicion remained with me as the dual lessons of school desegregation. Obstinacy and terror. Fearlessness and phobia. It is a puzzle to understand why I abstracted two seemingly contradictory emotions. In third grade, I was chosen to read the Bible at the school assembly at which my class was putting on the Easter show. My parents gave me a beautiful new Bible from which to read. It was an illustrated Bible, and I was particularly gripped by the beautiful painting of Esther approaching the throne of her husband, King Ahasuerus.

The story of Esther is my favorite Bible story. I often celebrated the Jewish holiday, Purim, with my friend, Sally. Purim celebrations re-create the story of Esther. I used to love to dance the part of Esther in those celebrations. I felt her power as if it were my force. I paid little attention to her fear.

But the Old Testament does not neglect that part of her story. As all familiar with the Book of Esther will remember, Esther was called on to save her people, who were to be massacred at the instigation of the evil Haman. Esther's uncle, Mordecai, told her, "You must go to your husband, the king, and plead for the Jews."

"But you know that I can't go to him unless he sends for me," she replied. "To go without permission is to risk death."

"If you don't go, you will die, as all the Jews will die," he countered.

Realizing she had no choice, she told her uncle, "Then tell my people to fast and pray for me for 3 days. My maidens and I will pray and fast, as well. On the third day, I will go to the king."

I know how Esther felt on the third day. I can imagine how it was when the morning dawned and she knew what a fearful thing she faced, knowing that she had to risk her life by entering the king's presence without his permission. I know how it was that she went anyway. Going in spite of her fear and buoyed by her faith: All that I can understand from my own life.

In my illustrated Bible, Esther is truly beautiful, and I do not doubt that the real queen was as well. It is, then, not so surprising that when she appeared before him, King Ahasuerus extended his scepter, which was the sign that she was welcome. Her courage saved the Jews. At Purim, this story is told in homes and synagogues around the world. When the name of the evil Haman is uttered, the people make a great hissing. That is my favorite part.

The beautiful Esther went in spite of her fear and was welcomed by her king. The little Mindy went, but I do not believe that I was welcomed at Heywood Avenue School. I do not believe that any of us who went felt wanted or beautiful. It is one thing to be deeply frightened and then triumphant. It is another to be so fearful but not succeed.

I lost my school, a place that had made me feel welcome, a place where I felt like hopping. It took no effort to move through space. If place is embodied in our bones, muscles, and minds, then Oakwood Avenue School was in me like a pocket rocket. I had to reconstitute myself at Heywood, an alien setting where I was allowed but not embraced. I hopped to Oakwood because that school empowered me, it gave me energy to dance and fly. I had to push myself to Heywood, the strength of my will pounding at my wish to stay at home.

All new settings, in my lexicon, became something to fear. To get there required a fight between will and wish. Each and every time, I had to battle this out. My will drew strength from my parents' values: The need to go was morally binding and hence nearly inescapable. I was a hero because I went, but no one knew just how much heroism it took to go and go and go.

That struggle did not end in the past. I still live with timidity and obstinacy warring in my bones. Go and die or stay and die. Every day is the third day. I usually go.

NOTE

1. Steffens (1931), who is eloquent on the change made in his life by having a horse, notes on this point, "I never played 'follow the leader,' never submitted to the ideals and discipline of the campus or, for that matter, of the faculty. . . . I think I learned this when, as a boy on horseback, my interest was not in the campus; it was beyond it; and I was dependent upon, not the majority of boys, but myself and the small minority group that happened to have horses" (p. 25).

REFERENCES

Coles, R. (1967). *Children of crisis: A study of courage and fear.* Boston: Little Brown.
Steffens, L. (1931). *The autobiography of Lincoln Steffens.* New York: Harcourt, Brace.

CHAPTER 15

Disturbances of Difference: Lessons from a Boys' School

MICHAEL C. REICHERT

Several decades into the postmodern moment, men wrestle with the gendered nature of our lives. First there were Books about Men (Carrigan, Connell, & Lee, 1985), an outpouring of polemic and scholarship reimagining men's lives in a postfeminist world. More recently boys have been a subject of preoccupation, publishers tripping over each other to produce the male Mary Pipher (1994). Where Kimmel (1996) detailed the historic bounds on masculine possibility and Gilmore (1990) the cultural, Connell (1998) has suggested that it is an emerging world gender order that lies behind the new focus on boys' lives. How boyhood is represented—in research, media, and institutions—is in contest and up for grabs.

A HISTORIC TURN AT A TRADITIONAL SCHOOL

At The Haverford School, an independent school for boys aged 4–18 in Philadelphia's suburbs, a century of commitment to educating boys was releveraged during a period of enrollment decline into a strategic decision to become "both a laboratory for providing the best practices for the education of boys and a beacon whose leadership in teaching them will be a model for other schools" (The Haverford School, 1993, p. 3). Confronted with market research indicating that many families had reservations about single-sex schools for boys, the school seized its own history and the historic opening, recommitting to boys and their education. An aggressive campaign to reach out as a boys' school was launched—to the broad community of less privileged boys in and around Philadelphia and to the world interested in educating boys. As part of the new campaign, the board of trustees encouraged the school to create an "On Behalf of Boys" Project, intended to serve as a center for research, discussion, self-reflection, and advocacy. Inviting national gender scholars onto a research advisory board, conducting a survey of the past 30 years' graduates, organizing symposia for parents on raising sons, and supporting teacher research as a means to self-renewal were some of the project's early moves.

Lessons about change and its limits came quickly. The survey of alumni provoked a minor storm of reaction. Many of the men perceived a foreign tone to the research instrument; one respondent scrawled in the margin, "This question must have been written by a woman!" There was outrage that the school would ask graduates questions about, for example, sexuality and relationships with women. Such matters had never been discussed publicly before, and there were many who felt strongly that the school should remain as it had always been.

But there were also many who responded to the survey and to the project with hope that "at last" the school's gender regime might be opening up. One man, 49 years old, wrote:

> My own experience at Haverford started out very badly. . . . I'd been pulled from the comfortable womb of a coed public school where I seemed to do well enough, socially and academically, without much effort, and thrown into the totally uncaring, all-male, stiff-upper-lip, cold-showers-in-the-morning, violent, almost brutal world of the British upper-class public school. As a 12-year-old, I was dismal at sports and Haverford required us to do sports. My parents—mostly my mother—contributed to the misery by becoming verbally abusive every time I did poorly or admitted weakness or lack of comprehension. Happily, the misery described above lasted only a year, although bits and pieces of it came back to haunt me every time I failed to "measure up" in one way or another. By and large, with the development of friendships among peers and mentor-type relationships with a rare and revered handful of excellent teachers and coaches, Haverford became a very comfortable world in which to live. I remember the deep satisfaction of walking into classes *knowing* I was prepared for anything they could throw at me. At the end of it all, I graduated a "winner" and that gives the Haverford experience a nice, rosy hue in memory—for the most part. I am proud of this project that my dear old school has taken on. If it results in insights that will relieve just a little of the suffering of some

future bewildered 12-year-old wondering why they are making him
play football, it will have been worth many times its cost.

As the school moved to fulfill the call of its strategic plan with new
emphasis on recruitment and outreach to new student populations, there
were further lessons. Growing numbers of graduates were returning to
their families and to the school with stories that they had found a much
broader racial, economic, and cultural diversity after high school than they
had been prepared for. This 26-year-old, for example, commented on his
college experience: "My freshman hall looked like the United Nations. And
you compare that to this school which is as milky white as you can get,
your eyes are opened to a lot of things once you leave this school."

These graduate stories and the school's market surveys and experiences with a new generation of parents shopping for their sons' futures
created a powerful pressure on the school. New admissions practices emphasized the school's intent to welcome a wide variety of students from
nontraditional backgrounds. As financial aid rose beyond the million-dollar
mark, new boys were attracted to the school in numbers and scope well
beyond the traditional pool.

How this elite school wrestled with the unintended effects of introducing boys from new backgrounds into what had always been a remarkably predictable experience is the story of this research. It is a cautionary
tale about the potency of difference and about pitfalls that can occur when
communities innocently launch themselves onto a more democratic trajectory. It is also, I hope, a tale about possibilities that can flow from a
careful effort to attend to the rich, irrepressible, and vivacious quality of
children's imaginations for the spaces they inhabit.

NEW BOYS, OLD RULES

In the throes of its diversity fervor, the school was thrown into an unexpected crisis when a group of boys from blue-collar families, many recruited
by coaches to enter the ninth grade, collectively refused to cooperate with
cherished school traditions. Powerful antagonisms developed between old
and new groups of students in the upper school. Teachers were at a loss to
deal with this surly, defiant gang of blue-collar students—the "Gauntlet,"
they were called—and parents of "Lifers" (more affluent families who had
attended the school since elementary school) complained mightily. The
headmaster responded to clamors for help by commissioning a Diversity
Research Project, consistent with the school's new commitment to research. Groups of students from various backgrounds—blue-collar, Asian,

African American, Jewish, "Lifers," "Recruits" (Black and White students who enter the school in the ninth grade)—were interviewed in focus groups. Four years later, some of the boys who had been freshmen were reinterviewed just before they graduated.

Immediately, the interviews revealed an aspect of boys' lives that had been little explored: School life at the ground level was a churning sea of competing masculine identities. The boys in the focus groups were stunningly aware of their contrasting and often conflicting notions of manhood, turning on axes of class, race, religion, and other differences. Lifers, for example, spoke at length about classmates "whose families have economic struggles." They called this group of boys "Recruits," promoting the stereotype that they had been brought to the school simply to fill out athletic teams. They noted the moral superiority of their own approach to work and achievement by contrasting it with that of the other group, distinguishing themselves from the "kids from poor backgrounds who make little effort": "They're angry tough guys with different morals and no regard for the rules. With their spitballs, snowballs, food fights, they intend to be malicious."

For their part, on the other side of this conflict the recruits were also quite conscious of their identities. Previously unnoticed differences—where they lived, how they talked and dressed, what cars they drove, or didn't, and what work their parents did—became definitive for them: "People look at you as if you were an alien. There's lots of snide looks as if to suggest, 'Get out of here.' We feel like Blacks must feel walking through a White neighborhood." They responded defensively, noting difference as well, especially in terms of their masculinity. Referring to the Lifers, they commented: "In grade school, when we would have a sissy in our class, we were the majority. Here it's just the reverse. The sissies are in the majority." "Never seen anybody run away from a fight before." "We've been brought up not to rat on each other; they're brought up to kiss ass and tell on others."

Schools' masculinity regimes, Connell (1996) asserts, are typically characterized by hierarchy and hegemony. Boys' collective identities—their masculinity politics—yield social positions in relation to each other. For example, in his English school, Mac An Ghaill (1994) found several classic identities—Macho Lads, Academic Achievers, New Enterprisers, Real Englishmen—that struggled among themselves for dominance and control in the school. Boys did not choose among such identities casually. Their choice of identity, driven by biography, culture, and opportunity, represented hope for social position within a hierarchical order. How they expressed themselves, whom they associated with, how they dressed—these and the many other facets of public gender identities were strategies for claiming the various rewards and other sources of attention and recognition in the school.

In this elite school, high-minded changes in admissions policy had the unanticipated consequence of inducing a new competition among groups of boys for coming out "on top" in the school's distribution system. While the administrators and faculty of the school may not have understood what all the turmoil and unhappiness—the confusing failure of gratitude—were about, there was considerable clarity among the newer groups of boys and their families. Financial aid, athletic attention, and greater numbers notwithstanding, the school had invited these boys into their community but had not otherwise opened itself up to them. The deck, in the eyes of the recruits, remained stacked in favor of the traditionally privileged identities. Apart from their physical inclusion, the school expected little else to change in its curriculum and practice.

The Diversity Research Project's focus groups revealed a serious contest, vicious and at times physical. There were threats, fighting, name-calling, exclusion, and jostling for attention. Many people were upset and stumped. Yet as we learned in our interviews, amidst all this noise and heat, Lifers registered little feeling of displacement. They continued to feel generally endorsed by the school's values and norms and enjoyed a sense of entitlement and ownership. They trusted that the school would not cede their place nor fundamentally alter its hallowed space. As the Diversity Research Project reported: "There was consensus among lifers that they felt at home here and looked forward to coming back at the end of summer and seeing old faces"(Bergh, Reichert, MacMullen, & MacMullen, 1993, p. 2). These boys emerged from their years at school with an identity like that calmly and confidently described by one Lifer:

> Cocky, confident, almost arrogant. Sort of elitist in a way. People who can and do excel. Self-important people. And that's because, in our own minds, we are the best.

Recruits, in contrast, were ever-conscious of being overlooked and undervalued, on foreign turf. In their focus-group comments, these boys were often quite bitter about the ways they felt disadvantaged in the school, feeling that they were always being evaluated in areas of comparative weakness. They felt left out of the school's narrow band for valuing boys by the fact that the achievements that conferred status and yielded appreciation were not generally their strong suits. For example, with respect to the school's formal reward and recognition structures—grades, honor societies, awards, college admissions—they commented: "Yeah, there's awards. It's so obvious who's going to get them. You can predict it. I could put $10 on who is going to get the next award, and I'd win."

Far from being grateful for their educational opportunity, these boys felt invited to dinner but denied a full place at the table. Children's hunger for social validation—for recognition (Mann, 1994)—left them vulnerable to feelings of deprivation as they participated in a public life "handicapped" by background and culture. Schools, we appreciated anew, provide children with real, material rewards around which they develop identities. Yet they do not do this idly or incidentally. In her study of a comprehensive high school in New York City, Fine (1991) observed how deliberate schools can be in this regard, expending their capital, lavishing resources in certain directions, to insure desired outcomes. The direction in which resources were spent was quite precious in her school, swaddled in rhetoric, custom, and explication. The rituals of public assertion were so elaborate, in fact, that she sought for a metaphor to convey their worshipful quality: "This high school, perhaps like other comprehensive high schools, was occupied and organized by a series of what I consider 'fetishes' which effectively order the experiences, beliefs, rituals and behaviors known as public schooling"(p. 180).

Rhetoric about "excellence" invites comparison, suggesting such a precious discourse in the lives of boys—with its own hidden underside. Organizing boys into hierarchies of merit by measuring and ranking particular behaviors succeeds primarily in privileging such behaviors—and the social experiences that produce them—and discounting others. In Fine's study, absent or hidden in the elaborate ritual of attending to the "responsible few" students who did not drop out was the school's failure with the rest of the students in its care. Similarly, in this boys' school the lavish attention to the boys at the top obscured the experience of the other boys, which is thereby deemed irrelevant. Institutional fetishes set the parameters of discourse: of what can be acknowledged, puzzled over, and cared about, and of what must be hidden.

Experiences with grades were a case in point. Being evaluated by teachers seemed a sore subject for many of the boys who shared the perception, across class and race lines, that teachers' often "pegged" boys for style and fluency of written expression and graded thereafter with abiding prejudice. One boy put it this way: "Sometimes it's just reputation. I know one kid who can write anything. He could write his name backwards for a paper and he would still get an A–, and it's not because he was writing good papers, it's because he is so and so and he is going to get that grade no matter what."

Feelings of arbitrariness and inequity were reported by many boys in our study. But it was the Recruits who felt particularly excluded by the warp and bias of the excellence discourse. One of the Recruits, a young man who was ultimately selected "Key Man" for his academic accomplishments, related stories of encountering abiding prejudice during his years at school:

> It's that kind of feeling that people were sort of, that you are expected to fail. At one of my Mom's parent–teacher conferences, with one of my teachers, I was doing really well and the guy, when it came out that I wasn't a Haverford student my whole life, he goes like, "Wow, I can't believe that your son comes from some other . . ."—I don't remember the quotation but it was, like, he was astonished that someone was doing well who came from another background.

Coming to the school community with considerable strengths that were relevant to their experience—strengths of character, intelligence, judgment, and wisdom, of family connections and a capacity for love, of insight into the human condition—boys such as this one found little interest in or validation for—what Gilligan (1993) terms "resonance" with—what they had learned and achieved. Their voice, mirrored back to them in grades and critical comments about their writing, needed "refinement." The fetish of excellence succeeded primarily in banishing discussion of other ways of valuing men, of other meanings to a man's life, from open consideration in the public life of the school community.

And banished also were the consequences for all those boys who learn that their existences will be dominated by a pressured competition to look and act in very particular ways under the regime of such a precious and lavish attention to particular qualities. Lifers as well as Recruits found themselves jammed through a narrow passage to manhood, forced to make sacrifices to gain the privileges conferred by the school. A Lifer, asked to look back on his experience within the school culture, described his years in this way:

> Like I was scared, very scared, about everything. I didn't really know what was going on, what I should be doing, what was expected, how aggressive you should be, how hard you should work, who you should be talking to, even.

The crucible through which boys had to pass deployed a wide variety of pressuring and sanctioning practices to produce preferred identities. As we realized the indifferent and impersonal, systemic nature of this practice, it occurred to us that the struggle underlying the Lifer/Recruit tension was not merely over tradition or even maintenance of preferential status but, more importantly, over the soul of the social space that was this boys' school, over its impact on the generations of men yet to come into it, over whether the school would merely reproduce privileged men or whether it might assist boys to imagine new possibilities for being male.

IDENTITIES AND POLARITIES

"You've got to leave some things at home to make it here. If you come to this school and bring the baggage of your background, you'll likely meet with more failure than success." This comment came during the Diversity Research Project from a Lifer who happened to be Jewish, a young man for whom religious calendar and rituals informed family life. He was a popular young man and generally successful. When questioned about how much his schoolmates knew of his religious practice, he answered that he had told almost no one. Matters such as these, he explained, matters of family or culture, matters of the heart, had no place in the public life of this private school.

All the Recruits and Lifers we interviewed, it turned out, had come to accept that school life was not a place for self-disclosure about such aspects of their lives or experiences. They accepted that this was the price they and their parents had paid for the possibilities offered by the school. Across the focus groups, boys from very different backgrounds yielded to the mandate that they dissociate personal from public, hiding everything but what might enhance their position and standing.

This finding was the strongest of our study. The display of personal differences was prohibited in the school's community life. Differences were presumed deficient. They became secrets. All boys we met strove to project a public self that reflected the dominant ideal. Yet we also noticed from the focus groups that some boys had no chance to follow the advice of this Jewish Lifer, to submerge parts of themselves, for the simple fact that their differences from this ideal were too obvious, too much a matter of skin color, clothing, or manners, to hide. Some, for reasons that were perhaps even more idiosyncratic, simply could not make the choice to hide. This default left these boys particularly vulnerable, without common retreat.

Forced to be visible, their experience was caricatured as "other," unwholesome or unnatural. Among the different focus groups in the Diversity Research Project (DRP), none was more subdued than the group of African American boys. In the report of the DRP (Bergh et al., 1993):

Of all the groups with which the task force met, the African-American students seemed least spontaneous. They were generally quiet, mannered, studied, careful and cautious. There was a pronounced lack of emotional expression in their responses. It seemed their reluctance to talk stemmed from the
fact that the business of conforming, assimilating and fitting in is so demanding, it's hard to relax and break loose from. (p. 3)

These males, in particular, seemed to be in an extreme position in the politics of the school. Like everyone else, only more so, they tried to keep their
difference to themselves, huddling with each other at lunch tables or in
hallways, passing through the schoolday unobtrusively. They expected little
from the school's peer culture, attending Haverford only for the credential
they would be presented upon graduation. And in marked contrast with
the White working-class group, these African American boys were not
overtly or even consciously angry, rebellious, or in contest with the dominant school identities. They stated that they were simply trying to make it
through. There were too many examples of boys of color who had not. Life
seemed even more precarious, their difference more consequential.

As we noticed this position occupied by African American boys, we
realized that boys' silence and loss of voice, their dissociative separation
of personal from public, had to do with their group identities—and the
position these conferred within the hierarchy—as much as with individual experience. Resonance, recognition—in extreme form, simply
safety and protection from hazing and humiliation—determined what
boys managed to show of themselves. The claims boys would make on
the public space of the school for personal expression depended on social invitation; it was granted in certain, careful ways to boys from majority groups, withheld or simply absent for boys from outside the center. African American boys "fit in," with a silence donned as manners,
to an unfriendly or indifferent school culture. The presumed "difference"
of their identities disappeared behind a veil of assimilation and
marginalization. Voice is socially accomplished.

For the less obviously different boys from White, blue-collar families,
this process of centering certain identities while marginalizing and exoticiz-
ing others produced a heightened consciousness of their group position.
In one interview I asked, "What are you a group of?" They answered:

Student 1: A lot of us, I guess, coming into the school really don't have the
money at all. As compared to what some of the people have here, you
know.
Student 2: Speaking for myself, I mean, I wasn't given everything these
people out here were given at birth. I think that is the main separation.

Student 3: I like a lot of these kids. I'm friends with a lot of them. But they
    don't have the same concerns like, you want to talk about neighbor-
    hoods, I mean, you have to watch yourself sometimes where I live, at
    night. You have to be careful. Out here you don't have to worry about
    anything. I don't feel, like, any animosity toward these people but I just
    feel, I can see the differences like when I go to people's houses, some
    people have maids and stuff like that. I'm like, the maids like live in the
    kind of neighborhood I live in, you know what I mean? So I feel kind
    of awkward at their houses sometimes. I think economically is like the
    biggest, biggest setting, the biggest difference.

Despite whatever personal friendships they may have formed, in the
school community they found themselves so distinguished by this othering
process, in fact, that the Recruits ultimately clung to each other, offering
understanding and resonance to themselves. By their senior year, just half
of the original Recruit group remained. In exit interviews, those who survived acknowledged their dependence upon each other:

Student 1: I definitely wouldn't have made it without these two guys here.
    These two guys were probably the most important ones to me, that
    helped me through.
Student 2: It was just understood pretty much, like, that there were four or
    five of us who are always together and we always just stayed together
    and associated with ourselves not because we didn't want to associate
    with other people but sometimes I didn't feel like, I never felt like a
    real part of my class.

They also acknowledged their separation from the Lifers:

They don't want us around. They want us around when we are
teammates and stuff, but for the most part, like, if the people went
to, say, a party, I tell you they wouldn't call any of us. It's like N.
said, they just don't, some of them don't call. They don't see what
you are doing or who you are.

Boys' identities, these recruits suggested, are forged in contexts in
which social meanings derive from group membership quite independent
of any personal agency. Class, in this case, but certainly also race, sexuality, and, in fact, almost any conceivable difference can signify to boys an
opportunity to distinguish themselves from the "other" and, thereby, gain
some advantage in a competition for recognition. "You are the company

you keep," some have said of children's peer groups (Jacklin, 1989). From the experience of these boys, we might rather say, "you become"—willingly, reactively, somehow—"the company you are presumed to keep." In social contexts so intent on excluding and differentiating as a basis for distributing rewards, boys are sorted into identities that reflect who they are thought to be and bear upon who they may become.

THE SURGING TIDE OF DIFFERENCE

Children, the work on behalf of girls has revealed, are both resilient and remarkably sensitive. While schools and communities have labored over the past decade, certainly since the research of Sadker and Sadker (1994) and the American Association of University Women (1992), to ensure fairness and equal access to resources for girls, the common experience in classrooms—of girls deferring to assertive boys, of teachers recognizing boys more readily, of girls following curricular pathways that track them toward the humanities and domestic arts and away from math and the sciences—suggests that fairness and access are as much psychological as structural. Or better, it teaches that the spaces relevant to children's sense of imagination, identity, and possibility are relational and psychological as much as they are concrete and material. Spaces are undergirded, configured, and circumscribed by practice, often unconsciously serving power and historic privilege, and by the meanings it enables and excludes.

We speak of the "co-construction of gender," an interplay between the overt and hidden curricula of our institutions and the choices of children. Children may do a variety of things with the gender "offers" available to them: They may collude with them, resist them, conform their lives to them (Connell, 1996). With respect to girls, works such as that of Pipher (1994), Brown and Gilligan (1992), and Fine (1988) have drawn our attention to the limits we impose on girls' choice by the force of our systems of recognition and regard. Our work suggests the constraints imposed on boys' freedom by the practice and politics of difference in their institutions and social spaces. Finding themselves in systems of recognition that are hierarchical and that pressure them to prefer certain kinds of masculinities and to hide, forswear, and even war with others, instead of learning that uniqueness is a rich and wonderful condition of being human, boys learn that being different can make or break you. Boys develop such views in schools in which they never know what might be cause for victimization. Their harshness toward each other is entirely arbitrary and unpredictable on an individual basis. What boys learn to depend on is that position in the hierarchical system of their school community is what confers relative safety. Who am I connected to and what power do we have? Who has clearance to show what? How much dare I risk to be myself?

Schools that hope to enable boys to imagine and live their own lives must assume more responsibility for the way they "do" difference. They must become more self-conscious, more sensitive to the power of groups and identities to occupy a space; they must develop pedagogy and curricula that can decenter the narrow hegemony of exclusive identities. Fine, Weis, and Powell (1997) describe this as the work of building "communities of difference," and everywhere schools now wrestle with the task of recreating a public life that invites the many selves floating through children's gender practice into the public eye.

At The Haverford School, of the original group of recruits interviewed, half remained 4 years later to graduate. In their exit interviews, while optimistic about the futures they had earned with their diploma, these boys also voiced regret at the compromises they had been forced to make to succeed at the school. In exchange for an educational class upgrade, for opportunities and privileges unavailable to their parents, these boys felt they had been forced to collude with a system that they found fundamentally unfair. Their embrace of the school, accordingly, was half-hearted and ambivalent. In fact, the community's polarizing attention to the difference of their experience reaffirmed their connections to these values and ideals. As one graduating recruit explained:

> I don't think any of us lost our identity, of who we are and where we came from, at all. I mean, I can see that in these two right here. They haven't lost where they came from. From the neighborhood, from the family. There is a way they keep you at home. They didn't change like some kids who pretend to be who they are not. A lot of kids do that to fit into the crowd. But I think among us all we have made it clear that we are not going to do that and who we are is who we are and if they don't like that they can stuff it.

Supporting each other, validating their experience not just of the school but of the neighborhoods and families that had sent them out as emissaries, these boys achieved the difficult task of referencing their worth by maintaining alternative, counterhegemonic standards, supporting each other to do so.

Their success revealed the limits of their recruitment to the school's predominant masculine identity and the inherent fragility of the school's reproductive project in this historic time. As schools respond to a postmodern surge of inclusion and diversity ideas, the assured reproduction of predictable identities and relations becomes more and more problematic. It seems harder to recruit boys to the narrow ways that had predominated before.

Even more hopefully, these boys hinted at actively imagined alternatives to the system of recognition and the gender, race, and class hierarchies it established, revealing also the disruptive force their different experiences, and the imaginations borne within, held for the school community:

> I think one problem is that this school gives a lot of academic awards and prizes to the kids who excel at the academics, you know, because the way the kids are getting real high SAT grades and stuff like that. When I think there should be more emphasis, a lot of times, on, on kids who put a lot more effort, you know, and do within the best of their ability. "You did a good job." "You got through."

Reflecting a yearning for fairness, for a school in which recognition might be based more broadly, more inclusively, in ways which acknowledged, embraced, and accommodated difference, these young men's political vision had been sharpened. Recruited to fit into a system that prided itself on producing men with a focused and restrictive sense of masculinity, enduring years of a competitive crucible that excluded those who could not yield, these boys were pragmatic, focused on getting where they wanted to go, and yet were also able to withhold some part of themselves from the bribes and bullying of the school culture. They had grown but not been remade. If anything, their experience had confirmed their faith in the worth of their fathers and families. They had come close to power identities, been invited to assimilate them, and yet had treasured something that did not offer them much reward in the school community.

In recent work to update this Diversity Research Project, a new group of freshmen Recruits were interviewed. From their comments, we learned that the school had indeed been moved by these earlier struggles, that the Recruits had not only stood their ground but had gained in the battle for recognition, inclusion, and change, to the point, in fact, where student identities were no longer crudely dichotomized into Recruits and Lifers. Leveling programs such as weekend outdoor challenge retreats had been added to the school's standard curriculum for all freshmen. Faculty had been hired and advanced expressly to offer boys from backgrounds new to the school models of success more likely to mirror their own experience. Support services for boys from many different educational backgrounds and learning styles grew tremendously, creating a new logic for more individualized pedagogy. Overall, boys who might just a few years earlier have thought of themselves as Recruits now laid claim to the resources and support of the school, even emboldened enough to request of the school that it "be partial to us" as it takes account of the nonlevel playing field of academic preparation.

The findings from this study may encourage those who wonder how boys will stand up to pressures for a more equitable distribution of resources, how they will deal with their decentering in an era of postmodern justice and multiculturalism. We found boys here who valued something in addition to getting ahead: belonging and a sense of loyalty seemed to lie behind their layered participation in the school's community. These blue-collar boys, in particular those who graduated, certainly achieved goals and rewards. Yet, perhaps because of their experiences of exclusion and prejudice, they did not merge themselves fully into the traditional mold. Like the Jewish boy—or the Black boy, the Asian boy, the gay boy—they participated in public life guided by instincts of personal survival and values of integrity. Their participation hinged on axes of flexibility and defiance, a determined decision to define themselves.

REFERENCES

American Association of University Women. (1992). *How schools shortchange girls.* Author.

Bergh, B., Reichert, M., MacMullen, R. & MacMullen, J. (1993). *Report of the Diversity Research Project.* Haverford, PA: The Haverford School.

Brown, L. M., & Gilligan, C. (1992). *Meeting at the crossroads.* New York: Ballantine.

Carrigan, T., Connell, R. W., & Lee, J. (1985). Toward a new sociology of masculinity. *Theory and Society, 14,* 551–604.

Connell, R. W. (1996). Teaching the boys: New research on masculinity and gender strategies for schools. *Teachers' College Record, 98*(2), 206–234.

Connell, R.W. (1998). Masculinities and globalization. *Men and Masculinities, 1,* 3–23.

Fine, M. (1988). Sexuality, schooling and adolescent females: The missing discourse of desire. In L. Weis and M. Fine (Eds.), *Beyond silenced voices: Class, race, and gender in United States schools* (pp. 75–99). Albany, NY: SUNY Press

Fine, M. (1991). *Framing dropouts.* Albany: State University of New York Press.

Fine, M., Weis, L., & Powell, L. (1997). Communities of difference: A critical look at desegregated spaces created by and for youth. *Harvard Educational Review, 67*(2), 247–284.

Gilligan, C. (1993). *In a different voice.* Cambridge, MA: Harvard University Press.

Gilmore, D. D. (1990). *Manhood in the making.* New Haven, CT: Yale University Press.

Haverford School, The. (1993). *Strategic plan.* Haverford, PA: Author.

Jacklin, C. N. (1989). Female and male: Issues of gender. *American Psychologist,* *44*(2), 127–133.

Kimmel, M. (1996). *Manhood in America.* New York: Free Press.

Mac An Ghaill, M. (1994). *The making of men.* Philadelphia: Open University Press.

Mann, P. (1994). *Micro-politics.* Minneapolis: University of Minnesota Press.

Pipher, M. (1994). *Reviving Ophelia.* New York: Grosset/Putnam.

Sadker, M., & Sadker, D. (1994). *Failing at fairness.* New York: Scribner's.

CHAPTER 16

"La Cultura Cura": Cultural Spaces for Generating Chicana Feminist Consciousness

AÍDA HURTADO

Cultural production can be a surprisingly fruitful source of feminist consciousness. For groups with a strong tradition of "folk" forms such as poetry, song, and plays, cultural production is a means by which young people can explore alternative forms of consciousness and social relations (McCarthy, 1998). For working-class people without access to traditional forms of theorizing, participation in cultural production is a way to grow and enlarge their sense of identity in the company of other artists.

In this chapter, I offer an analysis of a powerful cultural space, a theatrical space, in which culture and gender were worked and reworked, in an effort to argue the continued need for such spaces designed by and for Chicana girls and women. As public-school budgets are cut, as community-based programs evaporate, as the National Endowment for the Arts shies from controversy, as feminism is reduced to dreaded jargon, we must fight to preserve those sites in which poor and working-class youth can reclaim both cultural and feminist possibilities. The story I tell is a cautionary tale about male domination within a Chicano cultural space and, even more powerfully, about feminist resistance by young Chicanas. The lessons of reproduction and resistance should reverberate to all those spaces considered "coed"—male spaces to which girls and women are invited but given no place.

The focus of my story is *El Teatro Campesino*, a theatrical group that has proved to be a site of both liberation and restriction: *liberation* because it is one of the few sites that Chicanos have had in which to develop a vision of a theater that expresses their own culture and values; *restriction* because gender equality has not been central to the development of this vision. In this chapter, I explore this conflict by examining the oral

274

histories collected by Yolanda Broyles (1986, 1994) of Chicana actors in the troupe and comparing them to the themes emphasized here and to those that appear in another important cultural form—poetry written by Chicanas.

THE BEGINNINGS OF *EL TEATRO CAMPESINO*

El Teatro Campesino was formed in 1965 by Luis Valdez in Delano, California, to support César Chávez and the farmworkers' struggle to unionize. For the first 2 years, members of *El Teatro* improvised political skits urging workers to join the United Farm Workers Union (UFW) (Sánchez, 1985). In 1967, *El Teatro* severed its ties with the UFW and since then has operated as an independent theatrical company, counting among its most recent accomplishments the play (and eventual film) *Zoot Suit* and the film *La Bamba*, both directed by Valdez.

From the beginning, *El Teatro Campesino*'s goal was to represent the collective social vision of Chicanos and to reflect all that is valued in these communities: family ties, preservation of the Spanish language, Chicano culture, and political mobilization. The main dramatic device developed by *El Teatro* was *el acto*—short one-act skits with rapid dialogue and sharp wit, incorporating a critique of the day's events. The purpose of *el acto*, in Luis Valdez's (1971) words, was to "inspire the audience to social action," "illuminate specific points about social problems," and "show or hint at a solution" (p. 6). The point of *el acto*, then, unlike other dramatic forms, was to express not the individual vision of Valdez as a dramatist but the collective vision of the community. As such, the characters in *el acto* are archetypes that are supposed to be representative of *La Raza*[1]—a factor that makes them a revealing focal point for representations of gender in Chicano communities.

THE STAGE AS METAPHOR: THE DEFINITION OF CHICANA SEXUALITY

Of the many analyses of *El Teatro Campesino* (Broyles, 1986, 1994; Frischmann, 1982; Huerta, 1982; Yarbro-Bejarano, 1985, 1986), only a few (Broyles, 1986, 1994; Yarbro-Bejarano, 1985, 1986) focus on the position of Chicanas within the troupe. Most of the women characters in *El Teatro Campesino*, as well as in Chicano communities, are cast into one of two roles: whores or virgins [*putas/virgenes*]. In the interstices of this bipolar conception of Chicanas' sexuality is the *neuter woman*.[2] In *El Teatro*, this *neuter* role takes the form of allegorical characters such as *la Muerte* [Death] or *el Diablo* [the Devil]. In Chicano communities, the neuter woman is represented by what Abelardo Delgado (1978) calls the femme-macho, the woman who is attractive to men because she is strong and powerful—not meek, like a wife—without being a whore. A femme-macho can be sarcastic, funny, outrageous, aggressive, mean, or belligerent. She is never tender, loving (except in a political/abstract sense), frightened, or insecure. In fact, her psychological characteristics are so grotesquely exaggerated as to be inhuman—especially her sexuality, which, in effect, neuters her. The sexuality exhibited by femme-machos is not tied to emotional involvement and therefore is not a sexual expression at all but a *physical act* to gain power in a heterosexual world.

In *El Teatro Campesino*, as in Chicano communities more generally, the assignment of women into the categories of "virgins" or "whores" is based largely on physical characteristics, assertiveness, and strength. The *virgin* is the woman who is small, fragile, fair-skinned, and pretty. The potential whore is an Indian-looking woman who speaks up and is "difficult" (Broyles, 1986). Socorro Valdez (Luis Valdez's sister), a longtime actress in *Teatro Campesino*, describes the "rigidification process" as follows:

> The actresses that were "soft" offstage and just *muy buenas, muy buenas* [very nice, very nice] got the "soft roles." And the ladies that were *medias cabronas* [tough] and had a beer and a cigarette hanging out of their mouth, well, you know what role they got. . . . And I know there were moments in the group when there was to be a "girlfriend." Well, can Socorro be the girlfriend? No, Socorro can't be the girlfriend. Socorro is either the old lady or she's the jokester. But I was never in this company as a "soft" woman, because they confuse softness and hardness and they attach those two things to strength or weakness. But there is no such thing in my mind. (quoted in Broyles, 1986, p. 171)

The power of the femme-macho lies in her strong personality and in her ability to remain emotionally uninvolved though sexually active. Sandra Cisneros (1994), in the following excerpt from her poem "Loose Woman," exalts the characteristics of the femme-macho as a form of liberation.

LOOSE WOMAN

They say I'm a beast.
And feast on it. When all along
I thought that's what a woman was.

They say I'm a bitch.
Or witch. I've claimed
the same and never winced.

They say I'm a *macha*, hell on wheels,
viva-la-vulva, fire and brimstone,
man-hating, devastating,
boogey-woman lesbian.
Not necessarily,
but I like the compliment.

The mob arrives with stones and sticks
to maim and lame and do me in.
All the same, when I open my mouth, they wobble like gin.

Diamonds and pearls
tumble from my tongue.

Or toads and serpents.
Depending on the mood I'm in.

I like the itch I provoke.
The rustle of rumor
like crinoline.

I am the woman of myth and bullshit.
(True, I authored some of it.)
I built my little house of ill repute.
Brick by Brick. Labored,
loved and masoned it.

. . . .
My sin and success—
I think of me to gluttony.

By all accounts I am
a danger to society.
I'm Pancha Villa.

I break laws,
upset the natural order,
anguish the Pope and make fathers cry.
I am beyond the jaw of law.
I'm *la desperada*, most-wanted public enemy.
My happy picture grinning from the wall.

I strike terror among the men.
I can't be bothered what they think.
¡Que se vayan a la ching chang chong![3]
For this, the cross, the Calvary.
In other words, I'm anarchy.

I'm an aim-well,
shoot-sharp,
sharp-tongued,

sharp-thinking,
fast-speaking,
foot-loose,
loose-tongued,
let-loose,
woman-on-the-loose
loose woman.
Beware, honey.

I'm Bitch. Beast. *Macha.*
¡*Wachale*!
Ping! Ping! Ping!
I break things. (pp. 112–115; abridged)

If women are thought of as less human than men, the poet claims her bestiality outright ("I'm a beast," "I'm a bitch") and her dangerousness. She "feasts" on the idea of herself as "a danger to society," a "desperada" who "break[s] laws," all the while her "happy picture [is] grinning from the wall." She defies patriarchal power and usurps a male identity for herself by becoming "Pancha Villa" (in reference to the only Mexican hero to openly defy the U.S. army at the turn of the century), furthering her transgression by feminizing the name *Pancho* to *Pancha*. She rebels against all authority and violates all sacred boundaries, including that of hetero-sexuality ("*viva-la-vulva*"), and defies the holy father by "anguish[ing] the Pope" as well as "mak[ing] fathers cry." She has fashioned herself into a crime of nature and rejoices in her transgression ("man-hating, devastat-ing/boogey-woman lesbian"). She does not regret, apologize, or otherwise feel anything but passion and power ("Diamonds and pearls/tumble from my tongue/Or toads and serpents/Depending on the mood I'm in/I like the itch I provoke"). Her emotion is not tempered by sympathetic response to anybody but instead thinks of no one but herself "to gluttony." She relishes her selfishness and laughs out loud at being the creator of her own image (not real but made out of "bullshit" through the appropriation and mockery of hegemonic masculinity). She laughs deep and she laughs hard, and at the end only she is left standing, because all her accusers have run away in fear ("The mob arrives with stones and sticks/to maim and lame and do me in./All the same, when I open my mouth, they wobble like gin"). And all the while, she claims, sarcastically and with an implied wicked smile, this is what she thought "a woman was."

Whereas the femme-macho has her will, *whores have no volition.* In *El Teatro Campesino*'s portrayals, whores are not women who give themselves willingly in exchange for goods or money. As "fallen women," they are "damaged merchandise." At the root of the image of the *puta* [whore] is

Chicanos' dread of the symbolic meaning of sexual penetration, especially the equation of penetration with the Spanish conquest of México (Alarcón, 1981; Del Castillo, 1974; Paz, 1985; Pérez, 1991). Pivotal to the story of Mexico's conquest by Spaniards was an indigenous woman—*La Malinche*—who became the translator for Hernán Córtez. Paz (1985) proposes that the conquest of México is a violation and that *La Malinche* represents the violated mother country because she is the mistress to the leader of the conquest. *Mestizos* are *"hijos de la Chingada"*[4] or "the offspring of violation." All Mexican women are potential traitors, because they are the descendants of *La Malinche*.

The victim of the violence, *la Chingada*, is not deserving of pity or compassion but is considered worthless. When virginity, the only gift women have to offer men, is gone, women join the ranks of *las Chingadas*. According to Paz (1985), even if a woman willingly partakes in the act of lovemaking, the fact that she is "penetrated" constitutes a violation. The most desired among women is the virgin, followed by the once-married with children, then the divorced woman with no children (no evidence of having been penetrated), then the woman who lives with a man. More damaged than all of these is the woman who sleeps with different men, regardless of her motivations for doing so, and the ultimate violation is suffered by women who are opened by other women—lesbians (Trujillo, 1991). Once a woman opens herself to another woman, she can never again redeem herself—not even through motherhood.

Women's reward for saving their virginity until marriage is to become wives and, eventually, mothers and grandmothers. Mothers and grandmothers have authority in families, because in Mexicano/Chicano culture, as in many other cultures, there is an *idealization* of motherhood. Respect for elders facilitates the authority of mothers as they become grandmothers and great-grandmothers. Mothers are often seen as superhuman beings who heal the wounds inflicted by an oppressive, racist society (Zinn, 1975). As such, they are mythologized in Chicano creative production. For example, Mirandé & Enríquez (1979) conclude that:

> Mothers in Chicano literature are universally warm, enduring, and uncomplaining. Their home, whether a tent, a migrant shack, or a house, is their domain, and the hearth is almost synonymous with maternal soul. . . . Ties between mother and son are incredibly strong in Chicano literary works and might be called a trait inherent in Chicano culture itself. A mother's endurance in adversity endows her with strength that sustains her children as well as herself. (pp. 166–167)

Chicano mothers are central to the family through their nurturance and care. In many poems and novels it isn't uncommon for them to perform household chores while the rest of the family sleeps and then join their families in grueling work such as farm labor. Universally, however, Chicana mothers refuse to express needs, pains, or frustrations. Their silence is a direct measure of her sainthood and reinforces the Indo-Hispanic notion of devotion as equated with obedience (Alarcón, 1981). *La Madrecita* [The Little Mother] inculcates the cultural ideals of respect, devotion, and the legitimacy of gender hierarchies (regardless of how little she *actually* believes or follows them). As Carla Trujillo (1991) proclaims, "Martyrdom, the cloth of denial, transposes itself into a gown of cultural beauty" (p. 188). Much of this cultural production does strike a chord of truth for many working-class Chicanas and Chicanos, because the survival of the group has been possible precisely because of women's constant work, at home and in the fields (Trujillo, 1991).

The project of Chicana feminists by contrast, especially Chicana poets, is to allow the other to speak. Instead of celebrating silence, obedience, and devotion, Alma Villanueva's poem "Mother May I" painfully recalls how at the age of 18, when she got married, she began "the years of silence." She would open her mouth and no words would come out. Her isolation and "loneliness grew" as she sought her voice in her "husband's eyes" and in the eyes of her children. She looked for her voice in her daily chores of shopping in the supermarkets, in cleaning the oven, and in the dustpan. She concludes that her "emptiness grew" because ultimately she "hungered for myself" (quoted in Sánchez, 1985, pp. 323–324). Similarly, Elba Sánchez (1990) challenges the notion that silence is desirable in her poem "Women's Word":

> woman
> her story
> I sustain in my memory
> the want you want
> to erase
> to domesticate
> with your alphabet
>
> you have wanted me mute
> since childhood
>
> once
> my silence
> carved the place
> you called smile
> as frothing words
> spilled out
> your eyes sternly
> warned

—don't think
you're prettier that way

once
I would hide
my forbidden voice
in the pleats of my conscience
cities trapped in my throat

that was then

now
my tongue
has birthed the words
challenging
what is
no longer accepted

This poem could be a mother's reply to the cultural demand of silence. Silence that results in the loss of a voice with which to speak of her pain. Women's imposed silence results in a loss of self, because nobody, no matter how noble their intentions, can live entirely for others. More importantly, the *expectation* that Chicano mothers be self-sacrificing saints has its historical precedent in the Aztec codices as translated through the lens of the Spanish clergy (Mirandé & Enríquez, 1979):

tenacidad de aguantar las dificultades de la vida [tenacity in enduring the difficulties of life]
decencia y honestidad [decency and honesty]
devoción y piedad [devotion and piety]
conocimientos y habilidad en los oficios mujeriles [knowledge and mastery of feminine duties]
diligencia [diligence]
castidad [chastity]
obediencia [obedience]
modestia [modesty] (p. 99)

The communication of these *expectations* as the ideals for "true womanhood" is what subordinates and controls Chicanas. If Alma Villanueva stopped looking for her voice in her husband, her children, the oven, or the supermarket and instead said to her family "I think I hungered for myself," the arrangement between Chicanos and Chicanas would collapse. Silence is imperative to maintain the image of mothers as self-sacrificing saints.

As Chicanas acquire political consciousness about gender subordination, they become aware of the restricted social constructions of Chicana womanhood. As Socorro Valdez states:

It was like walking the same path over and over. There was the mother, the sister, or the grandmother or the girlfriend. Only four. . . . The way those females are laid out are for the most part very passive and laid back, *y aguantaban todo* [and withstanding everything]. I think that is what really chewed me up at the time. (quoted in Broyles, 1986, p. 166)

The female characters' ability to "withstand everything" is crucial in understanding the gender subordination of Chicanas. Many Chicanas are apparently "passive" yet *strong* enough to withstand their oppression (Castillo, 1991). The socioeconomic struggle to survive has not permitted many Chicanas to remain truly passive (as evidenced by the strong women labor leaders within Chicano/Mexicano communities). Furthermore, the social location of the femme-macho allows for the expression of *will* and leaves an aperture for Chicanas to enforce their power. Therefore, the apparent "passivity" of Chicanas is much more complex than it first appears. Their subordination lies in the contradiction between having strength and refusing to use it all of the time on those who obviously oppress them.

THE COMMUNITY AS *FAMILIA*—WHAT BINDS CHICANAS TO THE STAGE

For Chicanos, the basic unit of community organization has been *la familia* [the family], which is patriarchal in nature (Orozco, 1986; Zavella, 1988). Following the same pattern, *El Teatro Campesino*'s organization is headed by writer and director Luis Valdez—a symbolic father who works with actors typically much younger than himself. A very influential voice in the development of Chicano arts, he has worked diligently tried to portray Chicanos, especially poor Chicanos, with dignity and depth. Members of *El Teatro Campesino* live and work communally, and the relationship among members of the ensemble is characterized as a familial one. In addition, in 1971 *Teatro Campesino* moved to San Juan Bautista, California, a rural community, to farm and raise livestock, underscoring their philosophical position that "ultimate freedom for the farm workers means ownership of the land he [*sic*] works" (Bruce-Novoa, 1978, p. 68).

The roles for women in *El Teatro Campesino*, however, have remained fairly constant and oppressive throughout its history. Never is the world seen through their eyes (Broyles, 1986). Diane Rodriguez, who joined *El Teatro* at age 15, states: "Somehow at that point we didn't have the consciousness and we played these cardboard roles. Or maybe we did have some consciousness but we didn't know how to get it on stage" (quoted in Broyles, 1986, p. 165).

Broyles (1986) notes that the limited roles given to women during the 1960s in *Teatro Campesino* reflected "the efforts to address *raza*, and the reality of *raza* as a *whole* somehow precluded a special consideration of women's roles and problems" (p. 165, emphasis in original). Women's experiences in *El Teatro* paralleled those of Chicana feminists within the Chicano movement and in other leftist movements of the 1960s (Sánchez, 1985). Chicano activists used two types of rhetoric to keep Chicana feminists from raising women's issues within the movement: one that focused on the divisive nature of considering them and another that implied that joining the White feminist movement was a betrayal (Trujillo, 1991; Zavella, 1988). In the 1960s, the response of many politically progressive Chicano men to Chicana feminists' demands were similar to those of their White counterparts: appeals to reason ("Yes, there are problems, but changes can come only incrementally"), cries of confusion ("What is it that you want?"), requests for prescription ("Tell us what to do"), and, finally, outright anger (*"El problema no es el macho, es el gabacho!")"* [The problem is not the *macho*, it is the white man!] (Orozco, 1986, p. 12).

The *Teatro* women's dissatisfaction with their roles led to one of the longest and deepest struggles in the troupe's development. Men perceived the challenge by the women as an unnecessary provocation instead of as an avenue to expand *Teatro's* creativity. Whereas *Teatro Campesino* and the Chicano movement have both been at the forefront of progressive political action (unionization of farm labor, voter registration, and prison reform), both have consistently been unwilling to confront sexism. The men in *El Teatro* suggested that women create their own theater company. Eventually the women did leave and proceeded to write, produce, and act in their own plays. For example, Olivia Chamucero started to do theater work with the children of migrant workers and conducted drama workshops for women in battered women's centers and for youth in drug prevention centers. However, as Broyles (1986) observes, "Clearly the collective spirit suffered a collapse when gender roles were questioned. Suddenly an individual solution was suggested for what was a collective problem" (p. 168).

It is important to understand that Chicanas' loyalty to Chicanos derives primarily not from the hope of economic security but rather from their desire to gain *respectable* entry into the Chicano community. The Chicano community is the *universe* for many Chicanos, who often encounter hostility outside their segregated barrios. Attachment to a man is not merely for economic stability but also to insure woman's inclusion in the social and cultural life of the community. That is the crux of the hold that Chicanos have on Chicanas—the threat of the universe collapsing. In *Teatro* terms, it is *El Fin del Mundo* [The End of the World], the last play by *Teatro Campesino*, which was performed in Europe (Huerta, 1982). The fear is that the Chicano way of life will disappear if Chicanas step outside the boundaries of the narrow stage set for them by Luis Valdez and other symbolic fathers.

EL FIN DEL MUNDO—
CHICANAS WALK OFF THE STAGE

In 1980, when Chicanas in *El Teatro Campesino* walked off the stage, *El Teatro Campesino* ended as a collective enterprise, and the members of the ensemble went their separate ways. *El Teatro Campesino* still exists under Luis Valdez's direction, but it is now dedicated to "mainstreaming" its productions, and, as *La Bamba* shows, it has even had an effect on Hollywood.

Contemporary Chicana feminists, in and out of *El Teatro Campesino*, have claimed the right to invent themselves, and they have done so through many avenues, including creative and academic production. Central to their artistic production is the recognition of hybridity as a means of preserving their culture and communities and simultaneously recognizing the power of coalition building with other ethnic and racial groups. They see themselves as part of a global project in which they are "both reinventing and questioning the very constructs of [their] imagined national and racial communities" (McCarthy, 1998, p. 159).

Gloria Anzaldúa (1987) uses the borderlands [*la frontera*] as a metaphor to denote that space where antithetical elements mix, not to obliterate each other or to get subsumed by a larger whole but rather to combine in unique and unexpected ways.

> To live in the Borderlands means knowing
> that the *india* in you, betrayed for 500 years,
> is no longer speaking to you,
> that *mexicanas* call you *rajetas* [traitor],
> that denying the Anglo inside you
> is as bad as having denied the Indian or Black;
>
> *Cuando vives en la frontera* [When you live in the borderlands]
> people walk through you, the wind steals your voice,
> you're a *burra, buey* [beast of burden], scapegoat
> forerunner of a new race,
> half and half—both woman and man, neither—
> a new gender;
>
> To live in the Borderlands means to
> put chile in the borscht,

eat whole wheat *tortillas*,
speak Tex-Mex with a Brooklyn accent;
be stopped by *la migra* [the immigration service] at the border check-
   points;

To survive the Borderlands
   you must live *sin fronteras* [without borders]
   be a crossroads. [p. 195, abridged]

The borderlands are the place where individuals can put chile in their borscht and speak Tex-Mex with a Brooklyn accent. They are a space some women of Color—specifically Chicanas—can inhabit because of their ability to maintain multiple selves without feeling incoherent. In the borderlands it is possible to develop a "forerunner of a new race, half and half—both woman and man, neither—a new gender."

"LA CULTURA CURA"—THE CREATION
OF A "NEW GENDER"

Artist and scholar Amalia Mesa-Bains, in an interview for the film *La ofrenda: The day of the dead* (Portillo & Muñoz, 1990), proclaimed the healing powers of cultural production: "Art is a about healing. When people participate in art, when they make it, when they view it, it is the same as making yourself well." In the same film, psychologist Concha Saucedo concurred—"*la cultura cura*"—because it can be an antidote to the devastating effects of colonization.[5] An integral part of the political mobilization of the 1960s was the work of artists to reconstitute, rediscover, and create a Chicana/o imaginary. As Erika Apfelbaum (1979) reminds us, a subordinate group "must rediscover its own cultural roots and historical background" to "re-endow one's own collectivity with its main group support functions, by restoring a cultural heritage (such as literature or music), by establishing an historical chronicle, or simply by discovering the commonality of problems" (p. 203). Many of the well-known Chicana artists of today were young women in the 1960s who were leaders in creating art that specifically addressed the material and social conditions of Chicanas/os. They were the precursors to today's young artists like Marisela Norte, a spoken-word artist in her early 20s who produces her own audiotapes and CDs. According to Jennifer Gonzalez and Michelle Habell-Pallan (1994), Marisela Norte

   juxtaposes images found in popular culture to construct non-linear narratives. She contextualizes words in order to connote several meanings at once, and allows sound-images to build new meanings through repetition. She represents the unexpected and seemingly unconnected elements of a Chicana border identity in order to show, for example, how the life of a domestic worker is circumscribed by the objects she collects and keeps, "souvenirs *turistas* left behind." (p. 92)

Gonzalez and Habell-Pallan link the art production of Amalia Mesa-Bains (one of the pioneers of the Chicano art movement of the 1960s) and of Marisela Norte. Mesa-Bains is famous, among her other accomplishments, for her construction of altars—a cultural practice in many Mexican/Chicano homes to commemorate the dead, linking them with social issues of importance to the living. According to Gonzalez and Habell-Pallan, "If one could *hear* the altar installations of Mesa-Bains, they might sound like Norte's complex narratives. Each artist constructs multi-layered representations of the way cultural identity can change as it moves across different social spaces" (p. 92, emphasis in original).

Marisela Norte does not own a car and, therefore, produces most of her spoken-word work on her daily bus rides from her home in East Los Angeles to her office job downtown. It is in this "rolling space" that she "acts as a social critic who recognizes the importance of place and space in the construction of social being or identity. She is always mindful of how social space or geography determines, in part but not completely, the lives of women in their communities" (Gonzalez & Habell-Pallan, 1994, p. 94). Norte's cultural production creates a "critical social space, or a counter-site, in which to critique the confinements of social space and patriarchal practices" (p. 94).

There are numerous other young women artists who have advanced the struggles of the Chicana artists of the 1960s. While their forms may be new—including spoken-word, rap, and performance art—these young artists have not abandoned the preoccupation of their predecessors with the material conditions that affect their communities. In that sense, the legacy of Chicana artists is a "living" heritage that has been transformed by the experiences of younger women but not divorced from its initial impetus, which was the creation of a more just society for all.

Chicana feminists, like other feminists of Color, are struggling to develop a truly inclusive political consciousness that embraces all who have been rejected and does not lead to the abandonment of hope even in those who reject it. To refuse to separate from Chicano men and to understand their oppression does not mean excusing their brutality (Anzaldúa, 1987). What Chicana feminists advocate is a head-on engagement with Chicanos and with other members of their communities to achieve positive change for all parties involved.

Eventually Socorro Valdez was asked by Luis Valdez to return to *El Teatro Campesino* to play in his award-winning television special, *"Corridos."*

Socorro Valdez agreed, under the condition that she play the woman lead for the first time in her career. In her words:

> I didn't want makeup on my face. I didn't want lipstick. I didn't want false eye-lashes or fake boobs or nothing. I just wanted to be myself up there, just wanted to be the Indian person that I am. . . . I came back to him [Luis Valdez], but I said: "That's it. No more masks, no more *calavera* face [skull mask], no more *calavera* bones on my face. None of that shit. I'll go out there in a plain cotton dress and I'll have those people going." (quoted in Broyles, 1986, p. 182)

Just as Socorro Valdez wanted to keep her home in her theater community, Chicana feminists also want to remain in their communities and to link their struggle as women to the struggle of all oppressed peoples. And like Socorro Valdez, they are insisting that their participation be on their own terms.

NOTES

1. *Raza* refers to José Vasconcelos' (1979) notion of a unified "cosmic race" in North America and Latin America that would result in a new social order combining the best elements of all cultures.
2. The *Oxford Dictionary* (1973) defines neuter as "Of gender: Neither masculine or feminine. . . .Of a verb: neither active or passive, intransitive" (p. 1398).
3. This is a play on the word *chingar*, which means "to go fuck yourself."
4. *Chingada* literally means "the one who has been fucked." Chingón means "the one who *can* fuck."
5. In Concha Saucedo's (Portillo & Muñoz, 1990) words: "'*La cultura cura*' means, if it were to be translated literally, that culture heals. And, essentially what it means is that there are elements in all cultures that give health to the people if they retain those elements. Particularly for Latinos, we have, sometimes have had to separate ourselves from that culture, and that separation, dislocation has created an imbalance, which in effect is ill health. And when we are saying '*la cultura cura*' we are saying return to your culture, maintain your culture, because the basis of your health is there. You will be able to find within the richness of the culture that what you need to live today."

REFERENCES

Alarcón, N. (1981). Chicana's feminist literature: A re-vision through Malintzin/ or Malintzin: Putting flesh back on the object. In C. Moraga & G. Anzaldúa (Eds.), *This bridge called my back: Writings by radical women of color* (pp. 182–190). Watertown, MA: Persephone Press.

Anzaldúa, G. (1987). *Borderlands—La Frontera: The new mestiza*. San Francisco: Spinsters/Aunt Lute.

Apfelbaum, E. (1979). Relations of domination and movements for liberation: An analysis of power between groups. In W. G. Austin & S. Worchel (Eds.), *The social psychology of intergroup relations* (pp. 188–204). Belmont, CA: Wadsworth.

Broyles, Y. J. (1986). Women in El Teatro Campesino: ¿Apoco estaba Molacha La Virgen de Guadalupe?" In R. Romo (Ed.), *Chicana voices: Intersections of class, race and gender* (pp. 162–187). Austin: Center for Mexican-American Studies, University of Texas at Austin.

Broyles, Y. J. (1994). *El Teatro Campesino: Theater in the Chicano movement*. Austin: University of Texas Press.

Bruce-Novoa, J. (1978). *El Teatro Campesino* de Luis Valdez. *Texto Critico, 4*(10), 65–75.

Castillo, A. (1991). La Macha: Toward a beautiful whole self. In C. Trujillo (Ed.), *Chicana lesbians: The girls our mothers warned us about* (pp. 24–48). Berkeley: Third Woman Press.

Cisneros, S. (1994). *Loose woman*. New York: Knopf.

Del Castillo, A. (1974). Malintzin Tenépal: A preliminary look into a new perspective. *Encuentro Femenil, 1*(2), 58–77.

Delgado, A. (1978). An open letter to Carolina . . . or relations between men and women. *Revista Chicano-Riqueña, 6*(2), 33–41.

Frischmann, D. H. (1982). El Teatro Campesino y su Mito Bernabé: Un Regreso a la Madre Tierra. *Aztlán, 12*(2), 259–270.

Gonzalez, J. A., & Habell-Pallan, M. (1994). Heterotopias and shared methods of resistance: Navigating social spaces and spaces of identity. *Inscriptions, 7*, 80–104.

Huerta, J. A. (1982). *Chicano theater themes and forms*. Ypsilanti, MI: Bilingual Press/Editorial Binlingue.

McCarthy, C. (1998). *The uses of culture*. New York: Routledge.

Mirandé, A., & Enríquez, E. (1979). *La Chicana: The Mexican-American woman*. Chicago: University of Chicago Press.

Orozco, C. (1986). Sexism in Chicano studies and the community. In R. Romo (Ed.), *Chicana voices: Intersections of class, race, and gender* (pp. 11–18). Austin: Center for Mexican American Studies, University of Texas at Austin.

Oxford English dictionary, 3rd ed. (1973). Oxford, UK: Clarendon.

Paz, O. (1985). *The labyrinth of solitude* (L. Kemp, Y. Milos, & R. P. Belash, Trans.). New York: Grove Press.

Pérez, E. (1991). Sexuality and discourse: Notes from a Chicana survivor. In C. Trujillo (Ed.), *Chicana lesbians: The girls our mothers warned us about* (pp. 159–184). Berkeley: Third Woman Press.

Portillo, L., & Muñoz, S. (Directors). (1990). *La ofrenda: The day of the dead* [Film]. San Francisco: Xochitl Films.

Sánchez, E. R. (1990). Palabra de mujer [Woman's word]. In A. Anzaldúa (Ed.), *Making face, making soul. Hacienda cavas. Creative and critical perspectives of women of color* (p. 192). San Francisco: Aunt Lute Foundation.

Sánchez, M. E. (1985). *Contemporary Chicana poetry: A critical approach to an emerging literature*. Berkeley: University of California Press.

Trujillo, C. (Ed.). (1991). *Chicana lesbians: The girls our mothers warned us about*. Berkeley: Third Woman Press.

Valdez, L. (1971). *Actos*. San Juan Bautista, CA: Menyah Productions.

Vasconcelos, J. (1979). *The cosmic race = la raza cósmica*. Los Angeles: Centro de Publicaciones, Department of Chicano Studies, California State University, Los Angeles.

Yarbro-Bejarano, Y. (1985). Chicanas' experience in collective theatre: Ideology and form. *Women and Performance, 2*(2), 45–58.

Yarbro-Bejarano, Y. (1986). The female subject in Chicano theatre: Sexuality, "race," and class. *Theatre Journal, 38*(1), 389–407.

Zavella, P. (1988). The problematic relationship of feminism and Chicana studies. *Women's Studies, 17*, 123–134.

Zinn, M. B. (1975). Chicanas: Power and control in the domestic sphere. *De Colores, 2*(2), 19–31.

PART IV

REIMAGINING PUBLIC SPACES

We end this volume with an essay by Maxine Greene that invites us to play with the relation of space and imagination. Greene, a brilliant cultural critic, educational theorist, and advocate for "what must be," challenges us to conceive and enact spaces for and by youth, in which ambivalence can flourish, contradictions fill the air, and possibility sails on the winds of open windows and minds.

CHAPTER 17

Lived Spaces, Shared Spaces, Public Spaces

MAXINE GREENE

Artists know about spaces opening in imagination, even as they understand what it means to be situated in the world and to speak (or paint or sing or dance) from the vantage point of their situations. They tell us what happens when they experience new beginnings, when they are enabled to see through new perspectives. There is a clearing, a lighting, a reaching beyond what people are convinced they know. One critic writes that, for him, the arts are on the margins of most of our lives, the margin being the place for those feelings and intuitions that daily life doesn't have a place for and mostly seems to suppress. "Yet those," he says, "who choose to live within the arts can make a space for themselves and fill it with intimations of freedom and presence " (Donoghue, 1983, p. 129). To speak this way is not to confine oneself to what have been called the "high arts" or an elite education. It ought to take into account the many modes of attending in our culture, the many modes of creating. It ought to allow for those who are still nameless where majority audiences are concerned, long-silenced poets and lyricists, storytellers confined to their kitchens, those who treat rap as a craft as well as an art form, street singers, folk singers, protest balladeers, puppeteers. At once, it ought to mean expanding the communities where Shakespeare plays are wondered at and talked about, where Melville or Frost or Fitzgerald or Ellison or Kingston or Morrison can become accessible enough to enable their readers to find their own voices, to suggest ways of naming their worlds.

Adrienne Rich (1993) tells us that "most often someone writing a poem believes in, depends on, a delicate vibrating range of difference, that an 'I' can become a 'we' without extinguishing others, that a partly common language exists to which strangers can bring their own heartbeat, memories, images of strangers" (p. 85). Acutely conscious of the alienation, the brutalities, the muting of voices that mark our society, she makes the point that the arts have the capacity to speak to something different from dread and helplessness. Poetry, painting, dance, music can bring together those parts of human beings that exist in dread and those parts that strain toward a possible happiness, collectivity, community. This, as I see it, suggests the relevance of the arts and imagination in the spaces we need to bring into being. They are, they can be the kinds of spaces Adrienne Rich had in mind when she spoke of her search for a "common language."

Perhaps particularly in this country, the very notion of space has been associated with departure, with escape, with personal rebellion against confinement or extrinsic control. We might recall the initial paragraphs in *Moby Dick* and what it signifies to be a "watergazer," looking beyond the ordinary and the routine:

> There now is your insular city of the Manhattoes, belted round by wharves as Indian isles by coral reefs—commerce surrounds it with her surf. Right and left, the streets take you waterward. Its extreme down-town is the Battery, where that noble mole is washed by waves, and cooled by breezes, which a few hours previous were out of sight of land. Look at the crowds of watergazers there . . . these are all landsmen; of week days pent up in lath and plaster—tied to counters, nailed to benches, clinched to desks. How then is this? Are the green fields gone? What do they here? (Melville, 1851/1981, p. 3)

From their lived situations, clearly enough, the weekday world, their lived world is one that confines them—indeed (as Melville's metaphors suggest) crucifies them. So they look toward the distances, the open spaces, yearning to become, to find some way of attaining freedom. We might remember, too, Huck Finn feeling all "cramped up" when the Widow Douglas "allowed she would sivilize me" (Twain, 1884/1959, p. 11) and, after joining Tom Sawyer's gang and then being trapped by his father, joining Jim on his journey up the river in a fated quest for a "territory ahead." He, too, views the world—or southern society—from the perspective of his lived situation; and it is a world that threatens to make him an object, a world that has to be resisted if he is to be. Another instance (out of many) is the train ride taken by Violet and Joe in Toni Morrison's *Jazz* (1992). They are leaving the Virginia fields where they were migrant laborers in 1906 and taking the train to New York: "When the train trembled approaching the water surrounding the City, they thought it was like them:

nervous at having gotten there at last, but terrified of what was on the other side. Eager, a little scared, they did not even nap during the fourteen hours of a ride smoother than a rocking cradle" (p. 30). Again, it is not an objective train or tunnel or baggage rack; it is a reality that cannot but be contingent and provisional.

Violet and Joe feel the tremors of solitary break with the familiar. Like the "isoladoes" on Melville's whaling ship, they are turned in upon themselves. So are Huck and Jim, for all their apparent fraternity, condemned to what is called "otherness," unable (because of racial difference) to achieve mutual intersubjectivity. Each one's interest is in her or his own liberation. Whether they articulate it or not, they are seeking a freedom from what stands in the way of their fulfillment: the counters, benches, and desks; the pieties and constraints of Widow Douglas's slaveowner world; the accumulated doubts and fears bred in the humiliations of cotton-picking in the Virginia fields. They are all experiencing a lack in their lives, a closing in, a terrible incompleteness. There are gaps between what they are and what they ache to become, what they desire and do not yet have. Never thinking about changing things, they want their plight to change. They want to be self-determining individuals—free to go to sea, to ascend the river, to become "stronger, riskier selves" in a city they would come to love. Toni Morrison (1992) writes:

> And in the beginning when they first arrive, and twenty years later when they and the City have grown up, they love that part of themselves so much they forget what loving other people was like—if they ever knew, that is. I don't mean that they hate them, no, just that what they start to love is the way a person is in the City; the way a schoolgirl never pauses at a stoplight but looks up and down the street before stepping off the curb, how men accommodate themselves to tall buildings and wee porches, what a woman looks like moving in a crowd. (pp. 33–34)

In some intimate lived space they are connected with each other; but they are seldom concerned for the kind of common language that might link them to strangers and help them understand how it is with those others. They have little use for the metaphors that, as Cynthia Ozick (1989) sees it, enable people at the center to imagine what it is to be outside, enable the strong to imagine the weak, "we who are strangers to imagine the familiar heart of the stranger" (p. 283). They may release their imaginations enough to project changes for themselves; but the damage they have suffered keeps them from coming together with others to share available space in such a way that the obstacles or the injustices they face are viewed as common concerns, not only to be resisted and escaped from but also to be transformed somehow and overcome.

Pondering the move from lived space to shared space, I cannot but recall what happens in Albert Camus's *The Plague* (1948) when Tarrou, a stranger, comes to the pestilence-stricken town and organizes sanitary squads. Before that, most of the citizens are caught up in habit, in "doing business," in purely private ways of denying or escaping the plague. Tarrou keeps a chronicle with a "habit of observing events and people through the wrong end of a telescope. . . . He set himself to recording the history of what the normal historian passes over" (p. 52). Like his friend Dr. Rieux, he links solitude to exile and separation; he knows how important it still is to use "plain, clean-cut language . . . to speak—and to act—quite clearly." And he goes on: "That's why I say there are pestilences and there are victims, no more than that." He has decided, he says, "to take in every predicament, the victims' side so as to reduce the damage done" (p. 230). There is no reducing the damage if people remain solitary. Those who join the sanitary squads Tarrou founded:

> knew it was the only thing to do, and the unthinkable thing would then have been not to have brought themselves to do it. These groups enabled our townsfolk to come to grips with the disease and convinced them that, now that the plague was among us, it was up to them to do whatever could be done to fight it. Since plague became in this way some men's duty, it revealed itself as what it really was, that is, the concern of all. (p. 121)

For all Camus's neglect of the non-European citizens in Oran, for all his focus on Tarrou, Rieux, Rambert, and others to whom he gave French names, the novel holds implications for people willing to come together in our own time and place, to move from their lived spaces (so frequently private places) into a space where they can come together, not only to escape the pestilence but also to become (in their squads, in their emerging communities) what the narrator calls "healers."

The sanitary squads, by helping citizens realize that the plague is "the concern of all," create wider and wider spaces in which people are called upon to act rather than to resign themselves to the injustices of a plague-stricken city. That means intentionally coming together in speech and action to identify what they hold in common and what has given rise to their commitment—a commitment, one way or other, to fight the plague. In our present situation, especially in American cities, the plague takes the form of homelessness, of child abuse, of tracking devices in schools. It shows itself in the absence of child-care centers, in the juvenile justice system, in drug dealing, in the AIDS epidemic, in the many varieties of neglect and violation being suffered by the young. Individuals might unexpectedly come together in the way members of the French Resistance came together during World War II. They did so, writes Hannah Arendt (1961), "because they had become 'challengers,' had taken the initiative upon themselves and therefore, without knowing or even noticing it, had begun to create that public space between themselves where freedom could appear" (p. 4). Freedom for them was not an endowment. They had to achieve it, to bring it into being; and, in becoming "challengers," they had to open a space in which they could take initiatives and act on those initiatives in the light of a vision of a better state of things.

There is a signal difference between choosing to come together to sustain each other's desire to adjust, to accommodate to conditions assumed to be unalterable—and choosing to come together to transform somehow and to do so without guarantees. Paulo Freire (1970) writes that, for those who recognize themselves to be oppressed, there must be some shared perception of oppressive conditions as making up a "limiting situation" that can be changed. To view what surrounds them as a closed world without an exit is to lose the motivating force for liberating action. In another text Freire (1994) writes about the surprising ways in which the "culture of silence" can be broken when people begin analyzing the realities nearest at hand and move from there to national realities. Involved, trying to say everything that is on their minds, they find that their critical discourse on their own world is itself a way of remaking that world:

> It was as if they had begun to perceive that the development of their language which occurred in analysis of their reality, finally showed them that the lovelier world to which they aspired was being announced, somehow anticipated, in their imagination. It was not a matter of idealism. Imagination and conjecture about a different world than the one of oppression, are as necessary to the praxis of . . . agents in the process of transforming reality as it necessarily belongs to human toil that the worker or artisan first have in his or her head a design, a "conjecture," of what he or she is about to make. (p. 39)

Eager to replace the sectarian talk of too many educators with an authentic language of the "popular classes," he insists that, when people speak their own language and allow it to probe their lived realities, it will sketch out anticipations of a new world. "Here is one of the central questions of popular education," he concludes, "that of language as a route to the invention of citizenship" (p. 39).

The connection between this and creative and appreciative experiences with the arts seems clear. Involved with any sort of art-making, the individual cannot allow for a phenomenal world that is fixed in place and time. Monet, painting grainstacks at different times of day; Michelangelo rendering "captives" thrusting themselves free from the rock; Shakespeare's Hamlet groping for an explanation of what is "rotten in Denmark"; Alvin

Ailey's dancers ceaselessly making new patterns in space and time; the pulsations of love, jealousy, wonder, and hate in Ibsen's *The Doll's House*: Each shows forth a reality in process, forever in the making. Unlike arguments or scientific reports or newspaper articles, works of art do not come to conclusions that can be detached from the cumulative movement that is the works. Nor—whether the work is a Bach cantata or Sophocles' *Electra* or Antonioni's film *L'Avventura* or Van Gogh's bedroom in Arles—is there a meaning secreted in the work. It can only be achieved as an aware, reflective consciousness reaches out to bring the music or the text or the painting or the film alive. Its coming alive is an event occurring in a space between the perceiver and the piano, let us say, or the museum wall, or the screen, or the stage. When or if the meaning is achieved, it radiates through the experience of the one willing to lend her or his life to what is making itself audible, visible, present. Dewey talked about a funding of meanings; we may think of what is revealed through a reading of an Adrienne Rich poem, or *Moby Dick*, or an involvement with a film as adding to, enriching the fund. The philosopher Maurice Merleau-Ponty (1964) speaks, rather, of the layering of meanings on a perceived landscape, what he calls the "primordial landscape" in which our being in the world begins (pp. 4–5). The meanings we bring out of concealment, he writes, are not primarily conceptual or intellectual. That is because an intellectual synthesis does not allow for the multiple perspectival views in which each object or situation appears. The idea of multiple perspectives on any aspect of the human or natural world carries with it an idea of incompleteness, of partiality, of something still to be attended to, still to be seen.

Coming together, bringing a space into being, those who participate may find it particularly important to set aside the idea of a precisely forged association or any sort of totality, in which differences are subsumed under a single norm. More significant is the realization that, at most, we see aspects of each other, possible paths of becoming, and that there is always, always more. Merleau-Ponty (1964) speaks of the need to reflect, after a time, on the perceptual field and to come to understand how reflection and the search for meanings are grounded in the primordial landscape that, for so many, is overgrown with partially digested facts, what are taken to be "truths," assumptions, formulas. For Merleau-Ponty, "without reflection life would probably dissipate itself in ignorance of itself and in chaos" (p. 10). Without opportunities to reflect on the phenomena of our beginnings—the sounds, the colors, the fluid outlines of things, the textures—we would lose touch with our becoming, our formation, with who we have chosen ourselves to be.

The notion of multiple and provisional perspectives fuses with a vision of spaces that are not closed in, that are open on all sides to the unexpected and the possible. They are not and cannot be closed to the search for meaning, which takes so many forms. Reflection on, thinking about lived and perceived actualities is what gives rise to understandings and to meanings. And all of these are contingent on the need to communicate with others—to conversation and dialogue. When there is no need to communicate, experience is not shaped, not formulated; nor are the meanings that are found. To formulate, according to Dewey (1916), is to get outside an experience, "seeing it as another would see it, considering what points of contact it has with the life of another so that it may be got in such form that the other can appreciate its meaning, and this happens through acts of imagination" (p. 6). Again, there is a consideration of future possibility, of what Freire (1994) describes as a "future to be created, built politically, aesthetically, and ethically—by us women and men . . . the erstwhile future is a new present, and a dream experience is formed" (p. 91).

It may be the desire for a new dream experience and for opportunities to talk about it that draws people together in whatever spaces they can possess for themselves. The alternative for many is a silence with regard to their own experience. It is the sense of fixity, of *thereness* in what impinges and surrounds. On some level, there is a realization of the pain of being marginal; on another, there is a longing to say what is seen from the margins, to make available a perspective too many refuse. For too many, however, there remains the suspicion that inequities detected around them are inherent within an unchangeable system, the one they are presumably being trained to enter. Hannah Arendt (1972) once defined bureaucracy as the worst kind of dominion known to us because it is perceived as "the rule of an intricate system of bureaus in which no man, neither one nor the best, neither the few nor the many, can be held responsible, and which could properly be called 'rule by Nobody'" (p. 137). The young may not associate what they feel with bureaucracy; but they may well associate it with what shows itself in many works of art (as well as philosophy) as the will of the all-powerful gods, or some dread necessity, or the rule of patriarchy, or the spread of something called power masked in all sorts of authoritarian and even "democratic" ways. It has to be named; it has to be talked about; it has to be revealed through many perspectives; it has to be questioned as, above all, a "limiting situation" that has to be at some point transcended, understood, overcome. After all, we find here the sources of feelings of nobodiness and invisibility; and it must be questioned, thought about, raged at from many vantage points, many points of view.

Sonia Sanchez (1994), for one, has written a poem called "Song No. 3 (for 2nd or 3rd grade sisters)":

cain't nobody tell me any different
i'm ugly and you know it too

you just smiling to make me feel better
but i see how you stare when nobody's watching you.

i know i'm short black and skinny
and my nose stopped growin for it wuz sposed to
i know my hair's short, legs and face ashy
and my clothes have holes that run right through to you.

so i sit all day long just by myself
so i jump the sidewalk cracks knowin i cain't fall
cuz who would want to catch someone who looks like me
who ain't even cute or even just a little tall.

caint tell me any different
i'm ugly anybody with sense can see.
but, one day i hope somebody will stop me and say
looka here, a pretty little black girl lookin' just like me. (p. 111)

A work of art, yes, beginning in the "dread" Adrienne Rich described, ending with some hope, some reaching out toward possibility. Finding another may well be the beginning of discovering a shared space. And there is more. The perspective being expressed not only allows a reader to uncover an aspect of our society seldom noticed by members of the society who live at the center; it suggests the importance of multiple perspectives, especially when we place this up against as concrete a rendering of something as abstract as "rule by Nobody." Who comes closer to the truth—the poet or the political theorist? Is there a single vision that would settle what is true—and, to add to that, what there is to be done?

In the present context, in the midst of searches for "safe spaces" where unexpected inventions may take place and new visions opened up, there is hope that the arts will play an increasingly central role to the end of releasing social imagination. That means the kind of imagination that responds to the flaws and deficiencies viewed in our society with a sense of what ought to be in mind. It is difficult to set aside Jean-Paul Sartre's (1956) account of workers in the nineteenth-century factories who were lulled into acceptance even of exploitation by promises of reward in an afterlife. When people are immersed in their historical situations, wrote Sartre, they cannot even conceive of what is wrong or hurtful or demeaning. It is because they cannot imagine how they can exist otherwise. "It is on the day that we can conceive of a different state of affairs that a new light falls on our troubles and our suffering, and that we decide that these are unbearable." People resign themselves to cruel, inequitable conditions because they lack the "education and reflection" needed for conceiving a social state in which their suffering would not exist (pp. 434–435). If indeed, as Emily Dickinson (1914/1960) wrote, "The Possible's slow fuse is lit/ By the Imagination" (pp. 688–689), this gives rise to another hope that the arts will become more present for poor and working-class youth in their created spaces as well as in the schools. Not only should a full range of the arts be made available (with materials and media everywhere accessible). Art experiences should be encouraged in open spaces as well as in safe ones: spaces where diverse individuals can talk about their differing interpretations and about the light their encounters may be throwing upon their experiences, the pleasures now being offered to them, the perplexities, the ecstasies, the pain, the surprise. As important is the need to keep naming, to keep resisting what presses living beings into molds and categories. It needs continually to be recalled that we would not be able to perceive certain phenomena as impediments and obstacles if we did not have a field of possibles ahead, a consciousness of what might be, what ought to be. It is at least interesting to hold in mind that the most admired writers in our century have been those compelled to overcome terrible obstacles in order to tell their stories. When we think of African American women writers, Czech writers such as Milan Kundera and Václav Havel, Native American writers—we find people whose very creativity was unleashed by their felt needs to overcome censorship and indifference, and even the threat of imprisonment.

Through resistance in the course of their becoming—through naming what stood in their way, through coming together in efforts to overcome—people are likely to find out the kinds of selves they are creating. Most are aware that the identities they seek are not simply functions of their gender or their ethnic past or their economic class. Rather, they emerge from many kinds of intersection: There is no predefined essence in the humanity someone like Václav Havel or Toni Morrison or Bill Z. Robinson or Paulo Freire was trying to achieve. The action and speech that may go on among such men and women can become agent-revealing because of the reflection they have done on their original landscapes, on their experiences. Somehow or other, they come to disclose the kinds of persons who are capable of initiating the kinds of actions that take place in the public sphere. For Hannah Arendt (1958), the disclosure of the person responsible for an action and the full significance of that action require their appearance before others, their coming into the public sphere.

Disclosures like this can happen in classrooms, indeed ought to happen if teachers and learners are to be fully present to each other and to take responsibility for what they do and say. Only when there is a revelatory quality in the dialogue taking place is the distinctiveness of each individual made clear. Also made clear is the realization that each one's uniqueness is a function of togetherness, of being participant. It is difficult if not impossible to say what the human being is; it follows that who she or he is or is becoming is essential if there is to be a public sphere.

Arendt (1958) says that the interests with which a given group is concerned are worldly interests—curriculum, perhaps, a school lunch program, a mentoring program. Such interests "inter-est," lying between people and binding them together. Most words and deeds refer to such worldly interests, even as they become agent-revealing, disclosing who is taking responsibility, who cares. Arendt goes on to say that the physical in-between may become overlaid by a different in-between,

> which consists of deeds and words and owes its origin exclusively to people's acting and speaking directly *to* one another. . . . A subjective in-between is not tangible, since there are no tangible objects into which it should solidify; the process of acting and speaking can leave behind no such results or end products. But for all its intangibility, this in-between is no less real than the world of things we visibly have in common. We call this reality the "web" of human relationships, indicating by the metaphor a somewhat intangible quality. (pp. 182–183)

When we think back to the silenced ones, the ones who feel themselves to be excluded, this rendering of a public sphere pervaded by a reality of human relationships may provide a new perspective on how spaces, when opened and extended, may become a public space. It is acknowledged that people are differently located in whatever common world or concern may emerge. It is acknowledged as well that perspectives differ, and that people perceive what is common from different positions and against different backgrounds. This, says Arendt, is the "meaning of public life. . . . Only where things can be seen by many in a variety of aspects without changing their identity, so that those who are gathered around them know they see sameness in utter diversity, can worldly reality truly and reliably appear" (p. 57).

What may hold shared spaces together and bring them closer to a public space may be in part the phenomenon of storytelling. One way to keep the French Resistance alive is by incorporating it into the ongoing democratic traditions that feed some of our familiar narratives. Surely, the history of the civil rights movement and the antiwar protests of the 1960s ought to become part of the stories told in schools today, becoming part of our art forms, keeping alive a tradition that creates continuities and holds people mysteriously together who might otherwise fall apart. Storytelling, in fact, can become a beginning for political action when it focuses on the process of thinking about experience and the conditions of action. One commentator on Arendt has said that storytelling "addresses the question of how we understand what has happened from the point of view of the present. The story presents a past experience to us by recalling it to mind, thereby raising it to the level of understanding where we can imagine it for ourselves. This is the moment 'between past and future' when we can 'think what we are doing'" (Hill, 1979, p. 290).

Thinking about our thinking, imagining things for ourselves, seeking a community of concern in a public space: These may be the phases of our striving for social justice, our striving for collectivity, our striving for what is always in the making—what we call democracy. These may be our ways of reaching toward each other in safe and unsafe spaces, seeking equity, seeking decency, seeking for a common world.

REFERENCES

Arendt, H. (1958). *The human condition*. Chicago: University of Chicago Press.

Arendt, H. (1961). *Between past and future*. New York: Viking.

Arendt, H. (1972). *Crises of the republic*. New York: Harcourt Brace Jovanovich.

Camus, A. (1948). *The plague*. New York: Knopf.

Dewey, J. (1916). *Democracy and education*. New York: Macmillan.

Dewey, J. (1954). *The public and its problems*. Athens, OH: Swallow Press.

Dickinson, E. (1960). The gleam of a heroic act. In T.H. Johnson (Ed.), *The complete poems* (pp. 688–689). Boston: Little Brown. (Original work published 1914)

Donoghue, D. (1983). *The arts without mystery*. New York: Little Brown.

Freire, P. (1970). *Pedagogy of the oppressed*. New York: Herder & Herder.

Freire, P. (1994). *Pedagogy of hope*. New York: Continuum.

Hill, M. A. (1979). The fictions of mankind and the stories of men. In M. A. Hill (Ed.), *Hannah Arendt: The recovery of the public world* (pp. 275–300). New York: St. Martin's Press.

Melville, H. (1981). *Moby Dick*. Berkeley: Clarendon, University of California Press. (Original work published 1851)

Merleau-Ponty, M. (1964). *The primacy of perception*. Evanston, IL: Northwestern University Press.

Morrison, T. (1992). *Jazz*. New York: Knopf.

Ozick, C. (1989). *Metaphor and memory*. New York: Knopf.

Rich, A. (1993). *What is found there: Notebooks on poetry and politics*. New York: Norton.

Sanchez, S. (1994). Song No. 3. In M. M. Gillan & J. Gillan (Eds.), *Unsettling America: An anthology of multicultural poetry* (p. 111). New York: Viking Penguin.

Sartre, J.-P. (1956). *Being and nothingness*. New York: Philosophical Library.

Twain, M. (1959). *The adventures of Huckleberry Finn*. New York: New American Library. (Original work published 1884)

About the Editors and Contributors

A. A. Akom is a Ph.D. candidate in sociology at the University of Pennsylvania. He received his B.A. in political science/economics from the University of California at Berkeley and his M.A. in education from Stanford University. Currently he is a research fellow in poverty, urban education, and public policy at the Institute for the Study of Social Change at the University of California at Berkeley. His dissertation research investigates America's powerful achievement ideology by examining differential access to advanced placement courses in a California high school and in schools across the country.

Bernadette Anand is Principal of the Renaissance School, and co-author of "Revisiting the Struggle for Integration: An Oral History Project" (to be published in 2000 in the journal *Radical Teacher*).

Nancy Barnes is a cultural anthropologist on the faculty at Lang College at the New School University. She also teaches high school students in a collaborative project that involves small public high schools in New York City, about which she has recently written in *Curriculum Inquiry* (1999) 29(3). Her current research focuses on participatory teacher-research projects and the uses of ethnography to support progressive urban school reform.

Richard Barry holds an M.A. in psychology from the City University of New York. He also holds a B.A. in psychology and a B.S. in biology from Mercer University in Macon, Georgia. His research interests include the construction of community for gay men, lesbians, and bisexuals. Working within that rubric, he has in the past been co-principal evaluator for a community-based Asian and Pacific Islander AIDS organization. He is presently an adjunct professor at Hunter University in New York City and working toward the completion of his Ph.D.

Linda Brodkey, professor in the Department of Literature at the University of California–San Diego and Director of the Warren College Writing

Program, is the author of many articles on writing and literacy along with two books, *Academic Writing as Social Practice* and *Writing Permitted in Designated Areas Only.*

Doris Carbonell-Medina, Esq., received her J.D. from the State University of New York at Buffalo Faculty of Law and Jurisprudence and is licensed to practice law in New York State. Before working for Preventionfocus, where she runs most of the workshops connected to Womanfocus, she worked with Prisoners Legal Services of New York and was in private legal practice. Her legal expertise consists of civil rights litigation, including employment discrimination, police brutality, family law, and entertainment law. She currently practices law on a referral basis only.

Sarah K. Carney is a graduate student in social/personality psychology at the City University of New York Graduate Center. Her doctoral research is on women and legal discourse. Other research interests include the social production of psychological knowledge and cultural constructions of trauma survival/mental health.

Craig Centrie is a faculty member in the Latino/Latina Studies program, State University of New York at Buffalo. He completed his Ph.D. in the sociology of education, also at SUNYAB. He co-founded the only visual arts organization in western New York that is dedicated to the exhibition of visual art by artists of color.

Colette Daiute is professor of psychology at the City University of New York Graduate Center. Before joining that faculty, Dr. Daiute taught at Harvard University for 11 years, following a 3-year postdoctoral research program at Columbia Teachers College, where she also did her graduate work. She has received numerous research grants to study social development, focusing on how children in urban public schools use oral and written language with teachers and peers to construct knowledge and to critique society. Dr. Daiute has published in journals across diverse disciplines, including the *Journal of Narrative and Life History, New Directions in Child Development, Language Arts, Cognition and Instruction*, and *Research in the Teaching of English*, and has written several books, including, most recently, *The Development of Literacy Through Social Interaction.* (Jossey-Bass)

Michelle Fine is a professor of social psychology at the City University of New York Graduate Center. Her recent books include *The Unknown City* (with Lois Weis; Beacon Press), *Off White* (with Lois Weis, Linda

Powell, and Mun Wong; Routledge), and *Becoming Gentlemen* (with Lani Guinier; Beacon Press). She also helped to create a 30-minute, teacher- and adolescent-friendly video of the course described in Chapter 9 (*Off-Track*, produced by Teachers College Press, 1998).

Mindy Thompson Fullilove, M.D., is an associate professor of clinical psychiatry and public health at Columbia University and a research psychiatrist at the New York State Psychiatric Institute. Important publications include: "Psychiatric Implications of Displacement: Contributions from the Psychology of Place," in the *American Journal of Psychiatry*; "Promoting Social Cohesion to Improve Health," in the *Journal of the American Medical Women's Association*; "Injury and Anomie: The Effects of Violence on an Inner-City Community," in the *American Journal of Public Health;* and "Building Momentum: An Ethnographic Study of Inner-City Redevelopment," in the *American Journal of Public Health*.

Most recently, Dr. Fullilove has published *The House of Joshua: Mediations on Family and Place*, a collection of essays that explores the importance of place in shaping family life.

Maxine Greene is professor of philosophy and education (emeritus) and Director of the Center for Social Imagination, the Arts, and Education at Teachers College, Columbia University, where she still teaches. She is a past president of the American Educational Research Association and the Philosophy of Education Society. The "philosopher-in-residence" at the Lincoln Center Institute for the Arts in Education, she has written about 100 articles and chapters in journals and anthologies having to do with philosophy, the schools, social theory, curriculum, literature, and the other arts. She has written six books, the latest of which are *The Dialectic of Freedom* (Teachers College Press) and *Releasing Imagination* (Jossey-Bass.)

Aída Hurtado is a professor in the Department of Psychology at the University of California–Santa Cruz. Dr. Hurtado's research focuses on the effects of subordination on social identity, educational achievement, and language. Her most recent publications include *Strategic Interventions in Education: Expanding the Latino Pipeline* (co-edited with Richard Figueroa and Eugene Garcia; University of California, Latino Eligibility Study) and *The Color of Privilege: Three Blasphemies on Race and Feminism* (University of Michigan Press). Dr. Hurtado received her B.A. in psychology and sociology from Pan American University in Edinburg, Texas, and her M.A. and Ph.D. in social psychology from the University of Michigan.

Carlton Jordan is Research Associate at Education Trust (Washington, DC) and a former high school teacher.

Jennifer McCormick is an assistant professor of education at Brooklyn College. She is currently writing a book about how young women assert and explore their identities through poetry, despite the depersonalizing schooling practices prevalent in large urban high schools. She received a Ph.D. in English education from New York University.

Amira Proweller is an assistant professor of social and cultural studies in education in the School of Education at DePaul University. She received her Ph.D. in social foundations of education from the State University of New York at Buffalo in 1995. Dr. Proweller teaches courses in education in the social context and qualitative research methods. Her research focuses on gender and education, youth culture and identity, and multicultural education. Dr. Proweller is the author of *Constructing Female Identities: Meaning Making in an Upper Middle Class Youth Culture* (State University of New York Press).

Michael C. Reichert is a child and family psychologist who received his doctorate from the Graduate School of Education of the University of Pennsylvania. He is currently director of "On Behalf of Boys," a center for research on boys' lives sponsored by The Haverford School in Pennsylvania and project director of a youth antiviolence program, Peaceful Posse, which works with children exposed to high levels of violence in Philadelphia. Current research interests include the social dimensions of boys' learning, intersections of violence, and male development and diversity programming in schools. He recently co-authored *Bearing Witness: Violence and Collective Responsibility* (with Sandra L. Bloom, M.D.; Haworth Press) and has also published on the subject of boys' development. He has two boys of his own, ages 15 and 8.

Dana Sherman is a middle school teacher.

Janie Victoria Ward is an associate professor in the Department of Education and Human Services and the African American Studies Department at Simmons College in Boston, Massachusetts. She has been a visiting research scholar at the Center for Research on Women at Wellesley College, and she is a past recipient of a Rockefeller Foundation Postdoctoral Research Fellowship at the Center for the Study of Black Literature and Culture, University of Pennsylvania. Dr. Ward lectures frequently on racial identity formation and issues in the psychosocial development of African

American adolescents. She is the co-editor of *Souls Looking Back: Life Stories of Growing up Black* (with Andrew Garrod, Tracy Robinson, and Robert Kilkenny; Routledge). Her recent book, *The Skin We're In: Teaching our Black Children to Be Emotionally Strong, Socially Smart and Spiritually Connected,* will be published by The Free Press in fall 2000.

Constance Webster received her doctoral degree from the University at Buffalo in social foundations of education. She currently works for the New Jersey State Department of Education in the Division of Field Services. In this capacity, she assists school districts in implementing educational reform initiatives. In addition, she holds adjunct faculty status at the College of New Jersey.

Lois Weis is professor of the sociology of education at the State University of New York at Buffalo. She is the author and/or editor of numerous books and articles on the subject of social class, race, gender, and schooling. Her most recent publications include *The Unknown City: The Lives of Poor and Working Class Young Adults* (with Michelle Fine; Beacon Press); *Working Class Without Work: High School Students in a De-Industrializing Economy* (Routledge); *Beyond Silenced Voices* (with Michelle Fine; State University of New York Press); *Beyond Black and White* (with Maxine Seller; State University of New York Press); and *Off White* (with Michelle Fine, Linda Powell, and Mun Wong; Routledge). She sits on numerous editorial boards and is a former editor of *Educational Policy.*

Index